THE DEBATE

THE DEBATE

Edited by Yash Tandon
with an Introduction by A.M. Babu

Tanzania Publishing House
Dar es Salaam.

Tanzania Publishing House
P.O. Box 2138, Dar es Salaam
Tanzania

ISBN 9976 1 0011 6

Printed in India by Allied Publishers Pvt. Ltd., New Delhi-110064

CONTENTS

1

INTRODUCTION

A.M. Babu

Here is a vigorous, sometimes too vigorous, discussion on what are probably the most burning questions of the day – imperialism, finance capital, monopoly capitalism, neo-colonialism, and classes in the neo-colonies.

For the most part these questions have either been ignored in Africa or subjected to a rather simplistic and therefore misleading investigation by the opinion leaders who have themselves already developed vested interests in neo-colonialism and the status quo. For let it be said at once that the advocates of "third worldism" have now become shameless apologists of neo-colonialism which is a direct offspring of the dominance of finance capital in the entire capitalist world, developed and underdeveloped.

It is heartening that this excellent discussion by some of the finest brains in East Africa should have occurred at this moment when all of us need a clearer understanding of what is taking place under our very noses. Significant changes in our societies are occurring now and it needs a clear analysis which subjects them to serious scrutiny in order to bring out into the open their underlying causes and tendencies.

This is what these essays have succeeded in doing. Social change, like changes in the human body, occur slowly and unseen until they reach their maturity and reveal themselves with a bang. This maturation is known as the aggregate of objective conditions or, to use modern Marxist parlance, the *conjuncture*. Marxism is first of all about understanding these changes by observing them in their nascent form and to prepare ourselves for organising subjective initiative to coincide with the conjuncture, for the second task of Marxism is to change the world.

These essays are showing us these invisible changes through a penetrating analysis employing the well-tried and tested methodology of dialectical and historical materialism. This is the most reliable way of uncovering the hidden links that tie together the seemingly unrelated phenomena and thereby helps us to see reality as it exists in the real world.

Dialectical materialism which was first discovered and utilized by Marx and Engels in their investigations and studies has proved itself to be the only philosophy that answered *all* the questions which troubled orthodox philosophy throughout history, especially the most fundamental and critical question: what is the law of the motion and development of the universe? The correct answer to this question has developed into the Marxist philosophy.

This philosophy has discovered the most cardinal law which guides all objective life; i.e., the law of the unity of opposites. According to this universal law all objective things have two opposite tendencies which are independent and at the same time struggle against each other. This unity and struggle determines the life of things and pushes their development forward. This law, consequently, is the Marxist world outlook as well as methodology. Marx himself made all his important discoveries by utilizing this methodology. In discussing these important discoveries, such as the law of the *tendency for the rate of profit to fall*, Marx pointed out "this inner and necessary connection between two seeming contradictions."

As a *world outlook* this philosophy therefore regards all things as the unity of opposites in accordance with law of self-movement and development of objective things.

As a *methodology* it uses this law as the dialectical method of analysis in order to *know* and *change* the world.

On the basis of this law Marxism developed the theory of the evolution of classes through struggle and leaps. It showed the evolution of the working class from being a class-in-itself, i.e., the original identity of the hidden, underdeveloped conditions within things, to that of a class-for-itself, i.e., the coming into the open of the distinction and separation of these hidden and latent elements which is the starting point of their struggle and contradiction.

Prior to Marx the basis of philosophy was the formal logical method but this proved to be totally inadequate and unsatisfactory as a way of understanding the real world. As a rule we formulate our language logically but the real, objective world does *not* behave logically. This important fact was overlooked, sometimes deliberately, by orthodox philosophy and resulted in confusing language with reality. Herein lies their problem of understanding the world clearly. This is the first point to remember in reading these essays.

The second point worth remembering is that as Marxism sees process and development through the struggle of opposites and contradictory forces it traces decisive historical conflicts and changes to roots in the mode of production. These are known as the class struggles. Behind these struggles lie the essential economic relations. These are the most important elements which are isolated and analysed through abstraction. Earlier philosophers could not see the economic basis of contradictions and they resorted to logical illusions of the illogical world.

Thus contradictions, class struggle, modes of production, the economic base and its superstructure are the stuff of Marxist investigation and analysis. These are the substance of the essays contained in this volume.

The theme of the essays can probably be broken down to four main subthemes: classes in the neo-colonies; imperialism and the national question; the relationship between the economic base and the superstructure; and neo-colonialism.

In an introduction of this nature it is impossible to deal with each of the points raised or with each writer's position. To attempt to do that will require a whole new book. Thus only major issues will be dealt with, those which are likely to be of more practical value in our on-going struggle.

CLASSES IN NEO-COLONIES

There seems to be some misunderstanding on the question of the national bourgeoisie. One writer (Tandon?) argues that there is no national bourgeoisie in neo-colonies *because* under the imperialist world order they cannot accomplish the national bourgeois revolution due to the dominance of monopoly capital and their subservience to it. Here the argument confuses the *existence* of the national bourgeoisie with its *capacity* to lead or accomplish national bourgeois revolution.

That they exist there is no doubt. Their capital is "national" in the sense that it has been accumulated within the neo-colony concerned and it continued to appropriate surplus value generated by the workers under its employment, e.g., small soap manufacturers, etc.

Distinction must be made between these small (not petty) and the big bourgeoisie. The latter, like Madhvanis in East Africa, of course, derive the capital from, and it is therefore linked and tied to, imperialist finance capital. The small bourgeoisie has contradictions with imperialism because it impedes its expansion. The big bourgeoisie on the other hand is in harmony with imperialism because it is its final recourse. But neither of them can accomplish the national bourgeois revolution because, in the former case, it functions in the wrong historical epoch, and in the latter case it is subservient to imperialist finance capital and consequently it cannot revolt against itself. Historically, the bourgeoisie is a dying force.

Our small national bourgeoisie is not the same class as the petty bourgeoisie because of respective position in production, and this position is not determined by wealth. A petty-bourgeois, say a successful auctioneer, may be wealthier than a small manufacturer but because of his position in production i.e. appropriating no direct surplus value, the former will still remain petty-bourgeois and the latter full bourgeois. Wealth is not a Marxist criterion of class.

Again it is important to distinguish between the existence of the national bourgeoisie and the *national capital* in the neo-colonies. National capital is the capital which constitutes the basis of the political economy of a country. In the neo-colony this capital, through loans, grants, aid, foreign investments, etc. is a part of imperialist finance capital and to that extent it is not national.

If, say, a national marketing board or a milling corporation borrows from the World Bank to purchase agricultural commodities from the peasants the board or the corporation becomes an agent of imperialist finance capital by introducing it into the country.

The entire business operations of the board or corporation is thus subjected to finance capital. It appropriates surplus value in milling, ginning, textile mills, etc. on behalf of finance capital and it plunders peasants commodities through "exchange" on behalf of that same capital. This capital is not national; it is a part of the imperialist finance capital.

Our small national bourgeois, on the other hand, can conduct his business with or without recourse to this capital. An ex-colony which cuts off links with the capitalist world order, as in North Korea, China, or Vietnam, can still have a role for its national bourgeoisie although it cannot play a leading revolutionary one as did its counterpart before the October Revolution. Its non-revolutionary role in this case is not due to its being subservient to the imperialist finance capital but because this is no longer the epoch of the bourgeisie; this is the epoch of the proletariat.

There are thus two types of the national bourgeoisie: the small one which generates and accumulates capital without recourse to finance capital; and the big bourgeoisie whose capital is part of imperialist finance capital. This bourgeoisie must not be confused with the comprador capitalist who is exclusively in the service of, and an agent for imperialist finance capital and cannot survive after cutting off links with imperialism.

Analysis of classes in the neo-colonies is one of the most difficult studies in Marxism and it is thus no accident that most of the discussions in these essays are centred on the subject. African countries were annexed to European capitalist economy and they have evolved in a specific, historically determined way, in a definite mode of production which serves external interests.

Their economies have been penetrated by external capital from metropolitan economies and they suffer the pernicious subordination to those markets which siphon off their economic surpluses leaving hardly anything for internal accumulation. In a normal, non-colonial development, accumulation of capital leads to a situation where one class becomes economically dominant and constitutes the "civil society". Its economic strength leads it naturally, either by revolution or stealth, to take over the reins of power, i.e. the state. At this stage it constitutes the "political society", or the superstructure.*

In other words, the social organization evolving directly out of production and commerce forms the basis of the state and its ideology. They establish institutions for the mutual guarantee of their property and interests, and for further facilitating and strengthening their economic dominance. In this instance the economic base is said to be determining the superstructure.

In colonized countries this evolution did not take place because the dominant economic force remained the colonial power, and the economies remained only as extensions of the metropolitan economies. The normal development of classes was interrupted and economic groupings gravitated towards metropolitan interests. Our history ceased to be national history; we became part of bourgeois world history.

When independence came those who took over state power from the colonialists were the intellectuals of mostly peasant origin–son of a chief, of a parish pastor, of a rural school teacher, of a successful rich peasant – and their economic and social base, i.e., class origin, is consequently peasant. How then does this ruling stratum constitute a class independent of the peasantry? Obviously there is a problem here.

In countries where the land is privately owned and the peasants are already involved in commercial, or commodity production class struggle develops between the peasants and the landlords. The peasants are forced to pay in cash or in kind for the use of the means of production – the land – which has been appropriated by the landlord. Here we can see the essential but conflicting economic relations between the peasant and the landlord, the latter exploiting the former through his ownership of the means of production.

In the least developed countries where the vast majority of the peasants are not involved in commodity production and have not yet developed independent class interest the struggle may appear in individual form. For the vast majority the struggle is against nature because the peasants are still in the "realm of necessity." The struggle here is for survival and not yet for conflicting commercial, i.e. economic interests.

Where the land is communally owned, even if the peasants have advanced sufficiently to be involved in commodity production, their struggle will not be over the means of production because the landlord class does not exist. In this situation their struggle will take a different form. It will be a struggle against the forces that intercept and deny them the realization of the full return for their toil–the middlemen i.e. produce merchants, the money lenders, marketing boards, marketing co-operatives and so on. Again we see here conflicting economic relations between the peasant and the middlemen, the latter plundering the former through a predatory relationship.

In both of these economic relations the ultimate beneficiary is imperialist finance capital. However, some local groupings who facilitate this operation also benefit. These include, in addition to the national bourgeoisie, state bureaucrats, managers of private and state economic institutions, the emerging millionaires who take advantage of the economic chaos to enrich themselves, and so on. How do we classify these groups?

Some comrades in these essays, Shivji, for instance, suggest that this is in fact a new class and it is formed from the state level downward: they first take over state power and then develop an economic base through their control of economic enterprises, banks, corporations, whether private or public, and the comrades call

---

*This is not the "civil society" and the "political society" of John Locke

these the "bureaucratic bourgeoisie".

Other comrades, Nabudere and others, reject this proposition and say that since these managers of neo-colonies are nothing but agents of imperialist finance capital they cannot constitute an independent class, and that the economically dominant class still remains the world bourgeoisie. Here again the question arises: can there be an international ruling class, a class outside the nation-state?

There are difficulties in accepting either of these propositions. To accept the first one is to accept the logical rather than dialectical standpoint. We have seen above that classes are first formed at the economic level, the "civil society", before they reach the state level. To assume otherwise is to put Marxism upside down. We shall return to this problem when we discuss the relationship between the economic base and the superstructure.

The second proposition is also difficult to accept. The proletariat cannot lead the revolution against an unseen, abstract "international ruling class." It must have an identifiable, local and existing class to marshal its forces against.

IMPERIALISM AND THE NATIONAL QUESTION

On this extremely important subject too, there seems to be some misunderstanding. Do our countries constitute a nation in the Marxian sense? Stalin's famous definition of a nation is that a nation is a "historically constituted, stable community of people, formed on the basis of a common language, territory, economic life, and psychological make-up manifested in a common culture."

For historically determined reasons African nationalism comprises more than the above definition. In Asia there is no Asian nationalism: there is Chinese nationalism, Vietnamese, Japanese, Indian, Iranian nationalism, etc. There is no European nationalism either, only French, British, German, etc. In the US there are nationalisms within the artificial US nationalism.

In Africa, on the other hand, there is no Nigerian, Kenyan, or Tanzanian nationalism; they are subordinated to the stronger and more overriding one – African nationalism.

The reason is clear. Unlike any other continent, an African wherever he or she may be is categorized by his or her Africanness, his or her colour. This peculiarity has not been introduced by the Africans themselves but it has been imposed on them by the long and terrible recent history of slavery, the color-bar, segregation and now *apartheid*. It is part of an African's conscience, his psychology, his identity. We constitute a "nation" not by territory or common language but by our physical characteristics. That is why, unlike Pan-Helenism, Pan-Slavakism before it, Pan-Africanism has a much stronger appeal to all black people of African descent the world over.

The discussion on the subject in these essays is about the economies and politics of separate nation-states and consequently it is not comprehensive enough to include the currently most burning question of African nationalism. Practically all the contributors of these essays seem to be aware of this question but none seems to be prepared to discuss it at length. The reason is obvious: Marxist politics is about the class struggle; its economics is about social relations of production; there is no room for nationalism. The national question is discussed as a part of the general problem of the proletarian revolution, as a part of the problem of the dictatorship of the proletariat. Herein lies the difficulty which Marxists are confronted with in dealing with the phenomenon of African nationalism.

Some comrades, Nabudere and others, argue that since our countries are dominated by imperialist finance capital they do not constitute separate political economies independent of imperialism. Consequently, our struggle is essentially an anti-imperialist struggle and not exclusively a class struggle confined to each country or "nation". It is a struggle by the whole people against "national oppression". Our "national" bourgeoisie, or whatever we call it, is also oppressed by imperialism and therefore has the chance to join the popular united front against imperialism in the period of the "new democratic revolution."

The opposing comrades, Mamdani *et al*, argue that although imperialism is the main enemy it remains an external force and we must first identify the internal force which oppresses the people, on its own behalf and on behalf of the external imperialism; otherwise we shall be disarming the working class ideologically and allow their oppressors to shelter in the camp of the people.

Here we see nationalism as the preponderant consideration in the first case and the class struggle within a nation in the second.

Current developments in Africa show one interesting characteristic. Whereas African Marxist intellectuals tend to be reluctant to categorize fellow-Africans as the enemy, the new generation of African working class tends to be less so inhibited. The reason is that in general the intellectuals come from the same stratum as those who now comprise the "ruling class", whether these are in politics or business. They share the same background, they went to the same schools, they shared the same passion against colonialism and racial oppression, and so on. It is inconceivable for the intellectuals to think of them as their enemies, until, perhaps, when they send them to detention camps or subject them to personal or political humiliation.

The gradually emerging African working class and the ubiquitous lumpen proletariat, especially the younger generation who have no direct experience of colonial oppression, although they are constantly reminded about it by the political leaders – in schools, party meetings, etc. – who desperately wish to establish their legitimacy, appraise their situation differently.

It is true that they are not as articulate as the intellectuals but they express their disenchantment with their rulers by other means–through action. While their industrial action is still at the level of "economism", being still a class-in-itself, their enthusiastic response to the Master Sergeant Does and Lt. Rawlings speaks louder than words.

In other words it is difficult for an African intellectual to be objective on this question and the only valid test as to what is primary in our circumstances between anti-imperialism and class antagonism is through the inarticulate expression of the working class, and to some extent, the poor peasants, and by the observations of those not directly involved in this nationalism.

In discussing this question in the essays some ambiguity has crept in which needs to be clarified. This is in connection with the definition of the "New Democratic Revolution". One gets the impression that some comrades consider any form of a united front as new-democratic, provided it is anti-imperialist. To clarify this question to the general reader we should bear the following in mind:

New Democracy

(a) The establishment of the New Democracy does not come prior to but after a successful socialist revolution.

(b) New Democracy is not any kind of united front; it is of a specific kind. It is a united front in which the proletariat has already led a successful socialist revolution, smashed the oppressive state machine, and established its own democratic dictatorship in alliance with other oppressed classes and "nationalities" or "national minorities." This is a prelude to and a first step towards the dictatorship of the proletariat.

(c) New Democracy is a necessary transitional phase only in countries where the productive forces have not been fully developed and the existing relations of production have not yet become a fetter to their development. In other words, in advanced capitalist countries there is no need for New Democracy phase after the socialist revolution.

Anti-Imperialist United Front

(a) The anti-imperialist united front is not the same thing as New Democracy.
(b) This united front must be under the leadership of the proletarian party otherwise it cannot be revolutionary.
(c) It is anti-imperialist and its ultimate objective is social revolution, not just liberation.

Thus we have two kinds of united fronts: first, the anti-imperialist united front which will lead the struggle to socialist revolutions; and second, the united front under the New Democracy which will lead the struggle for laying the foundations of socialist construction. It is also anti-imperialist in essence. Both the united fronts are under the firm leadership of the proletariat.

This clarification is important for devising political strategy and tactics, i.e., the General Line.

RELATIONSHIP BETWEEN THE ECONOMIC BASE AND THE SUPERSTRUCTURE

This discussion is inevitably linked with the above discussion on classes. Does the economic base – the Civil Society – determine the superstructure all the time, or does the superstructure – the "political society" or the state – on certain occasions determine the base?

We have seen above the difficulty of resolving this question from the non-dialectical standpoint. Many Marxists are not clear on this question and there are a lot of disagreements around it. Those who support the contention that the superstructure does under certain conditions determine the economic base go by the authority of Chairman Mao who asserted that "politics" does determine the economic base under certain conditions.

Mao, of course, consistently urged "putting politics in command", i.e., the class struggle comes first, then economics and finally the superstructure. This is a revolutionary strategy whereby in order to win the economic struggle the masses must first strive to win the political struggle, establish a proletarian economic base after which the abolition of the ideological foundation of feudalism and capitalism, i.e., the superstructure will follow as a natural consequence of victory in the political and economic struggles. These are the "certain conditions" under which politics determine the economic base.

Conversely, when revisionism takes over state power in a socialist society they depart from the principle of the law of planned and proportional development, re-introduce competition and the law of value, and eventually the change in the superstructure will follow automatically to correspond with the new capitalist economic base. This is the process by which capitalist restoration is achieved. It does not mean that the proletariat has changed to capitalist. It only means that owing to some mistakes by the proletariat, at party and state levels, the remnants of the bourgeoisie have temporarily won an upper hand in the ongoing class struggle and seek to establish an economic base which will determine a capitalist superstructure.

However, this is not the same thing as saying that the superstructure can determine the economic base. Under our condition of neo-colonialism the "bureaucratic bourgeoisie" do not "determine" the economic base, they merely carry forward the peasant mode of production to the capitalist relations which is its logical destination. Left to itself the peasantry gravitates towards capitalism and not socialism; peasants are inherently capitalists. Only proletarian intervention and under its leadership can the peasants move towards socialism.

In other words, Mao's statement is not inconsistent with the dialectical principle that the economic base in the final analysis determines the superstructure, and not vice versa.

NEO-COLONIALISM

Another important issue in these essays is how and why does the gap between advanced capitalist countries and neo-colonies continue to widen? Why are these neo-colonies permanently subordinated to the capitalist world order?

We know that this is achieved by the huge transfer of value, i.e. wealth, from the neo-colonies to the metropolitan countries. The question is: how is it achieved? Is it through "unequal exchange" or through the "exploitation" of the peasants? First let us be quite clear that exploitation does *not* take place at the point of exchange because at this level no new value is created – it is only transferred from one party to another. It can take the form of legalized looting or plunder which we call "trade". There can never be equal or unequal exchange between commodities of the subjugater and the subjugated, and the law of equivalents cannot operate under the circumstances. Our exchange with imperialism is not determined by market mechanism or by the law of demand and supply, and consequently prices neither gravitate towards nor deviate from their value. These laws operate only within a single economy or between economies of more or less equal development where the "cost" of labour, or variable capital, roughly correspond.

Exploitation takes place only at the level of production where new value is created. In our case the developed capitalist countries exploit the surplus value created by the workers in mines, industries, as well as by agricultural workers, as distinct from commodity producing peasants, in much the same way as they exploit "their" workers at home. The cheap labour in neo-colonies helps to create a colossal return to the capital so invested. For instance, in developed capitalist countries the average return to capital is about 5% while in our countries it ranges from 40% to 200%, as in gold mining and petroleum. Thus the huge transfer of wealth from the neo-colonies to the metropolitan countries takes place through the exploitation of our workers and the looting of our peasants.

Why we allow this to happen is another question. The politicians and bureaucrats in underdeveloped countries who supervise this exploitation and plunder are not themselves underdeveloped. They enjoy as high a standard of living as their counterparts in the developed capitalist countries; and through bribery and corruption some enjoy even higher standards. They have therefore developed a vested interest in the system which they are reluctant to change, whatever they say to the contrary.

There is also emerging a new group of local millionaires who benefit from this exploitation and plunder of their people by their foreign masters; they also take advantage of the economic chaos which the system has brought about. Both groups are developing material bases for reproducing themselves as a class whose vested interest is inextricably bound to neo-colonialism.

We cannot discuss neo-colonialism without touching on the controversial question of "three worlds". Comrades have raised this issue in the essays but for some reason they did not go into it in a thoroughgoing way. Are there "three worlds" in this world of ours? The Chinese say there are, and they have categorized them as follows: First World–the Superpowers–i.e., US and USSR; Second World–Eastern and Western Europe, Japan, Canada, Australia, New Zealand; and Third World–The rest of us. They have also a thesis to support this division.

Briefly this thesis is as follows: since the advent of revisionism and capitalist restoration in the Soviet Union that country has now become a social-imperialist power, as vicious as US imperialism. And because they are new in the game they tend to be more ruthless than US imperialism.

The Soviet Union and the US have devided the world between themselves, each having its own hegemony over their respective spheres. They also struggle between themselves to expand their respective hegemony at the expense of the other.

Although they struggle between themselves these superpowers unite in their world domination. This quest for Soviet/US condominium has created contradictions between them on the one hand and the rest of the world on the other. In spite of the fact that the Soviet Union and the US respectively share ideological affinity with Eastern and Western Europe the national interests of the latter group of countries force them to resist condominium. Thus the interests of these European countries and Japan–the Second World–resisting superpower hegemony and those of the neo-colonies–the Third World–coincide, although there may be secondary contradictions between the Second and Third Worlds.

Socialists, according to this thesis, must support the national governments in the Second and Third Worlds in their objective contradiction with the superpowers even if the leaders of some of these countries are despotic, reactionary, and repressive, or subjectively pro-imperialists.

This thesis has been elevated to a theory by the Chinese Communist Party since the death of Chairman Mao who is said to be the originator of the theory.

As a result of pursuing this theory in diplomatic practice the new Chinese leaders have often found themselves in some awkward situations, the most dramatic ones being Iran and Angola. It has also resulted in China joining the World Bank and IMF, the leading organs of imperialist finance capital. All this has created a lot of confusion among Marxists the world over.

For instance, it is impossible for an Iranian Marxist, revisionist or otherwise, to support the Shah when the entire population of the country rejected him. It is equally impossible for an African Marxist to support Savimbi of Angola who is in shameless collusion with the South African fascists to dismember his country. Or to support Mobutu of Zaire or leaders like him.

Until the death of Chou-en Lai and Chairman Mao the Chinese government pursued this policy of "three worlds" only tactically. It was not elevated to a theory or strategy. They found it a useful guide with which to conduct a revolutionary diplomacy. Marxists found no difficulty in supporting this tactical guide at the time because it was accompanied by an important injunction which guided it from getting out of hand and turning it into an opportunistic diplomacy.

The injunction was that: *countries want independence, nations want liberation; people want revolution*. The last one–people want revolution–is the guiding principle and it is the main link of the whole injunction.

Where there was a clash between the socialist and imperialist camps the Chinese supported the socialist camp, as in Korea, Vietnam, and Sihanouk's Campuchea. Where there was a clash between Europe or Japan and the USA they supported Europe and Japan. Where there was a clash between the imperialist camp – USA,

Europe, Japan – and the colonial and neo-colonial countries, they supported the latter. Where there was a clash between a reactionary ruling class and the people in the neo-colonies they supported the people. The support for the people also extended to supporting the people in the US, Europe, Japan when they clashed with their governments.*

The "theory of three worlds" as interpreted by the present Chinese leaders and its practical consequences has thus become a very controversial question among Marxists.

Among the most outspoken critics of this theory are the Albanian Community Party leaders who have gone out of their way to attack not only the theory itself but to accuse Chairman Mao of having been more of a petty-bourgeois nationalist than a communist.

In these essays all the comrades seem implicitly to accept the categorization of the three worlds. For instance, one group asserts that winning concessions from the imperialists by the neo-colonies is objectively a victory for the Third World and a defeat for the imperialists. The other group concludes that such concessions are actually a decoy designed to entrap neo-colonies more firmly in the imperialist camp and thereby facilitate more intensive exploitation and plunder at this stage of the development of finance capital. The Lome I and II Conventions are said by the first group to be a victory for the African, Caribbean and Pacific (ACP) countries; while the second group regard it as a victory for the US and Japanese monopolies on the grounds that it is their capital which owns the factories in the neo-colonies whose products will now be exported to the European Economic Community with lesser restrictions.

The first group seems to view the world as a gigantic balance sheet whereby a plus on neo-colonies means a minus on the imperialists. But in the era of the IMF, World Bank, multinational corporations, free trade zones and finance capital under which the entire capitalist world, including the neo-colonies which comprise the OECD (Organization for Economic Co-operation and Development) the balance sheet view of the world seems to be unrealistic. Such a balancing can be relevant only in evaluating the gains and losses between the socialist camp and imperialism.

CONCLUSION

Finally, what is the purpose of these essays? They originate in response to the publication of three most important books to come out of East Africa. One of these is Issa Shivji's *Class Struggles in Tanzania*, one is Dan Nabudere's *The Political Economy of Imperialism*, and third is *Politics and Class Formation in Uganda* by Mahmood Mamdani. These books have inspired a lot of thinking among East African intellectuals [unfortunately they could not reach the masses because they are written in English] and especially among those with Marxist inclinations.

The purpose of these essays is obvious; Marxists do not engage in debates just for the fun of it as in school debates. Their principal task is to change the world. Their debates are about the correct understanding of the world around us. Once this

*Incidentally, the idea of the Third World came into being with the advent of the Cold War in the 1950s. The two worlds were then the Capitalist camp and the Socialist camp and the Third World was comprised of the so-called non-aligned countries. No Marxist accepted this obviously propagandistic categorization at the time on the grounds that there are only two ideologically opposing systems in the world and we are either in the one or the other, capitalist or socialist. But now both capitalist and socialist countries try to woo these countries to support their respective positions in international issues, the reason being that these "non-aligned" countries on many issues have a block vote at the U.N.

world is understood then the task is to outline policies which will guide their struggle – to draw up the general line. This is arrived at by concrete analysis of the concrete situation in any given area. To do this they use the dialectical methodology which is universally applicable and they relate it to their concrete situation.

The second point in Marxist debate is about state power: who controls it, what class interests does it serve, what is the role of the proletariat, and so on. If the state is the most important instrument in the class struggle how can the proletariat achieve state power – spontaneously, or through conscious, organized leadership? And having attained state power how should they use it in continuing the class struggle from that level?

The essays are limited to the first part only and have not touched on the second at all. This is unfortunate, especially when they are being published for the general readership. The most burning issue in people's minds at this crucial moment is: what shall we do to extricate ourselves from the horrifying situation in which Africa finds itself? Without tackling this question there is a danger that the essays might be dismissed as irrelevant and will be relegated to academic circles only. This will be a tragedy because the work which has gone into this debate would then be a wasted effort.

How do Marxists view the problem of extricating ourselves from our horrifying experience of hunger and misery? Marxists assert that to change the situation the proletariat must struggle to win state power first of all, and to do this it must organize itself under the leadership of the vanguard party. The party then trains its cadres as "professional revolutionaries" who carry out the day-to-day political work, to agitate and propagate. In other words, to take up issues which affect the masses and struggle for their resolution, and at the same time to educate the masses by raising the class consciousness of the working class and political consciousness of the masses. And also to train other cadres at the lower levels of the organization – the factory level, farm level, street and village levels, etc.

The cadres at both higher and lower levels develop a style of work which wins over people's confidence in their leadership. They do not lord it over the people but on the contrary constantly learn from them, because people may be ignorant but they are not stupid. The cadres learn what the people want, feel, aspire to, and so on as they are conveyed to them in a disjointed, sometimes incoherent and fragmented manner. They then analyse these feelings and aspirations, synthesize them in a coherent manner and formulate policies which reflect them. This style of work is known as: from the people and back to the people.

This form of organization is the surest way of leading to state power. After winning state power the proletariat is then faced with the task of establishing their own state machine on the basis of democratic dictatorship of the proletariat in alliance with the popular forces – the peasants, petty bourgeois intellectuals, oppressed minorities, etc. under their own leadership. This is the stage of the New Democracy.

Then comes the most important task of the administration of the country which is distinct from the political task of organizing state power. The basis of socialist administration is socialist accounting and control during the complex period of the transition from capitalist domination.

The economic task is more difficult than that of winning state power, and it begins by organizing it slowly, systematically and cautiously. The principal aim of such organization is the rapid development of the productive forces without which the country will be plunged into permanent and profound economic and political crises.

The aim is to improve as soon as possible the well-being of the majority of the

12

people, in our case the peasants, through increased production of material goods. This will in turn expand industrial production and the growth of the proletariat. The practical meaning of the worker/peasant alliance is for the proletarian state to help the small peasant develop their productive forces with state assistance. Without this development the worker/peasant alliance will break up and the peasants will go over to capitalism.

This assistance is based on the peasant's personal incentive during the whole period of the new democracy. If the peasants' condition is not improved, if agriculture does not flourish, then industrialization will not take place and the proletariat will not grow – they will in fact be a declassed proletariat as industrialization stagnates. Thus the industrial strategy must be linked with the development of agriculture and vice versa.

Every important branch of the economy during this period of the new democracy is built on the basis of personal incentive — collective discussion but individual responsibility. Meetings and discussions are encouraged among the people in order to remind themselves of their overall revolutionary tasks, summing up experience, setting new targets and so on, but at the same time learning to distinguish between what is appropriate for meetings from what is appropriate for administration, for production and for achieving new targets.

All this effort is to ensure that the condition of the people constantly improves and does not deteriorate. In an underdeveloped peasant country socialist revolution can triumph only on two conditions: by receiving timely support from the more advanced socialist countries; and by winning voluntary support of the peasantry. The interests of the workers and peasants differ and we must not assume that both can be satisfied by the same measures. To satisfy the peasants they must have a certain freedom of exchange; they must obtain commodities and industrial goods. Scarcity of these is the surest way of losing the confidence not only of the peasants but also of the workers. The proletariat cannot win the confidence of the people by merely telling them what they intend to do however nicely phrased this may be. The people want to see the results of what the proletariat say they can do. Once the confidence of the peasants has been won through concrete results, their enthusiasm for production will be aroused and sustained. This will pave the way for accelerated growth on the basis of planned and proportional development.

These essays are about knowing and changing the world. However much the writers may disagree, they give us an insight into what is happening around us. From this raw material we can marshal our forces to begin the first steps on our long march towards changing the world. The most hopeful event coming out of Africa today is that young Africans are asking questions.

These young people see their continent to have been turned into an imperialist playground. It is being manipulated, exploited, plundered at the expense of the people. Poverty is taken for granted, with regular interludes of plagues and famine. The three declared scourges of Africa at independence, poverty, ignorance and disease have proved to be unshakable and stubborn; if anything, they seem to be flourishing luxuriously on the fertile soil of neo-colonialism. These essays identify the core of our problems and articulate their finding in a scientific way. It is to be hoped that as many Africans as possible will read this book, for only in understanding what is at issue can we hope to move Africa to a truly prosperous future.

2

A LETTER TO APOLLINARIA

V.I. Lenin

I clearly see two trends also in your letter to a friend: one quite legitimately lays the stress on the need for economic struggle, the need to be able to make use of the workers' legal societies as well, "to respond in diverse ways to the day-to-day vital needs of the workers", and so on. All this is legitimate and correct. You are mistaken if you think that the revolutionaries "are opposed to legal societies", that such societies are "hateful" to them, that they "turn their backs on society", and so on. The revolutionaries too recognise the necessity of economic struggle, of responding also to the day-to-day vital needs, and of learning to make use of legal societies as well. Not only have the revolutionaries never and nowhere *advised* to turn one's back on society, but on the contrary have stressed that it is essential for Social-Democracy to *take the lead* in the social movement and to unite under the leadership of the revolutionary Social Democratic Party all the democratic elements. However, it is imperative to take care that the legal societies and purely economic organizations should *not separate* the workers' movement from Social-Democracy and revolutionary political struggle, but that they should, on the contrary, *link them as closely and indissolubly as possible*. But in your letter there is also that tendency (a harmful and, in my opinion, thoroughly reactionary one), the tendency to *separate* the workers' movement from Social-Democracy and revolutionary political struggle—to put off the political tasks, to replace the concept "political struggle" with the concept "struggle for legal rights", and so on.

How to draw the line between the sound and useful tendency and the harmful one? I believe there is no need for me to persuade you who have already had a taste of "meetings abroad" that we must not confine ourselves to mere talk. And would it not be ridiculous to fear examination of the question in print since it has already been discussed for a long time in letters and debates. Why should debates at meetings and writing letters be considered permissible and elucidation of controversial issues in the press a "most harmful thing capable only (???) of amusing our enemies"? This I cannot understand. Only polemics in the press can precisely establish the dividing line I am referring to, for some people are often bound to go to extremes. Of course struggle in the press will cause more ill-feeling and give us a good many hard knocks, but we are not so thin-skinned as to fear knocks! To wish for struggle without knocks, differences without struggle, would be the height of 'naivete', and if the struggle is waged *openly* it will be a hundred times better than foreign and Russian "Gubarevism", and will lead, I repeat, a hundred times faster to lasting *unity*.

Printed from the original

Written in October 26, 1900
First published in 1930 in *Lenin Miscellany* XIII

*Lenin, Collected Works Volume 43, Progress Publishers, Moscow 1969, pp. 47-48. A variant of part of the letter (*see present edition*, Vol. 34, pp. 51-54).—Ed.

3

COMBAT LIBERALISM*

Mao Tsetung

We stand for active ideological struggle because it is the weapon for ensuring unity within the Party and the revolutionary organizations in the interest of our fight. Every Communist and revolutionary should take up this weapon.

But liberalism rejects ideological struggle and stands for unprincipled peace, thus giving rise to a decadent, philistine attitude and bringing about political degeneration in certain units and individuals in the Party and the revolutionary organizations.

Liberalism manifests itself in various ways.

To let things slide for the sake of peace and friendship when a person has clearly gone wrong, and refrain from principled argument because he is an old acquaintance, a fellow townsman, a schoolmate, a close friend, a loved one, an old colleague or old subordinate. Or to touch on the matter lightly instead of going into it thoroughly, so as to keep on good terms. The result is that both the organization and the individual are harmed. This is one type of liberalism.

To indulge in irresponsible criticism in private instead of actively putting forward one's suggestions to the organization. To say nothing to people to their faces but to gossip behind their backs, or to say nothing at a meeting but to gossip afterwards. To show no regard at all for the principles of collective life but to follow one's own inclination. This is a second type.

To let things drift if they do not affect one personally; to say as little as possible while knowing perfectly well what is wrong, to be worldly wise and play safe and seek only to avoid blame. This is a third type.

Not to obey orders but to give pride of place to one's own opinions. To demand special consideration from the organization but to reject its discipline. This is a fourth type.

To indulge in personal attacks, pick quarrels, vent personal spite or seek revenge instead of entering into an argument and struggling against incorrect views for the sake of unity or progress or getting the work done properly. This is a fifth type.

To hear incorrect views without rebutting them and even to hear counter-revolutionary remarks without reporting them, but instead to take them calmly as if nothing had happened. This is a sixth type.

To be among the masses and fail to conduct propaganda and agitation or speak at meetings or conduct investigations and inquiries among them, and instead to be indifferent to them and show no concern for their well-being, forgetting that one is a Communist and behaving as if one were an ordinary non-Communist. This is a seventh type.

To see someone harming the interests of the masses and yet not feel indignant, or dissuade or stop him or reason with him, but to allow him to continue. This is an

*Mao Tsetung, *Selected Works*, Volume II, Foreign Language Press, Peking, 1967, pp. 31-33.

eighth type.

To work half-heartedly without a definite plan or direction; to work perfunctorily and muddle along–"So long as one remains a monk, one goes on tolling the bell." This is a ninth type.

To regard oneself as having rendered great service to the revolution, to pride oneself on being a veteran, to disdain minor assignments while being quite unequal to major tasks, to be slipshod in work and slack in study. This is a tenth type.

To be aware of one's own mistakes and yet make no attempt to correct them, taking a liberal attitude towards oneself. This is an eleventh type.

We could name more. But these eleven are the principal types.

They are all manifestations of liberalism.

Liberalism is extremely harmful in a revolutionary collective. It is a corrosive which eats away unity, undermines cohesion, causes apathy and creates dissension. It robs the revolutionary ranks of compact organization and strict discipline, prevents policies from being carried through and alienates the Party organizations from the masses which the Party leads. It is an extremely bad tendency.

Liberalism stems from petty-bourgeois selfishness, it places personal interests first and the interests of the revolution second, and this gives rise to ideological, political and organizational liberalism.

People who are liberals look upon the principles of Marxism as abstract dogma. They approve of Marxism, but are not prepared to practise it or to practise it in full; they are not prepared to replace their liberalism by Marxism. These people have their Marxism, but they have their liberalism as well–they talk Marxism but practise liberalism; they apply Marxism to others but liberalism to themselves. They keep both kinds of goods in stock and find a use for each. This is how the minds of certain people work.

Liberalism is a manifestation of opportunism and conflicts fundamentally with Marxism. It is negative and objectively has the effect of helping the enemy; that is why the enemy welcomes its preservation in our midst. Such being its nature, there should be no place for it in the ranks of the revolution.

We must use Marxism, which is positive in spirit, to overcome liberalism, which is negative. A Communist should have largeness of mind and he should be staunch and active, looking upon the interests of the revolution as his very life and subordinating his personal interests to those of the revolution; always and everywhere he should adhere to principle and wage a tireless struggle against all incorrect ideas and actions, so as to consolidate the collective life of the Party and strengthen the ties between the Party and the masses; he should be more concerned about the Party and the masses than about any private person, and more concerned about others than about himself. Only thus can he be considered a Communist.

All loyal, honest, active and upright Communists must unite to oppose the liberal tendencies shown by certain people among us, and set them on the right path. This is one of the tasks on our ideological front.

4

TANZANIA – THE STRUGGLE FOR NATIONAL INDEPENDENCE AND SOCIALISM

Comments on Issa Shivji's essay "Tanzania: The Class Struggle Continues"

Peter Meyns*

This article was stimulated by Issa Shivji's essay "Tanzania: The Class Struggle Continues" which is not only a major contribution to scientific analysis of the history of class struggle in Tanzania, but also contains much material to further the debate on Tanzanian *ujamaa – socialism*.

However, I differ with Shivji on certain essential points. These points do not so much touch the facts he gives or his description of recent history of class struggle in Tanzania, but his analysis of this development. Questions of class analysis, with concrete reference to Tanzaina, are therefore, the main subject of these comments.

The approach taken in this article is determined, as are Shivji's writings, by Marxist analysis. Taking the Marxist approach means analysing the concrete reality of development in Tanzania in the light of the historical experiences of the working class and the oppressed peoples throughout the world in their struggle for freedom, national independence and socialism, and of the theoretical generalizations of these experience.

The central question to be answered here is what concretely is the stage of development in Tanzania today. Is Tanzania building socialism, or is it fighting to defend and strengthen its national independence against diverse imperialist interests?

What line does Shivji follow in his analysis of the recent history of class struggle in Tanzania? He describes three periods in this development.[1]

(1) With regard to the pre-independence period, he says, "the petty bourgeoisie for various obvious reasons was the only class in a position to lead the Uhuru struggle against the colonial state" (p. 51), while "the concrete conditions in Tanzania itself did not favour workers' leadership." (p. 52) Summing up his assessment of the petty bourgeoisie Shivji's adds:

> Thus by the sheer method of elimination, the petty bourgeoisie was the most well-suited to lead the Uhuru struggle. More important, however, is the fact that it had immediate material interests to lead such a struggle. In a historical

---

* Peter Meyns is a Lecturer at the Free University in West Berlin (West Germany). He was a research associate at University College, Dar es Salaam, from January 1963 to April 1969 and revisited Tanzania in July/August 1973.

sense, it was a rising class whose interests coincided with those of the broad masses and hence progressive. The African petty bourgeoisie could only aspire to the economic position of a dependent commercial bourgeoisie. Unlike the classical national bourgeoisie, it was incapable of a national bourgeois revolution to build independent national capitalism. This would require disengagement from the world capitalist system – a radical structural change – a task which the petty bourgeoisie could hardly accomplish. It would, among other things, in fact, mean its own liquidation. Such a task could be accomplished only by a highly developed national bourgeoisie or by a workers/peasants alliance under the leadership of proletarian ideology. . . . The petty bourgeoisie was interested in political freedom as an end in itself and at most to facilitate its own struggle against the commercial bourgeoisie, not for the total emancipation of the whole society. (pp. 53-4)

(2) Following independence we find the petty bourgeoisie in political power and consolidating its position as ruling bureaucratic bourgeoisie through measures representing an "economic expression of nationalism", to use President Nyerere's own words.[2] This period culminated with the Arusha Declaration and the subsequent nationalizations. Of this period Shivji writes:

...the contradictions that were being ironed out during this phase were between the petty bourgeoisie and the commercial bourgeoisie. Objectively, the workers and poor peasants had limited interest in this struggle as a means to "clear the way" for *their* struggle which could only be carried out under this leadership and under the scientific socialist ideology. (pp. 72-3)

Historically, he adds, the 'bureaucratic bourgeoisie' has played and, to some extent, continues to play a progressive role... Firstly, the very class struggle between the petty bourgeoisie (led by the 'bureaucratic bourgeoisie') and the commercial bourgeoisie was not only inevitable but historically necessary as much as political independence was necessary for the conduct of this class struggle. In a way, this struggle is helping to clear the way for further struggles unencumbered by the obfuscation of radical divisions. Thus the liquidation of the inherited *racial* structures was *conditio sine qua non* for 'purifying' the class struggles. (pp. 88-9)

(3) The progressive role of the bureaucratic bourgeoisie is also seen in the following respect, particularly significant for the ensuing development of class struggle in Tanzania.

... by putting socialism on the agenda, it marked the beginning of class struggles for socialism and the discussions of the proletarian ideology. (p. 71)

Resulting from the contradictions within the petty bourgeoisie the adoption of the TANU Guidelines strengthen this line. "Mwongozo is the most progressive document to emarste from TANU and marks the beginning of the proletarian line." (p. 90) Though Shiviji is not blind to the fact that in the present historical situation in the Third World "even capitalism and neo-colonialism have to be wrapped up in socialist rhetoric and vocabulary", he underlines as more important "the fact that though material *class* forces may not immediately warrant it, a few progressive and revolutionary leaders manage to push through (officially) radical ideas and policies. The adoption of the Mwongozo by TANU, with its progressive features, was such an event." (p. 92)

What the advent of Mwongozo means for Tanzania, Shivji gives his view on this, by way of a conclusion to his article:

The road to socialism is a long one of continuing class struggles. In the process of its class struggles, the Tanzanian society has made substantial progress, but it has a long way to go. With the rise of the proletarian line, however, the long march has begun. Socialism cannot be achieved without class struggle, whatever the form. The class struggle must continue even beyond the first phases of socialism. The class struggle continues. (p. 108).

Having quoted a few passages from Shivji's essay let me point out from where I am going to take up my comments.

First, I disagree with his statement made with regard to the pre-independence period that the petty bourgeoisie "in a historical sense, was a rising class."

Second, the idea of "purifying the class struggle" used to explain the "historical necessity" of the class struggle between the bureaucratic and the commercial bourgeoisie, and the "progressive role" of the former itself needs clarifying.

Third, the bureaucratic bourgeoisie, according to Shivji, has put "socialism on the agenda" in Tanzania. By adopting *Mwongozo* it has marked "the beginning of the proletarian line", more generally it allows "a few progressive and revolutionary leaders to push through (officially) radical ideals and policies." What does all this mean with regard to the concrete stage of development in Tanzania today?

Fourth, the deficiencies of Shivji's analysis come to light in his last few sentences. "The class struggle must continue even beyond the first phases of socialism", he states. Who will disagree with that. But the essential question is: Has Tanzania reached the first phase of socialism or not? What historical stage precisely has development in Tanzania reached? And this is exactly the question to which Shivji does not give a clear, explicit answer. He does, however, give an answer implicitly. It is that Tanzania is on what some call the 'non-capitalist road of development', the '3rd' or 'middle road to socialism', and the 'road of peaceful transition to socialism'. When renowned Marxist writers, and Shivji is not alone here, appear to adopt this 'theory', though probably unintentionally, then it is high time that the issue involved in this theory as well as its relevance for Tanzania are openly discussed. The following article hopefully may serve as an opening contribution to this new line of debate on Tanzanian political and economic development.

1. WHO IS THE RISING CLASS UNDER IMPERIALISM?

The present historical epoch is that of imperialism, the highest and last stage of capitalism. It is the epoch in which the bourgeoisie, erstwhile a revolutionary class with the task of destroying feudalism and liberating the productive forces by establishing the capitalist order, having accomplished its historical task has turned into an outright reactionary force fighting to maintain its system of exploitation and oppression against the revolutionary forces created and strengthened by capitalism itself. In his lucid analysis of imperialism Lenin already made this quite clear.

> The struggle of rising capital emancipating itself nationally against feudalism has given way to the struggle of ultra-reactionary, outdated finance capital, which has outlived itself and is moving towards downfall and decay, against the new forces.... The bourgeoisie has changed from a rising, progressive class into a descending, decaying, internally walked, reactionary class. Quite another class has become – in the large historical sense – the rising class."[3]

The rising class under imperialism is the working class. This is true on a national level as it is in the context of the world-wide imperialist system.

In particular, this is also true of those countries under imperialist domination where the influence of feudalist and other pre-capitalist social orders is still widespread. Mao Tsetung made an important contribution to class analysis in underdeveloped countries when investigating the concrete conditions in his own country, China, a country with a numerically small working class and an overwhelming peasant population. Nevertheless:

> No matter which classes, parties or individual persons of an oppressed nation participate in the revolution–this revolution becomes, if only all of them fight against imperialism, part of the proletarian-socialist world revolution, and its participants become allies thereof whether they are conscious of this fact or not, whether they understand it or not.[4]

And he asserts that the responsibility of leading the people in this struggle against imperialism "inevitably falls on the shoulders of the working class."[5]

What is more, there is only one alternative. If the people's struggle does not become a firm part of the proletarian socialist revolution then its development will sooner or later lead back into the arms of the imperialists.

> Under the international conditions existing today the brave fighters of the colonies and half-colonies must decide whether to join the imperialist front and to become part of the forces of international counter-revolution, or to join the anti-imperialist front and to become part of the forces of world revolution. One of the two, there is no other way.[6]

"One of the two, there is no other way"–in a historical sense. This leaves no room for the petty bourgeoisie as a rising class. To claim such a role for the petty bourgeoisie, as Shivji does, can only be understood as the beginning of a '3rd road', a 'middle road' between that of the imperialists and the bourgeoisie on the one side and that of socialist revolution and the working class on the other side. Lacking clarity about the role of the petty bourgeoisie, in other words, is already part of my main criticism of Shivji's analysis, and so what follows is all part of my critique of the so-called 'non-capitalist road of development' in which petty bourgeois nationalist forces in political power play a central part.

We must look at the role of the petty bourgeoisie more closely, however, because empirical reality and the views of a leading African revolutionary, namely Guinea-Bissao's Amilcar Cabral, at first sight appear to give weight to Shivji's views on this question.

Not only in Tanzania, but in all African countries, the independence movement, was, in fact, led by the petty bourgeoisie. The neo-colonialist reality of these countries after independence starts from there. In other words, under the leadership of the petty bourgeoisie the anti-colonialist independence movement representing the interests and deepest desires of the oppressed masses of the people was led back into the arms of the imperialists. The independence movement in Africa was a broad people's movement which gained such strength after the 2nd Imperialist World War that by 1960 and the following years the main colonialist powers on the continent, England, France and Belgium, were forced to concede political independence to their former colonies. Nevertheless imperialist domination was not broken, neo-colonialist rule was established.

The petty bourgeoisie was well rewarded materially for having accomplished this feat. Of course, Shivji is fully aware of the limited interests of the petty-bourgeoisie. Its interest is not, he clearly sees, "the total emancipation of the whole society." But how can he write then of this same class that "in a historical sense, it was a rising class whose interests coincided with those of the broad masses and hence progressive"?

The interests of the petty bourgeoisie only to a limited extent coincide with the interests of the broad masses, and to this extent only is it progressive. This partial identity of interests is the basis of the alliance between the broad masses and the petty bourgeoisie in the independence movement. The other side of the picture is that the petty bourgeoisie on the basis of this anti-colonialist alliance betrayed the interests of the broad masses for total emancipation of the whole society. In this historical sense it is a reactionary force serving its own limited interests which remain dependent on the imperialist powers.

A class force characterised by such a contradictory nature can never be a rising class in a historical sense. Under conditions of imperialism a rising class is the class which most consequently represents the interests of the broad masses for total emancipation of the whole society – that class is the working class.

The given empirical reality of class structure in colonial Tanzania, or for that matter in colonial Guinea-Bissao, notably the fact that the working class is at an early stage of its development and numerically still small, may be even insignificant, does not mean that of necessity the leading role in the anti-colonialist movement must fall to the petty bourgeoisie.

Cabral, quite regarded as a leading spokesman – in theory as well as in practice – of the African revolution is frequently quoted in this context. Speaking of the situation in his country, Guinea-Bissao, Cabral writes: "Events have shown that the only social sector capable of being aware of the reality of imperialist domination and of directing the state apparatus inherited from this domination is the native petty bourgeoisie." But in his very next sentence Cabral hastens to add that given the contradictory nature of the petty bourgeoisie this "situation constitutes one of the weaknesses of the national liberation movement"[7] and clearly places it before the only possible historical alternative: subordination to imperialist capital or support of the native working classes.[8]

Cabral's analysis shows clearly that the petty bourgeoisie can only to a limited extent (one limitation is the colonial context itself[9] and due to certain *capacities* it has played a revolutionary role, that, in a historical sense, it does not even represent an independent class force.

Therefore, it is quite wrong to say, as Rodney does in his article "Some Implications of the Question of Disengagement from Imperialism, the battle of ideas is within the petty-bourgeois stratum"[10] and that "the working classes can choose between the different lines that emanate from the petty-bourgeoisie taken as a whole".[11] This is a distortion of Cabral's analysis. His point is that members of the petty bourgeoisie have the capacity to attain full awareness of the reality of imperialist domination. However, only to the extent that they side with the people and join their struggle can revolutionaries of petty bourgeois origin develop revolutionary ideas. It is not a question of the "class committing suicide"[12]–here Cabral himself coined a misleading phrase – but of individual members leaving their class to take a working class standpoint, and of the working classes developing an anti-imperialist alliance to include the progressive sections of the petty bourgeoisie.

It is important to dinstinguish these two aspects when analysing the role of the petty bourgeoisie. The one is the question of capacity[13] of developing a proletarian consciousness of the imperialist system. This is a point of general relevance to the proletarian class struggle already dealt with by Lenin. In *What is to be done?* he wrote (quoting the early and still Marxist Kautsky):

> Modern socialist consciousness can only develop on the basis of deep scientific insight.... However, the carrier of science is not the proletariat, but bourgeois intelligentsia; so modern socialism grew in individual members of this stratum and was passed on by them to intellectually outstanding proletarians who carry it into the class struggle of the proletariat where conditions permit. Socialist consciousness is, therefore, something carried into the class struggle of the proletariat from the outside, not something developed originally from within.[14]

And Lenin draws the following conclusion from these words:

> If now there can be no question of an independent ideology elaborated by the workers' masses themselves in the course of their movement, then the question can only be: bourgeois or socialist ideology. There is no middle road here (because) humanity has not produced a 'third' ideology, just as in any society turn to pieces by class antagonisms there can never be an ideology which stands outside or above the classes.[15]

The other aspect is the question of the petty bourgeoisie or certain sections of the petty bourgeoisie being capable of playing a leading role in the independence movement. This chance exists as long as proletarian leadership which is the only guarantee for ultimate success of the independence movement as far as the interests of the people's masses are concerned, has not been established. This was the situation in colonial Tanzania and to a certain extent, too, as Cabral's writings show at the beginning of the liberation struggle in Guinea-Bissao. It does not represent a strength, but on the contrary constitutes a weakness of every anti-imperialist movement, a contradiction which must be solved.

In Guinea-Bissao this contradiction has been solved in a revolutionary way, though this does not mean, of course, that petty bourgeois elements will not try to re-assert themselves. The murder of Amilcar Cabral was tragic proof of this, while at the same time turning into an outstanding example of the revolutionary strength of the PAIGC and the people of Guinea-Bissao and the Cape Verdes.

Shivji quotes Cabral at length (pp. 23-25) to show that from the beginning of the liberation struggle the leadership of the PAIGC recognised the need and went about establishing proletarian leadership.

In 1961 already in the manifesto of the UNTG, the national Union of Guinean Workers, it was stated:

> In this struggle the workers of our country, the wage-earners, peasants and employees, have and will play the decisive role until final victory under the leadership of the revolutionary party of our people.

This role they have assumed to an increasingly large extent in the course of the struggle, so that in 1971 Cabral could declare:

> If in the beginning the leaders of the struggle were from the petty bourgeoisie – like me – with only a few workers, gradually new people have come to lead the party and today most of the leaders are workers and peasants.[16]

To underline the main point here again; what is significant in, for instance, Cabral's contribution to the liberation struggle is not his petty bourgeois origin, as some seem to think, but his proletarian class standpoint. Only from this standpoint was he able to recognise the petty bourgeoisie not as "a rising class", but as an ambivalent force, at the same time a help and danger for the people's struggle.

And when talking about the transformation of the progressive elements of the petty bourgeoisie from the proletarian stand point one factor must be mentioned which has been the decisive one in this progress in Guinea-Bissao as well as in Angola and Mozambique: the fact that for over 10 years now the peoples in these countries have been leading an armed struggle for national liberation. When Cabral unequivocally states "that the only effective way of definitely fulfilling the aspirations of the peoples, that is to say of attaining national liberation, is by armed struggle"[17] he is drawing general conclusions from his own people's concrete experience.

Surely, when looking at Guinea-Bissao and at Tanzania the difference with regard to this decisive factor is more relevant than certain similarities in the class structure of the two countries at the beginning of the anti-colonial independence movement.

2. LEADING THE CLASS STRUGGLE–OR FOLLOWING IT

Turning to the development after independence we find TANU, the recognized leader of the independence movement, establishing itself as state party–the petty bourgeoisie establishing itself as bureaucratic bourgeoisie.

In his description of the development of class struggle in Tanzania since independence Shivji puts much stress on the progressive role "the 'bureaucratic' bourgeoisie has played and, to some extent, continues to play." The progressive elements in the politics of the bureaucratic bourgeoisie in Tanzania are not to be disputed. From the beginning its policy of using the peasant backing it had won during the independence movement to set up its predominance over the commercial bourgeoisie also involved measures to defend and consolidate the country's independence.

This inevitably led to contradictions between the Tanzania government and the imperialist powers. Early examples of this were the conflict with West Germany about the GDR diplomatic mission following Union with Zanzibar in 1964, and the rift with Britain over the Smith regime's unilateral declaration of independence in 1965.

These assertions of Tanzania's independence led to further contradictions in the form of reduced economic aid commitments and payments from the imperialist countries.[18] Such economic repercussions obliged the Tanzania government to reassess its own economic policies. The Arusha Declaration and the subsequent nationalizations were the result. The best explanation of these measures has been given by President Nyerere himself. Speaking at one of the plants taken over by the National Development Corporation he said: "Our purpose was thus primarily a nationalist purpose; it was an extension of the political control the Tanzanian people secured in 1961."[19] And the TANU Guidelines follow the same line when in face of new external threats (the military *coup* in neighbouring Uganda, the imperialist invasion in Guinea) and increasing internal contradictions (the capacity of important sections of the bureaucratic bourgeoisie which must inevitably undermine its anyway shaky alliance with the peasants and the workers) it characterizes the state party – TANU – still as Liberation Movement.[20]

These progressive elements in Tanzania's policies are proof of the nationalist aspirations of its government. They distinguish Tanzania from those independent African states whose bureaucratic bourgeoisies and state parties precipitated the sell-out of their country's resources to the imperialists after independence. However, they have not, as the TANU Guidelines correctly state, led to total liberation, to liberation from all form of imperialist domination.

The leading force in the development of class struggle in Tanzania since independence has been the bureaucratic bourgeoisie. Based on its alliance with the peasants and the workers it has successfully reduced the influence and strength of the commercial bourgeoisie and consolidated its own.

This struggle Shivji declares "was not only inevitable but historically necessary." There is no reason to dispute that this is the way the class struggle in Tanzania has gone, but what about the historical necessity of this way–*historical necessity*, in particular, for whom? Shivji asserts that this historical necessity existed for the workers and poor peasants, because the contradictions between the petty bourgeoisie and the commercial bourgeoisie, inherited social structures involved in this contradiction had to be "ironed out" and this "was *conditio sine qua non* for 'purifying' the class struggles."

Looked at from the historical task of the working class to lead the people's masses to total national liberation and independence two views on class analysis and the development of class struggle have to be distinguished. These two views have played a significant role in the working class movement for many years. In his book *What is to be done?* published in 1902 Lenin referred to them as "spontaneity" and "consciousness".

Shivji's view is that of spontaneity, that of relying on objective historical movements to go on, and to regard these movements as historically necessary preliminaries before the working class takes the lead. The idea of "purifying" the class struggles is an expression of this view. So is Shivji's further statement that in Tanzania the bureaucratic bourgeoisie, rather than the working class and the people's masses, "put socialism on the agenda" and thereby "marked the beginning of class struggles for socialism". More than that: by publishing the TANU Guidelines it even marked "the beginning of the proletarian line".[21]

There is obviously something wrong here. It is one thing to say that gaining political independence is a necessary step on the road to total liberation. But it is quite something else to identify this political goal with petty bourgeois leadership in this struggle. It is one thing to recognize the necessity of liquidating inherited racial structures, quite another to declare the leading role of the bureaucratic bourgeoisie in this process as a historical necessity. As Cabral clearly stated, petty bourgeois leadership in the national liberation movement is one of its main weaknesses as far as the ultimate aim of the people's masses, total liberation, is concerned. And he only envisaged it as a possibility at all during the colonial period.

Not to stress the historical necessity of proletarian in the earliest possible phase of the anti-colonial and anti-imperialist movement, as Cabral did, and to recognise this as a crucial factor in the liberation struggle and the main task of all conscious proletarian forces is to trust blindly the objective and spontaneous course of historical movement.

Where will the spontaneous struggle of the Tanzanian working class, which have taken place since 1971 and in which Shivji rightly sees a most significant development, lead if they remain without organized proletarian leadership? Lenin gave the answer to this question when he wrote:

> The spontaneous development of the workers' movement leads precisely to its subordination under bourgeois ideology, ... because spontaneous workers' movement is trade-unionism, is trade-unionism alone, and trade-unionism means precisely ideological enslavement of the workers by the bourgeoisie. Therefore, our task, the task of social-democracy, lies in the struggle against spontaneity. Our task is to get the workers' movement away from the spontaneous tendency of trade-unionism to place itself under the wings of the bourgeoisie, and to bring it under the wings of revolutionary social-democracy.[22]

From this standpoint what becomes most significant is the reaction of Tanzania's leadership to demand that organized proletarian leadership must be created, either within or without TANU as the national liberation movement, as a necessary condition of the struggle for socialism. When, to give just one example, Ngombale-Mwiru spoke in very general terms of the need for "a vanguard within the mass party"[23] his view was refuted in strong terms just one week later by the late Jacob Namfua then Regional Commissioner for Kilimanjaro, as "both misguided and

misplaced", and the reference of "dogmatic Marxism-Leninism" was not missing.[24]
And when next he spoke at Kivukoni College, of which Ngombale-Mwiru was
still Principal at that time, President Nyerere made his refutal of the vanguard
party a main theme of his talk, too.[25]

"The class struggle continues" – Shivji's last words on p. 108 are too general to be
relevant. The important question is: Who is leading it? The spontaneous strikes
notwithstanding, the leading force in Tanzania remains the bureaucratic
bourgeoisie. What does this fact mean for the ultimate aim of the working class and
the people's masses?

Shivji's analysis implies relying on the spontaneous continuation of the class
struggle. Similar proposals were made in Chile under the Allende government. The
Allende government's line of adhering to bourgeoisie legality, some argued, had its
disadvantages, but was historically necessary nonetheless and in the interest of the
working class and the people's masses because it would allow them to prepare for
the forthcoming battle with the bourgeoisie and its imperialist strongmen. In Chile,
too, the class struggle continued. Disarmed ideologically and unarmed militarily
by Allende's ideology of 'peaceful transition' to socialism the Chilean people
suffered immense losses at the hands of the fascist military junta. Notwithstanding
the heroic resistance of the Chilean people the Chilean revolution suffered its
biggest defeat for years.

The tragic events in Chile are a bitter practical lesson for Marxist class analysis,
too, one that we should not forget so soon.

3. THE 'NON-CAPITALIST' ROAD OF DEVELOPMENT

Chilean example is, in fact, of still more general significance. In Chile many
'radicals' propagated the view that the Allende government was a necessary stage in
the interest of the working class and the people as a whole notwithstanding its
compromise character, its adherence to bourgeois legality, and so on. Similarly, in
Tanzania Shivji comes to the conclusion that "a few progressive and revolutionary
leaders manage to push through (officially) radical ideas and policies."

Shivji does not make the position he takes here and in other remarks explicit.
Not so in Chile, however. There, the Allende government was widely propagated as
an example of the 'non-capitalist' road of development, as proof of the 'theory of
peaceful transition to socialism'.

Let us take a look at the content of this 'theory' in order to understand why all the
critical points I have raised with regard to Shivji's essay meet here.

Like all revisionist theory the 'theory of non-capitalist development' is derived
from an originally Marxist-Leninist standpoint. Raising the question whether the
peoples "who are liberating themselves now and among whom we recognize today,
after the war, a progressive movement necessarily have to pass through the
capitalist stage of development of the economy"[26] the 2nd World Congress of the
Comintern in 1920 answered with a clear: No. In his "Report From the
Commission in the National and Colonial Question" Lenin went on to say that the
Comintern must establish the guiding line "that the underdeveloped countries with
the help of the proletariat of the most advanced countries can reach the Soviet
order and via certain stages of development communism without having to pass
through the capitalist stage of development."[27]

In the same report Lenin also dealt with the difference between the reformist and
the revolutionary line within the national liberation movement. He said:

... The imperialist bourgeoisie is doing its best to bring to life a reformist
movement among the oppressed peoples, too. A certain approach has taken

place between the bourgeoisie of the exploiting countries and that of the colonial countries so that the bourgeoisie of the oppressed countries very often in fact, even in most cases – supports the national movements, but at the same time in agreement with the imperialist bourgeoisie, i.e. together with it, fights all revolutionary movements and revolutionary classes.[28]

Needless to say, only a revolutionary movement will lead to full national liberation. Liberation movements in Asia, Africa and Latin America have recognized the truth of the analysis made at the 2nd World Congress of the Comintern in the course of their own concrete struggles. So, for instance, the MPLA, the People's Movement for the Liberation of Angola, declared:

There are two roads which can lead a colonised people to independence; the reformist road, which leads to neo-colonialism, and the revolutionary one leading to complete independence.... The revolutionary road is certainly a much more difficult one. It requires a strong organisation, a national struggle, a ceaseless battle against tribalism, a dynamic guerilla war in which higher forms of struggle are developed, a tremendous spirit of self-sacrifice and discipline in all militants, an immense amount of work to raise the consciousness of the masses and active participation by leaders in the concrete tasks to be carried out together with the people. But the revolutionary road is the only one which will lead to complete independence and the restoration of the dignity of the Angolan People.... So let us follow the revolutionary road laid down by the MPLA.[29]

In contrast to this view the 'theory of non-capitalist development' propagates the reformist road as revolutionary. Speaking at the seminar on "Africa – national and social revolution" in Cairo in 1966 the Soviet theoretician Sobolev developed this line.

The specificity of the democratic stage of the social revolution in Africa furthermore lies in the fact that in by far the most cases it is really possible to avoid civil war between the antagonistic classes to isolate the inimical class elements with political and economic means by uniting the people and to submit them to the will of the domocratic majority.... It may be said that the gradual character of the revolution and the broad application of the reform method in Africa give to the revolution an extremely specific character.[30]

This is, in fact, according to this view that "makes the transition of the liberated countries to socialism on the peaceful road possible."[31]

Though the 'theory of non-capitalist' development in words strongly rejects the idea of a 3rd road between imperialism and socialism the definition it gives for the stage of 'non-capitalist' development cannot in fact be understood in any other way.

The transition of a number of liberated countries on the road of non-capitalist development means that already it no longer suffices to point to the specific position which they have within the capitalist world economy. These countries can no longer be regarded completely as part of the capitalist world economy even though they have not yet integrated themselves into the socialist world economy. It is a particular type of transitional, of intermediary state.[32]

These words give valuable insight into the interest behind this 'theory'. Its aim is to loosen the ties of the countries following the 'non-capitalist' road with the US-dominated capitalist world economy and to put them firmly into the orbit of the US-dominated 'socialist' world economy. It is only consequent, therefore, that "the overwhelming power of the socialist world system which in the international context fulfills the role of political vanguard towards the peoples who are struggling for full liberation from imperialism" is given out as "the decisive factor which today makes the development on the non-capitalist road in Asia and Africa possible and real."[33] This is a blatant contradiction to the aim of the oppressed peoples who are decided to struggle for complete independence and liberation from any form of exploitation by relying first of all on their own revolutionary forces.

The 3rd road character of the 'theory of non-capitalist development' becomes quite apparent when we look at the class character it gives to this stage of development.

> A specificity of non-capitalist development in the anti-imperialist nation states in Asia and Africa is to be seen in the fact that under conditions in which the national bourgeoisie proves to be incapable of realising a general democratic programme on the road of social progress, and in which the working class is not yet in a position to directly take over the leadership of the revolution, representatives of petty bourgeois intermediary strata, in particular revolutionary-democratic forces from within the intelligentsia, take over hegemony in the liberation movement and stand in for anti-imperialist and anti-capitalist transformations which can lead towards socialism if the revolutionary aim is respected and deepened.[34]

To underline the crucial point:

> The political basis of the new power is a broad alliance which is led by non-proletarian, petty bourgeois class forces.[35]

In other words, a state led by petty bourgeois class forces, forces whose class interests ultimately are inimical to socialism, is called upon to lead the country towards socialism. Here, class struggle, held by Marx to be the driving force of history, appears to have lost reality, and given way to class harmony.

This impression is strengthened when we learn that of all bourgeois institutions "in most countries with non-capitalist development the army has taken over a determining role as an element in the creation and functioning of the political basis of the state and as an instrument to enforce the hegemony of non-proletarian progressive class forces."[36] At this point, we only have to look at Chile again, at the faith put in the army by Allende and at the fascist military coup against Allende's 'non-capitalist' government, or at the 'non-capitalist' military regime in Peru[37], or at other examples[38] to recognize the illusionary character of the 'theory of non-capitalist development'–inimical to the interests of the working class and the people's masses.

From Chile we can learn that what Lenin wrote in a polemic against Kautsky, after Kautsky had left the Marxist standpoint to take a reformist, bourgeois position, is still true today:

> "Never–unless in the sweet phantasy of the sweet fool Kautsky–will the exploiters submit to the decisions of the majority of the exploited without having tried to retain their advantages in a last, desperate struggle in a series of struggles.[39]

* * * *

To what extent do Shivji and other writers on Tanzania follow the line of the 'theory of non-capitalist development'? They do not, as mentioned already, explicitly take this position. That important part of the 'theory' which asserts that the role of the Soviet Union is decisive instead of underlining the principle of self-reliance they reject.[40]

But the crucial aspect of any theory is its class content. And here both take the same line. Shivji says that the Tanzanian bureaucratic bourgeoisie by adopting the Arusha Declaration "put socialism on the agenda" and by accepting the TANU Guidelines "marked the beginning of the proletarian line". Revisionist theory declares that in Tanzania "the non-capitalist road of development was proclaimed by the Arusha Declaration".[41] Moreover, both see this stage of development where the state is in the hands of "non-proletarian, petty bourgeois class forces" as a historical necessity, given the present concrete conditions in Tanzania or in underdeveloped countries generally, on "the long march to socialism," as Shivji says.

In other words, by a simple act of proclamation a process of change, of "gradual evolution of power to the left"[42], of reforms, in short: of 'peaceful transition' is initiated. The most advanced section of the ruling class is led by the logic of this process to adopt elements of scientific socialism.[43] "Scientific socialism becomes more and more the foundations and content of the conception of society."[44]

This leads to new contradictions within the country because the reactionary forces oppose this process. Here, we recall Shivji pinpoints the progressive role of the bureaucratic bourgeois in that by allowing "a few revolutionary leaders to push through radical ideas and policies" it "purifies" the class struggle.

At this juncture in Tanzania's development Shivji, very detailed in historical description, but rather vague in theoretical conclusions, can only give the outlook of continuing class struggles. The 'theory of non-capitalist development' is more explicit again in envisaging the step by step isolation of the reactionary forces and the gradual process of "leading the working class closer to power".[45] This 'peaceful transition' ultimately is said to lead to the point where the working class itself takes over power and establishes the dictatorship of the proletariat. Against their material interest and without serious resistance power will have slipped from the bourgeoisie's and the imperialists' hands into those of the working class. I have tried to show that this is not the road history follows.

There is no reason to identify Shivji's position with the ultimate conclusions of and, in particular, the material interests behind the theory of 'non-capitalist' development. His description of class struggle in Tanzania, however, especially with regard to the role of petty bourgeois class forces, in the final analysis implies a '3rd road' of development towards socialism along the same line.[46] What is more, Shivji's essay is certainly a good description of the reality of Tanzanian development so far.

* * * *

The 'theory of non-capitalist development' justifies its position with the need to create a broad-based front uniting all classes and strata of the people in the common struggle against imperialism. The need for such a front is undisputed. It was an essential part of the position developed at the 2nd World Congress of the Comintern. In his already quoted report on this question Lenin stated that "the large mass of the population in the underdeveloped countries consists of peasants who are representatives of bourgeois-capitalist relations" and that therefore proletarian parties cannot develop a revolutionary line without "establishing certain relations to the peasant's movement and without actively supporting it."[47]

However, the main question in the national-revolutionary movement – as in all class struggle – is the question of state power.[48] And revolutionary struggle for state power involves the question of the class character of the state whose task it is to lead the people to total emancipation. Under conditions of imperialism there is only one answer to this question. There is no 3rd road. A state under petty bourgeois leadership most certainly can have progressive elements by virtue of which it will stand in partial opposition to imperialism, but if the class struggle is not solved in a revolutionary way, i.e. establishment of a people's democratic state under proletarian leadership[49], such a 'non-capitalist' state will follow its own logic–that of one other 'specific' road of imperialist-neo-colonialist development.

> The government of the *Unidad Popular* undertook a number of measures and implemented reforms whose aim was to consolidate freedom and national independence and to guarantee the independent development of the country's economy... But Allende's tragedy lies in the fact that he believed he could convince the reactionary forces with reason, that he could bring them to stop their hostile activity and to give up their old positions and privileges peacefully... History has proven and the events in Chile, which did not have a socialist, but only a democratic regime, have shown that the establishment of socialism via the parliamentary road is completely impossible.[50]

What, finally, of an underdeveloped country with an as yet insignificant working class? There are historical experiences of such countries. Albania, for instance, is one of them. The development in Albania is also a practical lesson for Marxism class analysis.

> Under the conditions of the underdeveloped countries where a revolutionary working class party does not exist the creation of the subjective pre-conditions for the victory of a true people's revolution must begin with the foundation of the Marxist-Leninist party, with the indispensable political leadership of the revolution. Without this leadership there can be no question of the taking-over of power by the toiling masses or of the uninterrupted development of the revolution in order to prepare the transition to the road of socialist development. The usually small number of the working class in the underdeveloped countries, their relatively low ideological and cultural level, their limited experience of organisation and in political class struggle–all that can be no argument to refute the necessity and the possibility of creating the party of the working class.[51]

4. TANZANIA–THE STRUGGLE FOR FULL NATIONAL INDEPENDENCE CONTINUES

Our final question must be, even if the answer in this article cannot be exposed in detail[52], where does Tanzania stand today? We remarked above that the road of development suggested by the 'theory of non-capitalist development' comes close to the reality of Tanzanian development described by Shivji. For the same reason, obviously, the ideological proponents of 'non-capitalist' development among African countries most frequently quote Tanzania, together with Guinea, Congo, Algeria and the UAR.[53]

It coincides with this picture that Shivji does not give a clear answer to the above question. On the one hand, he aptly describes the characteristics of neo-colonialism in Tanzania, particularly also in his earlier essay, "Tanzania–The Silent Class Struggle". On the other, he sees Tanzania in "the first phases of socialism" and states that "with the rise of the proletarian line the long march has begun". These statements cannot both be analytically correct.

The "rise of the proletarian line" finds its expression in the spontaneous strikes that the workers have sparked off since 1971, very frequently with direct reference to clause 15 of the TANU Guidelines. In these strikes Shivji rightly sees the sharpening contradiction between the workers on the one side, the capitalists and the bureaucratic bourgeoisie on the other side, –with state power as the decisive factor. Surely, however, these sharpening class contradictions involving the workers as an active – though as yet unorganised – class force are not a sign of "the first phases of socialism", but of the contrary. They show that the working class does not control state power in Tanzania, and state power is the deciding factor in class struggle. Shivji's use of the term "rise of the proletarian line" is therefore imprecise, too, and in particular blurs the understanding of the decisive factors of Tanzania's present situation.

What are the progressive characteristics of Tanzanian reality today? They are not that Tanzania has reached the first phase of socialism. They are that Tanzania is in the forefront of those countries in Africa engaged in serious endeavours to defend and strengthen its national independence, both internally and externally. The Arusha Declaration says: "Tanzania is not yet a socialist state." And *Mwongozo* defines TANU as a liberation movement. These are realistic statements.

Once this decisive question as to Tanzania's present stage of development has been answered then other questions can be answered more clearly. That Tanzania's policy of defending and strengthening its national independence is led by the bureaucratic bourgeoisie is a fact. This fact is, to recall Cabral's words, one of the main weaknesses of the liberation struggle.

It creates contradictions which endanger the steps made towards national independence by creating new entries for imperialist manoeuvres of different kinds. Examples are manifold. Calling on a US consultants agency to work out an organisational structure to decentralize the country's administration can hardly be qualified as a step towards the destruction of the bourgeois state apparatus. Such reforms accumulated will certainly not bring Tanzania any closer to socialist revolution.

The bureaucratic barriers to the implementation of the ujamaa village programme, which Shivji describes on pp. 99-101, are another example. These difficulties must be traced to their roots in the class character of the Tanzanian bureaucratic bourgeoisie which devised this programme.

The contradictions which arise in the process of implementation and which take the form of bureaucratic barriers result from the class interests of the Tanzanian ruling class. That is the class content of bureaucracy in Tanzania. Mass mobilization can only take place as long as it does not threaten state power. In other words, the interests of the bureaucratic bourgeoisie set the limits to the mobilisation of the masses, and these limits are imposed ultimately by the means at the disposal of this class, i.e. by administrative means, bureaucratically. The history of the Ruvuma Development Association, for instance, and the spontaneous workers' strikes since 1971 should be seen in this light. This brings us to a further point, that of socialist ideology in Tanzania. To the extent that socialist ideology and socialist debate in Tanzania emanates and is determined by the bureaucratic bourgeoisie, and this is certainly true of the ideology of ujamaa-socialism, it must be analysed on the basis of the class standpoint of this ruling power.

In a historical situation characterised by the contradictions of neo-colonialist national independence and the struggle against imperialist domination to speak of "building socialism" is to say the least misleading. In contrast to the position I have taken in this article ujamaa-socialism believes that in Tanzanian conditions "the peasant movement is the genuine, truly socialist and immediately socialist movement";[54] it "preaches an immediate socialist revolution, stemming from the peasant commune with its petty form of husbandry."[55] So Namfua in the already quoted interview blindly states: "We are already carrying out a socialist revolution."[56] And even Rodney emphasizes this position and understands the

Tanzanian ideology of ujamma-socialism as a concrete application of scientific socialism[57] "...of the theory and policy of Ujamaa", Rodney writes, "has logically determined that the key role in socialist construction has to be played by the Tanzanian peasants. This is in accord with the present stage of the development of productive forces within Tanzania..."[58]

However, "to the Marxist, the peasant movement is a democratic not a socialist movement."[59] Rodney says: "Tanzanian Ujamaa has begun to make the decisive break with capitalism."[60] Essentially, this statement is perfectly correct. Any state that strives to defend and strengthen its national independence has indeed begun to make that decisive break, and socialism is the only answer to the people's aim of full national independence. But the historical task to fulfil that break, beyond which socialist development begins, is not that of the peasants or the petty bourgeoisie, it can only be accomplished under the leadership of the working class and its organized vanguard. The conditions for the completion of the decisive break with imperialism and capitalism have yet to be created in Tanzania.

Postscript, March 1979

The article above was written in April 1974. The general questions of class analysis in the epoch of imperialism, in particular the role of the petty bourgeoisie in underdeveloped countries, which I was primarily concerned with, continue to be a main issue in the debate on development and development perspective in the Third World.

It is with regard to two points of concrete analysis that I want to make some additional remarks in the light of the developments during the past five years.

Third World - Unity or Diversity?

The historical necessity of proletarian leadership to achieve *full* national liberation and to build socialism is one thing. But what of social and political movement in Third World countries without such leadership? Are they automatically reactionary, because they are still submitted to imperialist influence? The answer clearly should be: No. Contradictions between the Third World and imperialism are manifold, and they encompass relations between the governments of Third World states and imperialist powers. However ambivalent the overall political line of movements or Third World governments led by petty bourgeois or bourgeois forces may be, to the extent that they take a stand against imperialism, their position must be looked upon as progressive – and supported by proletarian forces.

The Third World demand for a New International Economic Order, which has gained considerable momentum in the past few years and has developed into a major unifying force among Third World countries, is an important case in point.

The core of the ruling class in Tanzania is the "bureaucratic" or state bourgeoisie. Notwithstanding this fact, I stated: "Tanzania is in the forefront of those countries in Africa engaged in serious endeavours to defend and strengthen their national independence." The "Group of 77" conference in Arusha in February this year preparing the Third World stand for UNCTAD V once more underlined Tanzania's progressive position in the pursuit of national independence in face of the growing rift between rich and poor countries. In his speech to the conference President Nyerere emphatically presented the case for unity and based his line of argument on the national interests of each country. He said:

> The immediate reason for each nation joining the Group of 77 depended on the point at which it had experienced the economic frustrations of power

external to itself. . . I stress the fact that it was our nationalism which has forced us together because we have to understand ourselves in order to achieve our purposes. The Group of 77 does not share an ideology. Some of us are avowedly "scientific" socialists, some just plain socialists, some capitalist, some theocratic, and some fascist! We are not necessarily friendly with each other – some countries represented here are currently engaged in a war with each other... But our diversity exists in the context of one common and over-riding experience. What we have in common is that we are all, in relation to the developed world, dependent – not interdependent – nations. Each of our economies has developed as a by-product and a subsidiary of development in the industrialised North, and in externally oriented. We are not the prime movers of our own destiny. We are ashamed to admit it; but economically we are dependencies – semi-colonies at best – not sovereign states... If we are to maintain Third World unity we all have to work together when operating within non-Third World organisations for Third World objectives. I do not believe this means that we never protest about brutality, tyranny, and racism within the Third World; that would be intolerable – and it would not serve the interests of our peoples. It does mean, however, that we may have to co-operate functionally with governments which we intensely dislike and disapprove of. For the object is to complete the liberation of the Third World countries from external domination. That is the basic meaning of the New International Economic Order. And unity is our instrument – our only instrument – of liberation. But we have to do more than stand united when negotiating as the Group of 77. We have to work together; our nations have to co-operate economically. This is where the diversity of the Third World can be our strength also.[61]

In fact, though each Third World country has its own history and its own political system, the similarities in their situation given their dependence on the existing international economic order seem to be more substantial than the differences among them. After all, what is so different between the dependent structure of Kenya and Tanzania? And even the countries which reached political independence in the last few years after years of armed struggle, Angola, Guinea-Bissao, Mozambique, Vietnam, are grappling with problems of national independence and the construction of a national economy well known in Tanzania and elsewhere in the Third World.

Over 10 years of armed struggle did not prevent the MPLA in Angola from falling prey to Soviet hegemonism in 1975. And 30 years of armed struggle did not prevent Vietnam from engaging in open aggression, under which it had suffered for so many years itself, by sending troops of invasion to topple the government of neighbouring Kampuchea early in 1979. This was not only a disillusionment for all those who supported Vietnam during its liberation war, but also pointed to social scientists not to equate armed struggle with the advance of social revolution after independence has been achieved and/or the aggressor defeated. The development of these countries during the last five years has certainly underlined the need for all-sided class analysis in each concrete situation, taking into consideration national and international factors.

'NON-CAPITALIST' ROAD OF DEVELOPMENT AND SOVIET HEGEMONISM

Development in Angola, Vietnam and elsewhere, for instance Eritrea, since 1975 have shown to what extent the Soviet Union has gone into the offensive in its worldwide rivalry with the USA.

In dealing with the Soviet theory of 'non-capitalist' development I analysed its bourgeois class content and also pointed out that according to this theory successful 'non-capitalist' development is dependent upon close cooperation with the Soviet Union, integration into the international 'socialist' division of labour, recognition of the leading role of, and close alliance with the Soviet Union. In fact, this latter of the two main features of the theory must be regarded as the more important one as it becomes increasingly clear that it is embedded in overall Soviet hegemonic policy in the Third World. As two Soviet writers, Solodovnikov, at present his country's ambassador in Zambia, and Bogoslovsky state:

> Of vital importance to the countries on the non-capitalist road and their governments is the establishment and expansion of close ties of sincere cooperation with the Soviet Union...[62]

It is indicative of the stress now being put on the Soviet Union as the necessary condition for the independence of Third World countries that the term 'socialist orientation' has been introduced and is explicitly used as a term identical in meaning to 'non-capitalist' development. The most clearcut proof of the theory's prime content, however, is given by the practice of putting the label 'non-capitalist' and 'socialist oriented' onto a country one day and taking it away the next, using the respective country's attitude towards the Soviet Union as the only measure.

Somalia was defined as being on the 'non-capitalist' road until it cancelled its "treaty of friendship and cooperation" with the Soviet Union in 1977. Without the government, let alone the class character of the ruling class having changed, for Soviet theory Somalia had changed from a 'progressive' 'non-capitalist' to a 'reactionary' country. Egypt is another good example. In their book on 'non-capitalist' development Solodovnikov and Bogoslovsky praise Egypt page after page for its 'non-capitalist' line of close cooperation with the Soviet Union. They even go to the extreme of claiming that President Nasser, known and acclaimed throughout the world as one of the initiators and leading representatives of the non-aligned movement, regarded "friendship and cooperation with the Soviet Union as the strategic line (!) of the Arab Republic of Egypt's foreign policy,"[63] Egypt was finally fed up of being blackmailed by the Soviet Union and used as a pawn in that country's power struggle with the USA in the Near East, and cancelled its "treaty of friendship and cooperation" in 1976 all earlier songs of praise were forgotten, and for Soviet theory Egypt did not qualify for the label 'non-capitalist' any longer.

Embedded in Soviet hegemonic policy the formulations of the theory of 'non-capitalist' development have become more aggressive as the Soviet Union itself has gone increasingly into the offensive to increase its spheres of influence throughout the Third World and elsewhere. Ulyanovsky, a deputy director in the international department of the Central Committee of the CPSU, leaves no doubt about his view that without support from and cooperation with the Soviet Union there can be no 'non-capitalist' development, and the sooner the 'progressive' forces in Third World countries realize this the better for them! Ulyanovsky writes:

> The objective necessity of cooperation of the socialist countries with national democracy confronts the latter with certain requirements, too. The positions on which the foreign policy of the countries of the "third world" were based hitherto must be made more precise and developed further. Positive neutrality and non-interference today do not meet the requirements put before the foreign policy of the young nation states any more! Non-capitalist development is not possible on such a basis. In the interests of the common struggle against imperialism it demands moving closer to the socialist community, clear understanding of the social nature of socialism and imperialism as well as the refutal of the theories of the "poor and rich

countries" or of the "two superpowers" which are based on the negation of the class character of the two world systems. One still encounters relapses into these theories by a few national democrats; they lead to a certain distrust towards the socialist countries, to isolationist slogans overestimating one's own forces and similar appearances. Experience is the best teacher, it will bring national democrats to an understanding of the necessity of strengthening relations with the socialist countries, which sometimes still occurs with certain reservations."[64]

Experience is more likely to strengthen "certain reservations" already widespread among Third World countries, whether 'non-capitalist' or not. Quite rightly, they refuse to accept the view that their economic independence from the existing international economic order should mean entering a new dependence on the Soviet Union and the East bloc. For them the alternative is not between one of the two superpower systems, but between independence and dependence: In an editorial published during the "Group of 77" conference in Arusha the *Daily News* brought this point home when it wrote:

> In discussions concerning the New International Economic Order, there is a tendency for some of the socialist countries to uphold their system as the New International Economic Order and to sort of urge advocates of NIEO to join them.[65]

This view, the *Daily News* editorial refuted. It pointed out that among those countries generally referred to as socialist countries there is as much diversity as among poor countries. "With such diversity, it is not at all realistic for anyone to urge the poor countries to join the socialist camp as the only way to bring about a New International Economic Order." Rather than for the poor countries to join the Soviet Union, it is for the socialist countries to support the Third World in its struggle for a NIEO, and to support them on the basis of equality, mutual respect and non-interference. "It is our fervent hope", the *Daily News* editorial concluded somewhat uncertainly, "that they will not be found wanting in this regard."

Ulyanovsky's statements and, primarily, Soviet policy in the international arena and in international conferences debating the NIEO during the past years leave little doubt that the Soviet Union, for one, will continue to oppose the Third World demand for a New International Economic Order as well as all attempts to strengthen unity and cooperation among Third World countries. What is progressive for independent development perspectives in the Third World runs counter to superpower interests.

NOTES

1 The following page references to Shivji's paper are from the cyclostyled copy issued by the Department of Development Studies at the University of Dar es Salaam, 1973.

2 J. Nyerere, Economic Nationalism in: *Freedom and Socialism – A Selection from Writings and Speeches 1965-1967*, Dar es Salaam, 1968, p. 262.

3 Lenin, *Unter fremder Flagge* (Under a foreign flag). in: Werke, Bd. 21. 137-8 (Whenever a German title is given first the translation of the quotation is mine; P.M.)

4 Mao Tsetung, *Uber die Neus Demokratis* (On New Democracy). in: Auagewahite Werke, Bd. 11. p. 404.

5 Mao Tsetung, op, cit. p. 407.

6 Ibid p. 415.

7 Amilcar Cabral, The Weapon of theory. in: Revolution in Guinea. London, 1969, p. 88.

8 Ibid. p. 89.

9 Ibid. p. 88.
10 Walter Rodney, Some Implications...in: *The Silent Class Struggle*. Dares Salaam, 1973, p. 67.
11 Ibid. p. 68.
12 Amilcar Cabral, op. cit. p. 89.
13 It is not primarily a question of whether or not colonialism allowed the peasants or the petty bourgeoisie to gain deeper insights, as Rodney suggests. op. cit. p. 67.
14 Lenin, *Was Tun? (What is to be done?)*. in: Werke Bd. 5, p. 395.
15 Ibid. p. 396.
16 Amilcar Cabral, Our People are our Mountains – A. Cabral on the Guinean Revolution, London n.d. (1972). p. 7.
17 A. Cabral, *Revolution in Guinea*, op. cit. p. 87.
18 See Julius K. Nyerere, Principles and Development, in *Freedom and Socialism*, op. cit. pp. 187–206.
19 J.K. Nyerere, Economic Nationalism, in *Freedom and Socialism*, op. cit. p. 262.
20 TANU Guidelines, clause 4.
21 We will look more closely at this ambiguous phrase in section 4.
22 Lenin, *Was Tun? (What is to be done?)*, op. cit, p. 396.
23 *Sunday News*, 31.11.72.
24 *Sunday News*, 7.1.73 – The reference to 'dogmatic Marxism-Leninism' is a frequent theme in Tanzania, one with which unwelcome views on socialism are all too often refuted. For scientific analysis this raises the question: what is in question here, dogmatism or Marxism-Leninism?
25 *Sunday News*, 25.3.73.
26 Lenin, *Bericht der Kommission fur die nationale und koloniale Frage* (Report from the commission on the national and colonial question). in: Werke Bd. 31. p. 232.
27 Ibid. p. 232.
28 Ibid. p. 230.
29 Angola in Arms, Dar es Salaam n.d. (4th Feb. 1969). pp. 2-3.
30 Alexander Sobolev, Binige Problems des sozialen Fortschritts in Afrika (Some problems of social progress in Africa). In: G. Liebig, *Nationale und Soziale Revolution in Afrika*. Berlin (GDR) 1967, pp. 101, 103.
31 Klassen un Klassenkampf in den Entwicklungslandarn – 3. Bd.: *Die Wahl des Weges* (Classes and Class Struggles in the Developing Countries – 3rd Vol. I: 1 – The Choice of the Road) Berlin (GDR) 1970. p. 315 – This is a Soviet textbook.
32 Ibid. p. 329.
33 *Nichtkapitalistischer Entwicklungsweg – Aktuelle Problems in Theorie und Praxis* (Non-capitalist road of development – Present-day problems in theory and practice). Berlin (GDR) 1972. p. 7.
34 Ibid. pp. 22–3.
35 Ibid. p. 25.
36 Ibid. p. 26.
37 For the reality of this military regime, see e.g. A. Quijano, "Nationalism and Capitalism in Peru: A Study of Neo-Imperialism" in: *Monthly Review*, July/August 1971.
38 Even Amin's Uganda is quoted (!):"Rep. of Uganda successfully treads the non-capitalist road". Title of article in: *Die Wahrheit* (The Truth), 30.1.74 (daily published by the SEW, the revisionist party in West Berlin).
39 Lenin, *Die proletarische Revolution und der Renegat Kautsky* (The proletarian revolution and the Renegade Kautsky) in: Werke Bd. 28. p. 252.
40 W. Rodney, Tanzanian Ujamaa and Scientific Socialism. in: *The African Review*, Vol. I. No. (April 1962). p. 70.
41 *Tradition und nichtkapitalistischer Entwicklungsweg in Afrika* (Tradition and non-capitalist road of development in Africa). Berlin (GDR) 1971. p. 88.
42 *Klassen und Klassenkampf...* op. cit. p. 319 – We are reminded here of Uganda's proclamation of a "move to the left" under Obote which was abruptly stopped by Amin's military coup.
43 *Nichtkapitalistischer Entwicklungsweg*, op. cit. p. 34.
44 *Tradition und...*, op. cit. p. 313,

45 *Nichtkapitalistischer Entwicklungsweg*, op. cit. p. 19.
46 Shivji's theoretically erroneous differentiation of two "types" of class struggle, violent as against the "hundred and one ways" of 'everyday' class struggle, must also be mentioned in this context, see pp. 60-1. The ultimate consequence of class struggle is always the open clash between the classes in which antagonistic contradictions are solved – in one way or in the other, with no '3rd way' available. It is because Shivji persistently evades the question of the ultimate *solution* class contradictions that of he develops erroneous views in his class analysis. '
47 Lenin, *Bericht der Kommission...*, op. cit. pp. 229–30.
48 This point is stressed by Shivji, too, in his introductory chapter, but he does not pursue it consequently at all in his subsequent chapters on class struggle in Tanzania.
49 "The People's democratic dictatorship needs the leadership of the working class. For it is only the working class that is most far-sighted, most selfless and most thoroughly revolutionary. The entire history of revolution proves that without the leadership of the working class revolution fails and that with the leadership of the working class revolution triumphs. In the epoch of imperialism, in no country can any other class lead any genuine revolution to victory. This is clearly proved by the fact that the many revolutions led by China's petty bourgeoisie and national bourgeoisie all failed." Mao Tsetung, On People's Democratic Dictatorship in: *Selected Readings from the Works of Mao Tsetung*. Peking, 1967. p. 312.
50 *Die tragischen Ereignisse in Chile – Eine Lehre fur die Revolutionare in aller Welt* (The tragic events in Chile – A lesson for revolutionaries throughout the world). Supplement to Albanian Heute (Albania), No. 4 (July-August) 1973. pp. 2, 5.
51 Hekuran Mara (Albanian political economist), *Noglichkeiten, den Sozialismus aufzubauen, ohne die Phase des entwickelten Kapitalismus durchzumachen* (Possibilities of building socialism without passing through the stage of developed capitalism). in: *Albanien Heute* (Albania Today), No. 4 (July–August) 1973. p. 15 – This article is an excellent critique of the 'theory of non-capitalist development'.
52 This I will attempt to do in a larger work in preparation.
53 *Nichtkapitalistischer Entwicklungsweg*, op. cit. p. 10.
54 Lenin, Socialism: petty-bourgeois and proletarian, in: *Works* Vol. 9, quoted here from separate pamphlet p. 8.
55 Lenin, Ibid., p. 7.
56 *Sunday News*, 7.1.73.
57 Rodney, *Tanzanian Ujamaa...*, op. cit. pp. 71–3 and passim.
58 Rodney, Ibid, p. 72.
59 Lenin, *Socialism:...*, op. cit. p. 9.
60 Rodney, *Tanzania Ujamaa...*, op. cit. p. 73.
61 J.K. Nyerere, *Unity for a New Order*. Address by President Nyerere to the Ministerial Conference of the Group of 77. Arusha, 12th Feb. 1979. pp. 4, 5, 9.
62 V. Solodovnikov, V. Bogoslovsky, *Non-Capitalist Development. An Historical Outline*. Moscow, 1975. p. 249.
63 Ibid., 242.
64 R.A. Ulyanovsky, *Der Sozialismus and die befreiten Lander* (Socialism and the Newly Independent Nations). Berlin (GDR) 1973. p. 367.
65 *Daily News*, 15-2-1979.

5

A CRITIQUE OF ISSA SHIVJI'S BOOK

M. Mamdani and H. Bhagat

Comrade Issa,

We welcome your book on *Class Struggle in Tanzania* as an attempt to concretely analyze classes in Tanzania (mainland), and furthermore, to sketch in outline from the class struggle since independence. It is imperative, we believe, that what has emerged as an individual effort be collectively developed through study, criticism and transformation. Only then can we ensure the development of a scientific theory.

It is in order to begin such an ideological discussion among comrades that we undertake in this letter to outline our differences with the analysis in your book.

We propose to focus on the question of method, deriving from it a few remarks on your concrete analysis of classes, while leaving aside for further discussion the analysis of the concrete Tanzanian situation.

On Method

THE CLASS RELATION

The fundamental shortcoming of the book, we believe, is its failure to grasp that the class relation is a relation of production. Indeed, you yourself quote Lenin's definition of social classes as:

> Large groups of people differing from each other by the place they occupy in the historically determined system of social production; by their relation (in some cases fixed and formulated in law) to the means of production; by their role in the social organisation of labour, and, consequently by the dimensions and mode of acquiring the share of social wealth of which they dispose.[1]

Nevertheless, when it comes to your analysis of the Tanzanian situation you explain "the criteria that are implied in (1) marking off the petty bourgeoisie from the other classes and (2) intra-class divisions" as Income; Education; Standard of living and life-style (urban milieu); Control of or potentially effective participation in the decision-making bodies; the role occupied in the production process; and control of our proximity to state apparatuses.[2]

This is bourgeois social science, not historical materialism. Its political consequence is immediately evident in the example you give on the footnote to the same page: "A machine-operator, involved fully in the production process (a productive worker), may be earning as much as or probably more than a clerk (unproductive worker) coming close to the life-style and consumptive pattern of the 'lower salaried, the lower levels of the petty bourgeoisie, should he therefore be included in the petty bourgeoisie? Undoubtedly, the chart raises many such difficult questions for precise class demarcation. But such demarcation is not absolutely necessary for the analysis of class struggle. There are overlaps between classes and there are 'fringes' around the 'cores' of the classes. The problem is therefore statistical rather than political."

We may point out two things here. First, classes are here defined as income groups, not in their relation to the process of production. For a Marxist, a productive worker, no matter how high or low his payment, is a member of the proletariat. Secondly, unlike what the book claims, such demarcation is absolutely necessary for the analysis of class struggle; the question is not statistical, but political.

IMPERIALISM AND THE ANALYSIS OF CLASSES

The analysis of imperialism must be integral to that of classes in the neo-colony. The fact that the main discussion on imperialism has been relegated to the appendix has serious methodological consequences. First, the analysis of classes appears ahistorical. Second, class analysis is often abstracted from that of imperialism. Let us take what we consider to be the most important example here.

In its analysis of the commercial bourgeoisie, the book defines as comprador only "managers and executives, etc. employed by foreign companies" (p. 45). On the other hand, in the theoretical section, the national bourgeoisie in Africa is simply dismissed as non-existent, in fact as "neither national nor bourgeoisie."[3] If the vast majority of commercial bourgeoisie was neither comprador nor national, what was it? The book doesn't even raise the question. Even the occassion to raise such a question doesn't arise, principally because at no point does the book discuss the relation of the commercial bourgeoisie to the British monopoly bourgeoisie.

The whole of the bourgeoisie in the neo-colonies is dominated by imperialism. Whithin this subordinate bourgeoisie, we must classify different sections: comprador and national. Compradorism has had various forms historically, its classical form being the commercial bourgeoisie, based entirely on the colonial export–import trade, and with little autonomy from its imperial masters. The comprador industrial bourgeoisie, risen on the base of import–substituting industrialization, must however be seen as a different historical form, with its own secondary contradictions with imperialism, nonetheless principally defining its own interests in harmony with those of imperialism. Separate from this is the national bourgeoisie, a tiny fraction whose production is based on national resources and the national market, and which finds its interests threatened by the imperialist export of capital and commodities. It is national not because it exercises hegemonic control over the national productive forces, but because it has aspirations to do so. In the context of imperialist domination, the composition of the national bourgeoisie must be seen as constantly shifting. Economically of marginal importance, politically this bourgeoisie is of great significance given its ideological influence over the petty bourgeois masses.

As is obvious from the above, we would argue that the whole of the commercial bourgeoisie, and not simply managers and executives employed in foreign firms, was comprador.

SUBJECTIVISM

There are moments when the analysis in the book slavishly capitulates to the dominant ideology. Let us take two outstanding examples.

On page 14, we are told why the small Asian trader was a 'capitalist' but not the small African trader: "The determining characteristic marking off the Asian trader as a 'capitalist' was that a portion of his profits went for capitalist accumulation. Even the smallest of the Asian retailers, who in practice consumed almost all his profit, always worked with a view and an aspiration to 'save' for accumulation, the specific difference which marks out capitalist ideology. The small African producer, the peasant or retailer, on the other hand, consumed all his 'profits' thus distinguishing him from a typical member of the Asian community."[4]

What about the petty bourgeoisie from Kilimanjaro and Bukoba? One would want to ask. Nonetheless, the larger point is that what has been dished out here is colonial racial ideology, not even nationalist obfuscation.

Further on in the text, we come across an examination of the business practices of the commercial bourgeoisie in the process of 'death and disintegration'.

> Unofficial and illegal means have taken over. Bourgeois standards of 'history' ('Honesty is the best policy!') have been completely eroded. There has been a spectacular decline in respect for bourgeois law and bourgeois business ethics.... The crumbling of established channels and the conspicuous decline in 'business morality' are themselves signs of the declining nature of the commercial bourgeoisie.[5]

The implication, it would seem, is that there was once an age, not simply quantitatively but also qualitatively different, when bourgeoisie standards of 'honesty' and fair play held sway, when the bourgeoisie put into practice its own moral ideology. Bourgeois morality and ethics, however, have never been for practicing, always for preaching. Its morality is the posture the bourgeoisie presents to other classes. It is its self-portrait that it would have others take seriously. And, we might add, the principal captive of bourgeois ideology in this sphere has been the petty bourgeoisie! The fact is the morality that has eroded over the last decade has been that of the (Asian) petty bourgeoisie!

A MECHANISTIC APPROACH

At moments, the book shows traces of the mechanistic approach, especially in the historical thread that runs through the analysis. For one, there is a conception, we believe totally alien to Marxism, of class struggles that are 'pure' and those that are 'impure'. The theoretical section informs us that "While class struggle constitutes the motive force in history, it is not always clear and pure as class struggle".[6] In the middle of the text we are assured of "a 'purer' form of class struggle after independence."[7] And finally, towards the end, the claim is made that "the liquidation of the inherited racial structures was *conditio sine qua non* for 'purifying' the class struggles."[8] It would seem we have before us yet another interpretation of the history of class struggles: from the impure to the pure! Also, one might add, as the last quotation indicates, there is a strong tendency in the book to turn whatever political struggles have taken place in Tanzania into historically necessary struggles. The study of history thus turns into an historicism.

CONCRETE ANALYSIS OF CLASSES

THE COMMERCIAL BOURGEOISIE

The book most unscientifically takes a racial group, the Indians, and lumps them together as a commercial bourgeoisie. The vast majority of the Asian in Tanzania – traders, clerks, civil servants, teachers, artisans – must be scientifically characterised as petty bourgeois. This is so regardless of their domination by bourgeois ideology, failure to organize as a "political conflict group" separately from that small number who can scientifically be characterised as commercial bourgeois, social origin or rate of social mobility–all the reasons you give for assimilating this petty bourgeoisie into the commercial bourgeoisie and then presenting us with the transformation of an ethnic group into a class!

Once the book identifies all the Asians as a commercial bourgeoisie, it can then claim that the commercial bourgeoisie, (i.e. the Asians) begins to disintegrate with the Arusha Declaration and that this process is more or less complete with the nationalization of buildings. Thus the conclusion: "The commercial bourgeoisie is a dying class. The essential condition of its reproduction–accumulation of capital is eroded."[9] On the other hand, once we recognize that the Asians in Tanzania comprised two classes, the vast majority petty bourgeois and a small minority commercial bourgeois, it becomes clear that we must identify separately the response of each to the events beginning with the Arusha Declaration. We would argue that it remains an open question, open to empirical investigation, to what extent the crisis of the "Asian community" has been that of the petty bourgeoisie and the extent to which it has been the crisis of the commercial bourgeoisie. Also, the book claims that after the Arusha Declaration, Asian capital went principally into real estate property. We would question this and point out the importance of empirical study to identify the extent to which the capital of the commercial bourgeoisie was transformed into industrial capital with investments in import-substituting industrialization.

THE BUREAUCRATIC BOURGEOISIE

The term bureaucratic bourgeoisie, we believe, has been used most unscientifically in the book. To begin with, Chapter Seven indentifies the period after *Uhuru* as that of "the rise of the bureaucratic bourgeoisie."[10] Concretely, we are told that the bureaucratic bourgeoisie and not (as) a class distinct from the petty bourgeoisie."[11] Now, previously the petty bourgeoisie was merged into the commercial bourgeoisie, but here we have the bureaucratic bourgeoisie becoming a part of the petty bourgeoisie! An identity of opposites, one might say! Further more, the chart on page 88 once again identifies the bureaucratic bourgeoisi as a part of the petty bourgeoisie, now concretely indentifying its members as heads of government ministries, of parastatals, of the civil service, and of the military. The bureaucratic bourgeoisie is thus identified with heads of governmental bodies, that is, the state apparatus. We conclude that in the book the 'bureaucratic bourgeoisie' simply become another term for what the bourgeois political scientist calls the 'political elite.'

The fact that the concept of a 'bureaucratic bourgeoisie' has been used most unscientifically in the book should not lead Marxist-Leninists to discard it. On the other hand, it is crucial that we grasp it scientifically. Only when the state power becomes, through nationalizations of means of production, not simply the agent of oppression, but also that of exploitation; and a social group, because of its control over the state, exercises control over means of production, only then can we identify the emergence of bureaucrat-capital and thus of a bureaucrat-bourgeoisie. That property under concrete historical circumstances assumes another legal form, in this case the public form, should not blind Marxist-Leninists to the fact that it still remains private (class) property. It should thus be clear that the bureaucrat-bourgeoisie is neither the 'political elite' nor simply the bureaucracy. In this scientific sense, then, we can identify the emergence of a bureaucrat–bourgeoisie in Tanzania <u>after</u> the nationalizations accompanying the Arusha Declaration. Needless to say, this class emerged in the context of imperialist hegemony over the semi-colony and its domination by the monopoly bourgeoisie of imperialist countries must be concretely studied.

In conclusion, we believe the book to occasionally manifest an unfortunate eclecticism, evident, not only in the theoretical framework and the concrete class analysis, but also in its bibliographical references and suggestions to the reader. For example, we are told to read Baran, Fanon and Nyerere on why no independent capitalist development is possible in the third world countries.[12] Bettleheim and Sweezy on the transition to third world countries,[12] Bettleheim and Sweezy on the transition to socialism,[13] and E.H. Carr on the meaning of history,[14] even when the quote used is but a paraphrase of Engels in *Anti-Duhring*.

Nonetheless, we consider the book a step forward, representing a stage in the development of Marxist thought in our countries, a stage in which the struggle is to free ourselves from the influence of the dominant bourgeoisie and petty bourgeois ideology. For this same task, we believe it extremely important for a widespread ideological debate to develop among Marxist-Leninists using as a starting point the criticism of various attempts made by comrades to scientifically understand our reality. We hope this letter contributes to the beginning of this ideological debate.

With fraternal greetings.

NOTES

1 Issa Shivji, *Class Struggles in Tanzania*, Tanzania Publishing House, Dar es Salaam, 1976, p. 19.
2 Ibid. p. 87.
3 Ibid p. 87.
4 Ibid. p. 20. In fact, the book even suggests that the Third World bourgeoisies be termed 'lumpen-bourgeoisies.' *a la* Baran. This is in spite of the admission in the text that "lumpen appears to give the idea that the 'bourgeoisie' was *outside* of the social production process which is of course not the case." And yet, the term is salvaged because we are told "its limited use can be most descriptive!" (p. 21) And indeed, on p. 44 (note 24) it is used as such!
5 Ibid. p. 44.
6 Ibid. p. 84.
7 Ibid. p. 8.
8 Ibid. p. 48.
9 Ibid. p. 98.
10 Ibid. p. 82.
11 Ibid. p. 63.
12 Ibid. p. 67.
13 Ibid. p. 10.
14 Ibid. p. 63.

6

COMMENTS ON *THE POLITICAL ECONOMY OF IMPERIALISM*

M. Mamdani and H. Bhagat

Comrade Dan,

We welcome your manuscript on *The Political Economy of Imperialism* as a contribution towards attaining a scientific understanding of imperialism in our epoch. The manuscript raises numerous issues the discussion of which we believe will enhance ideological clarity among Marxist-Leninists in our countries. In this letter, we limit ourselves to outlining our differences with your analysis of modern imperialism. So long as we struggle in the midst of class society, we can expect ideological differences among Marxist-Leninists. Their principled resolution requires an open ideological discussion among comrades. Only such a method of work, in line with the the real movement of people's struggles, can ensure the emergence of a scientific theory. We are confident that a principled discussion on issues raised by your manuscript will lead to unity at a higher level.

ON IMPERIALISM

The manuscript attempts an historical analysis of the post-World War II ascendency of U.S. imperialism, through a multilateral strategy, to the position of global hegemony: 'This elaborate, octopus-like imperialist tie-up of neo-colonial economies to suit imperialism's global strategies is enabled to a great extent by the multilateral imperialist institutions set up in the post-war period to serve its interest.' (p. 470) Central to this multilateral strategy is the role of the World Bank and the International Monetary Fund which act as 'the coordinator(s) of world finance capital'. (p. 479) At one point in the analysis, in fact, the manuscript even suggests the centralization of this 'world finance capital' under the hegemony of a section of the U.S. imperialist bourgeoisie: 'Currently the [World] Bank is largely under the control of the Rockeffeller-Chase Manhattan-Standard Oil Group.' (p. 270)*

Although it makes occasional references to the fact of intra-imperialist rivalry, the principal thrust of the manuscript is to abstract from all contradictions except that between labour and capital. This is only possible because the manuscript absolutizes the concept of 'centralization of capital' arriving at a concept of 'world finance capital', emphasizing its unity in a one-sided manner. In other words, the manuscript comes perilously close to taking the stand of 'ultra-imperialism' which Kautsky explained as 'the joint exploitation of the world by internationally united finance capital in place of the mutual rivalries of national finance capits.' (Quoted in Lenin, *The Collapse of the Second International*, Moscow, p. 19).

*This statement is footnoted and the proof ascribed to J. Halliday, and G. McCormack, *Japanese Imperialism Today*, p. 51.

The establishment of U.S. hegemony over European and Japanese capital is in fact only one aspect of the process; the other and the central aspect is the intensifying contradiction whithin the camp of American imperialism since the Second World War. In its *Proposal Concerning the General Line of the International Communist Movement*, the Central Committee of the Communist Party of China correctly stated:

> The following erroneous views should be repudiated on the question of the fundamental contradictions in the world:...
>
> (d) the view which denies that the development of the inherent contradictions in the contemporary capitalist world leads to a new situation in which the imperialist countries are locked in an intense struggle, and asserts that the contradictions among the imperialist countries can be reconciled, or even eliminated, by international agreements among the big monopolies.

We believe that a political analysis of modern imperialism, if it is to show the way forward to a struggle against it, must analyse and reveal its various contradictions in both their particular importance and interrelations. In the rest of this section, we attempt short statement of these contradictions and, in doing so, underline in some detail our differences with the analysis presented in the manuscript.

A. Contradictions among the Superpowers

Conspicuous in the manuscript is the absence of any analysis of social imperialism. Coupled with this are references to the 'socialist one-third of the world' and the 'socialist camp' (p. 367). It is, of course, quite legitimate to attempt a limited investigation. Such would be the case if your project were confined to an analysis of Western Imperialism. But both the title and the preface claim to be analysing imperialism in its totality. To then exclude social imperialism from one's investigation is only to end up in reformism.

B. Contradictions within the Bourgeoisie of Imperialist Countries

Contrary to what the manuscript suggests, the financial oligarchy is not the entire bourgeoisie of the imperialist countries. It is, in fact, a stratum of the bourgeoisie, the monopoly bourgeoisie. Throughout the epoch of imperialism, alongside the contradictions within the monopoly bourgeoisie of an imperialist country, there exist contradictions between the monopoly and the non-monopoly bourgeoisie. As Mao Tse-tung analysed: 'When the capitalism of the era of free competition developed into imperialism...the contradiction between monopoly and non-monopoly capital emerged.' *(On Contradiction*, p. 43) Without a study of these contradictions in their totality, we shall be unable to comprehend such political events as, for example, the Watergate episode in the U.S. or the division in Britain over entry into the European Economic Community (E.E.C.).

C. Contradictions between the Superpowers and the Second World (E.E.C., Japan, Eastern Europe)

As the comrades of Communist Party of China (C.P.C.) have pointed out, the struggle between the superpowers does not take place as a direct confrontation over one another's territory, but as a struggle over intermediate territories, today the Third and Second World. Of course, the bourgeoisies of the Second World partake in the imperialist exploitation of the Third World; they are at the same time, however, oppressed by the superpowers. This relation begets on their part both a limited struggle against the superpowers and a limited 'strengthening (of) ties with the Third World so as to cope with the superpowers'. (Commentary by Hsinhua, correspondent, 3 March, 1977, 'What does the Lome Convention signify', in *Peking Review*, No. 11, 14 March, 1975, p. 19). We must learn from Lenin's insistence on the Soviet power building a front with states which are bourgeois but nonetheless oppressed:

> We now set as the main task for ourselves, to defeat the exploiters and to win the waverers to our side. This task is a worldwide one. The waverers include a whole series of bourgeois states, which as bourgois states hate us, but on the other hand, as oppressed states, prefer peace with us. (Report on the work of the All-Russian Central Executive Committee).

In our analysis of the contradictions between the First and the Second World, we should analyze two contradictions, both separately and in their interconnection, 'the contradiction among imperialist countries and among monopoly capitalist groups'. (*The General Line of the International Communist Movement*, p. 6). While attempting an analysis of the relations between monopoly capitals, the manuscript totally abstracts from the relations between imperialist states. In order to underline the importance of the above, we shall give but two examples.

First, without analyzing the contradictions between the First and the Second World countries, it is not possible to grasp the significance of either Gaullism in France or the politics of Heath's Britain. It was under the leadership of the French state that the European imperialist states took the step to establish Euratom and build the Concorde in order to combat the hegemony of American monopolies.

Second, the significance of the agreement signed at the Lome Convention can not be grasped without analyzing this particular contradiction. The analysis in the manuscript one-sidedly concludes that the Convention was a victory for 'the monopolies of the U.S. and Japan'. (p. 395) Yet the fact is that the nine E.E.C. countries signed the Convention in spite of the opposition of both the superpowers. Because the products of the European monopolies ceased to receive duty-free entry into the markets of the 46 African, Carribean and Pacific countries, the manuscript concludes that the Convention 'merely multi-lateralized the neo-colonial ties to other monopolies of the U.S. and Japan'. What is ignored is that the terms of the Convention–the access (duty- and quota-free, without any reciprocal treatment) to the E.E.C. countries for 99.2 percent of the products of the A.C.P. countries *and* the establishment of a fund by the E.E.C. to compensate the A.C.P. countries for any fall in the prices of primary products and raw materials–signifies a limited victory for the Third World. As the *Peking Review* commentary summed up, 'This development in relations between the Second and the Third World countries favours the worldwide struggle against superpower hegemonism'. (ibid. p. 13)

Marxist-Leninists in the semi-colonies must face two political tasks: to organize the people's democratic struggles against their own ruling classes and to give the strongest impetus to the ruling classes of the Third World to struggle against superpower hegemonism. There may, of course, be a contradiction between the two tasks at particular moments. The only response would be to resolve these in a concrete situation through a concrete analysis.

D. Contradiction between Imperialists and the Third World

Here, the manuscript touches on two issues, the 'nationalization measures' and the contemporary struggles for a 'New Economic Order', and presents what we

44

consider to be a static and partial analysis.

Nationalizations in the Third World were not simply 'granted' by imperialism, although it attempted an adjustment once they were a reality. We must view the question historically. Nationalizations were the product of a long historical struggle – beginning with the Mexican nationalizations of the 1940s through to Mussadegh in Iran, Arbenz in Guatemala and Nasser and the Suez crisis in Egypt – struggles that imperialism fought, lost and adjusted to in order to minimize these losses. The significance of these nationalizations must be grasped both economically and politically. The manuscript attempts only an economic analysis, here belittling them as simply 'a nuisance to imperialism'. (p. 449) Although it correctly analyses these measures as 'remain(ing) within the sphere of bargaining for higher prices', the manuscript incorrectly dismisses their significance for two reasons. First, since it denies that the Third World peasantries are exploited through unequal exchange (this we shall deal with later), it cannot grasp the significance of limited struggles 'within the sphere of bargaining for higher prices'. Second, the manuscript has an extremely one-sided conception of the objective tendency of imperialism to block the development of the productive forces in the semi-colonies. As Lenin emphasized in *Imperialism, the Highest Stage of Capitalism*, the general tendency of imperialism, of moribund capitalism, to block the development of the productive forces does not rule out in particular instances a limited development, as in the case of India, Egypt or Brazil. Such a limited development must be understood in the context of contradictions between the socialist and imperialist countries, intra-imperialist rivalries and anti-imperialist struggles.

Similarly, the struggle to alter commodity prices through forming commodity producers' organizations, which has today culminated in the call for 'A New Economic Order', has had a long history beginning with formation of the Organisation of Petroleum Exporting Countries (OPEC) in 1960. Of course, as you correctly point out the the struggle for a 'New Economic Order', as that for nationalization, does not seek to alter production relations and is not in itself a battle for socialism; nonetheless, these are anti-imperialist struggles and as such objectively form a part of the world socialist revolution, as Mao Tsetung pointed out in *New Democracy*.

Our analysis of the struggles of the Third World countries must also have a political dimension. As shown by the instances of the Vietnamese and the Cambodian revolutions, it is such struggles that give rise to a global anti-imperialist front whose main force are the Third World countries and which successfully win over, however temporarily, wavering elements from among the Second World countries.

E. Conclusion

We believe that any analysis of contemporary imperialism by Marxist-Leninists must take as its point of departure the great ideological debate of 1960–63 on *The General Line of the International Communist Movement*, and particularly the scientific contribution of the Central Committee of the Communist Party of China. In its letter to the Communist Party of the Soviet Union, the Central Committee of the Communist Party of China identified 'the fundamental contradictions in the contemporary world' as follows:

the contradiction between the socialist and the imperialist camp;
the contradiction between the proletariat and the bourgeoisie in the capitalist countries;

the contradiction between the oppressed nations and imperialism; the contradiction among imperialist countries and among monopoly capitalist groups. (p. 6)

While all these fundamental contradictions exist today, the principal contradiction is that between the oppressed nations and imperialism. As the C.P.C. stated:

The various types of contradictions in the contemporary world are concentrated in the vast areas of Asia, Africa and Latin America; these are most vulnerable areas under imperialist rule and the storm centres of world revolution dealing direct blows at imperialism.

We hold this analysis to be correct with regard to the international situation today.

The above analysis of is importance because various deviations within the Marxist movement can be traced ideologically to a one-sided exaggeration of one of these contradictions. As the C.P.C. document warned, 'These contradictions and the struggles to which they give rise are interrelated and influence each other. Nobody can obliterate any of these fundamental contradictions or subjectively substitute one for all the rest'.

The revisionists one-sidedly substituted the contradiction between the socialist camp and the imperialist camp in place of the rest. The populist 'Third Worldists' of today, on the other hand, see the contradiction between imperialism and the oppressed nations as not only the principal but also the only fundamental contradiction in the world, thus denying the importance of proletarian leadership and seeing the anti-imperialist revolutionary struggles in the Third World as not only the main content but also the leading force of the world revolution. We repudiate such a populist stance. Finally, the Trotskyist deviation one-sidedly emphasizes the contradiction between labour and capital and substitutes it for the rest. We believe the argument in the manuscript objectively takes this latter position. This is in spite of the position taken in the conclusion because, as we argue in the next section, the conclusion regarding the necessity of the people's democratic revolution doesn't follow from the argument in the manuscript.

ON THE PEOPLES DEMOCRATIC REVOLUTION

Towards the conclusion, the manuscript poses the question of the character of 'the international proletarian revolution':

Firstly what is the character of the revolution in the imperialist centres? Clearly this is a struggle betwen the metropolitan bourgeoisie and the proletariat in which the proletariat has first to settle accounts with its national bourgeoisie and financial oligarchy....In order for the working class to establish meaningful control over its labour, it must move to take political power to establish a socialist state. Here, therefore, a socialist revolution is clearly posed. On the other hand, the struggle in the colonial, semi-colonial and neo-colonial countries, still under the dominating influence of imperialism, require different strategies and tactics. The true understanding of these requires a scientific study of the concrete revolutionary situation in which these struggles have been or are being waged in order to establish basic principles. 'Pure theory' would not do. (497. 8)

Whereas the above passages draw out certain general principles on the character of the revolution in the imperialist countries (that it is a 'socialist revolution' in which 'the proletariat has first to settle accounts with its national bourgeoisie and financial oligarchy'), we find it incredible that they have nothing to say on the general principles of the people's democratic revolution in the semi-colonies. Instead, we are given an empirical ruse ('Pure theory would not do'). To underline the general principles of the people's democratic revolution, what is needed is a scientific analysis of imperialist exploitation in the neo-colonies, the resulting class relations and finally, the character of the semi-colonial state. The perusal of the Vietnamese and the Chinese experiences that follows towards the end of the manuscript can only augment such an analysis; it cannot be a substitute for it.

A. Political Economy: Forms of Imperialist Exploitation

While we agree with the critique of Emmanuel Arrighi's thesis on 'unequal exchange' in the manuscript we cannot accept the conclusion drawn from it, that is, the total rejection of any possibility of exploitation in the neo-colonies through the exchange of unequal values. The critique of Arrighi rightly returns to Marx's polemic against Proudhon to underline the fact that the worker's exploitation doesn't take place in the sphere of circulation but in the process of production. The point, however, is to explain the exploitation of the peasant producer.

Imperialism's inability to qualitatively transform the productive forces in the neo-colonies means that the vast majority of the direct producers remain as small commodity producers: peasants are not transformed into proletarians. The peasant doesn't sell his labour-power, he sells his product and his exploitation is the result of the undervaluation of his product. 'Unequal exchange' explains the exploitation of the petty commodity producer in the neo-colony, not of the worker. To emphasize, 'unequal exchange' here refers not to the exploitation of countries but to that of non-proletarian producers. Recently, a comrade in the *Peking Review* emphasized the significance of this form of exploitation:

> It is known to all that the present price relationships between primary products and finished goods in the international market came into existence as imperialism occupied a monopoly position. This relationship in itself represents an exchange of unequal values. The Soviet revisionists go one better than the capital-imperialists in buying cheap and selling dear.... Prices of Soviet exports to Third World countries are generally 15–25 percent higher than world market prices while the prices of Soviet imports from Third World countries are 10–15 percent lower. This means an additional exchange of unequal values on top of the imperialist exchange of unequal values, a case of double exploitation. (Non Ching, "Social-Imperialism, Rapacious International Exploiter", *Peking Review*, 45, 1974, p. 17)

The manuscript confines itelf to the exploitation of the workers but has not a word to say of the peasant's exploitation. While capital exploits both, what we have in the latter case is capitalist exploitation on the basis of pre-capitalist forms of production.

B. Class Relations

It is extremely important that we possess a scientific analysis of the classes that form in the neo-colonies under imperialist hegemony. Here we find the manuscript both unsatisfactory and confusing. Let us take but one example.

On class formation in the neo-colonies, the manuscript has the following to say: Out of exports of capital for production in the neo-colony, a "national bourgeoisie" emerged which in reality was but a petty bourgeoisie in the process of colonial production.' (p. 387) We must have a strictly scientific understanding of the distinction between the petty bourgeoisie and the bourgeoisie. The tendency to equate or merge the two is totally unacceptable. The petty bourgeoisie partakes in the labour process, whether manual or mental, even though a section of it (e.g., the rich peasantry) may appropriate surplus-value. The petty bourgeois masses, as Lenin called them, are part of the working masses. The relation of the bourgeoisie, on the other hand, to the production process is strictly that of the appropriation of surplus-value. A neo-colonial bourgeoisie may retain only a part of the surplus-value it extracts, the bulk of it accumulating as the capital of the imperialist bourgeoisie. Nonetheless, the division of this surplus-value must be seen as a division between two bourgeois classes on the basis of the relative strength of each.

On the question of the bourgeoisie, the manuscript has very little to say, it would seem because, for the most part, it denies that any such class exists in the neo-colonies. Though several references exist to the national bourgeoisie, the very term is put in inverted commas. If the purpose is to deny the validity of such a concept, it should be clearly stated. If not, we wonder why the inverted commas.

The whole of the bourgeoisie in neo-colonies is dominated by imperialism. Within this subordinate bourgeoisie, however, we must distinguish different sections, comprador and national. Compradorism has had various forms historically, its classical form being the commercial bourgeoisie, based entirely on the colonial export-import trade, with no role to play in production, and therefore with little autonomy from its imperial master. The comprador industrial bourgeoisie, risen on the base of import-substituting industry, however, must be seen as a different historical form, based on production, with its own secondary contradictions with imperialism, nonetheless principally defining its own interests in harmony with those of imperialism. Separate from this is the national bourgeoisie, a tiny fraction whose production is based on national resources and the national market, and which finds its interests threatened by the imperialist export of capital and commodities. It is national, not because it exercises hegemonic control over the national productive forces, but because it has aspirations to do so. In the context of imperialist domination, the composition of the national bourgeoisie must be seen as constantly shifting. Economically of little importance, politically this bourgeoisie is of great importance, given its ideological influence over the petty bourgeois masses. The national bourgeoisie's contradiction with imperialism must be objectively studied and exploited.

C. The Semi-Colonial State

While the manuscript has very little to say on this issue, we take this opportunity to make a few brief remarks so as to begin a discussion on this very important question.

The transition from a colony to a semi-colony must be principally understood as a *political* transition, in the form of the state. Both the colonial and the semi-colonial states are different forms of the bourgeois state. While in a colony political power exercised by a metropolitan bourgeoisie goes hand-in-hand with imperialist exploitation, in the case of a semi-colony there is a radical rupture between economic exploitation and political oppression. The state, the apparatus of oppression, is now managed by a class situated within the semi-colony; on the other hand, imperialist exploitation continues. This is why the ruling class in a semi-colony must be viewed in its dependent relation to a particular imperialism(s). Central to the concept of the semi-colony is an intra-imperialist rivalry politically mediated through classes (or fractions of classes) within the semi-colony. As Lenin emphasized in *Imperialism, the Highest Stage of Capitalism:*

> Since we are speaking of colonial policy in the epoch of capitalist imperialism, it must be observed that finance capital and its foreign policy, which is the struggle of the great powers for the economic and political division of the world, give rise to a number of transitional forms of state

dependence. Not only are the two main groups of countries, those owning colonies, and the colonies themselves, but also the diverse forms of dependent countries which politically, are formally independent, but in fact are enmeshed in the net of financial and diplomatic dependence, typical of this epoch. (*Collected Works*, Vol. 22, p. 263)

Mao Tsetung further clarified:

> When imperialism carries on its opression not by war, but by milder means – political, economic and cultural – the ruling classes in semi-colonial countries capitulate to imperialism, and the two form an alliance for the joint oppression of the masses of the people. ('On Contradiction', In *Four Essays on Philosophy*, p. 52)

Some comrades have advanced the position that the ruling class in a semi-colony is the international bourgeoisie. We find such a position highly economistic giving the international bourgeoisie a political unity it doesn't possess, not the least because there doesn't exist an international bourgeoisie state. While Lenin so well expressed the relation of politics to economics in his epigram 'politics is the concentrated expression of economics', he also found it necessary to specify that 'politics doesn't obediently follow economics'. The principal flaw in conceptualizing the international bourgoisie as the ruling class in a semi-colony is that it abstracts from intra-imperialist rivalry. We would emphasize that in a semi-colony the ruling class must be seen as situated within the social formation. The relative autonomy of such a dependent ruling class is based on three objective facts:

1. The contradiction between the imperialist and the socialist countries. A recent example here is the decision by the ruling classes of Tanzania and Zambia, in the face of united imperialist opposition, to go ahead with the construction of the Tanzam railroad, economically made possible by socialist assistance.
2. The contradiction between imperialist capital and that between imperialist countries.
3. The level of development of productive forces within the semi-colony depending on the extent to which capitalist relations have penetrated the particular economy.

D. Conclusion

Without a scientific explanation of the exploitation of the peasantry, the call for a worker-peasant alliance will remain but a subjective slogan; its content and its basis will remain inexplicable.

Secondly, a scientific analysis of both the petty bourgeoisie and the bourgeoisie – and furthermore, of the division between the national and the comprador sections of the bourgeoisie – is necessary to define the content of a united front for a people's democratic revolution. Not only does the manuscript fail to provide such an analysis, it summarily dismisses the petty bourgeoisie as the 'henchmen' of the monopoly bourgeoisie. (p. 400) With the petty bourgeoisie dismissed, the united front is thrown out of the window. Any attempt to construct one and bring the petty bourgeoisie within its fold would be sheer opportunism. We would argue, on the other hand, that the petty bourgeoisie, scientifically defined, forms a part of the anti-imperialist forces. The camp of the 'people' in the people's democratic revolution is an extremely broad front, including not only the petty bourgeoisie but also the national bourgeoisie. We are aware that the conclusion of the manuscript agrees with such a formulation. Our point, however, is that the conclusion doesn't follow from the analysis in the text; in fact, it flatly contradicts it.

Finally, it is important to correctly understand the nature of the semi-colonial ruling class and state in order to understand the character of the principal contradiction at different stages of the struggle. Mao Tsetung, generalizing from the experience of the Chinese revolution, points out that 'when imperialism carries on its oppression not by war, but by milder means...often employ(ing) indirect methods rather than direct action in helping the reactionaries in the semi-colonial countries to oppress the people...the internal contradictions become particularly sharp' (*On Contradiction*, p. 52). For those who argue that the international bourgeoisie is the ruling class in the semi-colonies, there can be no distinction between internal as opposed to external contradictions in a semi-colony. The proponents of such a position, to be consistent, must in fact maintain that the international bourgeoisie is the ruling class in all but the socialist countries. For them, the principal contradiction, globally and in every single capitalist country, from here unto the birth of world communism, must be that between the international bourgeoisie and the international working class. Thus we have the stage set for the world revolution which itself can no longer be conceptualized as covering an entire epoch, with different stages and an uneven development, *but* as one single world-historical act. In such a conception, there is no room for the people's democratic revolution. Marxist-Leninists, on the other hand, must conceptualize the revolutionary struggle concretely, in terms of stages. For each stage of the struggle, then we must identify concretely the principal contradiction, and following that, the content of the united front under the leadership of the working class.

Before we conclude, comrade, we would like to point out that, in the interest of beginning a process of collectively arriving at a scientific understanding of imperialism and the struggle against it, we have found it necessary to focus on our differences. The strength of the manuscript, particularly the relations it underlines between Marx's analysis of *Capital* and Lenin's theory of *Imperialism*, we consider to be a scientific contribution to the development of Marxist-Leninist ideology in our part of the world. We hope this letter will be but the beginning of a principled and disciplined discussion among East African comrades.

With fraternal greetings.

Mahmood and Bhagat

7

WHO IS THE RULING CLASS IN THE SEMI-COLONY?

Yash Tandon

Comrades Mahmood and Bhagat.

Your initiative at writing a critique of comrades Issa's and Dan's manuscripts is most welcome. It is to be hoped that through a principled and comradely discussion of the various issues you raise, we shall have enhanced both a scientific understanding of our present conjuncture and the methods of resolving contradictions amongst comrades. In writing this I do not intend to pre-empt either Issa or Dan, for it is ultimately for them to answer the issues you raise. However, I'd like to join in the discussion at this early stage, partly to give my support for your initiative, and partly to draw your attention to what, in my opinion, appear to be certain contradictions or apparent contradictions in your two critiques. I am myself, therefore, not commenting on the two comrades' works, only picking up on a few issues from your two letters.

The question of classes and the state in neo- or semi-colony

You draw a very important distinction in your letter to Issa. Talking about the bureaucrat bourgeoisie, you say:

> Only when state power becomes through nationalization of means of production not simply the agent of oppression, but also that of exploitation; and a social group, because of its control over the state, exercises control over means of production, only then can we identify the emergence of bureaucrat-capital and thus of a bureaucrat bourgeoisie.

Quite so. Exploitation cannot be conceived in terms of just control over the state apparatus, that is surplus must be seen to be appropriated not as a result of managerial control over the state apparatus, but in the process of production itself as a result of a proprietorial control over the means of production. The exploiting class cannot simply be subsumed within the state machine; it has to be shown to exist prior to and independently of the state apparatus, though, of course, it would use the state apparatus for purposes of organizing exploitative relations of production.

You draw a correct distinction, but you fail then to follow through your reasoning, for the obvious next question is: who has a proprietorial (not just in the legal sense) control over the means of production in a semi-colony like Tanzania? At least Shivji has shown in his book, even if the data appears in the form of an appendix, that the effective control over the means of production in Tanzania is not in the hands of the economic apparatuses of the state, that this control is shared with multinational corporations, and that this sharing puts the multinationals in a dominant relationship with the state parastatals.

Now to come back to your statement that only when a 'social group...exercises control over the means of production'—and not simply because it has a managerial control over the state apparatus—'only then can we identify the emergence of bureaucrat capital and thus of bureaucrat bourgeoisie'. How then can you say, a few lines later, that 'In this scientific sense, then, we can identify the emergence of a bureaucrat-bourgeoisie in Tanzania after the nationalizations accompanying the Arusha Declaration'—unless, of course, you were to deny the entire evidence in Shivji's book. Are you really, in terms of your own definition, justified in calling this 'social group' a bureaucrat-bourgeoisie? Perhaps your next sentence referring to 'imperialist domination over the semi-colony and its domination by the monopoly bourgeoisies of imperialist countries' leads in the correct direction, but this still leaves the question of whether you were right in calling the local segment of the ruling class in a semi-colony a 'bureaucrat bourgeoisie'.

Perhaps you will resolve this difficulty by the addition of the word 'comprador' in front of 'bureaucrat-bourgeoisie'. I don't know. But if you did that, and given the fact you have already described the entire 'commercial bourgeoisie' as comprador in character also because it is 'based entirely on the colonial export-import trade, and with little autonomy from its imperial masters' then where exactly is your 'national' bourgeoisie in a semi-colony like Tanzania? Is not Shivji then right in dismissing the 'national bourgeoisie' as non-existent?

If the reasoning is correct so far, I might add in parenthesis that Comrade Nabudere too would be right in dismissing the existence of this class in his manuscript.

Or is it perhaps the case that you regard the 'bureaucrat bourgeoisie' in a case like Tanzania to be 'national' in character rather than 'comprador'? Or, to put a subtler interpretation, national in aspiration, but comprador in reality? If this subtler formulation is the more correct, you would still be unjustified in referring to the Tanzania "bureaucrat bourgeoise as national in character. It would be more in line to call it 'national-comprador' in order to bring out its dual aspect, i.e., its subordinate position vis-a-vis imperialism, and its aspiration to be independent, which, unless we were to take one version of a contemporary Trotskyist position, we know will never be fulfilled in the epoch of imperialism. Perhaps Nabudere's 'national bourgeoisie' (in inverted commas) is aimed at emphasizing this complex peculiarity of this social group rather than, as you suggest in you critique, 'to deny the validity of the concept', as a concept.

Let me put the question squarely to you. Do you really think that there exists in a semi-colony like Tanzania a 'bureaucrat bourgeoisie' in your (correct) sense of the term? And if so, is it 'national' or 'comprador' (for you say in both your letters that a distinction must be drawn between these two)? Or is it neither? Or both?

To put yet another interpretation, would you regard the 'bureaucrat bourgeoisie' in a semi-colony like Tanzania as divided within itself, one fraction being 'national' in character and the other 'comprador'? If so, which do you think, is the dominant fraction?

Perhaps there is no answer to this question in the abstract, i.e. in abstraction from political practice. For is not the real point of analysis to provide a guide to action? And only in proletarian practice would the true character of the 'national compradorial' bourgeoisie reveal itself. In the meantime, it would be unnatural and unscientific to create a national bourgeoisie, anti-imperialist in character, if such a national bourgeoisie did not exist, in order that a front then might be formed with it against imperialism.

While we are at this point, let me also point out that I was somewhat surprised to read the following in your letter to Dan:

> We would argue... that the petty bourgeoisie, scientifically defined, forms a part of anti-imperialist forces. The camp of the 'people' in the people's democratic revolution is an extremely broad front, including not only the petty bourgeoisie but also the national bourgeoisie.

This unfortunately, emphasizes only one side of the character of the national and petty bourgeoisie, a side that comes to the fore only with correct proletarian practice. In the absence of correct proletarian practice, even the petty-bourgeoisie, let alone the bourgeoisie, can become actually reactionary and anti-revolutionary. Contrast Chile with Vietnam and you have a full understanding of the dual character of the petty and national bourgeoisies, under different circumstances and different political practices. For as Lenin pointed out in his *Two Tactics of Social-Democracy in the Democratic Revolution*:

> The peasantry includes a great number of semi-proletarian as well as petty bourgeois elements. This causes it also to be unstable and compels the proletariat to unite in a strictly class party. But the instability of the peasantry differs radically from the instability of the bourgeoisie, for at the present time the peasantry is interested not so much in the absolute preservation of private property as in the confiscation of the landed estates... While this does not cause the peasantry to become socialist or cease to be petty-bourgeois, the peasantry is capable of becoming a whole-hearted and most radical adherent of the democratic revolution. The peasantry will inevitably become such if only the progress of revolutionary events, which is enlightening it, is not interrupted too soon by the treachery of the bourgeoisie **and the defeat** of the proletariat. Subject to this condition, the peasantry will become a bulwark of the revolution and the republic. (emphasis added).

The question of the ruling class in a neo- or semi-colony

Here you create a disjunction between the political and the economic, which is completely un-Marxist.

> While in a colony political power exercised by a metropolitan bourgeoisie goes hand-in-hand with imperialist exploitation, in the case of a semi-colony, there is a radical rupture between economic exploitation and political oppression. The state, the apparatus of oppression, is now managed by a class situated within the semi-colony; on the other hand, imperialist exploitation continues. (letter to Dan)

Here you revert to a purely managerial concept of class, which you had earlier correctly criticized in your letter to Comrade Issa. There you reprimanded Comrade Issa for failing to grasp 'that the class relations is a relation of production' and correctly suggested that 'the analysis of imperialism must be integral to that of classes in the neo-colony'. In your critique of Comrade Dan, on the other hand, while admitting the importance of understanding imperialism, when it comes to integrating the analysis of classes with that of imperialism, once again you separate the two. You accused Comrade Issa of carrying out a 'class analysis (which) is often abstracted from that of imperialism', and then go on to do the same yourselves in your critique of Comrade Dan or at least this is what it looks like. You can't have it both ways.

The fault, in my opinion, lies in your understanding of the ruling class. You have, as the above quote shows, a purely managerial conception of the ruling class. That group which manages the state apparatus is the ruling class. But is it?

I can give you a number of instances of neo-colonies (from Diem's Vietnam Gabon or the Central African Republic/Empire) in which the group that you would identify as 'the ruling class' is neither 'ruling' in anything more than a purely formal sense of the term, nor can it be strictly defined as a 'class' located, that is, at the level of the relations of production.

Now perhaps it is difficult to formulate a general theory on the neo-colonial state that fits every case, but whatever it is, its essential components will have to be the relations between whatever group there is that 'manages' the state apparatus, and imperialism, whatever imperialist group is dominant in that particular social formation, and how these are related in reproducing the relations of production and exploitation.

You appear to find it hard to understand how at least a segment of the ruling class, if not the whole of it, can be external to the national boundaries of the neo-colony itself. For you the ruling class must be exclusively internal to the neo-colony. But why is it difficult to conceptualize a neo-colony such as, for example, Gabon, where nothing has changed after independence except the colour of the men who now manage the state apparatus; indeed in many cases not even that? Objectively, the state and the economy perform exactly the same function as before.

Part of your difficulty here is that you identify 'international bourgeoisie' to mean a monolithic, united bourgeoisie which, since it does not exist in this monolithic and united form, cannot form part of any ruling class, let alone part of the ruling class of a neo-colony. If that is your conception of 'international bourgeoisie' then you are indeed knocking down a man of straw. You quote from the General Line of the Central Committee of the Communist Party of China to argue against those who would deny that there are internal contradictions amongst imperialist countries, and who assert instead that the contradictions among the imperialist countries can be reconciled, or even eliminated, by international agreements among the big monopolies. I did not get the impression, reading Comrades Dan's manuscript, that he needed to be reminded about inter-imperialist contradictions with this quotation from the General Line, but I'd leave this for him to answer.

Of course, finance capital has internal contradictions – contradictions between national capitals, contradictions between monopoly capital and non-monopoly capital, contradictions within monopoly capital. But what prevents one or more of these groups of finance capital from acquiring hegemony over a particular neo-colony, and becoming, in effect, its ruling class, or at least a segment of the ruling class? How else would you describe American imperialism's hold over Diem's Vietnam? Would you say it was an 'alliance' between American imperialism and a puppet regime placed in power by American imperialism itself?

You are right that the contradictions between imperialist countries and between imperialist and socialist countries provide the basis for the relative autonomy of the dependent ruling classes in the neo-colonies. But these contradictions create the possibility, not necessarily the actualization, of this relative autonomy for every neo-colony, and the degree of this relative autonomy varies from state to state. Tanzania and Zambia were able to build the Uhuru Railway with Chinese help, but not every neo-colony is in a position to do so. One has to analyze the concrete situation in each case.

When one examines each situation concretely, one might find that it is not just the 'international bourgeoisie' which lacks monolithic unity free from contradictions, but also the local ruling classes which lack unity and freedom from internal contradictions. Different fractions of the local ruling classes might well be expressing positions of the different competing imperialisms. Take India, for example. The landlords might form one segment of the local ruling classes, but among the bourgeoisie located in industry within and outside the state sectors, the local ruling class segments may well be reflecting competing American and Soviet imperialisms. These local segments of the ruling classes to be analyzed in their symbiotic relationship with competing imperialism, and in terms of their relative hold over the economy and the state apparatus.

The conclusion I'm leading towards is that in taking the position that the ruling class of a neo-colony must be found within the neo-colony itself you have taken a rigid and unscientific position. You have reduced the ruling class into a mere formalism, i.e. it is that 'class' that manages the state apparatus. You have abstracted class analysis from imperialism, a charge that you yourselves level at Comrade Issa. You have not fully worked out the implications of your own analysis.

Unequal Exchange

I don't wish to say much on this, partly because I'm still in the process of reviewing the literature, and partly because you yourselves have not said much on it but you have left a few tantalizing statements in your exposition. This one, for instance: "unequal exchange" explains the exploitation of the petty commodity producer in the neo-colony, not of the workers'. Now if you take the law of equivalents, in normal course, commodities should exchange for their value. You have really to show why the law of equivalents will not apply to coffee that is produced by a petty commodity producer in Moshi, while it will apply to the khanga produced by workers in the Tanga Textile Mills.

But the law of equivalents does not always operate in practice, prices almost always deviate from values. It is this deviation that brings about 'unequal exchange', that is, an exchange of unequal values at the level of market where prices, not values, rule. And this can happen as easily with the products of workers as with the products of petty commodity producers, and it can happen in exchanges between the products of the capitalist countries themselves as well as in the exchanges between the produce of a capitalist country and those of a neo-colony.

Now if you want to explain exploitation, that is a different matter. I don't think, as you seem to, that 'unequal exchange' explains the 'exploitation' of the petty commodity producer, because exploitation, that is the appropriation of surplus-value, will have to be explained at the level of production and not at the level of exchange. And here I would say that we need to go into considerably detailed analyses of how exploitation of the petty commodity producers in a neo-colony takes place, which would involve us in the whole question of the absolute rent and differential rent, and the nature and forms of surplus appropriation under 'pre-capitalist'– if that is what it is–forms of agricultural production. That still remains largely an uncharted area.

Finally, I'm not sure I will agree with your evaluation of the Lome Convention, but this is a lesser issue in terms of theory, and I will pick this up with you verbally.

8

IMPERIALISM, STATE, CLASS AND RACE

(A Critique of Shivji's *Class Struggles in Tanzania*)

D. Wadada Nabudere

INTRODUCTION

Issa Shivji's *Class Struggles in Tanzania*[1] is the latest effort by him on the vital question of classes and class struggle in a particular imperialist-dominated country. It is a culmination of his earlier writings, *The Silent Class Struggle*[2] and *The Class Struggle Continues* (unpublished), which attempted essentially to deal with same issue. The present work is a re-writing of this last-mentioned paper.

In our considered view, Shivji's book fails to deal with the problem scientifically and therefore raises more questions than it purports to answer. He carries forward the same theoretical errors that occurred in his earlier writings, which, in our opinion, were not brought out clearly enough by many of his critics, with the possible exception of Professor Szentes, although the latter's critique had also its own problems. The other critics tended to compound the errors as, for instance, when Saul raises the question, 'Who is the immediate enemy?' implying thereby that it is the 'petty bourgeoisie' which is the immediate enemy and not imperialism. Saul draws his authority for this position from Debray, who states that this petty bourgeoisie which at first has no economic power, 'transforms the state not only into an instrument of political domination, but also into a source of economic power'.[3] Saul also quotes Gundar Frank.

This, as we have shown,[4] is exactly the same way Frank[5] puts the issue for Latin America and concludes: 'the immediate enemy of national liberation in Latin America is the native bourgeoisie...and the local bourgeoisie in...the countryside'.[6] This, he declares, is necessarily so 'notwithstanding the fact that strategically the principal enemy undoubtedly is imperialism'.[7] We showed that this type of analysis leads to adventurism and hence a wrong prescription of strategy and tactics against the imperialist enemy and is typically neo-Trotskyist.

To be sure, Shivji's attempt to analyze the Tanzanian colonial and neo-colonial social formation is deeply steeped in this neo-Marxist, neo-Trotskyite theoretical framework. This fact is not surprising in view of the deformed way in which Marxism was first introduced at the University of Dar es Salaam. Most of the first 'left' academics who came to the Hill, particularly after 1967, were, the neo-Marxist type, neo-Marxism being a by-product of Trotskyism in Western Europe, the U.S.A. and Latin America. This phenomenon was strengthened by the literature that was characteristic of the Dar es Salaam University Bookshop in the period 1968-72. These were mainly Trotskyite books by Isaac Deuscher and writers such as Trotsky himself. Then we had the *Monthly Review* group of Paul A. Baran and Paul Sweezy, and lastly, in the later period, the Gundar Frank Latin American 'under-development' school. This latter type of literature was later popularized on this continent by the prolific neo-Marxist, Samir Amin. The latest comer to this neo-Trotskyite pile-up was the British *New Left Review*. Marxist-Leninist classics were kept in the background and were not encouraged, for these neo-Trotskyites regarded the classical work as 'too difficult' and as not helpful in the present epoch.

In these intellectual circumstances, it is not surprising that Shivji's approach would be influenced in the way it was, and hence his analysis of classes and class struggle in Tanzania has lacked a clear and definitive concept of imperialism. His footnotes betray his leanings and concepts on the present world order which show a lack of scientific understanding of imperialism. Analysis of a particular country in these circumstances is seen as an academic exercise and intellectual fascination.

IMPERIALISM

When capitalism comes on the scene of history, it does so as a world system. Marx points out that in its embryonic form, capitalism exists as merchant capital which mediates between two modes of production and brings them into contact by way of exchange. Here capital hardly touches the other mode except by mediating between the two in the exchange relations. The plunder of this period, based on 'unequal exchange', constitutes in part the 'primitive accumulation', a pre-requisite to capitalist development proper. In its youth capitalism introduced itself in the formerly plundered world by initiating capitalist production and turning the peasantry into commodity producers, i.e. producers of products for exchange. This is industrial capital. In its old age capitalism begins to withold capitalist development by subjecting the backward countries to capital exports for the aim of producing cheap raw materials and food products required for the profitable employment of capital at home. This is finance capital. Lenin's analysis shows that in the era of monopolies which are formed out of small competitive firms and banks, a monopolistic bourgeoisie which he called the financial oligarchy – acquires control over basic industries and the credit system, and, on the basis of this control, exports finance capital for the exploitation of cheap labour and other resources in the backward countries.

This analysis of Marx and Lenin is important for the understanding of classes and social formations. It reveals to us that in its embryonic stage capitalism does not lead to the reproduction of its class because it does not succeed in fully freeing its opposite class, the direct producer, from old bonds. In its international mediation through trade, capitalism preserves and leaves intact the classes of the backward areas. In its youthful and competitive stage, capitalism encourages the reproduction of its class on the basis of survival of the fittest; and in its old age a monopolist stratum within it disposes of the others and increasingly turns them into a petty bourgeoisie, and turns some of the petty bourgeoisie into members of the proletariat, while creating and reproducing a petty bourgeoisie, proletariat and a commodity-producing peasantry on a world scale. These developments in class formation are in line with the development in the productive forces, in that survival of the fittest is a stage concentration of capital, and monopoly is the stage of survivors *par excellence* dominating the other bourgeoisie strata on the basis of their mutual interest to exploit the working class and the peasantry in the world. But all this is possible because the bourgeoisie as a class are not only in the control of the means of production but are in control of the means and instruments of suppression of the opposing classes. These instruments of suppression are called the state. Hence, wherever capitalist production introduces itself, it necessarily creates a state machine to protect and advance the reproduction of capital. This also applies to the colonial and neo-colonial territories and countries where colonial and neo-colonial states are created and perpetuated as a result of the internationalization of bourgeois class rule.

In analyzing classes and class struggles we have therefore first to grasp how capitalism and hence the capitalist class reproduce themselves and their antithesis, the working class, and how the product is appropriated under this system of production. These relations are production relations and have to be examined as such at all times. Here we have to draw a distinction between the total bourgeoisie and individual capitalists. The total bourgeoisie – to use Marx's words, this 'totality of capital' – is agreed on the 'exploitation of the total working class'. But this exploitation is possible only on the basis of competition. Thus the total interest of total capital can only prevail on the basis of one capitalist or monopoly competing against another. Thus what appears as a contradiction between the capitalist class (inclusive of the petty bourgeoisie) is a non-antagonistic competition in which each individual capitalist or monopoly attempts to reap a portion of the total surplus-value produced by labour. This distinction will become apparent when we examine Shivji's analysis of classes and 'class struggles' in Tanzania.

Having this background in view, let us now try to examine how Shivji goes about his analysis. Shivji starts with no such basic hypothesis of the movement of capital and this is his basic stumbling point throughout the book. Without a clear concept of imperialism, Shivji stumbles and falls over his material and hence proves incapable of synthesizing a case. Marxist-Leninist science requires that in analyzing a social phenomenon, we must begin from the whole to the part, from the general to the concrete. The general postulates, the general laws of motion of society constitute the basic ideological position and hypothesis within which the particular, the concrete, can be understood. The general hypothesis from which we must examine the Tanzanian situation is the theory of imperialism worked out by Marx and Lenin and other Marxist-Leninist leaders. Shivji tries to spell out this hypothesis but falters.

Drawing on the Latin American thesis, Shivji tells us that 'underdevelopment itself has to be analyzed as an integral part of the world capitalist system'.[8] He continues:

> It appears to me that these theoretical developments are fully applicable to the African countries. Though the degree of integration in the world on capitalist system may vary, none of them remains outside it. (p. 16)

This conclusion is justified probably because:

> The capital mode of production in fact constitutes the dominant mode of production because, as we pointed out in the above sections, the Marxist notion of the dominant mode of production is inseparable from the idea [sic!] of the dominant class-ruling class holding state power.... This is not to say that there are no other modes of production existing side-by-side. But they are in subordinate relation to the dominant mode.

Later Shivji reaffirms: 'The historically determined system of social production in Africa is the system of underdevelopment as an integral part of the world capitalist system.' (p. 19)

Although the above neo-Marxist way of dealing with the question is unsatisfactory from our point of view, one might have nevertheless gone along with it, if only Shivji maintained consistency. A few pages later, however, he begins to falter. Discussing the 'Colonial (Economic) Structures', he states: 'By the time of independence Tanzanian economic structures had more or less come to be integrated in the world capitalist system.' (p. 34) This in spite of the fact that earlier we are reminded of the dangers of the 'dualist view'. (p. 16) The weakened position reflected here is later turned into a new theoretical position of 'partnership', between 'state capital' and metropolitan capital in the post-Arusha period, in which the NDC, as a partner, enters into partnerships with multinational corporations. This is because NDC's 'main function appears to act as a catalyst fishing out and stimulating new projects in which foreign monopoly capital can combine with local state or private capital.' (p. 166)

The purpose of these partnership arrangements with multinational corporations is to allow them 'to serve the old ends of exploitation through new forms'. (p. 167) This latter statement might seem to suggest that Shivji realizes the weakness of the partnership thesis, but apparently this is not the case – for we are told in relation to the period of post-Arusha Declaration that the 'new class' of the 'bureaucratic bourgeoisie' became the controller of such capital. He states: 'Political power and control over property had now come to rest in the new class.' (p. 85) (Emphasis added). This is in spite of the fact that the 'bureaucratic bourgeoisie' is said by Shivji to be a dependent bourgeoisie – dependent on the international bourgeoisie' (p. 85). The way in which way it is dependent, if indeed it is a partner, is not analysed. Earlier in the 'theoretical' section we are told that juridical ownership is not social ownership, (p. 6) and again in the appendix we are told that 'nationalisation does not mean socialisation'. (p. 165) All these statements do not seem to mean much to Shivji. Later he recognizes that his 'state capital' is 'denationalised' and utilized by 'metropolitan capital'. (p. 169) He does not see that he contradicts himself, for when and at what point did this capital become 'national'?

These positions of Shivji should prove to us that he has no concept of imperialism as analysed by Lenin. A concept of finance capital is lacking and this is his basic weakness. His eclectic 'neo-Marxist' theories are not a sufficient basis on which to analyze a social formation. Although many of the statements Shivji makes on international capitalism and particularly on the multinational corporations are correct, they are not made in the context of theory but are merely assertions based on unsynthesized empiricist material. It is quite clear that Shivji found considerable difficulty in his work because of this lack of a scientific theory of imperialism to synthesize his material. This is confirmed by his extra wholesale parts of *Silent Class Struggle* and of his article on *'Capitalism Unlimited'* and attaching them at the back of his main work as appendices under the general title 'Underdevelopment and Relations with International Capitalism'. (See pp. 147-178.) Given this weak theoretical base on the 'dominant mode', Shivji finds considerable difficulty in analysing classes and class struggle in Tanzania.

CLASS AND RACE

We have already shown that when capitalism enters its monopoly phase it does so with the rise of a financial oligarchy which dispossesses other bourgeoisies and thus turns them into a petty bourgeoisie. Colonialism, which arises with this phase, implies exports of finance capital.

This capital produces a petty bourgeoisie in the colonies. It could not reproduce a national bourgeoisie when in the imperialist country itself such bourgeoisie is negated and destroyed, giving rise to a financial oligarchy. In colonies which arose before this phase, any national bourgeoisie which might have sprouted was routed by finance capital and was increasingly turned into a petty bourgeoisie. This petty bourgeoisie is stratified according to its role in the process of production and distribution. This to us must be the starting point in analysing classes in a particular country.

Shivji begins his 'class analysis' from an abstraction. This is because for him:

> Scientific historical analysis is neither to celebrate nor to criticise but to explain. Explanation implies nothing about an author's preference for this or that course of history. In any case this would be irrelevant; for history cannot be remade, it can only be interpreted and explained. (Preface)

Here Shivji introduces an idealist concept of history and his method follows this idealism obediently. Although we are later reminded that 'a committed intellectual'... 'explains and interprets the past to understand and demystify the present with a view to changing it', a dualism in method is introduced which pronounces itself at each stage. Within this framework, Shivji trots us on an arduous route. How could this be otherwise when he holds that 'the concepts of class and class struggle are probably the most elusive in Marx's writings'? (p. 4) The fact that classes are real people in daily activity and struggle is mystified by Shivji when he states:

> The development of classes and class struggle can only be talked about tendentially, in terms of historical trends. In fact, classes hardly became fully class-conscious except in situations of intense political struggle. Class consciousness does not fully dawn upon individuals until they are locked in political battles. (p. 8)

In this passage, Shivji's dualism is brought out. We are introduced to the idea that classes are not in struggle (in class sense) all the time because, he says earlier on, 'while class struggle constitutes the motive force in history, it is not always clear and pure as class struggle and may take varied forms under different concrete conditions'. (p. 8) Elsewhere he talks of 'muted' class struggles (p. 55), 'throttling' of class struggles (p. 55-6) and "pure" class struggles (p. 48). Inherent in this notion is the concept that although classes exist in reality, they are not always the only measure of all struggles. There are other situations that can explain relations between people and history is not a history of class struggles (although that is also true!). For this reason, since not all struggles are pure *class struggles (par excellence)*- for these come when classes are caught in 'political battles'- we can analyze struggles on the basis of ethnicity and race. The whole theory of classes and class struggle becomes a big idea counterposed to its reality. This is the objective idealism of Kant, and becomes Shivji's point of departure. Here we have an illustration of Plato's great gimmick of transubstantiation, in which reality is first transformed into an idea (the Ideal Form) and then the idea is transformed into reality via the interpretation of the idea.

With this petty-bourgeois apologia we are introduced to a static and unscientific analysis of classes and class struggle. History is brushed aside, so too the dialectical method. This is why the proletarian cultural revolution in China is examined completely out of historical context, betraying an opportunist attempt to appear revolutionary. Actually the whole analysis is electric and petty-bourgeois. This approach is reflected further in Shivji's egotisms like 'I don't agree', 'in my opinion', 'I think', 'I suggested' etc. (p. 19-21), which betray an individualistic and petty-bourgeois frame of thought which personifies and individualizes things.

In chapter 5 entitled 'Classes in History', we are introduced to a historical treatment of the 'colonial (economic) structures'. This gives us no basis for the analysis of 'classes in history'. On the contrary, we are treated to an ethnography in the tradition of bourgeois sociology. Taking Stavenhaven on Latin America as the inspirations, we are given a hotch-potch of 'African-Asian relations' as class relations and struggles. The Asian is seen as a 'link' between imperialism and the

'African'. The fact that the African trader, chief, *askari* and clerk are different levels of 'links' is done away with or at least mystified. But then the 'Asian', in order to accord with this 'African-Asian' relation, is dubbed 'exploiter' almost *par excellence* (to use Shivji's well known catch-word), and the African is the labourer, peasant, retail trader and consumer. To quote:

> Actually, the relations of extreme exploitation of the African could be seen at all levels: as wage-labourer; as peasant-producer and as a consumer of simple goods... the Asian trader was always a price giver and the African, a price taker. (p. 42)

Although these statements contain elements of truth, they are at the same time one-sided. In spite of the fact that the metropolitan bourgeoisie are held out as the 'major beneficiary', the Asian here is depicted as the central exploiter with power to fix prices. The fact that prices are monopolistically fixed by the financial oligarchy and that the Asian is merely a seller who in turn receives a segment of the surplus value, is obscured, imperialism, too. The relations between Africans and Asians are seen in racial terms rather than in class (production relation) terms. We shall see that this also is true of the Asian-Asian relation. These relations are seen in terms of race even though we are eclectically reminded by Shivji that 'The essential relationship between the two communities, therefore, is to be found in the sphere of production relations rather than in the area of ethnicity or culture.' (p. 44) This is not upheld at all when we also look at Shivji's analysis of class formations.

He begins here with the metropolitan bourgeoisie, whom he correctly calls 'the ruling class' in colonial Tanzania (the German financial oligarchy is forgotten), to which the 'Asian commercial bourgeoisie' provided the necessary link for the domination of the economy as a whole (p. 45). But who is this 'Asian commercial bourgeoisie'? The answer is given unswervingly: the whole Asian community. This 'commercial bourgeoisie' is categorized under four strata.

First, the upper stratum which consisted of the large estate and plantation owners, big wholesalers and produce merchants and a few 'really "successful professionals"' such as lawyers, doctors and accountants.

Second, another stratum which consisted of 'prosperous businessmen', 'well-to-do executives, etc. employed by foreign companies' (the comprador class).

Third, another stratum was composed of small retailers, 'self-employed people' such as tailors, shoemakers, 'middle-level public employees' and skilled craftsmen.

Fourth, manual workers, mostly carpenters, masons, poor retailers in the countryside and self-employed people such as pot-makers, repairers and so on. (p. 45) Shivji then tells us:

> It will be readily seen that the stratification is mainly based on income and therefore on the standard of living. This was a most important basis of stratification in the Asian community. Secondly, the broad divisions are extremely vague and rough. This is because hardly any close study has been made of the intra-ethnic stratification system of the Asians. However, for our purposes, the broad sketch derived from observation is adequate. (pp. 45-6)

Shivji then proceeds to give us a line of bourgeois sociological rationale for his categories. It will be seen that from the industrialist and the plantation capitalist farmer to an urban Asian worker, the whole group is classified as the commercial bourgeoisie. Furthermore, it will be seen that Shivji himself admits that his categories are not based on 'any close study...of intra-ethnic [not class!] stratification system of the Asians', but rather on 'observation' and income categories. We must conclude, on his own admissions, that the thesis is not

Marxist-Leninist scientific method of analyzing classes and accordingly must be dismissed as petty-bourgeois. Marxist-Leninist method treats classes on the basis of social production relations but not on the basis of ethnicity or racial differences. This is quite clear and the confusion that Shivji introduces on Tanzania must be rejected for what it is.

Shivji's analysis of the African petty bourgeoisie introduces the erroneous concept of the colonial state, and hence of the productive process under colonialism. The African petty bourgeoisie, according to Shivji, was 'destined' to become a 'ruling petty bourgeoisie, unlike its counterpart in Europe, where the petty bourgeoisie could hardly play a historical role.' (p. 49) This is historically incorrect for it can be shown that the petty bourgeoisies in Europe today are the main political force in the various countries. Quite apart from this erroneous historical position, Shivji introduces the distinction between the 'yeoman' of Kenya and the 'weak kulak' of Tanzania. This becomes the foundation for his designation of Tanzania and Kenya as neo-colony and neo-colony *par excellence*, respectively. Since the questions of the colonial state and the neo-colonial one are joined in this manner, we shall deal with them in the next section.

To sum up on this issue, Shivji's analysis of 'classes in history' has nothing in common with the Marxist-Leninist method. It introduces subjectivism and idealism. Indeed, within this chapter we are treated to diverse concepts which have nothing to do with the category of class in the Marxist sense. Thus we are told of 'political conflict groups', 'partners', 'sections', 'factions', 'wards', 'social group' etc. (p. 48) The analysis is clouded with profound mysticism and folklore in that it is in many parts referred to as 'analytical abstraction', 'pure abstraction', 'abstraction itself', etc. (pp. 44-45) Indeed, this pure theorizing is so rampant that, in our view, this chapter does not qualify for the title given to it. A better title would have been: An Abstraction in Class Analysis. Even then it would fail to grapple with the problem of classes as historical categories of social (production) relations.

UHURU, ARUSHA, THE STATE AND THE 'BUREAUCRATIC BOURGEOISIE'

In Part Three Shivji tries to posit his basic thesis: the historical movement leading to independence is incomplete. The *Silent Class Struggle* is supposed to have dealt with this aspect, but this is not the case; thus we are introduced to the transitional period to political independence with the scantiest of historical movement. As pointed out, the analysis of the African petty bourgeoisie introduces the line of thought on this period. We are informed by Shivji that this petty bourgeoisie was 'destined to become a ruling class'. This is because his concept of state is also faulty.

Marx and Engels teach us that the state is an oppressive instrument of a class. It is always controlled by the 'economically dominant class'. Its purpose in bourgeois society? which are beneficial to the total bourgeois class in spite of competition among them. The state is manned by people and these need not be the dominant class itself. The proletariat and peasants are frequently recruited into its machine. The petty bourgeoisie, a portion of the bourgeois class, has since the 1880s become increasingly the main source of the executive force of the bourgeois state of which the financial oligarchy (monopolist bourgeoisie) is the economically dominant class. In the words of Marx and Engels, as formulated in the *Communist Manifesto*. The executive of the modern (i.e. bourgeois) state is but a committee for managing the common affairs of the whole bourgeoisie.

The colonial state is a product of colonialism. It arises specially to advance the interest of the financial oligarchy and other portions of the bourgeoisie (including the petty bourgeoisie), first to ensure that a colony is maintained as a sphere reserved for the capital of a particular monopoly group against other monopoly groups, which are allowed in this sphere on condition that they open up their own spheres to the conceding group and secondly, to suppress and oppress all opposition coming from the peoples of the colony in order to assure cheap labour for the monopolies. Such suppression of uprisings as the *Maji Maji* rebellion testify to this role of the colonial state as an instrument of bourgeois class rule.

Opposition to colonial rule and imperialism in the era of the proletarian revolution leads to the imperialists conceding political independence to the colonial people. This advances the struggle of the people for democratic rights and enables these to be achieved at a very limited level, thus making it possible for the democratic revolution to advance. But this political independence does not do away with the grip the financial oligarchy has over the country. This is all well-known. But what does it mean concretely? In our view, it means that the financial oligarchy now under multilateral imperialism still continues to exploit the workers and peasants of the neo-colony through continued exports of finance capital. This finance capital has **magnetic power** of **tying** all the capital resources generated internationally to its **production** needs. Shivji gives an illustration of this power in what he refers to as 'de-nationalisation' of local capital. (p. 169) Thus the political achievement of the neo-colony are brought under the control of the financial oligarchy—a process that has never been disposed of. Under these circumstances, can there be any doubt that the economically dominant class in the neo-colony is the financial oligarchy of the imperialist countries, and that politics must reflect the base? The contradictions in the Third World over the last twenty years reflect this phenomenon and have clearly shown the limits of this phase of the national democratic revolution. Developments in China and Indochina have demonstrated how these contradictions can be resolved.

It is with this background in view that we consider Shivji's analysis in Part Three unsatisfactory. First Shivji begins by suggesting that the traders were the 'material base' for the transformation of Tanganyika African Association into a political organisation, with the teachers providing the link between the urban-based petty bourgeoisie and the 'rural peasants'. This is partly true. But the kulaks in Bukoba and Kilimanjaro, unlike those in Sukumaland, were opposed to the independence struggle. Shivji maintains that the African trader's dominant antagonism' was with the Asian, a commercial bourgeois (p. 57) The African traders therefore supported the independence struggle because they could 'only aspire to stand in the shoes of the Asian commercial bourgeoisie', which they could not do 'without seizing state power'. 'Hence the contradiction with the colonial state became primary; it had to be solved before the contradiction between the petty bourgeoisie and the commercial bourgeoisie could come to the fore'. (p. 59)

All this is one-sided analysis and does not delve into the underlying contradictions of the people of Tanzania with imperialism. What of the European trading houses? Did these not constitute 'a dominant contradiction' with the African trader, or was it that these trading however did not 'exploit' the African trader, since the Asian was 'the link'? What of the contradiction with monopolies? What sort of contradiction was this? All these and other questions are dealt with partially and one-sidedly.

The kulak question is also partially, if not erroneously, treated. It is claimed that the strong kulak in Bukoba and Kilimanjaro opposed TANU because in these areas the organisation took the form of tribal unions. It is not shown why this was so. This is because Shivji does not treat the situation here historically. If he had, he would have found that the pre-colonial class structure of these areas had a lot to do with this phenomenon. But then to do so would have taken Shivji 'too far afield'. (p. 60) Hence we have to be satisfied with a historical analysis!

This weakness comes out clearly when Shivji tries to treat us to the reasons why the 'weak kulak' in Tanzania gave rise to a powerfully growing 'bureaucratic bourgeoisie, while in Kenya the strong kulak or yeoman' farmer did not. Hence states, and we must quote him *in extenso*, since this is his real thesis:

> In an underdeveloped African country with a weak petty bourgeoisie, its ruling section, which comes to possess the instruments of state on the morrow of Independence, relatively commands enormous power and is therefore very strong. This was precisely the case in Tanzania. The situation becomes much clearer when contrasted with that in Kenya. In Kenya, there were important sections of the petty bourgeoisie–yeoman farmers and traders, for example–besides the urban–based intellegentsia, which had already developed significant 'independent' roots in the colonial economy. Thus the petty bourgeoisie as a class itself was strong (?) and different sections within it were more or less at par. This considerably reduced the power of the 'ruling clique' irrespective of its immediate possession of the state apparatus, and kept it 'tied' to its class base–the petty bourgeoisie. The Kenyan situation came closer to classical class rule in an advanced bourgeois country where, although there may be different contending groups or 'cliques' it is the bourgeoisie as a whole which continues to be the ruling or 'governing class'. Moreover, the group or 'clique' immediately in possession of the instruments of state power, cannot in normal circumstances cut itself off from its class base.
>
> The Tanzanian scene, on the other hand, comes closer to the 'Bonapartist' type of situation where contending classes have weakened themselves thus allowing the 'ruling clique' to cut itself off from its class base and *appear* to raise the state above the class struggle. Of course, it is not that the contending classes had weakened themselves in the independence struggle. But a somewhat similar situation resulted from the fact that the petty-bourgeoisie was weak and had not developed deep economic roots. This allowed the 'ruling group' a much freer hand. In other words the control of the state became the single decisive factor. For these and other reasons to be discussed later, it is proposed to identify the 'ruling group' as the 'bureautic bourgeoisie'. (pp. 63-64)

This overloaded thesis is a travesty of the facts. It groups together different historic situations and takes them to be similar or the same. Nothing is further from scientific method than to identify 'classical class rule' (whatever that may mean) and 'bonapartist "type" of sitution' (whatever that may also mean) to the neo-colonial situation in which the historical movement is dialectically quite different. Marxists do not discuss 'types' of situations. That is left to Weberians. Marxists discuss real and concrete historical situations. Anyone familiar with the Kenya situation will know that if anything, the African 'yeoman' farmer and trader were the weakest in East Africa. This was because, apart from his small plot in the 'reserve', his other alternative was to become a squatter in the 'White Highlands'. It is because of this that the *Mau Mau* struggle was basically a popular struggle with all sections of the population, except the few great chief families and a few loyalists. And it is because of this support to the colonialist that this 'loyalist' section was rewarded with land during this period. Land consolidation did not take place until 1954 and after, so that no 'yeoman farmer' arises in Kenya until the last eight years of colonialism. This is not the case with Tanzania and Uganda. Here, because of the feudal-type precolonial social structure and because of the collaboration of the ruling classes with colonialism, a strong kulak was allowed to develop. This Shivji himself acknowledges for Bukoba and Kilimanjaro. In Uganda, Buganda, and to some extent Busoga, Ankole, Toro, and Bunyoro, as well as a few outlying areas stood out in this regard.

The above evidence therefore must disprove Shivji's central thesis on the basis of the same evidence about formation of the 'bureaucratic bourgeoisie' in Tanzania as opposed to Kenya. If anything, on the basis of Shivji's thesis, this 'class' should have arisen in Kenya and not Tanzania. (Incidentally, another 'neo-Trotskyite' refers to Kenya as a 'Bonapartist type' of state.[9]) Indeed, on the same thesis, it could not have arisen in Uganda. Yet Shivji tells us that with the 'movement to the left' in Uganda in 1969, there arose 'many parallels with Tanzania' (p. 123) in spite of the fact that this 'bureaucratic bourgeoisie' itself was encouraging kulakism in Uganda at that very moment–a fact which, by-the-way, goes to falsify Mamdani's thesis on class formation in Uganda, as regards this issue.[10]

If this were all, the point would have been left to lie. But then Shivji's interpretation constitutes the sole theoretical and historical justification for a thesis of the 'bureaucratic bourgeoisie' in Tanzania and the 'class struggles' that are waged between it and the 'commercial bourgeoisie'. For this reason the matter has to be examined further.

What is this 'class' of the 'bureaucratic bourgeoisie? According to Shivji, before Arusha, 'this would consist mainly of those at the top levels of the state apparatus–ministers, high civil servants, high military and police officers, 'and such like'. (p. 64) The 'bureaucratic bourgeoisie' had not acquired its 'economic base' and after Arusha such a base was acquired through nationalizations. (p. 76) It then formed part of the African 'petty bourgeoisie', which as a whole may be 'grouped – in terms of their importance'–as follows:

(a) Income;
(b) education;
(c) standard of living and style of life (the urban milieu);
(d) control of or potentially effective participation in decision-making bodies;
(e) role occupied in the production process;
(f) control of, or proximity to, state apparatuses. (p. 87)

It is to be noted that 'bureaucratic bourgeoisie' are a class-within-a-class and chart 11 (p. 88) reflects this class of the petty bourgeoisie as as a whole. In this chart the 'bureaucratic bourgeoisie' constitutes the upper stratum which is said to comprise:

(a) The Politico-administrative: political heads of government ministries and departments (central and local) and their top civil servants; heads and top functionaries in the judiciary, police and security, and the top leadership of the party;
(b) The economic: heads and high functionaries of parastatals, public corporations and other quasi-economic institutions, either state-run or state-supervised (co-operatives, marketing boards, higher educational institutions included);
(c) Military: top military officers (majors, colonels, captains and lieutenants).

These contitute Shivji's 'bureaucratic bourgeoisie' which 'cut itself off from its class base' (p. 63) of the petty bourgeoisie after Arusha Declaration and established itself as a 'bourgeoisie' – within the petty bourgeoisie! As can be seen, these categories have nothing, with exception of a category (e) in the first set of criteria, in common with Marx's concept of class. As we have seen, Shivji allows himself this manner of defining class because, according to him, the 'concepts of class and class struggle are probably the most elusive in Marx's writings'. (p. 4) He is allowed, because of the dualism he brings in through this stratagem, to introduce 'impure' intra-class struggle' between the new class of the 'bureaucratic bourgeoisie' and the 'commercial bourgeoisie' breaks out in earnest after independence and is intensified after Arusha. To quote Shivji·

> The situation Tanzania found itself in after independence was precisely where power and property were separated. They simply could not remain separated for long. The incipient 'class struggle' between the petty-bourgeoisie and the commercial bourgeoisie could not be waged without state power. (p. 67)

This is written under a title 'The Class Struggle Unfolds', in which a collection of diverse incidents are collected to accord with his case. The 'climax' of this 'class struggle' results in a resounding victory for the 'bureaucratic bourgeoisie', witn the 'disintegration' of the commercial bourgeoisie. (pp. 80–84) This disintegration is witnessed with 'cultural exclusivism, tight-groupism, and racial prejudice among the Asians' because 'their vital class interests had been destroyed'. (p. 82) The old 'patriotism, morality and loyalty – the objective law of class struggle' were no more!

This epitaph is as hollow as it is contrived. All the vices above of 'cultural exclusivism' etc. cannot be said to have arisen after Arusha. Loyalty to the 'class' cannot be said to have ended. But if we are made to think that the class is dead, Shivji soon reminds us the class is alive and kicking. Beginning with 'NATEX', men (p. 83) and following it up with the 'top established merchants' (p. 84), he states that this class, through 'relations, acquaintances, and friends (has) woven (its) way into the state distribution organisations'. (p. 84) He continues: Thus, through bribery and corruption they continue getting supplies even when there are shortages and rationing. In this way these businessmen have made enormous amounts of money in the last four or five years. (p. 84)

This unfortunate situation arises because 'unofficial and illegal means have taken over' 'Bourgeois standards' of 'honesty, fair play' etc. ('Honesty is the best policy'), have been completely eroded. There has been a spectacular decline in respect of bourgeois law and bourgeois business ethics'. (p. 84).

This apologia for imperialism is uncalled for, in our judgement. Monopoly capitalism which comes with colonialism has no such claim for itself. How could 'honesty' decline when, according to Shivji himself, the 'Asian-African relation' before independence was characterized by one exploiting the other – one a price-maker and the other the price-taker? (p. 42) Corruption and bribery of state officials is a practice engaged in by the financial oligarchy in all the imperialist centres. Surely Shivji must have heard of the Lockheed scandals and the Shell/BP Italian political party briberies. Where in the world is the honesty of capitalism? It is simply a good idea entertained by Shivji in his native analysis.

Be that as it may, Shivji concludes that the control of the state apparatus is 'One of the most important conditions for the continued existence and reproduction of the "bureaucratic bourgeois" especially in the initial stages when its grip over the economy has not been fully established'. (p. 94).

This is coupled with the 'class control of the neo-colonial territorial economy through the state', and the 'continued reproduction of the system of underdevelopment within the world capitalist system'. (p. 94) In this system of reproduction the bureaucratic bourgeois 'only does the consumption' (p. 95) out of its share of the "surplus", which according to Shivji, takes the 'form of three categories: (a) surplus-value, (b) merchant profit *strict sensu*, (c) surplus-labour.

Because Shivji, like all the neo-Trotskyites, drops Marx's concept of surplus-value, he cannot conceive that splitting hairs by creating other categories of 'surplus'. These only go to confuse the analysis of capitalist relations. Marx's concept of surplus-value which is the total surplus product of labour, would reveal that merchant profit *'strict sensu'*, as Shivji calls it, and surplus-labour are part and parcel of surplus-value. But this concept would not accord with his analysis of classes. So other forms of 'surplus' must be created for the petty-bourgeoisie and commercial bourgeoisie, apart from the surplus-value for the 'metropolitan bourgeoisie'.

Because of these major weaknesses in method and analysis, Shivji's otherwise generally correct observations on Ujamaa Vijijini (Part Four) and the workers' strike actions (Part Five) which he calls (proletarian class struggles) are enveloped in narrowness of scope. The workers 'proletarian struggles' are aimed at the 'bureaucratic bourgeoisie'in spite of the fact that Shivji reminds us that the state, 'with all its vigour and under the guise of encouraging economic development, passes all sorts of legislation antistrike laws, ceiling on wages – which ultimately benefit the multinational corporations'. (p. 171)

As we have shown, Shivji ends in this eclectic position because he has no concept of class and state; and this is inevitable since he abandons the Marxist-Leninist position. His incapability to conceptualize consistently the state as an institution which exists for the total interest of the total class is responsible for his putting out the 'bureaucratic bourgeoisie', state officials, and functionaries as a 'ruling class'. He goes further to attribute to this class use of state power for its own interests, when that interest does not contradict fundamentally the total interest of the class as a whole on world scale. Thus we are left in a foggy situation where we do not see the forest for the trees. The fact that in every bourgeois state, of which a neo-colonial state is one, part of surplus-value in the forms of taxes, profits and rents accrues to the state for its maintenance is seen by Shivji to be the condition for the 'reproduction' of the 'bureaucratic bourgeoisie' as a class. This is erroneous and misleading. His lack of a clear concept of class is also responsible for a lot of juggling with petty situations which are magnified to accord with his petty theories. The fact that all Marx's writings are concerned with nothing but analysis of society, an analysis which is deep in class analysis, is obtrusively brushed aside as 'elusive'. As we have said, this gives Shivji a chance to smuggle in his own 'classes' which are but racial and ethnic groups and his 'class struggles' which are nothing but intra-class competitive struggles. The real class struggles of the proletariat and other exploited classes are mystified under this general idealist presentation.

CONCLUSION

We conclude therefore that Shivji's book is very bad. Since it claims to be a Marxist thesis, it puts Marxist-Leninist scholarship – if one may use that term – in an extremely bad light. Indeed it makes a beginner in Marxism extremely flabbergasted with the text. The text is abstracted from the real movement of history, and concepts are therefore unclear and misleading. It also gives an incorrect position on Tanzania, which even Marxist-Leninists not knowledgeable about the Tanzanian situation would find difficult to understand. A scientific exposition about society requires a scientific method. The scientific method of Marx requires an analysis, based on historical materialism, of the movement of history as a whole. The particular movement can then he analysed within this context. Failure to do this leads us into a dualistic view of society, and introduces idealist misconceptions which can only lead us back into darkness and ignorance about our societies. Marx's materialistically based scientific method enables our countries – which bourgeois historians banished from history – to be looked at afresh in their precolonial setting. Reginald Coupland, the official imperialist historian writing on the 'history' of East African came to the conclusion that, before Livingstone:

> The main body if Africans had stayed for untold centuries in barbarism: Such it might almost seem had been Nature's decree. So they remained stagnant, neither going forward nor going back. The heart of Africa was scarcely beating. (p. 11)

Such a view of our peoples is contradicted by the very movement in our societies before colonialism. A scientific study will reveal that a variety of social life existed – societies at various levels of social development – from classless to class societies, re-enacting the social progress of man throughout the world. The myth that Africa was classless, which Shivji correctly points out (p. 18), is a product of this colonialist ideology that holds our societies as having been stagnant, neither going back nor forward, a view contradicted by history itself.

Bourgeois scholarship therefore cannot enable us to delve into our past and establish the real dynamic movement. The Marxist materialist – based conception of history is the only tool available to us. It is for this reason that we take great exception to the way Shivji analyses the Tanzanian situation. By reintroducing the idealist world outlook we are pushed back into the lap of bourgeois obscurantism, via the despondent root of neo-Trotskyism, which we all must reject. Although Shivji may not personally think of himself as putting forward a neo-Trotskyist position, we have shown that his main source of inspiration and ideas is in neo-Marxist (neo-Trotskyite) literature, a fact attested to by his references and footnotes. It is for this reason that this analysis adopts an eclectic approach which takes us away from a scientific approach. We conclude that his contribution cannot be accepted as a Marxist-Leninist thesis on class struggle in Tanzania.

9

THE "MARXISM—LENINISM" OF PROFESSOR D. WADADA NABUDERE

Karim Hirji

Progressive circles in Tanzania have recently been surprised to learn that Shivji's *Class Struggles in Tanzania* is a "neo-Marxist", "neo-Trotskyist", "idealist", "obscurantist", "static", "unscientific", "eclectic", "bad", "subjective", "petty-bourgeois", "egoistic", etc. work, and that it has "nothing in common with the Marxist-Leninist method".[1] Thus it is at best "an academic exercise in intellectual fascination" and at worst, plain reactionary stuff. If these assertions be correct, the question that immediately arises is, what then is the essence of a correct Marxist-Leninist analysis of the contemporary situation? Before anyone starts scratching his head over this burning question, a brilliant "Marxist-Leninist" Professor has the following answer:

> ... when capitalism enters its monopoly phase it does so with the rise of a financial oligarchy which dispossesses other bourgeoisie and thus turns them into a petty-bourgeoisie. Colonialism, which arises with this phase, implies export of finance capital.

To remain consistent to his economism, the Professor, who maintains that politics must reflect the base should have said that exports of finance, an economic phenomenon, imply colonialism, the politics. However, he can be forgiven for his inadvertent neo-Marxist slip.

> This capital reproduces in the process of production a petty bourgeoisie in the colonies. It could not reproduce a national bourgeoisie when in the imperialist country itself such a bourgeoisie is negated and destroyed, giving rise to a financial oligarchy. In the colonies which arose before this phase, any national bourgeoisie which might have sprouted was routed by finance capital and was increasingly turned into a petty-bourgeoisie. This petty-bourgeoisie is stratified according to its role in the process of production and distribution.
>
> [N.B. This is an important contribution to Marxism. The petty bourgeoisie is reproduced in the process of production but is stratified according to its role in the process of production and distribution. This to us *must* be the starting point in analysing classes in a particular country.[2]

Elaborating on this profound thesis, the Professor goes on as follows:

> Marx and Engels teach us that the state is an oppressive instrument of class. It is *always* controlled by the 'economically dominant class'. Its purpose in bourgeois society is to protect and advance the production relations existing in society which are beneficial to the total bourgeois class in spite of competition among them. The state is manned by people and these need not be the dominant class itself. The proletariat and peasants are frequently recruited into its machine. The petty bourgeoisie, a portion of the bourgeois

class [Another brilliant contribution to Marxism: the petty-bourgeoisie is a part of the bourgeoisie] has since the 1880's become increasingly the main source of the executive force of the bourgeois state of which the financial oligarchy (monopolist bourgeoisie) are the economically dominant class. In the words of Marx and Engels, as formulated in the Communist Manifesto: "The executive of the modern (i.e. bourgeois) state is but a committee for managing the common affairs of the whole bourgeoisie." The colonial state is a product of colonialism. [Is it a state or part of a state?] It arises specifically to advance the interests of the financial oligarchy and other portions of the bourgeoisie (including the petty-bourgeoisie).

This Professor excels in inconsistency! First he tells us that in the era of imperialism the financial oligarchy constitutes the sole and entire bourgeoisie, but now he talks of portions of the bourgeoisie other than the financial oligarchy—another "neo-Marxist" error! Nabudere goes on:

First to ensure that a colony is maintained as a sphere reserved for the capital of a particular monopoly group against other monopoly groups, which are allowed in this sphere on condition that they open up their own sphere to conceding groups.[So the British monopoly bourgeoisie which controlled the colonial Tanganyikan State did not constitute a class but a monopoly group!] Secondly to suppress and oppress all opposition coming from the peoples of the colony in order to assure the monopolies cheap labour. Such suppression of uprisings as the Maji Maji rebellion testify to this role of the colonial state as an instrument of bourgeois class rule.

The opposition to the colonial rule and imperialism in the era of the proletarian revolution leads the imperialist conceding political independence to the colonial people. It advances the struggle of the people for democratic rights and enables these to be achieved at a very limited level thus making possible for the democratic revolution to advance. But this political independence does not do away with the grip the financial oligarchy has over the country. This is well-known. But what does it mean concretely? In our view, it means that the financial oligarchy now under multilateral imperialism still continues to exploit the workers and peasants of the neo-colony through continued exports of finance capital. This finance capital has magnetic power of tying all the capital resources generated internationally to its production needs. Shivji gives an illustration in his book (p. 169) of his power in what he refers to as 'denationalisation' of local capital. Thus the political achievements of the neo-colony are brought under the control of the financial oligarchy—a process that has never been disposed of. Under these circumstances, can there be any doubt that the economically dominant class in the neo-colony is the financial oligarchy of the imperialist countries and that politics must reflect the base? The contradictions in the Third-World over the last twenty years reflect this phenomenon and have clearly shown the limits of this phase of the national democratic revolution. Developments in China and Indo-China have demonstrated how these contradictions can be resolved.[3]

If politics must reflects the base, then surely the struggle of Marx against the mechanistic materialism of Feurbach, and the struggles of Lenin against economism were all not in the Marxist-Leninist tradition according to this profound Marxist-Leninist of our time! One wonders how he would react to Mao's assertion that under certain conditions politics determine the base!

As Lenin says, 'To criticise an author, to answer him, one has to quote in full at least the main propositions of his article.'[4] Having quoted Nabudere's main propositions, the confusion and basic departures from Marxism-Leninism that they represent have to be exposed. If allowed to go on unchecked, this eminent Professor's handouts are bound to cause tremendous ideological confusion, thus retarding the further development of the struggle against imperialism and its allies in this part of the world.

This self-styled "Marxist-Leninist" has to be reminded that his assertions are, in substance, nothing new. He is just reviving, under different conditions and in a crude manner, the ideas of eminent renegades like Kautsky and others against whom Lenin had to conduct intense ideological struggles in order to defend Marxism from being revised and caricaturised. Writing in 1915, Kautsky speculated as follows:

> Cannot the present imperialist policy be supplanted by a new, ultra-imperialist policy, which will introduce the joint exploitation of the world by internationally united finance capital in place of the mutual rivalries of national finance capital?[5]

According to the "considered" views of the Professor, the prophesy of his predecessor has in fact materialized. For finance capital has "destroyed and negated" all national capitals. Thus in this phase of "multilateral" imperialism, a world bourgeoisie, "the class as a whole on world scale", (Nabudere, op. cit., p. 20) i.e. the international financial oligarchy, is the economically dominant class which rules in both the imperialist countries as well as the countries dominated by imperialism. For Kautsky, imperialism is a "policy" but for the learned Professor, the "multilateral" imperialism of to-day being a product of "the U.S. multilateral strategy" represents "the rise of the transnational corporate strategy" resulting in the implementation of "the neo-colonial strategy"! (See Nabudere, *The Political Economy of Imperialism,* mimeo, 1976).* In the words of Lenin:

> Kautsky called ultra-imperialism or super-imperialism what Hobson, thirteen years earlier described as inter-imperialism. [And what to-day Nabudere calls multilateral imperialism.] Except for coining a new and clever catchword, replacing one Latin prefix by another, the only progress Kautsky [and also Nabudere–though he has substituted a whole new word instead of just a prefix!] has made in the sphere of "scientific" thought is that he gave out as Marxism what Hobson, in effect, described as the cant of English parsons.[6]

Exposing further Kautsky's 'lifeless abstractions", Lenin points out:

> Abstract theoretical reasoning may lead to the conclusion at which Kautsky has arrived–in a somewhat different fashion but also by abandoning Marxism–namely, that the time is not too far off when (the) magnates of capital will unite on a world scale in a single world trust, substituting an internationally united finance capital for the competition and struggle between sums of finance capital nationally isolated. This conclusion is, however, just as abstract, simplified and incorrect as the similar conclusion drawn by our Struvists and Economists of the nineties...[7]

Nabudere, however, repudiates these "neo-Marxists" polemics of Lenin. For he "has shown", as he monotonously reminds us, that the financial oligarchy has routed all national bourgeoisies. Thus to talk of a "national bourgeoisie" is to engage in mystification. The struggles between various imperialist "bourgeoisies" are just intra-class contradictions between monopoly groups which are part of the international financial oligarchy. It is precisely such reasoning which led Kautsky to speculate about "peaceful" imperialism, which Lenin termed a "silly little fable". As Lenin pointed out,

*Published into a book under the same title TPH and Zed Press, 1977.

Kautsky's theoretical analysis of imperialism as well as his economic and political critique of imperialism, are permeated through and through with a spirit, absolutely irreconcilable with Marxism, of obscuring and glossing over the fundamental contradictions of imperialism...[8]

These fundamental contradictions of imperialism include "the competition between several imperialism", i.e. the struggles between various imperialist bourgeoisies, which can be conducted either by peaceful means or through wars between imperialist states. Nabudere obscures and glosses over these issues dubbing all such contradictions as intra-class contradictions between monopoly groups. Contradictions between one section of the U.S. financial oligarchy and another section can be mediated by the U.S. state since this state basically serves the interests of the U.S. bourgeoisie as a whole. It is complete nonsense to think that these contradictions can lead to "war" between one "section" of the U.S. state and another. However, contradiction between the U.S. financial oligarchy and, say, the Japanese financial oligarchy can lead to a war between the U.S. state and the Japanese state. So to talk of all contradictions as contradictions between monopoly groups is to obscure the second type of contradictions and, objectively, to propound the Kautskyist fable of peaceful imperialism.

Of course, subjectively, Nabudere will deny these charges and may even quote some isolated passages from his writings to show that he takes into account the war-like nature of imperialism. The point, however, is what conclusions logically follow from his main arguments, even if the conclusions are not explicitly drawn by himself. At the same time, it should be realised that Nabudere excels in inconsistencies and self-contradictions. He quite often says something only to say its opposite soon after that. At times, political opportunism prevents him from drawing the obvious conclusion which follow from his argument. The case in point are his views on the state and ruling class.

Firstly, Nabudere claims that the international financial oligarchy is the "economically dominant class" in the imperialist world and asserts that politics must follow the base. But he refrains from concluding that therefore the financial oligarchy is the international ruling class in the imperialist world. Nabudere has also reminded us that each ruling class has a state machine at its disposal to protect and further its interests. But he refrains from concluding that this international ruling class therefore has at its disposal an international state to consolidate and further its interests. His views on this issue deliberately vague and one is left with the impression that he is talking about a single ruling class controlling many states! The inconsistency of this entirely un-Marxist view is obvious. To a single ruling class, there corresponds a single state. A separate state implies a separate ruling class. Lenin long ago exposed the opportunistic gimmics of "Marxists" who confused this issue.

The law of economic concentration, of the victory of large scale production over small is recognised in our own and Erfurt programmes. Kievsky [one of Nabudere's predecessors – K.H.] conceals the fact that nowhere is the law of political or state concentration recognised. If it were the same kind of law – if there were such a law – then why should not Kievsky formulate it and suggest that it be added to our programme?

... Kievsky does not formulate that law, does not suggest that it be added to our programme because he has the hazy feeling that if he did so he would be making himself a laughing stock. Everyone would laugh at this amusing imperialist Economism if it were expressed openly and if, parallel with the law that small scale production is ousted by large scale production, there were presented another "law" (connected with the first or existing side by side with it) of small states being ousted by big ones![9]

The modern peddlers of imperialist economism also shy away from drawing such conclusion. They cannot show that in the era of "multilateral" imperialism, and "transnational" corporations, there has occurred a merger of various national states into a "transnational" or "multilateral" state. They are content with muttering about "economically dominant class" and that "politics must follow the base". Such economism which distorts Marxism into an undialectical dogma has also been exposed by Lenin.

> We recognise – and quite rightly – the predominance of the economic factor, but to interpret it *a la* Kievsky is to make a caricature of Marxism. Even the trusts and banks of modern imperialism, though inevitable everywhere as part of developed capitalism differ in their concrete aspects from country to country. There is still a greater difference, despite homogeneity in essentials, between political forms in the advanced imperialist countries – America, England, France, Germany.[10]

Professor Nabudere's economism emerges starkly as soon as he starts discussing neo-colonialism. Having rapidly gobbled up some Marxist texts, what emerges from him is Marxism minus dialectics i.e. confusion. Thus he metaphysically maintains that since the financial oligarchy, "the class as a whole on world scale", is the "economically dominant class" before and after independence, the only change independence implies is a change of the pigment of bureaucratic personnel manning the state machine. Both the colonial and neo-colonial states are controlled by and directly serve the interests of the financial oligarchy!

The question here, as Lenin would put it, is one of:

> . . . the relation of economics to politics: The relation of economic condition and the economic content of imperialism to a certain political form.[11]

To grasp the relation of economics to politics one has not only to stress the predominance of economics but also the dialectical interaction between economies and politics. Only to stress the former is to propagate metaphysical economism about which Engels warned long ago. Striking at its roots, Engels wrote:

> The basis of this is the common undialectical conception of cause and effect as rigidly opposite poles, the total disregarding of interaction. These gentlemen often almost deliberately forget that once an historic element has been brought into the world by other, ultimately economic causes, it reacts, can react on its environment and even on the causes that have given rise to it.[12]

The emergence of monopolies, the rise of finance capital leading to export of capital and the struggle between monopolies to dominate the world formed the economic basis of modern colonialism. However, colonialism, which combined imperialist exploitation with national oppression, inevitably gave rise to anti-colonial struggles. These struggles were given a tremendous boost with success of the October Revolution. On the other hand, the position of the leading colonial powers was weakened with intensification of inter-imperialist rivalries leading to the Second Imperialist War and the emergence of U.S., a non-colonial power, as the leading imperialist power. Thus the anti-colonial struggles triumphed, leading to the disintegration of colonialism. With the rise of Social Imperialism and the further intensification of inter-imperialist rivalries, final blows are being delivered to the colonial system. Witness Angola! Lenin wrote of this long ago:

> All national oppression calls forth the resistance of the broad masses of the people; and the resistance of a nationally oppressed population always tends

to a national revolt. Not infrequently (notably in Austria and Russia) we find the bourgeoisie of the oppressed nations talking of a revolt, while in practice it enters into reactionary compacts with the bourgeoisie of the oppressor nation behind the backs of, and against, its own people... For what is a 'national' uprising? It is an uprising aimed at the achievement of political independence of the oppressed nation i.e. the establishment of a separate national state.[13]

Nabudere, being a master of mental acrobatics, will juggle out of these issues by retorting that these arguments are only applicable to Europe as there is no national bourgeoisie in the colonies. Here he will conveniently forget that according to him there is no national bourgeoisie anywhere in the world in the imperialist phase of capitalism. Lenin wrote the above in 1916, so he must be a neo-Trotskyist! In any case, Nabudere's predecessors who talked about "the unachievability of self-determination for colonies in the era of imperialism" used to remind Lenin that there is no proletariat in the colonies![14] The gimmicks of these economists did not fool Lenin.

Liberation of colonies, we stated in our thesis, means self-determination of nations. Europeans [and some learned professors!–K.H.] often forget that colonial peoples too are nations, but to tolerate this forgetfulness is to tolerate chauvinism... The slogan 'get out of colonies' has one and only one political and economic content: freedom of secession for the colonial nations, freedom to establish a separate state! If, as P. Kievsky believes, the general laws of imperialism prevent the self-determination of nations and make it a utopia, illusion, etc. etc., then how can one, without stopping to think, make an exception from these general laws for most of the nations of the world? Obviously, P. Kievsky's "theory" is a caricature of a theory.[15]

So the learned Professor must first realize that it is not correct to talk of a colonial state as a single entity. For it is part of the metropolitan state of the colonizing power, an extension of it adapted to the concrete conditions of the colony. What independence implies is the establishment of a separate state and thus of a separate class controlling the state. The bourgeoisie of the former colonial power no longer holds state power in the neo-colony. This does not mean that imperialist exploitation is done away with. It is in fact intensified. For the local ruling class that holds state power in the neo-colony is economically dependent on imperialism and thus, the neo-colonial state whilst specifically serving the interest of the local ruling class(es), also serves the interests of imperialism as a whole. The difference being that the neo-colonial state can act against the interests of a specific imperialist bourgeoisie or try to play off one imperialist power against another. It is in this sense only that one can talk of the relative autonomy of the local ruling class(es) vis-a-vis imperialism, The extent of this autonomy varies from neo-colony to neo-colony depending on concrete conditions. The genius of Lenin is attested by the fact that he realised this long ago.

Since we are speaking of colonial policy in the epoch of capitalist imperialism, it must be observed that finance capital and its foreign policy, which is the struggle of great powers for the economic and political division of the world, give rise to a number of transitional forms of state dependence. Not only are the two main groups of countries, those owning colonies and the colonies themselves, but also diverse forms of dependent countries, which politically are formally independent, but in fact, are emeshed in the net of financial and diplomatic dependence are typical of this epoch. We have already referred to one form of dependence – the semi-colony. An example of another is provided by Argentina. 'South America and especially Argentina,' writes Schulze-Gaevernitz in his work on British Imperialism, 'is so dependent financially on London that it ought to be described as almost a British commercial colony'. Basing himself on the reports of the Austro-Hungarian consul at Buenos Aires for 1909, Schilder estimated the amount of British capital invested in Argentina at 8,750 million francs. It is not difficult to imagine what strong connections British finance capital (and its faithful 'friend', diplomacy) thereby acquires with the Argentine bourgeoisie, with the circles that control the whole of that country's economic and political life. [Emphasis supplied – K.H.][16]

What the simplistic notions Nabudere fail to explain is how, in spite of the overwhelming dominance of British finance capital, Lenin can still talk of an Argentine bourgeoisie without any quotation marks or qualifications and in fact characterize this class as part of "the circles that controls the whole of that country's economic and political life" i.e. the ruling class(es). The professor can only go on chanting that if finance capital is economically dominant it also rules, and that the "Argentine bourgeoisie" is only a petty-bourgeosie! According to Nabudere, British finance capital must constitute "the circle that controls Argentine's economic and political life". He wants to reduce the whole world to labour and capital, a single bourgeoisie and, thus, a single proletariat, a world in which "capital rules".

Professor Nabudere has a peculiar knack for engaging in blatant generalizations which bear no relations to reality and upholding these as the gospel truth. He has completely forgotten what Lenin termed the living soul of Marxism i.e. concrete analysis of concrete conditions. Thus he claims that all national bourgeoisies have been 'destroyed and negated' by finance capital and that in the colonies just a petty-bourgeoisie remained. This is flatly contradicted by historical facts. Consider Le Duan's analysis of Indo-China.

> After World War I, the French Colonialists carried out their policy of exploiting Indo-China, completely subordinating the economy of the countries in this area to the French economy. The Economic conditions of Vietnam at that time could only produce a bourgeoisie which was economically weak and politically, compromised with imperialism and followed a policy of reformism.[17]

Thus, Nabudere, notwithstanding, the rule of French finance capital in fact produced a dependent Vietnamese bourgeoisie. Or consider Mao's analysis of semi-colonial China.

> About forty years ago, at the turn of the century China's *national* capitalism took its first step forward. Then about twenty years ago, during the first imperialist world war, China's *national* industry expanded, chiefly in textiles and flour milling, because the imperialist countries in Europe and America were pre-occupied with the war and temporarily relaxed the oppression in China.
>
> The history of the emergence and development of *national* capitalism is at the same time the history of the emergence of the Chinese bourgeoisie and proletariat.[18]

Compare these concrete analyses with Nabudere's "lifeless abstractions" about negation of national bourgeoisie and emergence of a petty-bourgeoisie. Nabudere makes a fundamental break with Marxism when he goes on to state that the petty-bourgeoisie constitute a part of the bourgeoisie.

> The petty-bourgeoisie: Included in this category are the owner-peasants, the master handicraftsmen, the lower levels of the intellectuals – students,

primary and secondary school teachers, lower government functionaries, office clerks, small lawyers – and the small trades.[19]

Since Nabudere can only visualise a petty-bourgeoisie in the neo-colonies, a Nigerian factory owner, a Kenyan capitalist farmer or any President in Africa are only petty-bourgeois! According to him, since the petty-bourgeoisie are part of the bourgeoisie and since today the international financial oligarchy is the sole bourgeoisie, then the petty-bourgeoisie are part of the financial oligarchy! Thus we end up with the strange conclusion that a rich peasant in Kilimanjaro, a primary school teacher in Tabora and a small trader in Mwanza are part of the financial oligarchy – the economically dominant class as a whole on the world scale!

Firstly, Nabudere is confusing the issue of social composition of a class with that of political class alliances. It is true that in certain circumstances the petty-bourgeoisie takes the side of the bourgeosie but it is also true that the petty-bourgeoisie, under proletarian leadership, takes the side of the proletariat. This does not mean that the petty-bourgeoisie is either part of the bourgeosie or of the proletariat. It is a separate class which allies with different classes under different conditions.

Secondly, Nabudere's assertions lead to reactionary political conclusions. By putting a factory clerk in the same class as the factory owner, a primary school teacher in the same calss as the controllers of the state apparatus, Nabudere confuses the enemies of the proletariat with their potential allies. If all are branded as "agents of imperialism" this leads to forgetting the potential allies and thus falling prey to adventurism. If all are regarded as part of the united front, this leads to supporting the existing ruling classes in the neo-colonies i.e. to opportunistic reformism. Lenin warned long ago that adventurism and reformism are the natural political policies of economism.[20]

It must be mentioned that Nabudere's silence about social imperialism has nothing to do with "tactics" or with lack of information. It follows directly from his abstractions about a world bourgeoisie. For otherwise he would have to show that the Soviet bourgeoisie is also a part of this global class and that the contradictions between the U.S. bourgeoisie and the Soviet bourgeoisie are just intra-class contradictions – a thing he knows that he cannot show!

Nabudere's ramblings about "the total class as a whole on the world scale" just serve the modern Trotskyist talk about a world revolution. Although Nabudere can retaliate by saying that he talks of national democratic revolutions, the fact remains this does not at all follow from his main arguments. These proletarian conclusions are just used as a defence for his reactionary theories.

To Nabudere and his fellow travellers, the warning which Lenin gave to the imperialist Economists of his time is quite appropriate:

> It is absolutely necessary again and again to warn the comrades concerned that they have landed themselves in a quagmire, that their "ideas" have nothing in common either with Marxism or revolutionary Social-Democracy. We can no longer leave the matter "in the dark": that would only encourage ideological confusion and direct it into the worst possible channel of equivocation, 'private' conflicts, incessant 'friction', etc. Our duty, on the contrary is to insist, in the most emphatic and categorical manner, on the obligation thoroughly to think out and analyse questions raised for discussion.[21]

76

NOTES

1 D. Wadada Nabudere, "Imperialism, State, Class and Race: Critique of Shivji's Class Struggle in Tanzania", mimeo, 1976.
2 Nabudere, op. cit., p. 7 (Emphasis supplied and comments in brackets by the author).
3 Nabudere, op. cit., pp. 12-13. (Comments and emphasis supplied - K.H.)
4 Lenin, "A Caricature of Marxism and Imperialist Economism", in Collected Works, Vol. 23, Moscow: Progress Publishers, 1974, p. 61.
5 Quoted in Lenin, Imperialism, The Highest Stage of Capitalism, Progress Publishers, Moscow, 1966, p. 109.
6 Lenin, op. cit., p. 109.
7 Lenin, "Preface to N. Bukharin's Pamphlet, Imperialism and the World Economy" in Collected Works, Vol. 1. 22, Moscow, Progress Publishers, 1974, p. 105.
8 Lenin, Imperialism...., pp. 113-114.
9. Lenin, A Caricature of Marxism..., pp. 49-50.
10. Lenin, op. cit., p. 69.
11 Lenin, op. cit., p. 45.
12 Engels, Letter to F. Mehring, July 14, 1893 in Marx and Engels, Selected Correspondence, Moscow, Progress Publishers, 965-p. 460.
13 Lenin, A Cariceture of Marxism..., pp. 61-62.
14 See Lenin, op. cit., p. 64.
15 Lenin, op. cit., pp. 63-65.
16 Lenin, Imperialism...p. 79.
17 Le Duan, On Some Present International Problems, Hanoi, Foreign Languages Publishing House, 1964, p. 67 (Emphasis supplied - K.H.)
18 Mao, "The Chinese Revolution and the Chinese Communist Party, Selected Works, Vol. 11, Peking Foreign Languages Press, 1955, p. 310. (Emphasis supplied- K.H.)
19 Mao, "Analysis of Classes in Chinese Society", in Selected Works, Vol. 1, Peking Foreign Languages Press, 1965, p. 15.
20 See Lenin: What is to be done? in Collected Works, Vol. 5, Moscow, Progress Publishers, 1973.
21 Lenin, The Nascent Trend of Imperialist Economism in Collected Works, Vol. 23, p. 14.

10

NABUDERE THE "KAUTSKYITE" AND HIRJI THE "MARXIST–LENINIST"

A.B. Kayonga and S.M. Magara

We would like to join in the on-going debate on the issues of imperialism, state and classes, in particular on the paper by Hirji in which he sets out to defend Shivji's theoretical conceptions and expound some of his own.

Hirji begins by implying that Shivji's theoretical work is not idealist, static, neo-Trotskyite etc. as Nabudere showed in his criticism of Shivji; neither does Hirji affirm that it is Marxist-Leninist. From Hirji's beginning, one would have expected him to go ahead and defend Shivji's thesis instead of simply stating that 'progressive circles' (whatever that means) have been surprised by the criticism.

Having swallowed his surprise, Hirji then rushes to unleash a tirade of slanders against the 'Professor'. Now he is 'blabbering Professor' and then a ['self-styled']! Marxist-Leninist. Since when did slanders become the Marxist-Leninist method of criticism? Who 'styled' this Hijri 'Marxist', so as to mistake the theoretical views for the person?

ON CLASSES

Hirji begins by misunderstanding and consequently misinterpreting Nabudere's thesis. This is because Hirji has preconceived ideas about the man. Does Nabudere say that the financial oligarchy constitutes the entire bourgeois class? No, he does not. Let us examine. Nabudere says in the critique that the petty-bourgeoisie are a portion of the bourgeois class. He goes on to show that the petty bourgeoisie have, since 1880, increasingly manned the state machinery in the capitalist countries where 'the financial oligarchy (monopolist bourgeosie) are the economically dominant class' (emphasis added). Nabudere also says that the financial oligarchy dispossesses other bourgeoisie. Hirji understands this to mean all bourgeoisie, so as to reach his abstracted and absurd conclusion that the financial oligarchy constitutes the entire bourgeois class. In his critique Nabudere shows that, in its old age, capitalism leads to the emergence of, in his words, a 'monopolist stratum' of the bourgeois class. Moreover careful study of Nabudere's work. *The Political Economy of Imperialism*, could have dispelled Hirji's illusion that Nabudere meant that the financial oligarchy constitutes the whole bourgeois class. In that work it is shown that in the process of production, at some stage of development, a capitalist class arises; that in the process of competition in capitalist production, characteristic of youthful capitalism, some capitalists are knocked out increasingly to join the ranks of the petty bourgeoisie and the proletariat; that in the final stage of capitalism a financial oligarchy arises because of the increasing concentration of capital and dominates all other strata of the bourgeoisie. Why then does Hirji understand the man to mean that the financial oligarchy is the entire bourgeoisie class? Or is it because to Hirji such analysis is 'economism'?

ON MONOPOLY GROUPS

The next query of Hirji's is where Nabudere uses the words 'monopoly group' when discussing the colonial state. He says that the colonial state arises to advance the interests of the financial oligarchy. To quote the man:

"...first to ensure that a colony is maintained for the capital of a particular *monopoly group* against other *monopoly groups* [emphasis added] which are allowed in this sphere on condition that they open up their own spheres to conceding *groups.*"

If Hiriji is scared of the use of the 'words monopoly group or groups', he should read (for reassurance) Lenin's. "The Report on the International Situation and the Fundamental Tasks of the Communist International at the 2nd Congress of the Communist International." (*Selected Works*, Moscow 1971, p. 450). There Lenin says of the First Imperialist War:

The First Imperialist War of 1914–1918 was the inevitable results of this partition of the whole world, of this *domination* by the capitalist monopolies, of this great power wielded by an insignificant number of very big banks two, three, four of five in each country. This war war waged for the repartition of the whole world. It was waged to *decide* which of the *small groups* [of monopolies, the authors] of the biggest states, the British or the German was *to obtain the opportunity and the right of rob, strangle and exploit the whole world*. You know that the war was setled in favour of the British *group*.... [Emphasis added].

Thus Lenin shows that the contradictions between these imperialist states are actually contradictions between monopoly groups of different countries, contradictions between the financial oligarchy located in different countries. Hirji's query in his 'critique' is thus shown to be baseless and bankrupt.

ON POLITICS REFLECTING THE BASE

Nabudere says that the economically dominant class in the neo-colonies is 'the financial oligarchy of the imperialist countries' and that politics (of the neo-colonies) must reflect the base. On seeing this Hirji rushes to misuse the authority of Chairman Mao. He says that Mao 'asserts' that under certain conditions politics determine the base. It is true that Mao says so, however <u>certain</u> conditions are the exception rather than the general rule. The general rule is that the politics reflect the base, which is but another way of saying that the economic base determines the politics. Hirji does not go on to show which are the certain conditions that Chairman Mao is talking of, neither does he cite a reference so that we can examine what it is exactly that Chairman Mao is 'asserting'. This suggests to us that Hirji is using Mao's authority out of context. Moreover Hirji should remember that for politics under certain conditions to determine the base, those politics must themselves have been in the first instance determined by the economic base. Under what circumstances therefore do politics determine the economic base? This is where the proletariat in the struggle with the bourgeoisie as to who should control the economic base emerges victorious and transforms the economic base. It is in such a context that Mao's quotation should be understood. Marxism-Leninism holds that the <u>material</u> is primary, while not denying the force of ideas having emerged on the economic base. To use Mao's authority, Hirji must show that the exception is the case in the neo-colonies in the era of imperialist domination.

Moreover if the politics of political independence and a 'new ruling class' determine the economic base, how is it that imperialist exploitation 'intensifies' as Hirji tells us?

The issues raised by Hirji on intra-class contradictions within the bourgeoisie do not refute Nabudere's thesis. It is true that the struggle between various 'imperialist bourgeoisies' are actually contradictions between monopoly groups. I refer Hirji again to Lenin's report to the Second Congress of the Comintern. Nabudere is not unaware that these groups are located in different countries. He shows very well his awareness of this in his manuscript. What Hirji calls 'several imperialisms' is actually monopoly groups located in different countries. The sum total of these groups located in different countries is what we call the financial oligarchy. The contradictions within the financial oligarchy *are* intra-class contradictions inspite of the fact that the class is located in different countries. The monopoly groups located in different countries achieve unity at a certain level, but this is not to say there is no contradiction among them. In all things there is at once unity and contradiction. This is a basic that tenet of dialectical materialism. The sum total of what Hirji calls 'imperialisms' is what we call imperialism. Thus Lenin entitles his book *Imperialism, the Highest Stage of Capitalism*. Does Hirji want to tell us Lenin forgot to put the "s" after the word imperialism? One is led to conclude that Hirji wants to absolutize only the contradictions within the phenomenon by introducing his concept of 'imperialisms'.

Later in the same section Hirji says that contradiction between the U.S. and the Japanese financial oligarchies may lead to war using the state in each country. This is true. Nabudere is aware of it *(Political Economy of Imperialism)*. Nabudere does not say that contradiction between one section and another of the U.S. financial oligarchy can lead to war between one section of the U.S. state against another. Hirji misunderstands Nabudere. Nabudere does not divide the U.S. state into sections; Nabudere uses the words monopoly group(s) in the sense that Lenin uses them in the Report to the Comintern, not in the way Hirji perceives.

Hirji asserts that Nabudere does not draw conclusions. Nabudere says that the oligarchy is the economically dominant class and that politics must reflect the base. It follows therefore that the oligarchy is also politically dominant in the capitalist world. Does Hirji need a Nabudere to draw conclusions for him?

As the financial oligarchy dominate the state of their own countries, so do they also politically dominate the states of other countries where they are economically dominant. Since the oligarchy is able to dominate other states and use them for its benefit there is no need for the financial oligarchy to establish an international state. The bourgeois class arises on the basis of the nation-state and is located in different countries where a proletariat also exists. So in each bourgeois country there must be a state. If all the bourgeoisie were in one country then there would be one state for them. There are many bourgeois states because there are many bourgeois countries where the class holds power. However, these states are similar and have the purpose of serving ultimately the interests of the dominant class. As international state is not the pre-requisite for the domination of the financial oligarchy. The oligarchy uses other states for its interests. Has Hirji not heard of the Lockheed scandals in Japan and the Netherlands, of the Shell B.P. scandals in Italy?

Hirji himself tells us that after political independence, after a separate state is set up, imperialist exploitation intensifies. Doesn't this testify to the fact that the financial oligarchy dominates other countries, uses other states to serve its interests? Why then does he want Nabudere to talk of an international state?

Hirji says that a separate state implies a separate ruling class. He wants to establish that the economically dominant class is not the politically dominant. He also says that independence implies the establishment of a separate state. He then goes on to tell us that after 'separate' neo-colonial states are set up, imperialist exploitation is nevertheless intensified. Is this how the politics of the 'new ruling class' determine the economic base? In these circumstances, in what sense is the separate 'ruling class' in the neo-colony a 'ruling class'?

If independence implies the establishment of a separate state, under which state, since Hirji tells us that imperialist exploitation intensifies, is Nabudere not correct in saying that, 'the political achievements of the neo-colony are brought under the control of the financial oligarchy...?

From Hirji's logic one arrives at the conclusion that the emergence of a separate state and a 'separate ruling class' means intensified imperialist economic domination. Can this be so without the corresponding political domination?

The fact that a neo-colony can play off one imperialist power against another does not make it any more independent if exploitation is intensified in any case. The fact that Hirji talks of relative autonomy implies that he recognises there is a dominating power. And what is that power if it is not the financial oligarchy.

The realisation of this domination is not to say political independence is of no significance. Nabudere says, "it advances the struggle of the people for democratic rights and enables these to be achieved at a very limited level thus making it possible for the democratic revolution to advance. But this political independence does not do away with the grip the financial oligarchy has over the country." (Emphasis added)

ON THE PETTY BOURGEOISIE

Hirji holds that the petty bourgeoisie is not a portion of the bourgeoisie class. Citing Mao's analysis of classes in Chinese society to prove that it is not so Hirji forgets that small manufacturers, small capitalists, shopkeepers, pawnbrokers, etc. are petty-bourgeoisie in relation to the big bourgeoisie. Marx, in the Communist Manifesto, says that,

"The lower strata of the middle class – the small trades-people, shopkeepers, retired tradesmen generally, the handicraftsmen and peasants – all these sink gradually into the proletariat, partly because their diminutive capital does not suffice for the scale on which Modern Industry is carried on and is swamped in the competition with the large capitalists, partly because their specialised skill is rendered worthless be new methods of production"

If the handicraftsmen, shopkeepers and peasants do carry on small capitalist production which 'is swamped in the competition with large capitalists', so long as this portion engages in small capitalist production, why should it not be called a portion of the bourgeoisie class, albeit a lower portion? Chinese analysis is not a model for the standard petty-bourgeois in all countries nor does it contradict the fact that they are a portion of the bourgeoisie. Thus saying that the petty bourgeoisie is a portion of the bourgeois class is not a 'fundamental break' with Marxism-Leninism. It is, however, true that not all petty bourgeois engage in capitalist production since the petty bourgeoisie is 'stratified according to its role in the process of production and distribution.'

NABUDERE, KAUTSKY AND HIRJI

Hirji accuses Nabudere of being Kautskyite. We must therefore examine whether

Nabudere's views are the same as Kautsky's. What are Kautsky's views on imperialism? Let Lenin tell us:

> Advancing this definition of imperialism bring us into complete contradiction to K. Kautsky, who refuses to regard imperialism as a 'phase of capitalism' and defines it as a policy 'preferred' by finance capital, a tendency of 'industrial' countries to annex 'agrarian' countries. Kautsky's definition is throughly false from the theoretical standpoint. What distinguishes imperialism is the rule not of industrial capital, but of finance capital, the striving to annex not agrarian countries, particularly but every kind of country. Kautsky divorces imperialist politics from monopoly economics, he divorces monopoly in politics from monopoly economics... *(Imperialism and the Split in Socialism Movement*, Moscow, Progress Publishers, 1975.)

Does Nabudere refuse to regard imperialism as a phase of capitalism? No, he does not. He shows in his manuscript how the imperialist phase of capitalism arises from competitive capitalism as a result of concentration of capital and the tendency of the rate of profit to fall.

Does Nabudere define imperialism as a policy 'preferred' by finance capital? No, he does not. He shows in his manuscript that concentration of capital and the tendency of the rate of profit to fall must lead to imperialism. Hirji would like to attribute Kautsky's definition to Nabudere because the latter talks of the multilateral strategy of imperialism. Is Hirji correct? No, he is not. Nabudere traces how imperialism rises in the process of *capitalist production*. He does not state *a priori* that imperialism is a policy. The multilateral strategy is the strategy championed by American imperialism, by the American financial oligarchy, to redivide the world in the era of proletarian revolution. The multilateral strategy does not lead to peaceful imperialism. This is a misconception in Hirji's mind. The multilateral strategy is at one and the same time the embodiment of the unity and struggle of the financial oligarchy. It holds that the monopoly groups shall exploit but on the basis of an open-door policy, on the basis of strength. It means open-door competition. It holds that there be no bilateral ties of certain colonies to a monopoly group of a particular country only. If Hirji had studied the history and functions of the GATT, the IMF, the IBRD – in short, the imperialists agreements at Bretton-Woods and elsewhere – he would have known what multilateralism is all about and that it does not mean peaceful imperialism, as he would have us believe.

Does Nabudere regard imperialism as a tendency of 'industrial' countries to annex 'agrarian' countries? No, he does not. Like Lenin, he shows that what distinguishes imperialism is the rule not of industrial capital but of finance capital. This is particularly emphasised in his manuscript where he vindicates Lenin's thesis on imperialism.

Does Nabudere divorce imperialist politics from imperialist economics? No, he does not. On the contrary, he shows that monopoly in economics leads to monopoly in politics. It is Hirji who would like to separate the two by smuggling in his new 'ruling classes', etc.

While Kautsky sees only unity in imperialism, Hirji sees only contradiction. Nabudere's views have nothing in common with Kautsky's and Hirji's because these two absolutize one aspect of the phenomenon. Their methods and conceptions are undialectical. Nabudere shows that imperialism has at once unity and contradiction.

CONCLUSION

We have shown that Hirji's 'criticism' and accusations are baseless. Hirji excels

82

more in slander than in criticism. He tells other comrades that they have 'landed in a quagmire' and have turned a principled debate into 'private' conflicts and incessant 'friction', not knowing that it is he who is in the quagmire, it is he who has turned a principled debate into 'private' conflicts and incessant 'friction', not knowing that it is he who is in the quagmire, it is he who has turned a principled debate into private conflicts and incessant friction by coming out to slander more that criticize. We would like to reaffirm Lenin's stand that, 'Our duty on the contrary is to insist, in the most emphatic and categorical manner, on the obligation thoroughly to think out and analyse questions raised for discussion'.

Severe criticism should never be mistaken for slander, neither should slander for criticism. by Marxist-Leninists-if indeed they are Marxist-Leninist!

11

A CARICATURE OF MARXISM-LENINISM
(A Reply to Karim Hirji)

D. Wadada Nabudere

["To a single ruling class, there corresponds a single state. A separate state implies a separate ruling class. For the financial oligarchy to rule internationally there must be an international state" – Universal Logical Edict enacted by Karim Hirji, on the 22nd day, of August, in the year of our Lord one thousand nine hundred and seventy six A.D.]

We have recently been served with a contribution to the unfolding debate – long overdue – on the vital issues of imperialism, class and state from Karim Hirji. We are happy that many wrong views that have been thrown around as "Marxism – Leninism" are being exposed to a broad democratic opinion in this form. Indeed the quotation he ends up with from Lenin puts our position squarely and we reproduce it:

> It is absolutely necessary again and again to warn the comrades concerned that they have landed themselves in a quagmire, that their "ideas" have nothing in common either with Marxism or revolutionary social-democracy. We can no longer leave the matter "in the dark": that would only encourage ideological confusion and direct it into the worst possible channel of equivocation, "private" conflicts, incessant "friction", etc. Our duty, on the contrary is to insist, in the most emphatic and categorical manner, on the obligation thoroughly to think out and analyse questions raised for discussion.

Thus those of his like who wanted matters kept "in the dark" and encourage "ideological confusion" cannot claim to be advancing Marxism-Leninism. Our open "Critique" will remove this darkness and the basis for private "conflicts and incessant frictions" that Hirji might have had in mind. In this way a correct line on these issues will emerge. What clearly is becoming obvious already is the panic that this great debate is causing in the camp to which Hirji belongs. No longer is the myth held, hitherto the rule, that what was uttered by his like was sacrosanct truth which if challenged by those who expressed doubt were arrogantly rebuffed. Now the exposure of their confusion by our open "Critique" forced them to explain themselves, and the manner they have adopted in doing so clearly shows the bankruptcy of their position, letting us know for the first time some of the dogmas that have formed the basis of their theses on Tanzania to which we shall advert later. Indeed, what had originally been regarded as innocent mistakes committed in the course of learning have clearly come out as firm ideological positions which no longer can be excused, after their erroneousness has been exposed in our earlier criticisms.

To begin with, Hirji sets himself out at the very beginning of his paper to express "surprise" about our "Critique" of Shivji. To quote him:

> Progressive circles in Tanzania have recently been surprised to learn that

Shivji's *Class struggles in Tanzania* is a 'neo-Trotskyist'. 'idealist', 'obscurantist', 'static', 'unscientific', 'electic', 'bad', 'subjective', 'petty-bourgeois', 'egoistic', etc., and that it has 'nothing in common with Marxist-Leninist Method'. Thus it is at its best 'an academic exercise in intellectual fascination and at worst [which we do not say] plain reactionary stuff.

Having gone to this extent, one then expected him to go on and show, in order to justify his "surprise", that Shivji's book has neither of these untruths that we ascribe to it and to demonstrate that it is a Marxist-Leninist thesis. In other words he would be expected to defend Shivji's thesis against our "Critique" and show our criticism to be the empty *'Marxism-Leninism' of Professor D. Wadada Nabudere'.* But what do we get? We are treated to emotional rambling, calling to his aid a barrage of quotations from Lenin, Mao Tse-tung, Le Duan etc., to support arguments picked up at random from the "Critique" and our "manuscript" on the *Political Economy of Imperialism*, out of context. Before we embark on the task of disentangling Hirji's confusion we would make a few prelimianry observations.

Firstly, what are these "progressive circles in Tanzania" that he talks about? We know many progressive Tanzanians and non-Tanzanians who have approached us to express appreciation for the "Critique". The Hirji's must have sensed this, and that explains their last ditch effort to put up face; otherwise there would be no need for them to reply with such outbursts. What is clear to us is that this so-called "progressive opinion" in Tanzania is no more than the diminishing group around Hirji and his clique which has hitherto held their thesis on Tanzania to be an original contribution to Marxism-Leninism, but which alas is being shocked to hear that this is far from the truth.

It is pointless to go over the issues we have already answered in our "Manuscript" and "Critique" and other documents and in this connection if he had cared to study our "Reply" to Mamdani and Bhagat entitled "The Politics and Political Economy of Imperialism", he would have found it necessary to go over issues like "ruling class", and state. But since he raises them again we are forced to go over some of the fundamental issues in order to correct errors which are clearly intended to create more confusion. Moreover, as we regard these differences to be important we think they should be approached with seriousness. Hirji's effort to reduce them to absurdity by introducing vulgar expressions will not assit to clarify issues, and we intend to stick to the errors raised strictly without engaging in his trickery.

Secondly, Hirji continues to commit the idealist errors of Shivji. We pointed out in our "Critique" that the basic weakness with idealism was that it abstracted the idea from reality and examined the idea "itself" as the reality. This Plato did through his method of transubstantiation wherein the reality was transformed into the idea which, then joined other similar ideas to form the "Ideal Universal" from which individual things (reality) could be judged and understood. Kant perfected this idealism by re-affirming the dualistic nature of phenomena. He pointed out that univesality and necessity could not be arrived at by the empirical method. The principles which lie at the base of knowledge, have no intrinsic necessity or absolute authority. They belong to human reason and can be verified by fact. But nevertheless they are conditions of self-experience, of our knowledge of appearances and useless for the construction of a philosophic theory of things in themselves, for there is a world of things as they appear to us and a world of things-in-themselves. Real knowledge could only be obtained *a priori* and not from empirical sense experience. Knowledge according to Kant, comes from ideas shaped and conceived or developed by the human thought. Human knowledge does not therefore come after (*a posteriori*) but before (*a priori*) independent of human experience and reality. This is idealism *par excellence*.

We regret that we have to revert to this question, but it is necessary to clear the debate. In our view, as we shall show, Hirji operates within these idealist environs by dealing with reality *a priori*. He does not analyse the thing as it is but as it ought to be in order to conform to his *a priori* position arrived at in the abstract. This is what is called dogmatism which is a basic weakness of Hirji's camp. Dialectical materialism does away with this dualism and establishes monism, in which phenomena exist on the basis of unity of opposites. As the old and earlier Greek philosophers said a thing is and is not. Dialectical materialism scientifically developed this concept and demonstrated how the transformation takes place from is to is not leading to a new unity again existing on the basis of struggle of opposites. For dualists like Hirji, for instance, to talk about a thing in the singular is to obscure the contradiction within it. So we must talk of "financial oligarchies" in order to show that there are contradictions among the monopolies. Hirji and his like do not see unity in opposites – indeed they do not see that no existence is possible without this unity of opposites including the entity we know as Hirji. Thus in order to show that the existence of Hirji is contradictory, we must speak of Hirjis. Equally in order to see contradiction in imperialism Lenin must talk of *"Imperialism(s) the Highest Stage of Capitalism(s)"*, and in order to show that there is contradiction in capitalist production, Marx should have entitled his works: CAPITAL(S)!! This point is important because Hirji hangs on these philistinistic semantics to talk about "Kautskyism"!!

Thirdly, the accusations against Marx, Engels and Lenin about "economism", or "materialism" made by their opponents early in the century continue to be made in disguise by many a neo-Trotskyist. These have nothing in common with the debate carried on by Lenin against economism in the working class movement. The first accusations made against Marx and Engels about "economism" were petty-bourgeois. They were aimed at dealing blows at the Marxist materialist method. Thus the first of the bourgeois scholars in sociology who raised this bogey were Durkheim and Weber. Although accepting philosophical materialism in words they nevertheless went on to fight materialism and in this way fell prey to neo-Kantianism of Rikert and Dilthey which asserted that there cannot be any complete scientific description of reality, since reality consists of complex divisible profusion of phenomena. Even if we were to focus our attention on a concrete element of reality, it too was infinite. Social science, therefore, must select from this multitude of phenomena only some aspects for study. This neo-Kantian world outlook, therefore, castigated a scientific study of phenomena based on materialist dialectics as metaphysical and hence encouraged the dualist world outlook of Kant. Hirji's accusations of "economism" against the "Manuscript have this ring and have nothing in common with Lenin's polemic. We shall later demonstrate that this is so by tracing at length Lenin's polemics if only to finish this question once and for all.

Surface it to say here that Engels' letters, which he wrote between 1890-1894 on this question, re-affirmed that although he and Marx and over-emphasized the economic element against their adversaries, nevertheless it remained true that "the ultimately determining element in history is the production and reproduction of real life". (To Joseph Bloch, September 21-22, 1890). We point this out because Hirji abstracts from our "Critique" the five words "economics must reflect the base" (emphasis his) to conclude that this is "economism" and that this distorts "Marxism-Leninism", without caring to understand the context. Although he quotes it extensively, it apparently does not make any meaning to him. If he understood the context he would find no difficulty in this question. We stated and we quote again:

86

> The opposition to the colonial rule and imperialism in the era of the proletarian revolution leads the imperialists conceding political independence to the colonial people. It advances the struggles of the people for democratic rights and enables these to be achieved at a very limited level thus making it possible for the democratic revolution to advance. But this political independence does not do away with the grip the financial oligarchy has over the country. This is well known. But what does this mean concretely? In our view, it means that the financial oligarchy now under multilateral imperialism still continues to exploit the workers and peasants of the neo-colony through continued exports of finance capital. This finance capital has magnetic power of tying all capital resources generated internationally to its production needs... Thus the political achievement of the neo-colony are brought under the control of the financial oligarchy – a process that has never been disposed of. Under these circumstances, can there be any doubt that the economically dominant class in the neo-colony is the financial oligarchy of the imperialist countries and that politics must reflect the base?

What, if we may ask, is wrong with the above analysis? Hirji merely sticks to the last five words, abstracts them from the context and calls them "economistic". Where does the above quote deny the interaction between the base and the superstructure? Indeed, if it denied it, how could the politics reflect the base; and without interaction how could the "multilateral strategy" (a policy) lead to multinational corporations (the base). I bring this out because Hirji seems to be indulging in small talk about "Kautsky's" imperialism as "a policy" and comparing it to that of "the learned Professor, [whose] 'multilateral' imperialism of today (is) a product of the 'U.S. multilateral strategy'", without attempting in any serious way to grapple with this question apart from engaging in quotations from Lenin which he cannot even digest. Hirji does this because he does not have the slightest acquaintance with the history of this period and also because he makes no effort to study and understand what we are talking about.

If Hirji had gone deeper into the question he would have found that he is accusing us on the first score of being "economistic"; while on the issue of Kautsky, he would logically accuse us of seeing imperialism as "a policy" if he understood Lenin's criticism of Kautsky, which is not that of "economism" but of "politicism". Hirji does not do this because he is electic and idealist and regards the two as being "economistic" because this happens to be a jargon stuck somewhere in the corner of his brain.

But what are the politics that must reflect the base in the context of the quotation reproduced above? It is the politics of finance capital in its effort to justify its continued exploitation of the neo-colonial workers and peasants and its domination and oppression of the neo-colonial peoples in general. It is the politics of the petty-bourgeoisie, *inter se*, of pious hopes, of reformism and of subservience. It is the politics of the proletariat, its ideology and the politics of its alliances in order to fight the imperialist enemy. All these politics are created by imperialism in the colony that are inherited by the neo-colony and are a reflection of the base, namely the continued grip by finance capital on the neo-colony. Do you deny these facts? Which other politics, Hirji, which do not spring from this base, are reflected in the superstructure in the neo-colony?

The reader can see that Hirji's conception of "economism" is that of the bourgeois and petty-bourgeois who deny the materialist conception of history which places the production of real life to be the basis of all ideas. This is done by him because he prepares the ground to state that it would be "economistic" to deny the rise of "a new ruling class" which must come into being with a "separate state". In other words, according to him, since Engels says there is interaction between the base and the superstructure, and since Marx carried out a struggle against Feurbach's mechanistic materialism (without indicating what the debate was all about) and since finally Mao Tse-tung "asserts", that under "certain conditions, politics determine the base" (without indicating what "certain conditions" Mao Tse-tung had in mind), Hirji then concludes from these that it is "implied" that a ruling class, upon the rise of a separate state, would emerge apparently "non-economically"! These are *a priori* assertions which are intended to deny the dominant place of economics vis-a-vis politics. Lenin stated and we must repeat: "politics is the concentrated expression of economics".

1. RULING CLASS

Indeed this turns out to be the very issue on which Hirji betrays Shivji – whom he set out to defend. He took three-quarters of his paper to show that a "national bourgeoisie" arose in the colonies and that this became a ruling class under neo-colonialism. But this is the very issue on which Shivji is in part in agreement with us! Shivji states in his *Silent Class Struggle* that the class that exists in the neo-colony is petty-bourgeois. For this reason, Walter Rodney commended him in his comment 'for not inventing classes where they do not exist – a tendency of Mechanistic Marxists" [p. 62. Note this Hirji!] In *Class Struggle in Tanzania*, Shivji also asks "Is there such a thing as a national bourgeoisie in Africa?" (p. 7). He goes on to answer this question in the negative (p. 7). Again coming back to the issue later he states: "The so-called 'national bourgeoisie' in Africa, in this sense, (i.e., of bourgeois revolution) are neither national nor bourgeois" (p. 20). This is contradictory but the point is clear. It is contradictory because the petty bourgeoisie, although not "national" – but petty, i.e. it is not big bourgeoisie but a small bourgeoisie.

Shivji here clearly agrees that no national bourgeoisie exists in Tanzania. Our disagreement with Shivji is the effort by him to try to create such a bourgeoisie in the state machine which he calls "bureaucratic bourgeoisie" and this he does because his understanding of imperialism and his concept of state and class are faulty. We have argued in our "Critique" that this has nothing in common with the Marxist-Leninist method, because Marx and Lenin and Mao Tse-tung locate ruling classes in the process of production and not in the bureaucracy. This Hirji calls class "economism", because he says "a separate state" emerged at independence and "therefore" a separate ruling class must have emerged and did emerge. These are dogmas. We shall come to this point again later. Suffice it to say here that not only does Hirji contradict Shivji on the question of the "national bourgeoisie", but he also betrays him by not defending Shivji against our "Critique" which clearly states that a ruling class is not a bureaucracy. This is because our evidence and argumentation against Shivji on his central thesis is supported by the historical record. We argued that on the basis of Shivji's *rationale*, a bureaucratic bourgeoisie should have emerged in Kenya and not in Tanzania. Hirji does not controvert this and we must conclude that he finds the "Critique's" arguments on this issue compelling, and hence his "surprise" has no basis.

We do not wish to go any further into Hirji's inconsistent arguments on this question because they are not relevant to this main issue. The only point we want cleared is the accusation he makes that we make the error of joining the petty-bourgeoisie to be part of the bourgeoisie which, according to him, is a "separate class". Because of this alleged error he accuses us of equally making the petty-bourgeoisie part of the financial oligarchy. He makes these infantile accusations because although he claims to have read the "Manuscript" and the "Critique", he does not understand them. It is not we who make "a Nigerian factory owner, a Kenyan capitalist farmer, or a President in Africa" petty-bourgeois. The *Communist Manifesto* groups "small manufacturer, the shopkeeper, the artisan, the peasant" as belonging to the "lower middle class" i.e. petty-bourgeois (*Selected Works*, Vol. 1, p. 117) and regards them as "portions of the bourgeoisie" (p. 115). Comrade Chou En-lai in his interview with Hinton to which we referred in our "Reply" to Mamdani and Bhagat, re-affirms this position, when discussing the class struggle in China in the contemporary period, and focussing on the events of the class struggle during the cultural revolution when he stated:

> According to a Marxist point of view the petty-bourgeoisie belong to the bourgeois class and not to the working class or proletariat.

More than this we have not stated.

The word "petty-bourgeois" for Hirji's information means "small capitalist". A President of Africa does not become bourgeois because he is President. He is bourgeois if he engages in production of that scale, and he is petty-bourgeois because of his class base. So is a Wilson or a Brandt. The conclusion Hirji draws that a trader, because he is regarded by the "Manuscript" as portion of the bourgeoisie, is part of the financial oligarchy would have to be drawn in relation to the *Manifesto* as well. If he had cared to study the "Manuscript" and the Critique", he would have found that we draw a distinction between the petty-bourgeoisie and the financial oligarchy. Indeed this comes out of the numerous quotations he makes from the "Critique" without understanding their importance – for instance, the one he quotes on the very first page of his paper. His failure to understand this fact springs from his dualistic world outlook, which cannot enable him to conceive of the existence of a thing on the basis of unity of opposites. Indeed, with the same type of theorizing that he introduces in this idealist way, the concrete analysis of classes within the bourgeoisie is impossible. For instance, take the petty-bourgeoisie as a class; although a portion of the bourgeoisie, it is not homogeneous. In this class you have small manufacturers, traders, artisans, peasants etc, etc. Among the peasants you have rich peasants, middle peasants and poor peasants. On he basis of Hirji's logic if one spoke of a poor peasant as forming a portion of the petty-bourgeoisie, one would then have to see him as a manufacturer or a trader, or at worst a rich peasant although in fact he has his concrete class position as a portion, or part, of the petty-bourgeoisie. Indeed, on the basis of the same logic if peasants is financial oligarchy then it follows logically that financial oligarchy is peasant. The whole question of analysis of classes would be reduced to this absurdity. You can see, therefore, that Hirji's accusation on this issue is as hollow and baseless as it is petty-bourgeois, and reveals the level of vulgarism to which he has sunk.

We have insisted that the question of class analysis must be a concrete one which is approached from a Marxist-Leninist standpoint. An analysis of classes in he colonies, semi-colonies and neo-colonies must have pre-colonial class structure and the imperialist impact on these societies and the resultant class formations clearly in mind. Our treatment of this question in the "Manuscript" is general, indicating only general observations of classes in the neo-colony. Analyses of classes in the course of the struggle are shown by two concrete examples of China and Vietnam. Hirji and his friends want us to engage in generalities of a dogmatic type. We dealt with this question in the "Reply" to Madani and Bhagat. Hirji engages in the same historical abstractions when he quotes Lenin on Argentina, Le Duan on Indo-China and Mao Tse-tung on China. In all these cases he does not comprehend the historical situations that were being discussed. Indeed Mao Tse-tung and Le Duan pointed out that this bourgeoisie which arose in those historical circumstances was a "flabby" bourgeoisie.

What does that mean to the Hirjis? To us it means that this bourgeoisie cannot be compared to national bourgeoisies which arose in Europe, USA and Japan on the basis of the old bourgeois-democratic revolution. Why are they flabby? Mao Tse-tung says that this is because "national capitalism" in China did not play a considerable part in Chinese social economy and this was so because this bourgeoisie was "mostly associated with foreign imperialism and domestic feudalism in varying degrees" (*Selected Works*, Vol. 11, p. 313). Since Hirji does not have a concept of finance capital, nay, since he repudiates it as "Kautskyian" this latter part of Mao Tse-tung's analysis is a "lifeless abstraction".

What we have left with him are "lifeful" dogmas such as that there is a national bourgeoisie in Tanzania because Lenin, Mao, and Le Duan speak of such a bourgeoisie in the case of Argentina, China and Indo-China respectively. He gets fascinated with the word "bourgeoisie" and constructs dogmas out of it. We cannot accept this and we repudiate it, because then according to his thesis and that of Mamdani and Bhagat, in line with Shivji, Gundar Frank and a host of other neo-Trotskyists: "The immediate enemy is the local ruling class" and must be fought first (Frank). Mamdani and Bhagat also conclude from this that:

> Marxist-Leninists in the semi-colonies must face two political tasks: to organise the peoples' democratic struggles against their own ruling classes and to give the strongest impetus to the ruling classes of the third world to struggle against super-power hegemonism...

To us in Tanzania, Kenya and Uganda, the principal enemy is imperialism, and with the exception of a handful of local reactionaries the national democratic revolution will be supported by a broad spectrum of the people, including sections of the petty-bourgeoisie although some of them are agents of imperialism, but who, in spite of being agents, are oppressed by the financial oligarchies of the imperialist countries through the objectified power of finance capital. This brings us to the issue of economism and the national question, that Lenin was concerned with in his polemics.

2. ECONOMISM AND THE NATIONAL QUESTION

As we have indicated, the struggle that Lenin waged against economism had nothing in common with Hirji's understanding of the question. Indeed, in our view, he does not understand this polemic of Lenin against those whose aim was to weaken the proletarian struggle by putting forward purely economistic postulations and thereby underestimating the political factors on such issues as the national question and working class movement. The polemics in *What is to be done*, in the *Critical Remarks on the National Question*, and in *A Caricature of Marxism and Imperialist Economism* were aimed at this disease. This polemic was against an opportunist trend in the Russian Social-Democratic Party towards the end of the last century and early this century wherein Russian economists argued that because of the level of capitalist development in Russia, political struggles of the working class were "impossible", and therefore concluded that the working class should restrict itself to the economic struggles for better working conditions, higher wages, etc. With this narrow and one-sided approach, they advanced the erroneous thesis that the working class should not advance its cause politically. Other opportunists used similar arguments on the national question and asserted that national self-determination of oppressed nations is unachievable under imperialism. They went further to say that political struggles for political independence are "illusory" and impracticable, thus ignoring the fact that the struggle of the working class and other oppressed and exploited peoples for socialism was not a single act but a whole epoch of acute class struggles on all fronts, political and economic, which had to be utilised to advance this cause.

We would now like to deal at some length with Lenin's polemic against: (A) Kautsky, (B) Rosa Luxemburg, and (C) Kievsky. This is because Hirji has quoted extensively from the critique of Lenin against Kievsky, even then only partially, but ignored the debate with Luxemburg and Trotsky – his fellow travellers – whilst his small quotations on Kautsky have concealed the essence of the polemic. It is our intention to bring out the context, the wrong positions of these opponents of Lenin, and to show how Lenin dealth with them. This will help remove the veil and mystery around these issues which Hirji's terror of quotations envelopes them with.

(A) Lenin v Kautsky

In the course of writing his now famous booklet, *Imperialism, the Highest Stage of Capitalism*, Lenin found it necessary, in the course of his analysis, to rebut the views of the renegade Kautsky, who having been a leader of the Marxist movement in Germany, turned revisionist and reverted to the advocacy of propaganda against the working class movement. Lenin had analysed imperialism as the result of the contradictory development of capitalism, which as it developed increased concentration in production, and with the merger or coalescence with bank capital led to the era of monopolies. The era was characterised by the imperialist countries' striving to annex not only agrarian territories, but even the most highly industrialised regions. This was because of the fact that the world was already partitioned and this obliged those powers contemplating a redivision to reach out for every kind of territory. The second feature of imperialism was the revalry between several great powers in striving for hegemony, i.e., for the conquest of territory, not so much for themselves but mainly to weaken the adversary and undermine his hegemony. Lenin then put forward the five-point characteristics of imperialism which are well known.

In his analysis of imperialism, Kautsky in contrast, painted a picture of imperialism as a non-contradictory development and slurred over or denied the existence of these contradictions. He conceived of imperialism as a product of highly developed industrial capitalism. It consisted in the striving of every industrial capitalist nation to bring under its control or to annex all large areas of agrarian territory, irrespective of what nations inhabit them. This definition Lenin regarded as a political definition which abstracted from the economics, in which finance capital and not industrial capital was the rule. Lenin recognised this definition as "correct but incomplete" because imperialism, politically strives for "violence and reaction". Moreover, Lenin insisted, by putting forward the fact about the annexation of agrarian territories by industrial countries, the role of the financier was obscured. He further stated that Kautsky's defintion was not only wrong and un-Marxist, but also that it served as a basis for a whole system of views which signified a rupture with Marxist theory and Marxist practice all along the line. Kautsky detached the politics of imperialism from its economics, and spoke of annexations as "a policy 'preferred'" by finance capital, and opposed it to another bourgeois policy which, he alleged, was possible on the very same basis of finance capital. It followed from all this that monopolies were compatible with non-monopolistic, non-violent, non-annexationist methods in politics. It also followed that the territorial division of the world, which was completed during that very epoch of finance capital, and which constituted the basis of the then peculiar forms of rivalry between imperialist powers, were compatible with a non-imperialist policy. Because of these conclusions that inevitably followed from Kautsky's treatment of imperialism, Lenin pointed out that it resulted in a slurring-over and blunting of the most profound contradictions of the latest stage of capitalism, instead of the exposure of their depth, thus leading to bourgeois reformism instead of Marxism. (Lenin: *Imperialism*, Ch. VII).

Kautsky also had tried to treat imperialism from a "purely economic point of view". In this eclectic treatment Kautsky came to the conclusion that it was conceivable that capitalism would yet go from the then existing imperialist policy through a new phase, that of cartels, a phase which he called the phase of "ultra-imperialism", a phase of a union of the imperialisms of the whole world without struggles among them, a phase when wars would cease under capitalism, a phase which would introduce the "joint exploitation of the world internationally united finance capital". Lenin opposed this treatment not because there was no "joint exploitation of the world" nor that international finance capital had no unity in this exploitation. On the contrary in the realities of the capitalist system this was possible on the basis of agreements., etc., during periods of "truce" between wars. But because of the rivalries that are inherent in the system of monopolies, wars break out forcing a redivision or a repartition of the world. Peaceful alliances prepare the ground for wars, and in their turn grow out of wars:

> The one conditions the other, producing alternate forms of peaceful and non-peaceful struggle on one and the same basis of imperialist connections and relations within world economics and world politics (op. cit., p. 115)

He continued:

> This is because the only conceivable basis under capitalism for the division of spheres of influence, interests, colonies, etc., is a calculation of the strength of those participating, their general economic, financial, military strength, etc. And the strength of these participants in the division does not change to an equal degree, for even development of different undertakings, trusts, branches of industry, or countries is impossible under capitalism. (p. 114)

But in his banal and philistinistic fantasies, Kautsky conceived this unity as frictionless decided by the imperialists as a policy. This thesis of Lenin is a correct method of Marx based on dialectical materialism. Here capital develops on the basis of unity of opposites, that of capital and labour. Within the camp of capital it is also a unity of opposites – unity by capital to exploit but only on the basis of competition among capitals. It is this contradiction in capital that leads free competition to monopoly concentration wherein a new unity based on monopoly control and the division of the world on the basis of agreements, cartels, syndicates and wars is possible. But this does not do away with monopolistic competition. The rivalry of monopoly groups is the reflection of this bitter monopolistic competition.

After outlining this polemic, we ask Hirji to tell us where in our "Manuscript" or "Critique", when read as a whole, we commit the errors of Kautsky? Where in the "Manuscript" do we speak of imperialism as a policy "preferred" by monopolies and not arising out of its contradictory development? Where do we suggest as "thinkable" that "ultra-imperialism" of one trust being the union of all finance capital, will emerge "peacefully" doing away with all wars between the imperialists? Where about do we engage in these "lifeless abstractions"? Hirji has to show this concretely and not hide behind a barrage of undigested quotations from Lenin on this question! What evidence can he bring forward to "prove" that we put forward a Kautskyite position or Trotskyist one-sided position of internationalisation of capital leading to the rise of the working class on world scale thus leading to a "world revolution"? Where are the "blabberings" that he so uprightly exposes?

A look at his paper will reveal that he picked out little portions of incomplete sentences and mixed them together to show that the "learned professor" is a Kautskyite. He seems to hang on words like "multilateral imperialism", "financial oligarchy" and "the class as a whole on world scale" as being of any particular significance which are not so obvious to us. He disputes the "negation of national capital in the colony and neo-colony" without any proof to the contrary apart from engaging in mere *a prior* assertions. Do we have to remind him that here he again contradicts his friend Shivji who sees the same negation but which, in his manner, he calls "denationalisation". According to Hirji, at least on this issue, Shivji, whom he purports to defend but in fact contradicts, is a Kautskyite! Let Hirji check in case he had not thought about it! Having said nothing as shown above, he then states:

> For Kautsky, imperialism is a policy but for the learned professor, the 'multilateral' imperialism of today being a product of the 'U.S. multilateral strategy' represents the rise of the transnational corporate strategy, resulting in the implementation of 'the neo-colonial strategy'!

Where in the "Manuscript" does he get the above tit-bits without any analysis whatsoever of the contradictory development of capitalism? He indicates that this is from the "Manuscript" put he does not indicate the page reference, What is the page reference? Having put up these tit-bits of 19 words collected from here and there from a whole "Manuscript" of 550 pages, he then unleashes a whole line of quotations to refute these tit-bits; a conglomeration of quotations amounting to over 200 words, all intended to bombard the 19 words!

His tit-bits seem to underline the word "strategy" because it has meaning of "policy" which Kautsky used. Now if he really wanted to find complete sentences where the word "policy" is used, there are plenty of them in the "Manuscript", which is further evidence that he has never studied it. We will give a few examples which could help him out in his next "critique".

> The U.S. thus saw advantage in the circumstances and was quick to seize its chance and emerge as the leading imperialist power, not only over the vanquished and their empires but over the whole imperialist camp. This was a new imperialist policy of redivision based on "Open Doors" which the U.S. had been pursuing during the inter-war years. This new policy was reflected in high monopoly circles.

This is followed by a quote from these monopoly circles. Is it un-Marxist to talk of a "policy" because Kautsky used the word? Wasn't the "multilateral strategy" a U.S. dictated policy? We would like those who dispute it to prove it was not. But what brought about this policy? The "Manuscript" shows how U.S. economic position had become strengthened during this period due to increased concentration of production and capital which required outlets. It states:

> The rationale behind the U.S. policy was basically to get rid of imperial and colonial markets which its allies enjoyed to the detriment of the U.S.

Is this "politicism", or "economism" or "interaction between the base and the superstructure"? The analysis does not stop there. In fact this policy of "Open Doors" was pursued by the U.S. for over 20 years because of its growing concentration of capital leading to the need for sources of raw materials and new markets. This is analysed in Part Three of the "Manuscript". The redivision dictated was a sign of this power. Does the "Manuscript" paint a picture of non-contradictory development of capitalism leading to this new strategy? The burden is on Hirji and his like to show this.

The Manuscript right from the first page analyses this contradiction in capitalist development. In Part One, we analyse historically the rise of merchant capital and its antagonism, which lead to the genesis of industrial capital. In Part Two, we go into the rise of competitive capitalism and its laws of motion, in the course of which we carry out a polemic against Luxemburg on the market question. We restate Marx's "Law of the Tendency of the Rate of Profit to Fall" and later polemicise with Baran and Sweezy, Hirji's leading neo-Marxist bedfellows, who do away with this law, which Marx had described as "the most important law of political economy, and the most essential for understanding the most difficult relations." These neo-Marxists had brushed it aside in their book *Monopoly Capital*, whose theoretical roots had been worked out in their earlier books, namely *Political Economy of Growth and Theory of Capitalist Development*, by calling the Law a "time-honoured theorem" which had become time-barred by "new developments".

We went further to illustrate the relevance of this law to modern conditions and insisted that without this law it is impossible to analyse modern imperialism and its contradictions and rivalries–which are mere words to Hirji–the essence of which he cannot grapple with in any satisfactory theoretical manner. Indeed, how could he when he, Shivji and their like freely accept concepts like "economic surplus", which do away with Marx's concept of "surplus value" and see no contradiction, like Baran and Sweezy, in the "ever increasing accumulation of capital" on the basis of their new law. Their theoretical conception of capitalism at this stage cannot adequately enable them to comprehend the contradictory development of today, however much they may assert that they do.

In Part Three, we presented Lenin's analysis of imperialism, showing theoretically how Lenin's analysis springs directly from Marx's Law of the Rate of Profit. This much, at least Hirji's fellow travellers–Mamdani and Bhagat, admit. We go further to analyse finance capital, showing how the world was divided among monopoly groups on the basis of agreements and how the division among powerful imperialist states on the basis of partitions was completed; and demonstrate how wars based on rivalries arising out of monopolistic competition led to the Two World Wars, and polemicise against modern attackers of Lenin. We demonstrated the growing strength of the U.S. in these inter-war years and prepared the historical background to the analysis of multi-lateral imperialism on the basis of Open-Doors, which we follow up in Part Four. We show how Europe and Japan were weakened by wars, how the U.S. emerged the leader, seeking new markets for its products and outlets for its capital, how a multilateral system of institutions worked out–the Bretton–Woods system–to uphold this new redivision based on this Open-Door strategy (no other than neo-colonialism), how this redivision leads to the crumbling of the European colonial empire, how the U.S. on this basis builds a military machine to project its partners against "communism" and to combat liberation wars in the neo-colonies. We then go on to show how in these changed circumstances, where colonies are no longer preserves of particular colonial powers, the U.S. and then other imperialist monopolies have to re-arrange monopolistic competition on the basis of multinational corporate strategy. The multinational corporations, which Shivji deals with in his book and appends at the end is the same phenomenon. Hirji cracks small jokes about this as "Kautskyism"!

In this general analysis of imperialism do we deny monopolistic competition and rivalries amongst the imperialist powers? We have demonstrated in our "Reply" to Hirji's friends, Mamdani and Bhagat, that this is not the case. We demonstrated that although Europe was forced to accept the Open-Doors policy of neo-colonialism, it soon erected its own "common market" to stand against U.S. monopoly. European countries set up new links through association agreements (Yaounde, Arusha, Lome), to continue indirect contacts with their former colonies in Africa and Asia. Japan at this time was still occupied by the U.S. but later emerged with her own monopolies, which increasingly competed alongside U.S. monopolies in S.E. Asia, Africa and Latin America, and in time entered the U.S. market itself. At one point we state, and we quote again from the "Reply":

> This central contradiction of imperialism cannot be resolved by table resolutions to be 'united'. Hence war is still the central instrument of imperialism. Capitalist monopoly groups in the U.S. and Europe still continue to compete for markets and outlets for capital exports leading to 'vertical cohesion and division of labour' with the third world as we shall see. The transnational corporation cannot remove this basic contradiction. So long as this struggle for markets, and raw materials continues (which it must) wars among imperialist states are inevitable, although these may, due to the existence of the socialist camp, be eased.

The emphasis is added to bring out the point that our analysis of multinational corporate strategy, based on multilateral imperialist strategy, has nothing in common with Hirji's mechanistic understanding of Kautsky's "ultra-imperialism", which, as can be seen in our summary of Lenin's polemic with him, posed "peaceful" imperialism under one monopoly trust as "thinkable". Lenin had accepted this development as an "abstract new phase" but which he said in practice led to dreams instead of facing the "sharp" tasks of today. Lenin said:

> There is no doubt that the development is going in the direction of a single world trust that will swallow up all enterprises and all states without exception. But the development in this direction is proceeding under such stress, with sharp tempo, with such contradictions, conflicts, and convulsions – not only economical, but also political, national etc., etc., that before a single world trust will be reached, before the respective national finance capitals will have formed a world union of "ultra-imperialism", imperialism will inevitably explode, capitalism will turn into its opposite. (Introduction to Bukharin's book on – *Imperialism and World Economy*, Monthly Review 1973, p. 14)

In the manuscript we do not even go to entertain this "Kautskyism" of Lenin as "abstract" possibility, precisely because what Lenin said is happening today, namely, the whole colonial and imperialist system is crumbling down, with still many monopolies in the field competing for areas of exploitation. Because Hirji does not comprehend what Lenin is talking about he naively states:

> Nabudere, however, repudiates these 'neo-Marxist' polemics of Lenin. For he has 'shown', as he monotonously reminds us, that the financial oligarchy has routed all national bourgeoisie!

Where does Lenin deny that the financial oligarchy has routed all "national bourgeoisie"? In the above analysis he talks of "national finance capital". This "national finance capital" is controlled by the financial oligarchy which can only survive on *international exploitation*. But this routing of capitalist competitive enterprises by monopolies does not remove contradictions among "national monopolies". Later we shall show how Lenin re-affirs this international rule of the financial oligarchy.

(B) Lenin v Luxemburg

We bring in this polemic because Hirji ignored it completely. Because of its importance on the national question and the issue of a separate state we reproduce it here. The errors of Hirji's attitude of not taking Marxism-Leninism as a science with its basic orientation and not just a matter of brilliance, have been further exposed by his formulations on the national question. He has shown that he does not have the grasp of the essence of a Marxist-Leninist analysis of issues. This type of analysis requires that a given question be examined "within definite historical limits" ("Critical Remarks" p. 51), so as to be able to bring out its general and particular features. In relation to the national question, this categorical requirement implies "that a clear distinction must be drawn between the two periods of capitalism (i.e., the period of competitive capitalism and the period of monopoly capitalism - D.W.N.) which differ radically from each other as far as the national movement is concerned ("Critical Remarks" p. 51). This is the approach that would guide a Marxist-Leninist in examining issues bearing on the national question. But with the Hirjis we are treated from start to end to ahistorical logical deductions.

First in his haste to deny the concept of "international financial oligarchy", and therefore the whole concept of capitalist imperialism, he blocks all consistent examination of the national question when he states as follows:

"... to a single ruling class there corresponds a single state. A separate state implies a separate ruling class" (Emphasis added – D.W.N.).

Once he has coined such an absolute proposition applicable for all ages, he can then go on to further abstract that "what independence implies is the establishment of a separate state and thus of a separate class controlling the state (Hirji's emphasis). We dare say that such a position amounts to non-recognition of the national question. It is actually sheer opportunism when he smuggles in his grand thesis the reservation that imperialist exploitation continues and intensifies after the establishment of a separate state with its separate ruling class. The flat statement that the local ruling class(es) is economically dependent on imperialism does not tell us much theoretically; for this class(es) and its attribute of dependence must be proved historically and analytically and not merely proclaimed.

Secondly, he philistinely attributes to Lenin's analysis his neo-Marxist petty bourgeois views when he boldly proclaims that "...a separate state implies a separate ruling class" and that "independence implies (emphasis added – D.W.N.) the establishment of a separate (Hirji's emphasis) state and thus a separate ruling class". We ask Hirji to point out where in Lenin's entire analysis this tie-up is stated, let alone implied. We could give Hirji a whole lifetime and we are sure that he would be forced to admit that this tie-up is nothing but his own "blabbering". No wonder then that he opportunistically abstracted from Lenin's profound work on "Questions of National Policy and Proletarian Internationalism" the lone phrase of "separate state" and conveniently put away the entire analysis it contains. This is, to say the least, a childish attitude of going about serious issues with the interest of merely scoring points. It is in this light that we view Hirji's one-sided interest in Lenin's other work *A Caricature of Marxism and Imperialist Economism* which he vainly called to his help. We can assure him that Lenin's major work on the national question remains and will continue to haunt Hirji and his like. Moreover, they should have no illusions that it is they alone who have a privileged access to the revolutionary works of Marx, Engels, Lenin, Stalin, Mao, Le Duan, etc., and that they can thus indulge themselves in selective references to their ideas as and when it suits them.

Thirdly, Hirji makes a grave error when he vainly attempts to obscure and repudiate the democratic nature of the national question under the pretext of fighting economism. Again this is at the level of denying the concept of imperialism when he scoffs at our statement that political liberation means a partial change. He childishly reduces this to a laughable colour nonsense when he misinterprets it as "...the only change independence implies is a change of the pigment (note this puerility – D.W.N.) of bureaucratic personnel manning the state machine. Both the colonial and neo-colonial states as states are controlled by and directly serve the interests of the financial oligarchy"! Because he is steeped in economism of the worst type, no wonder he cannot have an idea at all that the national question is one of the points of the democratic programme of Marxist-Leninists. In the chapter "The Socialist Revolution and the Struggle for Democracy (Critical Remarks)" Lenin links up the right of nations to self-determination to the struggle for democracy thus:

> The socialist revolution is not a single act, it is not one battle on one front, but a whole epoch of acute class conflicts, a long series of battles on all fronts, i.e., on all questions of economics and politics, battles that can only end in the expropriation of the bourgeoisie. It would be a radical mistake to think that the struggle for democracy (emphasis added – D.W.N.) was capable of diverting the proletariat from the socialist revolution, or of hiding, overshadowing it, etc. On the contrary in the same way as there can be no victorious socialism that does not practice full democracy, so, the proletariat cannot prepare for its victory over the bourgeoisie without an all round, consistent and revolutionary struggle for democracy. It would be no less a mistake to remove one of the points of the democratic programme, for example, the point on the self-determination of nations on the grounds of its being 'impracticable' or 'illusory' under imperialism (p. 111. Emphasis added – D.W.N.)

It is clear from the above analysis of Lenin that the national question belongs to the sphere of political democracy (later we shall have occasion to refer to Lenin's elaboration of this point) and its achievement, short of the socialist revolution, means partial change. Lenin made this analysis to awake the Rosa Luxemburgs who could not visualise such a democratic change because of the economic strength of imperialism. The Rosa Luxemburgs of today, the Hirjis, pass over to the other extreme. They accept that self-determination is achievable but they surreptitiously put words in the mouth of Lenin by their insistence that "a separate state implies a separate ruling class", which now with its own ruling class exploits the masses and is the immediate target of the struggles of the masses. This is economism in its extreme, and objectively serves to mask the main enemy of the people, i.e, imperialism. Where the proletariat and the other toiling masses to be misled by this pseudo-revolutionary petty-bourgeois position, there is no doubt that they would end up trapped in a rut of fighting endless losing battles, nay, coup d'etats.

At this point we consider it necessary to refer the reader to the context of the national question, that is to go over Lenin's debate with the economists of the Luxemburg type as published in the book *Questions of National Policy and Proletarian Internationalism.* We do this for several reasons. We have already stated the first reason when we repudiated Hirji for abstracting the lone phrase of "separate state" (without even acknowledging that it is taken from Lenin's analysis). As we pointed out, he did this deliberately in order to obscure the Marxist-Leninist position and even brazenly to attribute his extensions of "Marxism-Leninism" to Lenin. Secondly, we must bring out the context so that the unbiased reader can judge for himself whether our position is economistic, that is, whether we do not recognise the right of nations to self-determination in the Marxist-Leninist sense. Thirdly, we refer to the context of the national question, so that we highlight certain points which are not covered by our refutations of his neo-Trotskyist positions.

Lenin put out this work in order to clarify the significance of the struggles for national independence by the colonised and semi-colonial peoples and the attitudes and tasks of the proletariat of the oppressor and oppressed nations in relation to the Right of Nations to Self-Determination. Lenin was prompted to unleash this theoretical struggle against the opponents of Marxism and the proletarian struggles because personages like Rosa Luxemburg, a Polish Marxist, who being unable to grasp the "revolutionary tactics" of the proletarian revolution, derived the concept and propagated the "unachievability" of self-determination by the oppressed nations on grounds that it would be made "impracticable" by the economic dependence of these nations on the big imperialist nations. Further, Rosa Luxemburg maintained that because of the existence of the bourgeoisie in the oppressed nations, the support for self-determination of the oppressed nations meant support for the nationalism of the bourgeoisie in these nations.

In this reply Lenin first of all emphasises the "bounden duty" of the Marxists "... to defend one special demand in the national question that is the right of nations to self-determination. . . to political secession" (p. 7-8). The Marxists were duty-bound to support this "if they do not want to betray democracy and the proletariat". The tremendous importance of the question derived from its being a component part of the national programme of working class democracy which Lenin sketches out as:

> Absolutely no privileges for any one nation or any one language. The solution of the problem of the political self-determination of nations, that is their aspiration as states by completely free democratic methods, the promulgation of the law for the whole state by virtue of which any measure, (rural, urban or communal, etc., etc.) introducing any privilege of any kind for one of the nations and militating against the equality of nations or the rights of a national minority, shall be declared illegal and ineffective, and any citizen of the state shall have the right to demand that such a measure be annulled as unconstitutional, and that those who attempt to put it into effect be punished. (p. 15)

The question that we must ask Hirji is whether he has ever heard of such programme, attempted to study its implications and whether he accepts it unconditionally? Certainly his ability to identify a local ruling class "on the morrow of political independence" is a peculiar treatment of this aspect of the general democratic programme that has nothing in common with Marxism-Leninism. This peculiar manner of handling the question is also revealed by Shivji in his now famous statement.

In contrast to those Marxists who either supported unconditionally nationalism or rejected it altogether Lenin pointed out clearly the opposition of Marxism to all forms of nationality in a bourgeois society and the full recognition by Marxism of the historical legitimacy of national movements, i.e., the tendency towards the formation of national states. In this way, Lenin was able to set out the narrow limits of the recognition of the national movements in so far as the democratic struggle of the proletariat are concerned. It is appropriate to quote Lenin at length on this question:

> Marxism cannot be reconciled with nationalism, be it even of the most just, purest, most refined and civilised brand. In place of all forms of nationalism

Marxism advances internationalism [note this our Hirjis and ask Lenin what he means by this word since there is no international state!]. The amalgamation of all nations in that higher unity, a unity that is growing before our eyes with every mile of railway line that is built, with every international trust, and every workers association, that is formed (an association that is international in its economic activities as well as in its ideas and aims) [Emphasis added – D.W.N.].

The principle of nationality is historically inevitable in bourgeois society and, taking this society into due account, the Marxist fully recognized the historical legitimacy of national movements. But to prevent this recognision from becoming an apologia of nationalism, it must be strictly limited to what is progressive in such movements, in order that this recognition may not lead to bourgeois ideology obscuring proletarian consciousness. [Emphasis added – D.W.N.]

The awakening of the masses from feudal lethargy and their struggle against all national oppression, for the sovereignty of the people, of the nation are progressive. Hence it is the Marxist's bounden duty to stand for the most resolute and consistent democratism on all aspects of the national question. This task is largely a negative one. But this is the limit the proletariat can go to in supporting nationalism, for beyond that begins the "positive" activity of the bourgeoisie striving to fortify nationalism. [Lenin's emphasis.]

Let us now examine briefly Rosa Luxemburg's arguments and their refutation by Lenin. In the first place we should point out that Lenin's ideological struggle was directed at Rosa Luxemburg because of all the opponents of the Marxist programme she represented the most dangerous current. Without Lenin's adherence to Marx's and Engel's teachings and his sharp ideological vigilance and combativeness Rosa Luxemburg with her well established reputation as Marxist would easily have passed off revisionsim for Marxism. Rosa Luxemburg's views on the national question fell into two broad categories. First, in her opposition to *Clause* 9 of the Social Democratic Labour Party Programme, Rosa Luxemburg denied the Marxist principle of nationality in bourgeois society, arguing that the formation of national states as the economic entities best suited for the development of capitalism was not inevitable. She argued:

This 'best' national state is only an abstraction which can easily be developed and defended theoretically, but which does not correspond to reality. (p. 48)

Lenin rebuffed the intellectual disquisition of Rosa Luxemburg on this score by pointing out the crux of the matter, i.e., whether an understanding of self-determination lay "… in legal definitions deduced from all sorts of 'general concepts' of law or in a historico-economic study of the national movement" (p. 46). In other words the question must be treated concretely and not simply generally. Lenin went on to examine the issue from "a historico-economic study of the national movements" noting that:

… throughout the world, the period of the final victory of capitalism over feudalism has been linked up with national movements. For the complete victory of commodity production, the bourgeoisie must capture the home market, and there must be politically united territories whose population speak a single language, with all obstacles to the development of that language and to its consolidation in literature eliminated. Therein is the economic foundation of national movements… Therefore the tendency of every national movement is towards the formation of national states under which these requirements of modern capitalism are best satisfied. The most profound economic factors drive towards this goal and, therefore, for the whole of Western Europe, may, for the entire civilised world, the national state is typical and normal for the capitalist period [p. 47, Lenin's emphais].

On the basis of "historico-economic conditions of national movements" Lenin maintained "... we must inevitably reach the conclusion that the self-determination of nations means the political separation of these nations from alien national bodies, and the formation of an independent national state... It would be wrong to interpret the right to self-determination as meaning anything but the right to existence as a separate state." [p. 47, emphasis added – D.W.N.]

So there we have the phrase "separate state" on which today's brilliant Marxists have staked their everything and all in a vain bid to make Marxism-Leninism more profound. But as we can see, there is no tie-up of a separate state with a separate ruling class in the way our learned Hirjis have attempted to make it appear. If Lenin had stopped here maybe he would have had a chance to get away with the vulgarisation of Marxism-Leninism.

After Lenin had routed Rosa Luxemburg on the inevitability of the principle of nationality in bourgeois society, the latter then turned around to dismiss the right to self-determination of small nations on the grounds that it had been made "illusory" by the development of the great capitalist powers and by imperialism. Lenin pulled the ground from under the feet of Rosa Luxemburg on this issue thus:

> For the question of the political self-determiantion of nations and their independence as states in bourgeois society Rosa Luxemburg has substituted the question of their economic independence. This is just as intelligent as if someone, in discussing the programmatic demand for the supremacy of Parliament, i.e., the assembly of people's representatives in a bourgeois state, were to expound the perfectly correct conviction that big capital dominates in a bourgeois country, whatever the regime in it. (p. 49)

So as not to leave room for any doubt about what precisely Lenin was talking about, he went on to point out:

> ...From the standpoint of national relations, the best conditions for the development of capitalism are undoubtedly provided by the national state. This does not mean of course that such a state, which is based on bourgeois relations, can eliminate the exploitation and oppression of nations. It only means that Marxists cannot lose sight of the powerful economic factors that give rise to the urge to create national states. It means that 'self-determination of nation's in the Marxists' Programme cannot from a historico-economic point of view have any other meaning than political self-determination, state independence and the formation of a national state [p. 50. Emphasis added on "political"]

It is clear from the above quotation that Lenin's analysis took account of the production relations of a nation that has emancipated itself politically from bondage of alien national bodies and has set up a separate state. The question as to whether such political transformation leads to complete rupture of national exploitation and oppression has to be considered on the basis of existing production relations taking fully into account the definite historical period of a capitalist development. It cannot be decided *a priori* and generally or by mere logical deductions of the Hirji type – "a separate state implies a separate ruling (controlling) class"! We contend that it is only from the scientific standpoint of Lenin that we can explain the dawn of national independence for the ex-colonies and the continued and intensified imperialist exploitation and oppression by the financial oligarchy.

Lenin went on to clarify why the colonial peoples after political liberation would still suffer exploitation and national oppression by the financial oligarchy:

> ... There was formerly an economic distinction between the colonies and the European peoples – at least the majority of the latter – the colonies having been drawn into commodity exchange but not into capitalist production. Imperialism changed this. Imperialism is among other things, the export of capital. Capitalist production is being transplanted [Hirji you want to substitute "extend" for "transplant"!] to the colonies at an ever increasing rate. They cannot be extricated from dependence on European finance capital. From the military standpoint, as well as form the standpoint of expansion, the separation of colonies is practicable, as a general rule, only under socialism; under capitalism it is practicable only by way of exception or at the cost of a series or revolutions both in the colonies and the metropolitan countries. [p. 42, Lenin's emphasis]

We have now a scientific, historical explanation of the origins and roots of imperialist exploitation and domination of the neo-colonies long after their attainment of national independence. Contrary to obscurantist formulations of our brilliant Hirjis, our countries are now suffering intensified imperialist exploitation and domination not just because we are controlled or ruled by economically dependent classes, for dependence is not such a generality, in Marxist-Leninist terms, but by the continued and now internationalised exploitative grip finance capital has over our countries. It is necessary to ditinguish historically forms of dependence, instead of generalising them as the Hirjis do. Again, let Lenin tell us how this may be approached:

> ... in a commodity-producing society, no independent development, or even development of any sort whatsoever, is possible without capitalism. In Europe the dependent nations have both their own capital and easy access to it on a wider-range of terms. The colonies have no capital of their own, or none to speak of, and under finance capital no colony can obtain any except on terms of political submission. (p. 1243)

Is this not type of "economism" that Hirji and his colleagues accuse us of? Hirji may want to exclaim that this is bad or dismiss the analysis on grounds that Lenin was referring to colonies and not neo-colonies. But precisely this is the pointed question that he has to answer unequivocally, how has political liberation ruptured the grip of finance capital on our countries?

Earlier, we pointed out that the national question is one of the points of the democratic programme of the proletariat. Luxemburg made a vain attempt to ridicule and trample on the democratic significance of the right of nations to self-determination in a typically bourgeois manner by contending that it was "impracticable". Lenin dealt with this attack by exposing it as the attitude of the bourgeoisie towards the position of the proletariat on the national question. In the course of refuting Rosa Luxemburg's views, Lenin characterised further the political nature of the right to self-determination of nations, as having to do with the "relationships of capitalism and of political democracy", and set out the revolutionary manner of handling the entire question in a way that links it up ultimately with the proletarian struggle for the socialist revolution, the maximum solution to the national question. Because of the great significance Lenin's analysis bears on our further struggles against imperialist exploitation and domination, we prefer to set it out fully:

> . . It would be no less a mistake to remove one of the points of the democratic

programme, for example, the point on the self-determination of nations, on the grounds of it being 'impracticable' or 'illusory', under imperialism. The contention that the right of nations to self-determination is impracticable within the bounds of capitalism can be understood either in the absolute economic sense, or in the conditional, political sense.

In the first place it is radically incorrect from the standpoint of theory. First in that sense, such things as, for example labour money or the abolition of crises, etc., are impracticable under capitalism. It is absolutely untrue that the self-determination of nations is equally impracticable. Secondly, even the one example of the secession of Norway from Sweden in 1905 is sufficient to refute 'impracticability' in that sense. Thirdly, it would be absurd to deny that some slight change in the political and strategic relations of, say, Germany and Britain, might today or tomorrow make the formation of a new Polish, Indian, and other similar state fully 'practicable'. Fourthly finance capital in its drive to expand, can 'freely' buy or bribe the freest democratic or republican government and the elective officials of any, even an 'independent' country. The domination of finance capital and of capital in general is not to be abolished by any reforms in the sphere of political democracy, and self-determination belongs wholly and exclusively to this sphere. This domination of finance capital, however, does not in the least nullify the significance of political democracy as a freer, wider and clearer form of class oppression and class struggle. [Emphasis added]. Therefore all arguments about the 'impracticability', in the economic sense, of one of the demands of poilitical democracy under capitalism are reduced to a theoretically incorrect definition of the general and basic relationships of capitalism and of political democracy as a whole. In the second sense the assertion is incomplete and inaccurate. This is because not only the right of nations to self-determination but all the fundamental demands of political democracy are only partially 'practicable' under imperialism, and then in a distorted form and by way of exception (for example, the session of Norway from Sweden in 1905). The demand for the immediate liberation of the colonies that is put forward by all revolutionary social democrats is also 'impracticable' under capitalism without a series of revolutions. But from this it does not by any means follow that Social-Democracy should reject the immediate and most determined struggle for all these demands – such a rejection would only play into the hands of the bourgeoisie and reaction – but one the contrary it follows that these demands must be formulated and put through in a revolutionary and not a reformist manner going beyond the bounds of bourgeois legality, breaking them down, going beyond speeches in Parliament and verbal protests, and drawing the masses into decisive action, extending and intensifying the struggle for every fundamental democratic demand up to a direct proletarian onslaught on the bourgeoisie, i.e., up to the socialist revolution that expropriates the bourgeoisie.

. . . increased national oppression under imperialism does not mean that social democracy should reject what the bourgeoisie call the 'utopian' struggle for the freedom of nations to secede but, on the contrary, it should make greater use of the conflicts that arise in this sphere too, as grounds for mass action and for revolutionary attacks on the bourgeoisie. [pp. 111–113. Lenin's Emphasis]

Such is the Marxist–Leninist line on the democratic revolution. It is up to an honest reader to compare the historical, revolutionary and dialectical analysis of Lenin and our appreciation of it and the arrogant, ignorant, simplistic tie-ups of Hirji and his fellow travellers on this issue. This is done in spite of Lenin's clear emphasis ". . . liberation of oppressed nations implies a dual transformation in the political sphere: (1) the full equality of nations and (2) freedom of political separation" (p. 127). The conclusion is irresistible that the motive of the Hirjis in avoiding to treat the national question in the context of Lenin's specific work on the matter, and instead abstracting a lone phrase – separate state – was none other than to misuse the revered authority of the great Lenin in the vile and vain endeavour of presenting a distorted and one-sided viewpoint of Marxism-Leninism. We wholly repudiate them for this childish but nonetheless dangerous attitude.

(C) Lenin vs. Kievsky

Hirji draws a lot of his "fire" from Lenin's pamphlet, *A Caricature of Marxism and Imperialist Economism*, in order to fight against our views on imperialism, etc., and prove that they are "a caricature" of Marxism-Leninism because they are "economistic". He quotes from this important 61-page pamphlet seven times in his 12-page hodge-podge of quotations. The reader is led to believe that he has read that pamphlet carefully and that he knows the context and the arguments in the quotes he has uplifted as they were put forward by Lenin against the economistic Kievsky. However, in his great haste to hit back and due to his now familiar dogmatic, eclectic approach, he completely forgets to give us the proper context of the arguments so that the readers of his so-called critique could be enlightened, on the nature of the debate that went on between Lenin and Kievsky. However, to have done so would have totally ruined his case for there is nothing in the pamphlet that supports his new concepts, his dogmatism and pure "logical" abstractions.

Now let us see in a summary form what the debate between Lenin and Kievsky was all about and the context within which it took place.

In the opening paragraphs of the pamphlet referred to above, Lenin set out the general context of the discussion as being that of a continuing theoretical (ideological) struggle between Marxism and "a caricature of Marxism" which had began in "the early nineties" (1890s). In his struggle against the new trend he pointed out that "caricature of Marxism" had assumed "the shape of Economism, or 'strikeism'" to which we have already referred. The Iskrists (Marxist-Leninists) had won that first round of the fight both "against petty-bourgeois Narodism" and "bourgeois liberalism". The Bolsheviks (Lenin's revolutinary wing of the former Social Democratic Labour Party of Russia) had now to fight relentlessly against a similar trend during the unsuccessful first Russian bourgeois revolution of 1905 and later in 1908–10. He then indicates that the views of Kievsky, the subject of debate in the pamphlet, regarding the first imperialist World War, were economistic and thus apolitical. To quote him:

> . . . Recognition of the present war as imperialist and emphasis on its close connection with the imperialist era of capitalism encounters not only resolute oppenents, but also irresolute friends, for whom the word 'imperialism' has become all the rage. Having memorised the word, they are offering the workers hopelessly confused theories and reviving many of the old mistakes of the old Economism. Capitalism has triumphed – therefore there is no need to bother with political problems, the old Economists reasoned in 1894-1910, falling into rejection of the political struggle in Russia. Imperialism has triumphed – therefore there is not need to bother with the problems of political democracy, reason the present-day imperialist Economists. Kievsky's article ("The Proletariat and the 'Right of Nations to self-determination' in the epoch of Finance Capital"). . . merits attention as a sample of these sentiments, as one such caricature of Marxism [p. 7–8. Emphasis is Lenin's – D.W.N.]

Having thus put the points at issue in these broad terms, he then proceeded to deal one by one with the main points of "Kievsky's disquisitions". Already, however, we can see what in the main, was Kievsky's error. And even here we see that the concept of "Economism" in the context of imperialism has nothing in common with the meaning Hirji attaches to it, as we have shown in our preliminary remarks.

Lenin first dealt with what he called the "central" point of Kievsky's disquisitions, i.e., Kievsky's disagreement with the famous clause of the Russian Social Democratic Labour Party programme adopted at the Second Congress of the Party in 1903, "dealing with national self-determination". This is the same clause against which Rosa Luxemburg and others, as we have demonstrated, had unsuccessfully waged a spirited struggle, dubbing it a betrayal of the proletarian cause since it encompassed the "interests" of the proletariat in the oppressed nations and those of the "national bourgeoisie" in these nations, thereby, they thought, obscuring the contradictions between Labour and capital. Kievsky argued thus:

> 'This demand (i.e., for national self-determination) directly (!!) leads to social-patriotism', and that it implied sanctioning the treason of the French and Belgian social-patriots, who are defending this independence (the national independence of France and Belgium) with arms in hand! They are doing what the supporters of 'self-determination' only advocate . . . We categorically refuse to understand how one can simultaneously be against defence of the fatherland and for it. [p. 9. Brackets exclamations and emphasis are Lenin's – D.W.N.]

Clearly these views were not new nor was the reply by Lenin new. Kievsky's views on *clause* 9 were the same as those that had been refuted by Lenin in the *Critical Remarks on the National Question* not very long before. Lenin argued that one had to approach the issue of self-determination historically and concretely. He showed that the Party's stand "On the Defence of the Fatherland" slogan had correctly put forward the position that "The present (1914–1919) war is, in substance [an imperialist war since it was waged in furtherance of an imperialist policy], unlike the 'genuinely national wars', which 'took place especially (especially does not mean exclusively!) between 1789 and 1871' and whose 'basis' was a long process of mass national movements, of a struggle agaisnt absolutism and feudalism, the overthrow of national oppression", [p. 9, Quotes as adopted by Lenin – D.W.N].

In relation to this, contrary to the eclectic Hirji who sees no connection between the general and the particular within it, Lenin observed:

> The present imperialist war stems from the general conditions of the imperialist era and is not accidental, not an exception, not a deviation from the general and typical. Talk of defence of the fatherland is therefore a deception of the people, for this war is not a national war. In a genuinely national war the words 'defence of the fatherland' are not a deception and we are not opposed to it. [p. 10]

To further elaborate the same point, he continued:

> Marxism, which does not degrade itself by stooping to the philistine's level, requires an historical analysis of each war in order to determine whether or not that particular war can be considered progressive, whether it serves the interests of democracy and the proletariat and, in that sense, is legitimate, just etc. [p. 11]

And a little later he stressed further the same point:

> National self-determination is the same as the struggle for complete national liberation, for complete independence, against annexation, and socialists cannot – without ceasing to be socialists – reject such a struggle in whatever

form, right down to an uprising or war. [p. 13, All emphasis are **Lenin's** – D.W.N.]

Such are the main points on the "central" issue of self-determination made by Kievsky and Lenin, respectively. We would like the dogmatic Hirji to tell us in which way our views differ from those of Lenin, if indeed, they are concerned with the same issues.

The second point dealt with by Lenin in the pamphlet is headed "Our Understanding of the New Era". Under this rubric, Lenin rebukes Kievsky for his mechanistic use of the term "era" by which he substitutes "ridiculous stereotype" for "concrete analysis" of social phenomena:

> Kievsky has flagrantly distorted the relations between the 'era' and 'the present war'. In his reasoning, to consider the matter concretely means to examine the 'era'. That is precisely where he is wrong. An era is called an era precisely because it encompasses the sum total of variegated phenomena and wars, typical and untypical, big and small, some peculiar to advanced countries, others to backward countries. To brush aside these concrete questions by resorting to general phrases about the 'era' as Kievsky does, is to abuse the very concept of 'era'. (p. 16)

Before we go into Kievsky's actual errors, let us observe here that in our "Manuscript" we painstakingly, by following closely Marxist-Leninist views and analysis, restate the Marxist-Leninist position on the various 'eras' and stages of 'capitalist development and the various "imperialism", in the context of a general movement, identifying "the sum total of variegated phenomena and wars . . . As regards the struggles of oppressed countries, we only refer to two "phenomena" – the Chinese and Indo-Chinese Revolutions – as concrete but variegated phenomena within the era of "finance capital" or "capitalist imperialism" as Lenin called it. We deliberately avoided making general views about otherwise concrete phenomena. Mamdani, Bhagat and now Hirji insist on substituting the general for the particular and then turn round to accuse us of that very error by turning our general observations, which are correct at their level, into concrete analysis of concrete situations of their choice.

We must put a pointed question to them: In our analysis of the eras of mercantilist, free-trade and modern imperialisms as such, where do our views differ from those expressed by Marx, Engels, Lenin, Stalin, Mao, Le Duan and all the other Marxist-Leninists? In what way have we distorted the concept of "finance capital" as developed by Lenin – not as distorted by philistines of the Hirji type? In what way, indeed, are our views dogmatic when we deal concretely with China and Viet-Nam? In what way are we dogmatic in our concrete discussion of Tanzania while criticising Shivji's "very bad book"? Such are the questions that our self-acclaimed Marxist-Leninists have to answer in order to show that their viewpoints are scientific and that ours are wrong on these two issues.

Let us see how Kievsky, whom Lenin was refuting, put his views on the "era" and concrete phenomena:

> The right of nations to self-determination is one thing in the era of the formation of national states, as the best form of developing the productive forces at their then existing level, but it is quite another thing now that this form, the national state, fetters the development of the productive forces. A vast distance separates the era of the establishment of capitalism and the national state from the era of the collapse of the national state and the eve of the collapse of capitalism itself. To discuss things in general out of context with time and space, does not befit a marxist. [p. 16]

Obviously this was a mechanistic presentation of the question at issue. Lenin thus rightly dubbed it "a sample of caricaturing the concept 'imperialist era' ". He showed how he had dealt with the question in his theses on the *National Question* which concretely distinguished the national question in three types of countries:

> First type: the advanced countries of Western Europe (and America), where the national movement is a thing of the past; Second type: Eastern Europe where is a thing of the present (1916); Third type: semi-colonies and colonies, where it is largely a thing of the future. (p. 17)

Our "Manuscript" assumes and indeed clearly argues that countries which used to be in the third category, "here the national movement was a thing of the future" in 1916, have for decades now become countries where the national movement has become "a thing of the present". We took pains to show how imperialist domination and exploitation have continued in spite of political independence which therefore means "neo-colonialism". Is this a caricature of Marxism? Do not hide behind phrases like "it does not follow logically" (!!) from the main thesis, or phrases like, ' ' "the main thrust" of the Manuscript abstracts from contradictions' (Mamdani and Bhagat). For this kind of observation stems from their failure to comprehend our discussion, based on Lenin's analysis of imperialism and of finanace capital after the Second imperialist World War. Logical deductions are not a method for studying the concrete.

Now, just because Hirji shows a very limited understanding of the Marxist-Leninist tactical and yet strategic position on the issue of national movements, we shall quote two short excerpts from the pamphlet on which he relied on this issue before we comment on his errors:

> ... In England, Germany, etc.; the 'fatherland' is a dead letter, it has played its historical role, i.e., the national movement cannot yield here anything progressive, anything that will elevate new masses to a new economic and political life.
>
> History's next step here is not transition from feudalism or from patriachal savagery to national progress, to a cultured and politically free fatherland, but transition from a 'fatherland' that has outlived its day, that is capitalistically overripe, to socialism.
>
> The position is different in Eastern Europe ... only a Martian dreamer could deny that the national movement has not been consumated there, that the awakening of the masses to the full use of their mother tongue and literature (and this is an absolute condition and concomitant of the full development of capitalism, of the full penetration of exchange to the very last peasant family) is still [1916] going on there. The 'fatherland' is historically not *yet* quite a dead letter there . . . whereas the English, French, Germans and Italians lie when they speak of defending their fatherland in the present war, because actually what they are defending are not their native language, not their right to national development, but their right to national development, but their rights as slave-holders, their colonies, the foreign "spheres of influence" of their finance capital, etc. (p. 18-19)

We have in effect argued, although not using exactly the same words or phraseology as the above, that the national question in our countries was not fully resolved and that therefore "the national movement has not been consumated" and, in line with Lenin, Stalin and Mao, that such consumation will only be effected by the total overthrow of imperialism from the economy from where it springs to have a controlling power over the politics of the neo-colonies in general, although the degree of such power definitely differs from neo-colony to neo-colony, depending on the internal alignment of class forces and the level of development of the productive forces. We have devoted the whole of Part VI of our "Manuscript" entitled "The End of Imperialism" to argue that the new-democratic revolution is the way out for the neo-colonies. Is this "economism"? Don't our self-acclaimed Marxist-Leninist realise that by posing the local petty bourgeois (which have been nurtured and yet are oppressed by dominating imperialist economic interests) as the true "ruling classes" and as the immediate enemy against whom "the struggle" must be waged, they are in effect denying continued imperialist exploitation and domination and the necessity for continues revolution under the leadership of the proletariat? Must we remind Hirji and his friends of Lenin's concept of the financial oligarchy as the rentier (usurer) class that thrives on "clipping of coupons" based largely on the exploitation and plunder of the backward countries (mainly neo-colonies and semi-colonies in the Third World)? Does he need to be reminded too that the backwardness and lack of transformation into fully fledged commodity producing regions of these neo-colonies with genuine local industry, etc., is the very *conditio-sine qua non* of such usury? When we advocate the furtherance of new democratic revolutions for neo-colonial countries you accuse us of advocating the Trotskyist nonsense of "world revolution" because you do not comprehend the dialectical relationships that finance capital objectifies in real world.

The third point that Lenin dealt with in the pamphlet is "What is Economic Analysis"? under whih he refuted once again the mechanistic view of Kievsky, which had been advocated by his predecessors like Rosa Luxemburg . . ., that self-determination of nations is, under modern imperialism, "unachievable" in the economic sense. Lenin once again shows that the issue of self-determination does not relate to overthrowing the entire system of finance capital but rather of one aspect of that system, political domination through annexation or colonial rule. He refutes once again Kautsky's opportunistic concept of imperialism which we have already discussed and which Kievsky was emulating. Then Lenin gives a more scientific "economic definition" of imperialism by removing the dualism that Kievsky and the other opponents of the necessity of the proletarian parties to recognise the right of oppressed nations to self-determination had introduced thus:

> Economically, imperialism (or the "era" of finance capital – it is not a matter of words) is the highest stage in the development of capitalism, one in which production has assumed such big, immense proportions that <u>free competition gives way to monopoly</u>. That is the economic essense of imperialism. Monopoly manifests itself in trusts, syndicates, etc., in the omnipotence of the giant banks, in the buying up of raw material sources, etc., in the concentration of banking capital, etc. Everything hinges on economic monopoly. [p.21/2. Emphasis and brackets are Lenin's -D.W.N.]

Then he discusses the political structure corresponding to this phenomenon:

> The political superstructure of this new economy, of monopoly capitalism (imperialism is monopoly capitalism) is the change *from* democracy to political reaction. Democracy corresponds to free competition. Political reaction corresponds to monopoly. 'Finance capital strives for domination, not freedom', Rudolf Hilferding rightly remarks in his *Finance Capital*. [p.22]

Now this being a crucial point in the discussion at hand, let us see how Lenin deals further with the issue of self-determination in this context. But to start with, let us see how he poses the questions. To quote him:

> And how does imperialism 'combine' its economies with the republic? Can

wealth dominate under this form of government? The question concerns the 'contradiction' between economics and politics. [p.25]

These questions were raised specifically because Kievsky had made a rather strange argument that "imperialism far from smiles on the republic, [among other things], and [its] achievement is therefore extremely difficult". Lenin then proceeded to answer the questions, as incidentally as he had so clearly done in *State and Revolution:*

> Engels replies: 'The democratic republic officially knows nothing any more property distinctions (between citizens). In it, wealth exercises its power indirectly, but all the more surely. On the one hand, in the form of the direct corruption of officials* of which America provides the classical example;** on the other hand, in the form of an alliance between governments and stock exchange . . .
> There you have an excellent example of economic analysis on the question of the 'achievability' of democracy under capitalism. And the 'achievability' of self-determination under imperialism is part of the question.
> The democratic republic 'logically' contradicts capitalism, because 'officially' it puts the rich and the poor on an equal footing. That is a contradiction between the economic system and the political superstructure. There is the same contradiction between imperialism and the republic, deepened or aggravated by the fact that the changeover from free competition to monopoly makes the realisation of political freedom even more 'difficult'.
> How, then, is capitalism reconciled with democracy? By indirect implementation of the omnipotence of capital. There are two economic means for that: (1) direct bribery; (2) alliance of government and stock exchange (that is stated in our these – under bourgeois system). Finance capital 'can freely bribe and buy any government and any official'. [p. 26]

Now let Hirji and his friends dub this as "lifeless abstraction", let them rumble about "politics does not always reflect the base" (a thing of course we never said !!), let them do as they may, but they won't run away from this shattering blow of the great Lenin on the state. Must we explain yet again such basic, very fundamental Marxist-Leninist concepts to those who claim to be Marxist-Leninists, who show such great acquaintance with the Marxist-Leninist writings on the question by their numerous quotations? Let the great Lenin finish the job, for indeed, he, on the basis of Marxism and against similar philistine views like those of Hirji & Co., finished it long ago. How did Lenin view the contradiction between monopoly capital, which negates democracy in general, and democratic forms of states? He viewed it in substantially the same way as Marx and Engels had done with regard to the contradiction between competitive (industrial) capitalism and democracy. He said:

> What, it can be asked, is altered in this respect when capitalism gives way to imperialism, i.e., when pre-monopoly capitalism is replaced by monopoly capitalism? [Lenin asked and then answered thus:]
> Only that the power of the stock exchange increases. For finance capital is industrial capital at its highest, monopoly level which has merged with banking capital. The big banks merge with and absorb the stock exchange . . .
> Further. If 'wealth' in general is fully capable of achieving domination over any democratic republic by bribery and through the stock exchange, then

---

*Issa Shivji and his followers like the eclectic Hirji regard them as the "ruling class" and call that Marxism-Leninism!!

**So even in America and even during Engels' time, wealth exercised its power "indirectly, but all the more surely"!! How about the Hirji & Co.?

> how can Kievsky maintain, without lapsing into a very curious 'logical contradiction', that the immense wealth of the trusts and the banks, which have thousands of millions at their command, cannot 'achieve' domination of finance capital over a foreign, i.e., politically independent, republic?? [The double question marks are Lenin's – D.W.N. p.26-27]

In these very clear terms, which the learned Hirji does not seem to undertand, Lenin, in following the Marxist analysis of the bourgeois state and in repudiating Kievsky and his kind (the Hirjis), re-emphasises the point that, both in theory and in practice there is no dualism between state and economy but that the economically dominant class is, as a rule, also the politically dominant class. It is open to any reader to see that Lenin is saying that finance capital, and hence its owning class, the financial oligarchy [united by capital yet in antagonism because of the private nature of appropriation of the surplus value produced by socialised labour and socialised capital] 'achieve domination' over any democratic republic by various means, two of which are the most significant. Where then lies Hirji's basis for saying by implication, that Lenin meant that political "independence implies . . .the establishment of ... a separate class controlling the [independent] state ..."? If Hirji and Co. have been looking for rationalizations of their petty-bourgeois, neo-Trotskyist theories in Marxism-Leninism, they had better give up the search there, for Marxism-Leninism is totally opposed to their neo-Trotskyist, dualist ramblings.

Having reached this point of Lenin's refutation of Kievsky, we have reached the end of his discussion of the three "central" points of Kievsky's "disquisitions". Lenin went on to illustrate further the scientificity of these views in their application to "The Example of Norway", to "Monism and Dualism" and to "The Other Political Issues Raised and Discussed by P. Kievsky", We shall not go into these aspects in detail except to quote from these sections those excerpts which further prove that Hirji's use of this pamphlet as a source of authority for his philistinistic views is totally untenable with the spirit and letter of the pamphlet. We shall restrict our summary and observations to the issue of what is meant by the right of nations to self-determination as explained in this pamphlet in order to show further that Hirji's presentation of it is anti-Leninist, although he quotes from this pamphlet on this issue. He does so in order, as we have seen, to rationalize his rather curious "idea" (it is nothing more) that every separate state implies a separate ruling class.

On the example of Norway which "achieved" her right to self-determination from Sweden in 1905 and thus presenting a clear and concrete proof of the "achievability" of that right "in the era of the most rampant imperialism", Kievsky had ventured a refutation of the Leninist position. His refutation was based on a mere *a priori* reasoning by negative deduction. As Lenin presented it, Kievsky in effect said: "enactment of a law against trusts does not prove their prohibition is unachievable" (p.27). Then Lenin made the following observations which in fact further expose the dualism of Hirji and his freinds:

> The example is an unhappy one, for it militates against Keivsky. Laws are political measures, politics. No political measures can prohibit economic phenomena. Whatever political form Poland adopts, whether she be part of Tsarist Russia or Germany, or an autonomous region, or a politically independent state, there is no prohibiting or repealing her dependence on the finance capital f the imperialist powers, or preventing that capital from buying up the shares of her industries.
> The independence Norway 'achieved' in 1905 was only political. It could not affect its economic dependence nor was this the intention . . .(p.27-28)

These views are clearly the same in substance as those we have summarized and quoted elsewhere on the issue of the relationship between politics and economics which Hirji vainly tried to refute as "economistic". The mere political independence of a country; the mere form of its political existence, does not mean that it is out of reach of the domination of finance capital, for finance capital has various ways of asserting its power, both directly and indirectly. Under capitalism as is very well known by all who are least acquainted with Marxism-Leninism, the law of uneven development regions supreme. This manifests itself not only at the level of the base (the economy), but also at the level of the superstructure (politics). Once we accept the dominance of finance capital in any given country with whatever form of state structure, can we turn round and advocate the idea of a separate ruling class (and hence of "separate politics") unless we can show how that class has arisen historically and at the level of production, of economy?

Thus we can understand Lenin's rebuff against the one-sided viewpoint of Kievsky who maintained that self-determination, or political independence, or the right to secede, or the right to set up a separate state (all essentially mean the same thing), was "economically unachieveable" simply because in the era of finance capital, "national" capital cannot hold its own against the rapacious finance capital - a very clear fact, by the way, which our backward-looking Hirjis do not seem to understand, namely that political independence is possible under the rule of finance capital at the level of the economy.* Kievsky and Co., who failed to understand that capital (including finance capital) can and does rule under various forms of state structures, deserved the following rebuff which Hirji himself quoted out of context:

> The law of economic concentration, of the victory of large-scale production over small, is recognised in our own programme . . .Kievsky conceals the fact that nowhere is the law of political or state concentration recognised. If it were the same kind of law if there were such a law – then why should not Kievsky formulate it and suggest that it be added to our programme? Is it right for him to leave us with a bad, incomplete programme, considering that he has discovered this new law of state concentration, which is of practical significance since it would rid our programme of erroneous conclusions? Kievsky does not formulate that law, does not suggest that it be added to our programme, because he has the hazy feeling that if he did he would be making himself a laughing-stock. Everyone would laugh at this amusing imperialist economist if it were expressed openly and if, parallel with the law that small-scale production is ousted by large-scale production, there were presented another 'law' (connected with the first or existing side by side with it) of small states being ousted by big ones! [pp. 28-29]

Hirji by asserting that since political independence under capitalism means, in the Marxist-Leninist sense, "a separate state", it must follow that it also means "a separate ruling class" for that "separate state", caricatures Lenin in vain. It is true to say, in a sense, as we have stated, that all colonial territories form part of the territorial expanse (realm) of the metropolitan state and its economy. It is not true, however, that a separate state for a former colony necessarily negates the continued dominance of the economic interests of the metropolitan bourgeoisie (which after independence and because of that independence under given historical social conditions, become challenged and joined by the 'interests of the imperialist-bourgeoisie of other imperialist countries). If the annexation of territory implies concentration of states under given historical circumstances, it does not follow that as a rule, there is a tendency towards the concentration of states just like it is true

---

*Which by the way is not the same thing as "separate politics", which the Hirji's imply as well in a one-sided manner – D.W.N.

that, as a general rule of capitalist development, there is a tendency towards the concentration of capital and production, the negation of free competition by monopoly or of small capital by big capital or of national capital by finance capital. Hirji seems to suggest this idea to himself when he talks of an international ruling class implying an international i.e., concentrated state! This idea stems from his own confusion. For to say that the emergence of "a separate state" from the imperialist state (concentrated state) necessarily implies, by itself, the emergence of " a separate ruling class" means that the concentration of capital and production necessarily goes hand in hand with the concentration of state and thus the separation of state must necessarily imply the separation of "economy", meaning the separation of "national capital" from finance capital. This would be a very strange thing since finance capital negates and absolves any subsisting national capital, and the negation of finance capital cannot be by "national capital" but by socialism. Hirji's dogma that a separate state implies a separate ruling class (under capitalism) leads him to imagine the springing up of national capital in the face of finance capital on the basis of the mere fact that a separate state has sprang up in the face of finance capital. Such is the muddled "logic" of Hirji and his friends, but surely such is not Marxism-Leninism as indeed Lenin yet shows:

> Economically, imperialism is monopoly capitalism. To acquire full monopoly, all competition must be eliminated, and not only on the home market (of the given state), but also on foreign market in the whole world. Is it economically possible, in the era of finance capital to eliminate competition even in a foreign state? Certainly it is. It is done through a rival's financial dependence and acquisition of his sources of raw materials and eventuality of all his enterprises – which [by the way Karim Hirji & Co.- D.W.N.] took place in the case of neo-colonies during the period of colonisation between 1870-1914. [p.22]
> National self-determintion means political independence. Imperialism seeks to violate such independence because political annexation makes economic annexation easier, cheaper (easier to bribe officials, secure concessions, put through advantageous legislation, etc.) more convenient, less troublesome – just as imperilaism seeks to replace democracy generally by oligarchy but to speak of the economic "unachievability" of self-determination under imperialism is sheer nonsense. [p.23]

Would Hirji, in line with his logic, not agree that his dualist reasoning leads to the same "sheer nonsense", because, once we agree that a mere creation of a separate state under finance capital does not and cannot give rise to a separate "national" capital and its personification in a ruling "national bourgeoisie", then, on Hirji's premises political independence would be "unachievable" under finance capital.

Thus we can conclude, without going into other important but not directly relevent points in the pamphlet (*A Caricature of Marxism and Imperialist Economism*), from which Hirji quoted so extensively, by reproducing one of his quotes from this same pamphlet – but this time in full:

> To criticise an author, to answer him, one has to quote in full at least the main propositions of his article. But in all of Kievsky's propositions you will find that every sentence contains two or three errors or illogicalities that distort Marxism. [p.40]

We have in this part and elsewhere in this critique shown how Hirji not only commits illogical errors but also fundamentally distorts Marxism-Leninism, including using quotations from Marxist-Leninist writings without taking the trouble of acquainting the reader with the context from which the quotes were uplifted and misused. As we have already observed, to have put the quotations in their proper context would have ruined Hirji's case and would have made his case without content, but as it is the case turns out to be no case at all. Having shown his failure to grasp and present the context and the substance of his quotes from the pamphlet under discussion, it is not necessary for us to disprove particular quotations he made except by way of shattering his central arguments, which we have partly done here and which we will revert to in the next section.

Having unravelled the confusion that Hirji and introduced into Lenin's thesis on imperialism and the national question, we now turn to deal with specific areas of his arguments and try to bring to a conclusion our reply to him. We have already dealt with the issue of RULING CLASS and we now turn to the question of the STATE, in order to round up our arguments.

3. THE STATE

The views which Hirji bring out on this issue of the state touch very closely on the issue of the ruling class. Hirji's paper must be praised for the fact that for the first time it brings out in stark openness the positions which appear to us to be the very basis of the petty theories that his clique put forward on the state and classes in Tanzania and as we shall show in a later critique of Mamdani on Uganda. We must now summarize these views again in order to deal with them in detail, in order to round up the discussion. This is necessary although this issue has been touched on at various points already. Hirji's position starts from the proposition that the colonial state was "part of the metropolitan state, adopted in the concrete conditions of the colony", in which the metropolitan bourgeoisie" is the ruling class. It is a single state, because:

> To a single ruling class, there corresponds a single state. A separate state *implies* a separate ruling class.

Leaving aside a quotation from Lenin, which we have shown not to have the contextual relevance, he proceeds:

> What independence implies is the establishment of a separate state and thus of a separate class controlling the state. The bourgeoisie of the former colonial power no longer holds state power in the neo-colony. This does not mean that imperialist exploitation is done away with, it is in fact intensified. For the local ruling class that holds state power in the neo-colony is economically dependent on imperialism and thus, the neo-colonial state whilst specifically serving the interests of the local ruling class(es), also at the same time serves the interests of imperialism as a whole. The difference being that the neo-colonial state can act against the interests of a specific imperialist bourgeoisie or try to play off one imperialist power against another. It is in this sense only that one can talk of the relative autonomy of the local ruling class(es) vis-a-vis imperialism. The extent of this autonomy varies from neo-colony to neo-colony depending on concrete conditions. [All emphasis added except over the words separate, specific, relative autonomy and vis-a-vis.]

Again leaving out Hirji's quotations from Lenin (on Argentina), Mao Tse-tung (on China) and Le Duan (on Indo-China), which were abstracted by him, we now proceed at this stage to try to disentangle the dualism heaped up in these bundles of verbiage.

A. Colonial State
Hirji's proposition that the colonial state was "part of the metropolitan state" is

substantially true. In our view even if Hirji maintained (which is more correct) that it was a separate state created to accord with the concrete conditions of each colony and tailored to serve the interests of the financial oligarchy, he could still logically maintain that some transformation took place at independence. But this is no accident because he also maintains that because of this it was the ruling class in the colony. He could still maintain the same with the second proposition we advance, since we have already demonstrated from a Marxist-Leninist position of Engels and Lenin, the financial oligarchy can have recourse to and does rule through any form of (separate) state. But furthermore, what Hirji fails to distinguish here is the dialecticalconnection between political control of the colony through its appointed Governors and Commissioners as well as local chiefs or traditional rulers in the colony and the economic control by the financial oligarchy which alone identifies them as a ruling class and thus of having the right of presiding over the political superstructure. There is a dialectical relation which he does not have in his abstractions. His proposition stated above suggests the former control (political) as being the determinant in identifying the metropolitan bourgeoisie as ruling class in the colony. This is evidenced by such formulation as "the bourgeoisie of the former colonial power no longer holds state power". This is because he separates the political from the economic. This is un-Marxist and introduces dualism between the economic and the political. If Hirji thinks we are falsely accusing him on this issue, treatment of the neo-colonial phase will clearly prove our observation correct, since, furthermore, his concept of "state power" is one-sided (i.e., only political).

B. Neo-Colonial State

His proposition here is that on "the morrow of independence", a separate state comes into being severing itself from the metropolitan state. Nay! To paraphrase him exactly "independence implies the establishment of a separate state". In other words, a new entity comes into being. But since a separate state has arisen, this also "implies a local ruling class", which now utilises this separate state power "specifically" to serve its interests and, at the same time, those of "imperialism as a whole". As we indicated above in relation to the second proposition we advanced of a separate colonial state but tailored to serve the financial oligarchy, he still could have argued logically that what "independence implies is the taking over of political power", but since this power cannot be exercised without a ruling class, he could then still argue that a separate ruling class is "implied" and that would be all right at that level of his logic.

But Hirji's formulations are important and underline his dualism, a dualism which, as we demonstrated in the polemic of Lenin against Luxemburg and Kievsky, is done away with. If these formulations are to be defended as Marxist-Leninist views, it has to be shown how the "establishment" of a separate state with its ruling class arises dialectically. Is this ruling class the one which rules in the economy? If it is, it has to be shown how its "national capital" arises during colonialism, which then on the "morrow of independence" enables this local class to rule as a class in itself. If this cannot be demonstrated historically, then it has to be shown with what magical powers this "national capital" comes into being on this morrow.

If these two facts are proved then it has to be asked why this "national bourgeoisie", a ruling class endowed with its "national capital" becomes "dependent" on the "imperialist bourgeoisie" and why this national, economically ruling class should allow its separate state, while serving its specific interests, "also" to serve those of the "imperialist bourgeoisie"? Hirji's possible recourse to Lenin in the quotation . . . on the issue of "transitional forms of state dependence", will not help him out here since clearly Lenin did not have in mind a colony and neo-colony but semi-colony which, as we argued in the "Reply" to Mamdani and Bhagat, are not the same thing. Moreover, to accept this interpretation of Lenin's point is to generalize and absolutize the idea of "state dependence" as we have argued earlier, and apply it to qualitatively and historically different situations. State dependence in these circumstances becomes a norm for all countries except the super-powers. Thus Britain, Japan, Argentina, Tanzania and a colony would all be in "transitional forms of state dependence", say on the U.S. This is a vulgarization of Lenin. While it cannot be denied (indeed it is the rule) that one financial oligarchy allows its state whether directly or indirectly to serve the interests of the other, Hirji has to demonstrate that this "national bourgeoisie" allows its state to serve the interests of the "imperialist bourgeoisie" on the basis of give and take and reciprocity, or that the neo-colonial state also on the basis of bribery uses the metropolitan state. If he cannot demonstrate this (which he can't) his formulations remain mere verbiage.

This idealism explains Hirji's vagueness and lack of concreteness, as for instance his talk of independence "implying" a separate state and a "new ruling class"! Is the new state and class "implied" or is it real? It is impossible for him to be concrete with his dualist method. This is because he creates a dualism between political power and economic power, and this dualism arises out of his idealist world outlook which is based on *a priori* positions, and which fails to see the concrete in its interaction. This is so although he is unconscious of it and his talk about "economic dependence" of this bourgeoisie on "imperialist bourgeoisie" and about exploitation being "intensified", as we have argued elsewhere, means nothing. He cannot also demonstrate the dependence of European sovereign states on the more powerful monopoly states. Is it of the same category?

How can "national capital" arise in a colony while it is even negated in the centre by finance capital – a capital that can only exist internationally. Was Lenin wrong when he said, and we quote him once more:

> In Europe the dependent nations have both their own capital and easy access to it on a wide range of terms. The colonies have no capital of their own, or one to speak of, and under finance capital no colony can obtain any except on terms of political subordination. (On the National Question, p. 129–143)

How did independence change this political subordination when finance capital continues its grip on our countries. This question is repeated and requires his concrete theoretical answer. Following this thesis of Lenin, the "Manuscript" states:

> The historical record clearly shows that multilateral imperialism has intensified the exploitation of the neo-colonial world through increased capital exports, and thereby subordinating these countries to the financial oligarchies of the imperialist countries. (p. 433)

It follows that Hirji's dualism cannot permit him to comprehend post-war developments and his mutterings about "relative autonomy" which allows the local ruling class to "play off one imperialist power against another" mystifies the significance of this stage of development on the whole issue of the national question. Because of this, as we have already argued, the new democratic revolution cannot be explained by him in any theoretically convincing manner.

C. The Financial Oligarchy

With this petty-bourgeois dualistic viewpoint, Hirji feels himself qualified to deal blows at those who see the financial oligarchy (divided but also united to exploit) as the economically dominant class on world scale, exercising rule in the economy of the neo-colony and hence ultimately determining the politics, as "economistic"! To quote him:

> Having rapidly gobbled up some Marxist texts, what emerges from him is Marxism minus dialectics, i.e., confusion. Thus he metaphysically maintains that since the financial oligarchy, 'the class as a whole on world scale' is 'economically dominant class' before and after independence, the only change independence implies is a change of the pigment of bureaucratic personnel manning the state machine. Both the colonial and neo-colonial states are controlled by and directly serve the interests of the financial oligarchy.

We have already demonstrated that the confusion is with Hirji. The summary of Lenin's contention against Luxemburg and Kievsky should by now have dispelled any illusions he entertained of having said anything profound in his paper. His formulation above is a mere caricature of Lenin, and of our position. It has nothing in common with what we have to say. Our formulation is brought out in the "Manuscript" and, indeed, Hirji quotes us correctly. If he removes his interjections inside the quotation which injects his own confusion, our formulation takes full recognition of this stage of the national democratic revolution. We state that the struggle of the colonial peoples at this stage "leads to the imperialists conceding political independence to the colonial people. It advances the struggle of the people for democratic rights and enables these to be achieved at a very limited level, thus making it possible for the democratic revolution to advance". But at the economic level the financial oligarchy continues its grip on the neo-colony. The contradictions in the third world over the last twenty years reflect this phenomenon and have clearly shown the limits of this phase of the national democratic revolution. This much, in short, we say in the passage.

It is true that only political power in the superstructure is wielded by local class, or bureaucracy, or whatever you call it. The fact remains, however, that the neo-colony continues to be under the grip of finance capital and in Hirji's own words "exploitation is intensified". It is so intensified for Hirji's information, because the financial oligarchy continues to be the economically dominant class in the neo-colony. His words, on the other hand, remain empty verbiage without an analysis of how this exploitation is "intensified". If he had taken the pains to do this, he would have had no cause for going around the issues we raise about the omnipotent power of finance capital, which is personified in the financial oligarchy. Talking of this phase of capitalist development, Lenin, whom Hirji is fond of quoting but whose message he does not understand, states:

> At present imperialism and the domination of the banks have 'developed' into an exceptional art both these methods of upholding and giving effect to the omnipotence of wealth in the democratic republics of all descriptions... Another reason why the omnipotence of 'wealth' (read 'financial capital') is more certain in a democratic republic is that it does not depend on defects in the political machinery or on the faulty political shell of capitalism. A democratic republic is the best possible political shell for capitalism, and, therefore once capital has gained possession of this very shell ... it establishes its power so securely, so firmly, that *no* change of persons, institutions or parties in the bourgeois-democratic republic can shake it. [*State and Revolution*, pp. 295/6, Lenin's own emphasis.]

Our Hirji sees the neo-colony as exception to this "economistic general rule", and prates the "relative autonomy" of "local ruling class"!! His conception of "relative autonomy" enabling the local ruling class to "play off" one monopoly group against another would cease to take on the one-sidedness he attaches to it if he grappled with Lenin seriously. But this would require him to undertake a much more painstaking study of Marx in his analysis of capitalist development and of Lenin's further development of the theory on the issue of imperialism and state. But being so scantly equipped on these issues, he thinks that his "blabberings" are a substitute for study. Moreover, if he did he would find the actual roots of the contradictions within capitalism. He would further find that it is not "glossing over contradictions" to call intra-monopoly, or intra-imperialist contradictions, intra-class contradictions. What does Hirji imagine is so profound about this criticism below advanced in in his paper:

> Thus to talk of a "national bourgeoisie" is to engage in mystification. The struggle between various imperialist 'bourgeoisies' are just intra-class contradictions between monopoly which are part of the international oligarchy. It is precisely such reasoning which led Kautsky to speculate about 'peaceful' imperialism, which Lenin termed a "silly little fable" . . . [Then follows a quotation from Lenin in which Lenin critises Kautsky for obscuring and glossing over the fundamental contradictions of imperialism – D.W.N.]. These fundamental contradictions of imperialism include the competition between several imperialisms, i.e., the struggle between various imperialist bourgeoisies, which can be conducted either peacefully or through wars between imperialist states. Nabudere obscures and glosses over these issues dubbling all such contradictions as intra-class contradictions between monoply groups.

If we may pause here to disentangle this verbiage before proceeding further, what has the question of the negation of national capital go to do with intra-monopoly contradictions? Was this negation not achieved on the basis of this contradiction when the monopolies divided up the whole colonial world among themselves? Where did Lenin tell Kautsky that the "struggles between various imperialist bourgeoisies' are not "just intra-class contradictions"? This is important because he then concludes that "it is precisely such reasoning which led Kautsky to speculate about 'peaceful' imperialism". Have we not demonstrated that it was not "precisely this reasoning" that led Lenin to accuse Kautsky of glossing over contradictions in imperialism? Do we have to repeat it? Is the contradiction between the bourgeoisies, whether monopoly or non-monopoly, not an "intra-class contradiction"? Has it got to be non-class in order to qualify as a fundamental contradiction? Does its fundamentality spring from its not being an intra-class relation?

Since Hirji does not comprehend the laws of motion of capitalism, he cannot possibly conceive that this contradiction, intra-class as it is, is called fundamental because of the fact that it is inherent in capitalist production itself and cannot be done away with until this mode of production is not more. Yet fundamental as it is, it is determined by yet another fundamental contradiction, that between capital and labour which is anti-calss and antagonistic. Thus, Hirji fails to prove that we gloss over this contradiction by calling it "intra-class". Indeed, on this evidence alone, without more, it proves our awareness of this contradiction, and his little stories turn out to be no more than the "silly little fables" that Lenin talked about. All intra-monopoly contradictions are settled in the final analysis by war. We assert no less. But because they are settled by wars, they are no less intra-class. Please note. His little story about war between monopolies within a state is not worthy of attention. Hirji should do his homework!

When will Hirji and his fellow travellers understand the distinction between the general movement of capital and its particular movement. Our analysis of imperialism deals with a general movement and when we come to neo-colonialism we restrict ourselves to general tendencies plus specific case studies of China and Vietnam. Hirji starts from the particular and then proceeds to turn it into the general. The issue of capitalist development towards greater concentration is a matter that Marx emphasized as a general tendency, and is not something that can be brushed aside by vulgar debate. Was Marx a Kautskyite when at the very early phase of capitalist development, he pointed out this phenomenon as growing with time. "One capitalist always kills many", Marx said! Nay, he said more:

> Hand in hand with this capitalisation. . .on an ever extending scale, the co-operative form of the labour-process. . . the economising of all means of production by their use as means of production, combined socialised labour, the entanglement of the peoples in the net of the world-market, and with this, the international character of the capitalist regime. Along with the constantly diminishing number of the magnets of capital, who usurp and monopolise all advantages of this process of transformation, grows the mass of misery, oppression, of the working-class, a class always increasing in numbers... .and disciplined and united, organised by the very mechanism of the process of capitalist production itself. The monopoly capital becomes a fetter upon the mode of production, which has sprung up and flourished along with, and under it. Centralisation of the means of production and socialisation of labour at last reach a point when they become incompatible with their capitalist integument. Thus the integument is burst asunder. The knell of capitalist private property sounds. The expropriators are expropriated. [*Capital*, Vol. 1, p. 714–715. Emphasis added.]

Lenin carries this scientific analysis of Marx further and states, please note Hirji:

> At a certain stage in the development of exchange, at a certain stage in the growing of large scale production, namely, at the stage that was reached approximately at the end of the nineteenth and the beginning of the twentieth centuries, commodity exchange had created such an internationalisation of economic relations, and such an internationalisation of capital, accompanied by such a vast increase in large scale production, that free competition began to be replaced by monopoly. The prevailing types were no longer enterprises freely competing inside the country and through intercourse between countries, but monopoly alliances of entrepreneurs, trusts. The typical ruler of the world became finance capital, the power that is peculiarly mobile and flexible, peculiarly intertwined at home and internationally, peculiarly devoid of individually and divorced from the immediate processes of production, pecualiarly easy to concentrate a power that has already made peculiarly large strides on the road of concentration, so that literally several hundred billionaires and millionaires hold in their hands the fate of the whole world. [Introduction to Bukharin, *Imperialism and the World Economy*, op. cit., p. 11. Emphasis added]

Where, we may ask Hirji, is the Kautskyism and economism of "professor D. Wadada Nabudere"? Who is turning his back on scientific analysis? We or him? Have we not demonstrated that while Kautsky say one-sided unity in imperialism, our anti-Kautskyites see only contradiction. If Lenin saw only contradiction in the bourgeoisie, would he have said this of them:

> On boards of joint-stock companies we find capitalists of different nations sitting together in complete harmony. At factories, workers of different nations work side by side. In any really serious and profound political issue sides are taken according to classes, not nations. (*Critical Remarks*, p. 24.)

Indeed if Marx saw only contradiction and not unity in capitalist production could he have said, in discussing the equalisation of the general rate of profit, the following:

> It follows from the foregoing that in each particular sphere of production the individual capitalist, as well as the capitalists as a whole, take direct part in the exploitation of the total working class by the totality of capital and in the degree of that exploitation, not only out of general class sympathy, but also by direct economic reasons. For assuming all other conditions among them the value of the total advanced constant capital – to be given, the rate or profit depends on the intensity of the exploitation of the sum total of labour by the sum total of capital. (*Capital.* Vol. 1, pp. 396/7)

We have already demonstrated in summarizing Lenin on Kievsky, how the financial oligarchy, through direct and indirect means, including bribery of officials and control of the stock exchange and banks, make use of the sovereign states of independent countries for the exploitative activities internationally. This is the Marxist-Leninist understanding of how the financial oligarchy excercises its political power internationally. Lenin's observations are drawn from Engels on the *Origin of the Family, The State and Private Property*, and are brought out by Lenin himself in the *State and Revolution*. These scientific observations of Engels and Lenin have generally been vindicated by reality and the recent Lockheed and BP/Shell scandals are, indeed, the exposed examples of a general hidden practice. In both cases monopolies of the U.S. and Britain have for years engaged in bribery in order to advance their sales and production in many bourgeois republics. The briberies have resulted in criminal proceedings against former prime ministers (Japan), army officers (Italy and Germany) and the resignation and censure of husbands of reigning monarchies (Holland).

If U.S., British, and other monopolies can so bribe and exercise power within borders of other equally monopolistitc states, how can Hirji imagine that the "national bourgeoisie" in the neo-colony cannot be used even more directly for the same purpose, particularly as they have to rely on them for finance? Is this not how the power of the financial oligarchy is exercised? This is our view of the exercise of economic power by the financial oligarchy over the neo-colonial world in enforcing its international rule, and, as Lenin said after the 1890s: "The typical ruler of the world became finance capital".

This is the reality with which we are concerned. We have no room for entertaining the dogmas Hirji puts forward: "To a single ruling class there corresponds a single state. A separate state implies a separate ruling class"! This absolute law is enacted in Hirji's head and cannot be shown to be Marxist-Leninist. It is not open to us to go further and show, as Hirji demands, that there should occur a merger of various national states into an international state if the financial oligarchy is to be regarded as ruling internationally. We are content indeed with "muttering" that "the economically dominant class on international scale is the financial oligarchy" because that is what the reality is, consistent with the teachings of Marx, Engels and Lenin. We have established that the achievability of self-determination at political level by itself does not rule out the international rule of finance capital at economic level. This stage of development only opens new avenues for furthering the struggle in the economic and political fields which can only be eliminated in the neo-colony with the success of the new national democratic revolution under proletarian leadership. We leave it to the dualists to draw the conclusions based on "Ideal Universals" of pure logic.

The financial oligarchy and the bourgeoisie in general can never do away with the nation-state, for that is its creation and the very basis of its existence. The bourgeois state and the bourgeoisie exist because of the uneven development of countries which under capitalism becomes a law. Without the nation-state under these conditions, capital cannot exploit labour and that is why Marx and Engels, emphasized that the state has always been an instrument of the owners and controllers of property. In the era of monopolies where such property (capital) can only exist internationally, such rule will be enforced through existing state structures internally. Yet on the basis of the most democratic republic, finance capital rules best and internationally whether this be directly or indirectly. It is only the proletariat, doing away with uneven development, that can create the conditions for the withering away of the nation-state. The logical necessity of the international state to arise in order to accord with the international bourgeoisie (the financial oligarchy) as a ruler on international scale in areas under the control of finance capital is the ahistoric logical deduction arising out of Hirji's dualism. It cannot arise concretely from our discussion which he quotes. Like the other dogmas it is his abstract logical conclusion.

4. CONCLUSION

We would like to conclude by pointing to some philosophical and political consequences that flow from Hirji's propositions. We have shown that his conclusions on imperialism, the state and classes are not scientific and concrete. They arise out of *a priori* positions logically postulated but not related to or based on reality.

We have further demonstrated that his recourse to Lenin is a prostitutions to back up his petty-bourgeois propositions. These *a priori* assertions are, however, important because of their harmful impact on revolutionary theory and practice.

Hirji asserts that it is "economistic" to hold that the political necessarily flows from the economic, Indeed, under "certain circumstances" (because to him, according to Mao) the political can determine the economic. Having come to this, he then turns these certain "special circumstances" to be the general rule at least as far as imperialism and neo-colonialism are concerned. Through this logical abstraction he arrives at his first partially correct proposition that the colonial state was "part of the metropolitan state". But at independence there was separation of state and a new neo-colonial state came into being, and because of the "establishment" of this separate state there was implied a separate local ruling class, which now ruled and used the state to serve its "specific" interests as well as those of the "imperialist bourgeoisie". What emerges from all this up to this point is that the rise of the neo-colonial state is a "certain special circumstance" in which the politics determined the economics, thus creating room for a local ruling class as opposed to the bourgeoisie in Europe because it has assumed political power and through this political power it now protects its "specific" economic interest. This much Debray, Gundar Frank, Shivji, Mamdani and the self-acclaimed Trotskyist Nicola Swainson assert.

The other approach, which we call "the economic approach", to Hirji's confused thesis may be stated as follows. Under colonialism, a national bourgeoisie emerges, because Lenin on Argentina, Mao Tse-tung on China and Le Duan on Indo-China say so. This national bourgeoisie with their accumulated national capital "on the morrow of independence" become the local ruling class and now with the separate state utilize the state to serve its "specific interest". This national capital (and hence its bourgeoisie) is not negated by finance capital. Indeed it, through the state, resists the encroachments of finance capital and in that way rolls back the concentrating, centralizing and internationalizing tendency of capitalism that Marx and Lenin talked about. Thus national capital was juxtaposed to finance capital and began to compete with it "for all capitals are interdependent and competitive" [Swainson, Rohini Banaji etc.]. Thus national capital exists side by side with finance capital. But, then, as we pointed out, Hirji has to explain why the exploitation by finance capital under neo-colonialism becomes "intensified".

These two positions, the political and the economic basically come out of Hirji's paper and are, from a materialist dialectical standpoint, irreconcilably contradictory. They are both held by Hirji because of his dualism although he is unconscious of this. From this it is easy to see that Hirji, although he so claims, is far from being a dialectician. He is an out and out idealist. This is the first and the *philosophic* conclusion to be drawn from his paper and, as we said to Shivji, we reject it.

The second conclusion is a political one and flows from Hirji's dualistic conception of the rise of national capital. It is of crucial importance because it affects the very character of political struggles in our countries. If, according to him, national capital arose either during colonialism and established itself against finance capital, or "impliedly" arose on "the morrow of independence" through use of political state power, thus establishing itself against finance capital, then it would follow that such national capital is either monopolistic itself, in which case it would exist at some relative parity with the finance capital, or it is competitive and free in its relations internally to the neo-colony or in its internal relationships as "partner" to finance capital. Whatever is the case, it would follow that this ruling class in the "neo-colony", nay in a capitalist country, has accomplished its bourgeois revolution and completed it. This would seem to be the position of the Trotskyist Jairus Banaji on India, but logically flows from Hirji's analysis as well. In this case the character of the revolution posed in the "neo-colony" would be a socialist one and not a new democratic revolution, although Hirji in his "Marxist-Leninist" purity claims the latter. This position is put forward by Gundar Frank on Latin America and by Banaji on India. We have shown that in fact Shivji, Mamdani and Bhagat pose the same task variously.

But the issue we wish to raise is this: if, indeed, Hirji denies that this is the correct conclusion of his arguments about the existence of a monopoly capital in the neo-colony or a free competitive capital (in which case he would be expected to say what else it is), the he would be assumed at least to entertain the theoretical possibility of its existence. This likelihood we would draw from the use of the word "implied" in relation to the rise of the separate state and separate ruling class, whereby this new ruling class "impliedly" arises with its capital. If this be true, and we cannot see how he can deny it without self-contradiction – for the term "dependent bourgeoisie" or "dependent capital" unless scientifically defined will not do – then we submit that Hirji is propounding an illusory and reactionary position which gives the petty-bourgeoisie a hope that national capital, if not in existence, can at least develop under neo-colonialism in the long run. In other words if it is not existent, it is achievable through the aid of the state. This is not stretching the argument too far, because in actual fact neo-Marxists like Bill Warren and Trotskyist Nicola Swainson argue the same on similar theoretical grounds. Both hold that Lenin's *Imperialism* had led to a mistaken "harmful" view that imperialism is parasitic and decadent. Bill Warren argues that this in fact is not the case because capital exports have led to the developoment of the productive forces in the "undeveloped countries". Nicola Swainson argues that national capital is growin in Kenya and, with the use of state power, a national bourgeoisie, able to resist finance capital, is emerging. It is clear that laws in parliament cannot do away with operation of economic laws of capitalism. We have already quoted Lenin in this reply to this effect, wherein he states:

> Laws are political measures, politics No political measures can prohibit economic phenomena. Whatever political for Poland adopts, whether she be part of Tsarist Russia or Germany, an autonomous region, or politically independent state, there is no prohibiting or repealing her dependence on the finance capital of the imperialist powers, or preventing that capital from buying up shares of her industries.

Today's mechanisms of control by finance capital are more refined, thus help tie-up more than even before a neo-colony to the imperialist countries.

These illusions of national capital, "competing" or sustaining itself against finance capital militates against the very basic contradiction – the tendency which is so more pronounced today than at the time Marx and Lenin wrote, the movement towards concentration and centralization of production and capital on world scale. In the colony because of this, according to Lenin, no capital, or if any very insignificant capital, is possible. It is a pious illusion that gives the petty-bourgeoisie hopes to restore old conditions of free competition. In his philistinistic views on imperialism, Kautsky entertained these illusions on trade between England and the colonies or semi-colonies and in particular Egypt. Kautsky speculated that such trade "would have grown more" without military occupation, without imperialism, and without finance capital. Lenin answered:

> What does this mean? That capitalism would have developed more rapidly if free competition had not been restricted by monopolies in general, or by the 'connections', yoke (i.e., also the monopoly) of finance capital, or by the monopolist possession of colonies by certain countries?
>
> Kautsky's argument can have no other meaning; and *this* 'meaning' is meaningless. Let us assume that free competition, without any sort of monopoly, would have developed capitalism and trade more rapidly. But the more rapidly trade and capitalism develop, the greater the concentration of production and capital which gives rise to monopoly. And monopolies have *already* arisen – precisely *out of* free competition. Even if monopolies have now begun to retard progress, it is not an argument in favour of free competition, which has become impossible after it has given rise to monopoly. (*Imperialism*, p. 108/9.)

Are these pious hopes of the petty-bourgeoisie which Hirji's propositions generate, not the ones that the *Communist Manifesto* rebuffed as "reactionary"? Although talking of the 1840s, Marx and Engels who classified the small manufactures, shopkeepers, artisans and peasants as "the lower middle class" (i.e., petty-bourgeoisie) noted that in their struggle against the bourgeoisie they "try to roll back the wheel of history", because they are not a revolutionary class. (*Selected Works,* Vol. 1)

It is only the working class which can do away with all old conditions. Its programme, according to Hilferding whom Lenin quotes approvingly, is not to "contrast the more progressive capitalist policy with that of by gone era of free trade and of hostility towards the state. The reply of the proletariat to the economic policy of finance capital, to imperialism, cannot be free trade but socialism. The aim of the proletariat policy cannot today be the ideal of restoring free competition – which has now become a reactionary – but the complete elimination by the abolition of capitalism." [Quoted in Lenin, op. cit., p. 108]. Those who piously hope that competition of national capital exists against finance capital, should listen again to what Lenin said:

Economically, imperialism is monopoly capitalism. To acquire full monopoly, all competition must be eliminated, and not only on the home market (of the given state), but also on foreign markets, in the whole world. Is it economically possible, 'in the era of finance capital', to eliminate competition even in a foregin capital', to eliminate competition even in a foreign state? Certainly it is. It is done through a rival's financial dependence and acquisition of his sources of raw materials and eventually of all his enterprises.

Lenin gives examples of American trusts activities of a hundred years ago in which he demonstrates the achievability of such elimination of competition, and then adds:

Big finance capital of one country can always buy up competitors in another, politically independent country and constantly does so. Economically, this is fully achievable. Economic 'annexation' is fully 'achievable' without political annexation and is widely practical. [Lenin then gives examples of Argentina and Portugal which through indebtedness "enable Britain to 'annex' these countries economically without violating their political independence. *Caricature*, pp. 22/23.]

We have already quoted Lenin on this question but we feel obliged to quote him again to remind our philistinistic Hirjis who talk of national capital, home market, etc., in the colony and the neo-colony where free competition was negated by the very movement that led to colonialism, piously expect us to see free competition re-emerge under monopoly (finance) capital itself! Can they give us any one single example of a third world, neo-colonial state, over which "financial dependence" has not been established by finance capital, and whose sources of raw materials have not been acquired by finance capital? Whence then do the home market and local resources of the neo-colony arise, markets and resources not monopolized with today's super-monopoly of giant corporations? Are these gentlemen unaware that they are rejecting the very analysis of Marx in *Capital* and in particular his *Law of the Tendency of the Rate of Profit to Fall*, which alone explains to us present day contradictions in imperialism? Are they not aware that they are denying the very movement in capitalist development which Lenin took over from *Capital* and analysed in *Imperialism*, the era of the omnipotence of finance capital?

Any talk by Hirji and his friends about the *new democratic revolution* in these circumstances is therefore possible only by what he himself calls "mental acrobatics" How can a new democratic revolution arise when a "neo-colony" has achieved its financial independence and has established control over its raw materials as is logically implied by Hirji's arguments. Do all these arguments not mean that a country is embarked on capitalist development? And how can a country do this without having gone through a bourgeois revolution of the old type? Mao Tse-tung thesis on this question arises directly from Stalin's analysis of the National and Colonial Question, which in turn is based on Lenin's theses which we have analysed, on the *National Question and the Right of Nations of Self-determination*. A national question cannot arise when a national bourgeoisie is able to establish itself against finance capital. Mao Tse-tung in analysing the Chinese revoluton observed that it had moved from the old bourgeois revolution in the period of the Revolution of 1911 to the new democratic bourgeois revolution. We quote him *in extenso:*

Why? Because the first imperialist world war and the first victorious socialist revolution, the October Revolution, have changed the whole course of world history and ushered in a new era. It is an era in which the world capitalist front has collapsed in one part of the globe (one-sixth of the world) and has fully revealed its decadence everywhere else, on which the remaining capitalist parts cannot survive without relying more than ever on the colonies and semi, in which a socialist state has been established and has proclaimed its readiness to give active support to the liberation movement of all colonies and semi-colony in which a socialist state has been established and has proclaimed its readiness to give active support to the liberation movement of all colonies and semi-colonies, and in which the proletariat of the capitalist countries is steadily freeing itself from the social-imperialist influence of the social-democratic parties and has proclaimed its support for the liberation movement in the colonies and semi-colonies. In this era, any revolution in a colony or semi-colony that is directed against imperialism, i.e., against the international bourgeoisie or international capitalism, no longer comes within the old category of the bougeois-democratic world revolution, but within the new category. It is no longer part of the old bourgeois, or capitalist, world revolution, but is part of new world revolution, the proletarian-socialist world revolution. Such revolutionary colonies and semi-colonies can no longer be regarded as allies of the counter-revolutionary front of world capitalism; they have become allies of the revolutionary front of world socialism.

Although such a revolution in colonial and semi-colonial country is still fundamentally bourgeois-democratic in its social character during its first stage or first step, and although its objective mission is to clear the path for the development of capitalism, it is no longer a revolution of the old type led by the bourgeoisie with the aim of establishing a capitalist society and a state under bourgeois dictatorship. It belongs to the new type of revolution led by the proletariat with the aim in the first stage, of establishing a new-democratic society and a stage under the joint dictatorship of all the revolutionary classes. Thus this revolution actually serves the purpose of clearing a still wider path for the development of socialism. In the course of its progress, there may be a number of further sub-stages, because of changes on the enemy's side and within the ranks of our allies, but the fundamental character of the revolution remains unchanged. Such a revolution attacks imperialism at its very roots, and is therefore not tolerated but opposed by imperialism. However it is favoured by socialism and supported by the land of socialism and the socialist international proletariat.

Therefore, such a revolution inevitably becomes part of the proletarian-socialist world revolution. ["On New Democracy", *Selected Works*, Vol. II, pp. 343/4, Emphasis added.]

The Indo-Chinese Revolution confirms Marxist-Leninist thesis of Mao Tse-tung, and contradicts our Hirji's who talk of "new democratic revolution" but deny it is essence by playing down its anti-imperialist mission. The new democratic revolution in China was necessary because again as we pointed out, Mao Tse-tung saw China's national bourgeoisie as "flabby" and therefoe "neither willing nor able to overthrow imperialism". He also pointed out that capitalism in China played a minor role in its social economy. This was so because again "international capitalism, or imperialism, will not permit the establishment in China of a capitalist society under Chinese bougeois dictatorship" [*Selected Works*, Vol. II, p. 354]. Further on he stated: "it is not China that is developing Chinese capitalism in our country; and it is not the Chinese bourgeoisie but Japanese bourgeoisie that is exercising dictatorship in our country". Let our brilliant Marxist-Leninists, the Hirjis, who see "nascent ruling classes" under every neo-colonial bed, shudder at these "Kautskyite, life-less abstraction" of Mao Tse-tung. In colonial semi-colonial China, the Japanese imperialist bourgeoisie and not the Chinese "national bourgeoisie", exercised dictatorship, because they and not the Chinese counterparts were the "dominant ruling class". "What"?, our Hirjis will exclaim, "the old man must have lapsed into 'economism', for does he not also say that in 'certain circumstances', politics determine the base, and is this not why we arrive at the conclusion that 'a separate state, implies a separate ruling class' "?!!

Such fuming and fretting will be misplaced, for nowhere did Mao Tse-tung suggest any such dogma. In case our Hirjis should try to find other reasons to wriggle out of this one, Mao Tse-tung explains in a Marxist-Leninist manner, the reasons why China was so dominated. He state:

> True enough, this is the period of the final struggle of a dying imperialism – imperialism is 'moribund capitalism'. But just because it is dying, it is all the more dependent on colonies and semi-colonies [and neo-colonies, we should add today – D.W.N] for survival and will certainly not allow any colony or semi-colony [or neo-colony – D.W.N.] to establish anything like a capitalist society under the dictatorship of its own bourgeoisie. [*Selected Works*, Vol. II, pp. 354/5]

Elsewhere Mao Tse-tung pointed to the fact that "imperialism controls not only China's vital financail and economic arteries but also her political and military power . . . China's economic, political and cultural development is very uneven, because she has been under complete or partial domination of many imperialist powers [*Selected Works*, Vol. II, p. 313. Emphasis added.] Here Mao Tse-tung is clear as to who the principal enemy is, and therefore what character of revolution China had to see through – that which led to socialist and not to capitalist construction because neither the international situation nor the domestic situation permitted capitalist development. [p. 354]. Hirji picks up a lone phrase "national bourgeoisie" from all this to construct dogmas out of it – and substitutes it for analysis. Here Mao Tse-tung's shows that this bourgeoisie never ruled. Mao Tse-tung's analysis in general applies to neo-colonial territories, as Indo-China demonstrated, precisely because the national question in its new democratic setting is still a thing of the present. National exploitation, oppression and domination continues unabated in spite of the political independence, but because of this fact excellent conditions exist for the total overthrow of imperialism and its minor local lackey cliques on the basis of the new democratic revolution, the motive forces of which must be analysed concretely to accord with the reality of each neo-colony. No amount of word juggling, of substituting "semi-colony" for "neo-colony" will help the Mamdanis and Bhagats and indeed the Hirjis to run away from this task.

Hirji's positions undermine and underrate the question of "national domination and oppression" by imperialism, a tactical question that is important to the proletariat in its tasks of mobilizing other classes exploited, dominated and oppressed by imperialism. As we have already indicated, these other classes are the great majority of the people. The alliance built by the proletariat with the peasantry is capable, on the basis of a national democratic programme, to mobilize a broad sprectrum of the people in isolating small reactionary elements supporting imperialism. Hirji's emphasis on the "local ruling class" as the immediate enemy only helps to isolate the proletariat from the broad mass of the people, and his talk about the "proletariat with their potential allies" is such empty talk. Lenin, on this question, also stated:

> In Europe, in 1871, the proletariat did not constitute the majority of the people in any country on the continent. A "people's revolution, one actually sweeping the majority into its stream, could be such only if it embraced both

the proletariat and, the peasants. These two classes then constituted the "people". these two classes are united by the fact that the 'bureaucratic-military state machine' oppresses, crushes, exploits them. To smash this machine, to break it up, is truly in the interest of the 'people', of their majority, of the workers and most of the peasants, is 'the precondition for a free alliance of the poor peasants and the proletarians, whereas without such alliance democracy is unstable and socialist transformation is impossible. (State and Revolution, *Selected Works*, Vol. II, pp. 314/5.)

In today's neo-colonial world as the Vietnamese revolution shows and as the earlier revolution in China showed, a broader alliance even with other petty-bourgeois strata and their "flabby national bourgeoisis" is possible and a "pre-condition" for the success of the new democratic revolution.

As we said, Mamdani and Bhagat see the task of the proletariat as essentially one concerned with the fight against its "local ruling classes". Hirji's propositions lead to the same conclusions. Indeed, in a recent article on Makerere, Mamdani even castigates what he calls "the democratic petty-bourgeoisie" for seeing the enemy as being imperialism which to him is "outside Uganda". To quote him:

For the democratic petty-bourgeoisie the enemy lies principally outside Uganda. This simplicity has the virtue of seeing Amin and the 'group'visibly around him as just the agents of external forces in some cases vaguely defined as 'imperialism', in others equally vaguely as the 'international bourgeoisie'. Since the ruling class is outside Uganda, the enemy internally is simply those individuals who occupy visibly important positions in the state power, and not any class with its own concrete interests. Thus anti-imperialist action need only dislodge this group from its prominent positions. Meanwhile the internal class in whose interest the state objectively functions is left intact. The 'revolutionary strategy' of the democratic petty-bourgeoisie turns out to be no more than a call for a coup d'etat.

While its anti-imperialism is quite real, if the democratic petty-bourgeoisie assumes leadership of the movement, it objectively shelters the ruling class in the camp of the people, disarming the revolutionary forces ideologically thus organisationally. (*Maji Maji,* No. 27, August 1976, pp. 72–73. All emphasis in original.)

Whatever these so-called "democratic petty-bourgeoisie" may be, Mamdani exhibits here "simplicity" of confusion. If this "democratic petty-bourgeois" opposition to imperialism is real how come that its concept of imperialism is "vague"? How come that their opposition is real to something that is to them vague and unreal, and if their opposition to imperialism is real how can their "revolutionary strategy" lead to a coup d'etat? If Mamdani understands imperialism in Uganda, as he claims to do by implication, how can he see it as "outside Uganda"? Is present-day Uganda not a creation of imperialism, and since when did imperialism leave Uganda's "internal" structures? Does political independence eliminate imperialism internally? If this is the case, then what is the new democratic revolution about: What are the "concrete interests" of this ruling calss which are counterposed to those of the imperialists? Do these "concrete interests" contradict in any fundamental way those of imperialism? What is this nascent commercial bourgeois class – commercial for who? Since when did "commercial capital" become a producing capital able to withstand finance capital? If indeed imperialist exploitation and national oppression are defeated in Uganda, does it not follow that the interests of this so-called "commercial bourgeoisie" would equally be eliminated and its class position demolished? How can it be "sheltered in the camp of the people"?

These simplistic formulations of Mamdani, nay petty-bourgeois formulations, to which Hirji subscribes, pose the danger of misleading the Uganda proletariat and young Ugandans to adopt the Trotskyist line of adventurism and hence our determined effort to expose them for what they are, including their class nature. If Mamdani claims to be a Marxist-Leninist, he should have a better concept of imperialism than the one he exhibits here and indeed in his forthcoming book. He has even begun already to abandon his "dependent bourgeoisie" thesis and is on the road to degeneration! As we have argued, Hirji's and Mamdani's dualism is responsible for their seeing imperialism as external to Uganda. This is because they detach the politics of imperialism from its economics.

But what is the "proletarian strategy" that Mamdani prescribes for the Uganda "working class" and peasantry in this, his latest theorizing? According to him:

> The enemy of the Ugandan revolution, at the present stage of the struggle are both imperialism and the internal [i.e., nascent commercial bourgeoisie] ruling class. [p. 73].

This is because "the working class position understands [sic!] that the enemy inside Uganda is not simply Amin but this nascent commercial bourgeoisie". According to Mamdani, the struggle in Uganda is an "internal" one. To quote him again:

> So long as a specific imperialism does not physically invade Uganda, as in the case of Vietnam and Combodia, the class struggle remains principally internal. The field of the battle remains inside Uganda. [p. 73.]

Here we are "simply" given rigorous and profound "analysis". Here we see the same Mamdani, who has the advantage of being an idealist and presenting imperialism as external to Uganda, advising the "proletariat" in Uganda to fight "imperialism". How, if we may ask, will this "proletariat" fight this external imperialist enemy "internally" if the enemy does not "invade" Uganda, as happened in Vietnam? Where will the "proletariat" find it? Will it push the battlefield to the U.S.? Did the Vietnam revolutionaries and patriots fight the U.S. "externally" because of U.S. intervention? Did not the "battlefield" remain not only "principally" but internal to Vietnam at all times? Does it not follow that if the "proletariat" of Uganda has not the misfortune of having Uganda being invaded by "a specific imperialist country", any talk of anti-imperialism is empty? Does it not follow further that the only enemy then is the local ruling class, the nascent "commercial bourgeoisie"?

What type of "proletariat" is this that Mamdani breeds in his brain, but wants us to see in Uganda? Have we not shown in a long quotation from Marx that the proletariat Marx was talking of was the one which arose out of the same ever-concentrating and ever-internationalizing capitalism that he analysed – a capitalism which, as it developed socialized labour, brought about "the entanglement of the peoples in the net of the world-market, and with this, the international character of the capitalist regime"? Have we also not shown that Lenin, following in the footsteps of Marx, analysed imperialism and pointed out how finance capital became the ruler of the world, where a few "hold in their hands the fate of the whole world?" Since Mamdani sees this concentration (i.e., imperialism) as external to Uganda, how then is this "proletariat" of his exploited by imperialism and how come that imperialism becomes its enemy to be fought alongside the "nascent commercial bourgeoisie"? Does it follows that Mamdani's "proletariat" is of his own creation, the one exploited "iternally" by this "nascent commercial bourgeoisie and not by finance capital of this "international regime of capitalism"? Does it not follow further that this "proletariat" is equally a "local" one, created not by imperialism, but by the "commercial bourgeoisie"? Marx Never devised his scientific tools and ideology for "local working classes", created by "nascent commercial capital", as we have seen. We challenge Mamdani to produce a new ideological blueprint for his "local proletariat" in Uganda, and not hide behind Marx and Lenin. Is it not clear that Mamdani is putting forward to us a petty nationalist thesis? Marx and Engels called on "Workers of the world unite" because of the fact that capital, in its internationalist growth, creates this class also on international scale:

> Alongside with the constantly diminishing number of the magnates of capital . . . grows the oppression of the working class – united by the process of capitalist production itself.

Lenin added to Marx's call "and all oppressed peoples of the world", because of the national question at the bottom of which imperialist exploitation and domination of the colonial and semi-colonial and today of the neo-colonial peoples was the basic factor for this call. Mamdani and Hirji want to lull us into believing that imperialist exploitation and domination is no longer that much! Whom do Mamdani, Hirji and Co. think they are deceiving with this out-and-out reactionary petty-bourgeois nationalism? How can they expect us to believe in their talk of new democratic revolution with this type of theorizing? Since they do not conceive of imperialism as internal as well as external to Uganda, are they not in effect putting out a plan for coup d'etat, since the overthrow of the "commercial bourgeois" does not mean the overthrow of imperialism? These gentlemen should be openly told to call a bluff to their tricks. When the debate organized by the TANU Youth League on the question *"Who is the real enemy in Uganda?"* took place at the University, Mamdani kept silent, contenting himself with making copious notes of the speeches. The resounding answer to this question that came out of the debate was: Imperialism is the real enemy in Uganda. Mamdani now turns up and puts forward his answer: The real enemy in Uganda is not imperialism but the local ruling class of the nascent commercial bourgeoisie!

These reactionary strategems that obscure the facts of history – which prove beyond doubt that imperialism is the internationalization of production and capital, the internationalization of bourgeois class rule and hence of its grave-diggers the proletariat of the imperialist countries and of the oppressed countries – leave the Ugandan proletariat isolated with no international scientific ideology (Marxism-Leninism). That is why we challenge him to spell out this new local ideology for the Ugandan "proletariat". We can assure him that it does not matter how long he takes over it, he can only produce a petty-bourgeois "Uganda Proletariat Manifesto". Good luck to him! Mamdani may not be aware that he is putting forward the Gundar Frankist thesis on Latin America, which Gundar Frank had said would also apply to Asia and Africa except that to him a "tactical attack" on the local bourgeoisie would hold to "produce a stronger confrontation with the principal imperialist enemy than does direct anti-imperialist mobilization". He sees the struggle in this way because he too is a dualist who sees no unity between imperialism and tis local bourgeoisie. We answered this neo-Trotskyist postulation in our "Manuscript". These erroneous views of Mamdani would equally flow from Hirji's positions and we must make it quite clear to them that have landed themselves in "a quagmire" and we refer them once more to the quotation from Lenin with which Hirji closed his paper. Their hideous theories of fighting "local ruling classes" directly lead to "revolution at one stroke", "left"-wing phrase-mongering that Mao Tse-tung refuted in his *New Democracy* (Chap. VIII.)

Finally, since, as we have shown, Hirji sets out to defend Shivji, but on the contrary contradicts him, the task he set out to do has not been accomplished. On the other hand his dogmatic propositions and edicts on ruling class, state and imperialism have helped us sharpen our understanding of these questions by delving deeper in Lenin's polemics with Kautsky, Luxemburg and Kievsky. This analysis has led us to conclusively demonstrate that Hirji's concept of "economism" has nothing in common with Lenin's. On the contrary, we have argued that Hirji's logical edicts and dogmas which enable him to conceive of the rise of a local ruling class and hence of national capital poising itself against finance capital and hence against the financial oligarchy, leads him into the worst type of, nay a perverted, economism. This is because his proposition that the establishment of a separate state *implies* the existence of national capital (and its owner the local ruling class), must logically lead to the conclusion that without such national capital and its class, political independence becomes impossible, and/or unachievable under the domination of finance capital. Hirji can only deny this at the expense of lapsing into great logical contradiction, since logic is the method of his analysis. This is out-and-out vulgar economism. It is: A caricature of Marxism-Leninism. It is Luxemburgism, Kievskyism and neo-Trotskyism. It is no wonder that neo-Trotskyists like Foster-Carter and his like were the only ones who described the analysis of Shivji in "Class Struggle Continues", as "almost a model of what Marxist analysis should be"; comparing Shivji's caricature with "Marx's own creative work on classes", a caricaturing which was raised to the skies and called "living Marxism", and "a major contribution to Marxism", and finally as "original and as being in the 'Mao Cabral Camp' (*Maji-Maji*, No. 11, August 1973, pp. 12–24). We reject such vulgarization and such a caricaturing of Marxism-Leninism.

12

THE MAKERERE MASSACRE

Mahmood Mamdani

After the assassination attempt on Amin last July (1977), an officer in the Uganda army thundered: 'The army will teach the people of Uganda a lesson if they do not behave.' That lesson yet another instance in the regime's campaign of terror against the people, was the massacre of Makerere students following the demonstration of Tuesday, August 3. The immediate reasons behind the demonstration – the regime's terror (the murder of the warden of Africa Hall and the open presence of security guards in student residences), Amin's own arbitrariness (the admisson of his illiterate son, Taban, to the Faculty of Linguistics) and the impact of the economic crisis of the students (scarcity of food and the early closing of the library due to lack of light bulbs) – have been well reported in the official East African press. Also reported has been the carnage left behind by the soldiers: 102 killed, over 700 injured and nearly 500 jailed, of which at least 50 are reportedly confirmed dead, bringing the death toll to at least 150. Bayonet wounds, chopped breasts, lobbed ears – the grim details gradually trickle out of Uganda as individual students flee the country.

While the bourgeois observe a minute's silence and the petty bourgeoisie weep, it becomes necessary to grasp the meaning of this event and draw lessons for the living: what conditions made for the students' revolt and what are the forces that stand behind the executors?

THE CRISIS OF THE AMIN REGIME

The students demonistration was not an isolated affair. It came in the context of a long, drawn-out resistance of the working people, workers and peasants, a resistance for the most part unorganised and economic in its expression. The apex of the workers' struggle was last year's strike as the Kilembe Mines. The regime's response was bloody suppression, extended this year to the Kenyan workers employed in the Jinja plantations* and manufacturing industries. Employed initially in the sugar cane plantations during the inter-war years as part of the colonial policy of drawing on migrant labour so as to hamper the growth of a firmly rooted working class, and used later in the textile industry established in the 1950s, when they fled the colonial repression of the Mau Mau, Kenyan workers formed 10% of Uganda's industrial work force. Historically the most militant section of the working class, their killing, jailing and intimidation was at the same time an attempt by the Ugandan military regime to discipline the entire working class.

The peasants are the producers of Uganda's prinicipal export crops, coffee and cotton. Ever since the coming of the military regime, added to their neo-colonial exploitation through the exchange of unequal values has been appropriation through straightforward armed plunder. The small commodity producer's

*Kakira Sugar Plantations.

response has been to revert to natural economy, from cash to food crops, from the production of exchange-value to that of use-values for direct consumption. As early as 1974, the Finance Minister admitted in his budget speech that cotton production had declined 60% in a year. Soon after, the Minister, disappeared. There has not been a budget speech in Uganda since! But facts, as Lenin was fond of quoting the English proverb, are stubborn things. Reality compels recognition.

The ensuing political crisis has robbed Amin of his social base. The 1971 coup that brought Amin to power was internally supported by the coalition of traders, southern kulaks and the Catholic petty bourgeoisie, a social base that Amin consolidated with the expulsion of the Asian commercial and petty bourgeoisie. As it took over the property of the departed Asians and also their positions (principally export-import), the upper stratum of the petty bourgeois traders began to mature into a commercial bourgeoisie. A section of the officer corps joined the ranks of these property owners-on-the-march. This nascent commercial bourgeoisie was the class base of the state power.

The result of peasant refusal to grow export crops was the scarcity of commodities and following it, price rises and the disruption of town-country exchange – a crisis for not only the petty but also the commercial bourgeoisie. It was not long before property demanded power and sections of the army allied with the new wealth began attempts to dislodge Amin. Amin's response was, on the one hand, to direct the apparatus of repression against the most advanced and ambitious sections of the commercial bourgeoisie and to terrotize them into submission. The businessmen, the ardent supporters of Amin's rule at the time of the '71 coup and the '72 expulsion then delighted with this rule-by-proxy which had brought them the wildest fruits of their dreams, suddenly found the taste turn bitter in their mouths. On the other hand, Amin sought to neutralize the 'unreliable' sections of the army by simply blocking their access to arms and countering them with a core of over 4,000 heavily armed mercenaries, recruited from the ranks of the non-Ugandan Sudanese, ex-Anyanya guerrillas. As Amin's repressive apparatus increasingly turned into a non-national mercenary force, his political crisis intensified. Without a social base among any of the classes in Uganda, his rule was transformed into a naked dictatorship by arms. With contradiction between the regime and its class base intensifying, different sections of the commercial bourgeoisie were not amenable to allying with competing imperialism to make a bid for power.

SUPERPOWER RIVALRY

The British and the Israelis were the first firm supporters of Amin's '71 coup. Obote's breaking relations with Britain over the Rhodesian UDI and his attempts to form a 'progressive bloc' at the '71 Singapore Commonwealth Conference were sufficient to sour British-Ugandan relations. Israel's disenchantment with Obote was even deeper. Ever since 1963, Israel had a 'presence' in Uganda, later even training the army, the police and the air force. After 1969, Uganda occupied a central place in Israel's Arab-African strategy. Northern Uganda was the base the Israelis used to assist materially the Anyanya guerrillas in Southern Sudan. But with the rise to power of General Nimeiri in the coup of 25 May, 1969, Sudanese-Ugandan relations improved visibly. An end was put to Israeli training of the police force and the intelligence; at the same time Israeli use of northern Uganda to fan the flames of the Sudanese civil war was terminated.

Neither the British nor the Israelis expected the treatment Amin meted out to them in the two years after the coup. The pro-Obote soldiers had run south to

Tanzania and north to Sudan, establishing guerrilla training camps in both places. In return for a promise from Nimeiri to close down the Obote camps in Sudan, Amin maintained the ban against Israeli use of northern Uganda for military purposes. Israel attempted economic blackmail but Amin retaliated by summarily expelling them. Relations with Britain soured as Amin's economic war against the Asian businessmen went into a second stage, this time engulfing British banks, the financiers of Asian merchants and industrialists.

Israel, and along with it Britain, attempted to organize an economic and military boycott of Uganda, but without active American assistance they could do but little. When Britain boycotted Ugandan exports after the Asian expulsion, the Americans refused to follow suit; instead, they bought most of Uganda's coffee crop, over 50% of its net exports. Meanwhile, their efforts to dislodge the Amin regime from within were fruitless for in the aftermath of the Asian expulsion the regime was at the height of its popularity: without the assistance of an organized social force from within, there was little any imperialist power could do short of an invasion. Amin meanwhile astutely exploited intra-imperialist rivalries, not turning to the social imperialists for his arms supplies.

What changed the American position was the Soviet thrust into sub-Saharan Africa with the Angolan civil war. In the following months, American imperialists feverishly strove to recoup their losses. There followed Henry Kissinger's African visit of early May; then in mid-June came the U.S. Secretary of Defence Donald Ruxsfeld; on his heels was the U.S. Ambassdor to the U.N., William Scranton; and finally in July the American Assistant Secretary of Defence, William Schaufele, Jr. According to the *New York Times*, the Defence Secretary was to discuss 'arms aid' to 'meet growing Soviet military influence in Africa'.

With the social imperialists attempting to ride on the crest of liberation struggles in southern Africa, the U.S. was left, on the one hand, to relying on its only firm allies in the region, Zaire and Kenya, and on the other hand, to its old coup-making devices. This fact underlines the political weakness of U.S. imperialism in the region today. If the guerrilla war in the south was to be halted, the U.S. needed the support of what it considered the key state in the region—Tanzania. This past year a flurry of visits by the luminaries of American diplomacy to the Tanzanian capital were part of an attempt to get the regime to accept the American plan to abandon guerrilla war and instead rely on an American-sanctioned invasion to secure 'black rule' in Zimbabwe. Failure to secure acceptance of the plan compelled American imperialism to alter its strategy. The strong internal base of the Tanzanian state power ruled out any successful coup-making. Instead, the U.S. sought a realignment of forces in East Africa in an attempt to isolate the Tanzanian regime regionally and 'destabilize' it. The internal crisis of the Amin regime and its military support by social imperialism qualified it as the immediate target of American imperialism. A successful strike against the Amin regime would achieve two regional goals: isolate Tanzania and undermine Russian influence.

Soon after Kissinger's visit to Nairobi, there followed a series of decisions by the Kenyan regime accelarating the break up of the East African Community. On July 4, the Kenyan regime put an embargo on the supply of oil to Uganda. The Kenya press openly encouraged any and all forces in Uganda to seize the opportunity and dislodge Amin. Meanwhile, at a press conference in Philadelphia attended by the former U.S. Ambassador to Uganda and the Israeli consul, there was announced the formation of the so-called Popular Front for the liberation of Uganda.

Given the blatant imperialist sponsorship of this formation, its announcement was probably a cover for American activities nearer to Uganda. As the American – orchestrated crisis in Uganda's foreign relations intensified internal political contradictions, Amin moved to ruthlessly crush any sign of opposition at home.

ROLE OF THE STUDENTS

In the history of revolutions, students have often acted as the catalysts of a movement. On the one hand, having no articulate class interests, on the other, threatened by unemployment and an adverse economic situation once they complete their studies, the radicalization of student action is rapid. Its political significance, however, is defined by the demands they advance and the classes with which they objectively ally. The demands put forth by the Makerere students, whose social origin is principally the urban petty bourgeoisie and the commodity-producing peasantry, reflected the democratic demands of the petty bourgeoisie. The character of its action during the Amin regime underlines the duality of what has been basically a democractic movement: spontaneous but courageous, incapable of sustaining action but nonetheless capable of igniting a spark.

The student struggle unfolded very soon after the 1971 coup. In 1972, both the Makerere Student's Guild and the National Union of Student Organizations (N.U.S.O.) pointed out that the Asian expulsion amounted to no more than a change of intermediaries in imperialist exploitation of the neo-colony. Amin's response was an attempt to intimidate and subordinate the student leadership. Beginning in 1974, student organizations voluntarily dissolved themselves and the leadership went underground. Students boycotted officially called elections and refused to elect a leadership which once exposed, would become the target of official terror.

The University student's struggle assumed a larger significance early this year. Following the disappearance of a Kenyan student at the Makerere campus in February, there was a massive student demonstration which spilled over from the university grounds to the city centre. Large numbers of city workers and petty bourgeois joined the students. Amin was either unable, or failed, to use the army to smash this popular outburst against official terror. For the first time it was publicly demonstrated that the regime could be defied and successfully at that.

Ever since those February days, Amin has waited to deal a firm blow to the students. In July, the army issued its not-so-veiled threat about 'teaching the people of Uganda a lesson' if the people did not 'behave'. After the demonstration of August 3, Major-General Mustafa, the army chief-of-staff, announced at the Makerere campus that 'the army will finish off the students if they don't keep quiet. In that Tuesday demonstration the regime found the occasion it had been waiting for to unleash a savage terror against the students.

WHO IS THE ENEMY?

With the increasing unpopularity of the Amin regime among all sectors of Ugandan society, with all classes acutely feeling the need for change, various programmes have been advanced before the people. As the crisis intensifies and different political tendencies begin to mature, the question is posed: who is the enemy?

There are today three clear responses to this question – the bourgeois, the petty bourgeois and the proletarian. For the bourgeoisie – various imperialist bourgeoisies, the nascent commercial bourgeoisie in Uganda and its political representatives within the petty bourgeoisie – the problem is simply an individual, Amin. This bourgeois conception overlooks both the internal intermediaries of imperialist exploitation and the alliances of this class with specific imperialist bourgeoisies. Its consequence is to leave the entire system of oppression and exploitation intact. Bourgeois ideology thus safeguards its own interests.

For the democratic petty bourgeoisie the enemy lies principally outside Uganda. This simplicity has the virtue of seeing Amin and the 'group' visibly around him as just the agents of external forces, in some cases vaguely defined as 'imperialism', in others equally vaguely as the 'international bourgeoisie'. Since the ruling class is outside Uganda, the enemy internally is simply those individuals who occupy visibly important positions in the state power, and not any class with its own concrete interests. Thus, anti-imperialist action need only dislodge this group from its prominent positions. Meanwhile, the internal class in whose interest the state objectively functions is left intact. The 'revolutionary strategy' of the democratic petty bourgeoisie turns out to be no more than a call for a coup d'etat. While its anti-imperialism is quite real, if the democratic petty bourgeoisie assumes leadership of the movement, it objectively shelters the ruling class in the camp of the people, disarming the revolutionary forces ideologically and thus organizationally.

Who, then, is the enemy in Uganda? Proletarian analysis must be concrete. The existence of a military dictatorship in Uganda bears testimony to the weakness of classes both for and against Amin. We have seen that the Asian expulsion created conditions for the emergence of a commercial bourgeoisie from both the upper stratum of the trading petty bourgeoisie and sections of the army officer corps. Amin's rule objectively represented the interests of this nascent commercial bourgeoisie. The period since 1972 has seen a relative consolidation of this class. The contradiction today, between the state power and the class economically dominant internally (the nascent commercial bourgeoisie) is necessarily a momentary contradiction. It must be resolved with the regime once again firmly anchored to the interests of the commercial bourgeoisie, either through a renegotiated relation between the two, or more likely, through the replacement of Amin.

The working class position understands that the enemy inside Uganda is not simply Amin but this nascent commercial bourgeoisie, hitherto the class base of the state power. At the same time, different factions of this class, as they seem to resolve the present crisis without any fundamental change in the character of the state power, buttress their position through alliances with particular imperialism. Imperialism continues to oppress the people of Uganda, but indirectly.

To ignore the imperialist alignments of the commercial bourgeoisie is bourgeois ideology; to abstract from the internal class struggle is populism. The working class can only draw a dialectical relation between the class that is the objective base of the state power in Uganda and its changing alliances with different imperialist bourgeoisies outside. So long as a specific imperialism does not physically invade Uganda, as in the case of Vietnam and Cambodia, the class struggle remains principally internal. The field of battle remains inside Uganda. What cannot be forgotten is that it is not an individual, nor a group, but class which will defend the Ugandan state power in the oncoming struggle.

The proletariat thus demarcates its ideology very clearly from that of the democratic petty bourgeoisie. The enemy of the Ugandan revolution, at the present stage of the struggle, are both imperialism and the internal ruling class. From this follow its tasks, both national (to overthrow imperialist exploitation) and democratic (to overthrow the rule of internal reactionary forces). The leading force of this revolution, the new democratic revolution, is the proletariat, while its motive forces also include the peasantry and the democratic petty bourgeoisie.

13

A REPLY TO MAMDANI AND BHAGAT

D. Wadada Nabudere

We have received and read your comments on my manuscript with interest.

Looking at your comments on Shivji's book on the issue of imperialism in analysing classes, we were a bit encouraged that some progress was being made on this general question of imperialism. Indeed we felt that our work on the manuscript was paying dividends. Unfortunately your criticism of Shivji is inadequate and in our view comes too late. We are therefore unable to accept it as a genuine and principled criticism. As for Mamdani, the whole of his thesis on Uganda is Shivjist and for Bhagat, his defence of Shivji's thesis hitherto has been total. For Mamdani to repudiate Shivji he must therefore first repudiate himself. Both their positions remain the same in spite of the 'criticism'. No wonder that after your criticism of Shivji, which in many places shows that he fails to comprehend his task, you conclude: 'Nevertheless we consider the book a step forward representing a stage in the development of Marxist-Leninist thought in our countries. . . .'

This is because, although you disagree in form, you are basically in agreement in substance.

We shall have occasion in the near future to say something on Mamdani's book. We have already written a critique of Shivji's book, copies of which have already been given to you. Furthermore Mamdani's insistence that our critique of Shivji be restricted is a clear betrayal of his effort to conceal fundamental errors of theory and ideology which are already widely disseminated in book form, a fact to which Mamdani himself has lent active support in recommending the book to the whole world over the BBC without indicating in any serious way the errors contained in it.

Coming to your comments on my manuscript we find that the criticisms are only "left" in form but right in content. We find the use of Chinese comrades' references to support your positions unacceptable. They exhibit a certain amount of petty-bourgeois dogmatism and stereotyped analysis. This kind of prostitution is tantamount to opportunism of the highest order. We shall show that the references to the Chinese comrades' texts do not in fact support your criticisms. Now we turn to your specific comments.

1. IMPERIALISM AND CONTRADICTIONS

One important fact to note about your comments is the glaring effort on your part to find every fault with the manuscript. In the end you fail, not because there are no faults, but because either you were pressured by the desire to criticize and looked for what struck you as erroneous and rushed to criticize it, or you read the manuscript but did not study it with sufficient sympathy or care to understand it. This is revealed by the first accusation you make that I 'claim to analyse imperialism in its totality'. To support this accusation, you hang on the title and the preface. There is nothing in these two to support you. Anybody reading the manuscript as a whole will not fail to see its scope and its purpose. Indeed, beginning with the first sentence in the introduction up to the last chapter, there can be no doubt that my purpose is to defend Lenin's thesis, *Imperialism, the Highest Stage of Capitalism*, and to try in a theoretical manner to connect it with Marx's *Capital*, a task I try to do in Part Two and Part Three of the manuscript. Incidentally, in conformity with the eclecticism which is revealed so glaringly in your comments, you recognize this (on the other hand!) when you state:

> The strength of the manuscript, particularly the relation it underlines between Marx's analysis of *Capital* and Lenin's theory of *Imperialism*, we consider to be a scientific contribution to the development of Marxist-Leninist ideology in our part of the world.

Thank you! We never undertook to do nor have we claimed to have done any more than that.

You can see, therefore, that your criticisms are drawn from outside the manuscript and you try to join issue with us on theses we have not advanced. This comes out glaringly when you accuse that the main 'thrust' of the manuscript has been to 'abstract from all contradictions except that of capital and labour' on the ground that we 'absolutize' the concept of centralization of capital 'arriving at a concept of "world finance capital" emphasizing its unity in a one-sided manner. You accuse us also of suggesting 'ascendancy of U.S. imperialism' in the post-war period, and of stating that the World Bank is currently under the control of the Rockefeller-Chase-Manhattan-Standard Oil Group. Because of these alleged faults, you assert that the manuscript 'comes perilously close to taking the stand of ultra-imperialism' of Kautsky. In disproof of these 'faults' in the manuscript you then proceed to show that:

> The establishment of U.S. hegemony over European and Japanese capital is in fact only one aspect of the process; the other and the central aspect is the intensifying contradiction within the camp of American imperialism since the Second World War.

You go on – quite unnecessarily – to seek the support of the *Proposal Concerning the General Line of the International Communist Movement* from the Communist Party of China, which state, in short, that to *deny* these contradictions is to be erroneous. Having gone to all this trouble, you would be expected to quote a passage in the manuscript where we deny the existence of this contradiction, or at least to show in any way, apart from mere assertion, that we do not deal with the question. Any casual reading of Part Four of the manuscript will reveal that this criticism has no foundation.

A. Contradiction within the Imperialist Bourgeoisie

Now coming to the substance of your accusations: do we 'abstract' centralization of the capital into a 'World Finance Capital'? No, we do not. We do not even create it. It is a reality which Lenin analyses. World finance capital is the total finance capital of the total financial oligarchies in their unity aimed at exploiting the total working class of the entire world under their hegemony. Does this unity in finance capital deny contradictions among the financial oligarchies? No, it does not. The manuscript is clear on this. The manuscript takes a whole Part Three to survey the historical roots of the rivalries between the imperialist powers resulting in the two imperialist World Wars. It points out that the U.S., which emerges solid after the war, soon carries out in the post-Second World War period, a redivision of the world under its hegemony. We go further to show the opposition of Europe and Japan to the multilateral strategy under U.S. hegemony resulting in rivalry;

wherein Europe decides to set up a common market; and we argue that this market was aimed against the working class in Europe and the workers and peasants of the Third World. Towards the end of Chapter XVI, we state:

> This central contradiction of imperialism cannot be resolved but table resolutions to be 'united'. Hence war is still the central instrument of imperialism. Capitalist monopoly groups in the U.S. and in Europe still continue to compete for markets and outlets for capital exports leading to 'vertical cohesion and division of labour' with the Third World, as we shall see. The transnational corporation cannot remove this basic contradiction. So long as this struggle for markets and raw materials continues (which it must), wars among imperialist states are inevitable although these may, due to the existence of the socialist system, be eased.

You can see that your criticism on this point is baseless and not worthy of any debate. You even query the fact that the World Bank is currently under control of the U.S. financial oligarchy, without even attempting to challenge our assertion of this effectively. You suggest that I come 'perilously' close to Kautsky without making the slightest attempt to quote Lenin correctly. You quote him from a source where he doesn't even discuss the issue. You do not quote him where he discusses the issue of Kautsky's attempt to treat imperialism in his booklet on the same subject. If you had done this, you would have found that Lenin, in refuting Kautsky's thesis on imperialism, was also refuting all obscurantists who attempt to separate the political from the economic. This you try to do when you eclectically require us to bear in mind the 'political dimension', and when you remind us that Lenin postulated that 'politics doesn't obediently follow economics' as if we had tried to do that anywhere in the manuscript.

In his definition of imperialism, Kautsky had said:

> Imperialism is a product of highly developed industrial capitalism. It consists in the striving of every industrial capitalist nation to bring under its control or annex all large areas of agrarian territory, irrespective of what nations inhabit it.

In repudiating this definition, Lenin said it is of no use at all because it one-sidely, i.e., arbitrarily, singles out only the national question (p. 87). He continues:

> The essence of the matter is that Kautshy detaches the politics of imperialism from its economics, speaks of annexation as being policy 'preferred' by finance capital, and opposes to it another bourgeois policy which, he alleges, is possible on this very same basis of finance capital. (p. 89).

You will see, therefore, that your attempt to identify your dualist views with those of Lenin does not support, but on the contrary refutes, your case. We have already shown that the manuscript deals with contradictions among monopolies. Your comparing out thesis with Kautsky is therefore based on your lack of understanding of this question. Lenin also pointed out that by bringing out the question of 'annexation of agrarian countries by industries countries' as an imperialist 'policy', the 'role of merchant capital is put in the forefront'; and the 'predominance of the financier over the merchant is over-shadowed'. (p. 89). This, as we shall show in our criticism of your forthcoming book on Uganda, is the very thing you try to do when you talk of 'Indian merchant capital', dominating production.

You further accuse us of obscuring the contradiction within the bourgeoisie. Again, you do not understand the manuscript and, as we have said, you do not even bother to refer to Part Three where the rise of the financial oligarchy is treated historically. If you had done so, you would have found that you have no ground for the complaint and there would have been no need for you to quote Chairman Mao Tse-tung *On Contradictions* on this issue. Indeed, in the only long passage you quote from the manuscript, you can see that a distinction is drawn between the 'national bourgeoisie' (who are the non-monopolist bourgeoisie as opposed to the petty-bourgeoisie) and the financial oligarchy. Perhaps you still find it difficult to accept this as a distinction solely because we don't use the word 'non-monopoly bourgeoisie' as it appears in Mao Tse-tung. In our entire analysis, we put emphasis on the financial oligarchy since this is the bourgeoisie involved directly in imperialism. We had no cause to enquire into Watergates and debates over EEC entry since we were not analysing this level of the contradiction. We were examining a major movement and even then there could be no confusion from the manuscript as to what is meant by the financial oligarchy.

B. Contradictions Between the Superpowers and the Second World and Relationship with Third World

You accuse us of failing to analyse contradictions between the superpowers and the 'Second World', since the <u>intermediate</u> zones are also 'oppressed' by the superpowers. In typical one-sidedness, you absolutize this 'oppression' to the point of seeing no unity between this 'Second World' and the superpowers, although you say they also 'partake' in the imperialist exploitation of the Third World. We have already shown that a contradiction exists between monopolies, whether intermediate or otherwise, but this contradiction is over who should have the upper hand in exploiting labour both in the 'Second World' and the Third World. This contradiction, generally non-antagonistic as it is within the same class – the bourgeoisie – for a greater share of the oppressed Third World, at time breaks out in open war. You state that if we do not 'grasp' this contradiction we cannot understand the formation of Euratom, Gaullism, etc. But we have shown that by grasping the 'fundamental contradiction' among imperialist countries (do not forget the *General Line*), we have also grasped the contradiction between the superpowers, among imperialist countries and among monopoly capitalist groups. All these stem from this fundamental contradiction. That is why we earlier explained the rise of the EEC as expressing this fundamental contradiction.

You also say that the manuscript one-sidedly 'concludes that the (Lome) Convention is a victory for monopolies of the U.S., and Japan'. Here you are seen unable to comprehend the paragraph from which you bring out only six words! You also fail to comprehend what we say in this paragraph because you do not consider the <u>historical</u> background to the Lome Convention, which can only be understood if the Yaounde Conventions, the Lagos Agreement and the Arusha Agreement, as well as a host of others between EEC and Third World countries, are analysed. If this analysis were made, one finds that the African, Caribbean and Pacific (ACP) countries fought tooth-and-nail to remove the preferential treatment in their countries formerly given to the EEC countries alone. They insisted that their markets should be open to other countries, which in present-day conditions could only mean U.S. and Japanese monopolies since, as we all know, trade among the 53 ACP states is almost non-existent. The same is true of the trade with the socialist countries. In the short term it therefore meant open door neo-colonialism. In the long term, with the socialist world, such a policy should be defended. This goes also for the so-called rights of establishment. We refer to the pressure by U.S. imperialism, in which Nixon insisted that Europe must not insist on 'reverse preferences' in her relations with ACP countries. It is only in this connection that we state that the multilateralizing of neo-colonialism in the Lome Convention was a victory by U.S. and Japanese monopolies, since the Convention allowed them the same privileges in the ACP states.

> The new convention, while purporting to do away with 'reverse preferences' by which products of the European monopolies ceased to receive 'duty-free entry' in return for so-called 'markets' for products of the [then] 46 ACP states, merely multilateralised the neo-colonial ties to other monopolies of the U.S. and Japan. Whereas the old Convention excludes these two imperialist groups, the new Convention opens up to them the same advantages and privileges the European [monopolies] enjoyed in these neo-colonial countries. Thus the exploitation of the Third World continues unabated under conditions of multilateral imperialism [p. 0]

You conclude that this signified a 'limited victory for the Third World' without showing how. You quote the *Peking Review* without understanding the context in which the *Peking Review* piece is written and to whom it is addressed, which betrays, as we already said, an opportunistic recourse to the Chinese comrades' texts. Whereas it is true that the superpowers in their struggles over the other imperialist countries oppress them, we cannot accept your interpretation of this contradiction to imply that the competitive struggles by all monopoly groups, including those of the Second World over Third World territories, are a sign of 'oppression' by the superpowers of the Second World imperialist powers. To accept this interpretation is to concede and accept the oppression of Second World imperialist powers over the Third World which is utterly dangerous and unprincipled; yet that is what is implied by talk of Lome as a 'limited victory' for the Third World in this context.

It does not mean that the struggles of Third World countries for control over their resources are not progressive and therefore not to be supported by the proletariat. The proletariat must view this step as a struggle for deepening the contradiction between imperialism and the oppressed peoples in the Third World. These struggles also reveal the contradiction between the 'national bourgeoisie' and petty-bourgeoisie with the financial oligarchy, which is the reflection of the objective dominaton of finance capital over the national bourgeoisie, limiting the area in which they can compete. So the proletariat has the greatest interest in deepening the contradiction between the oppressed peoples and imperialism, in order to be able to popularize and generalise its case against imperialism on a broader front. This is the context in which the *Peking Review* piece on the Lome Convention is written and also the context which the struggle against the superpowers is raised. You will see that our position on the 'New Economic Order' and on nationalizations holds this broad position.

In our view, you are unable to comprehend the contradictions leading to nationalisation measures in Third World countries because of your eclecticism. Although you point out that the significance of these measures 'must be grasped both economically and politically', you yourselves take a rather one-sided view of these measures. You accuse us of attempting 'only an economic analysis' and of 'belittling' them (the measures) as simply "a nuisance to imperialism". Characterising commodity producer organisations culminating in the call for a 'New Economic Order' as falling within price struggles, and not going to the root of production relations, you conclude, 'Nevertheless, these are anti-imperialist struggles and as such objectively form part of the world socialist revolution, as Mao Tse-tung pointed out in *New Democracy*'. This is clearly a one-sided treatment of the question of nationalisations and the struggle for the 'New Economic Order', 'perilously close', to use your catchword, to asserting a revisionist non-capitalist road. You misuse Comrade Mao Tse-tung's authority on this question because he was describing the character of the two democratic revolutions – the old and the new. He was no where discussing nationalisations and the "New Economic Order" in *New Democracy*. Indeed, you contradict yourselves where, in a similar comment on Shivji's book, you state one-sidedly:

> That property under concrete historical circumstances assumes another legal form, in this case a public form, should not blind Marxist-Leninists to the fact that it still remains private (class) property.

Here you are putting forward 'only an economic analysis', which you accuse us of doing! You have not successfully shown that the manuscript bears these faults, but your two criticisms exhibited them. "You cannot have it both ways". If you had looked at the manuscript carefully, you would have seen that we express a political appreciation of this form of struggle in spite of the fact that the change in legal form does not change the property relations; this led us to conclude that nationalizations and the struggle for a New Economic Order were a nuisance to imperialism, since the property remained basically bourgeois property. The manuscript nevertheless acknowledges these measure to be 'important developments' and further points out that 'whilst one must not underestimate the long-run implications of this contradiction between the peoples of the neo-world and imperialism', these struggles 'remain within the sphere of bargaining for higher prices' (pp.). The manuscript concludes on this point:

> Here we see that a neo-colony under these conditions can only get out of this octopus-like exploitative production relations by revolt. No amount of policy manipulation outside the class struggle can bring about the desired end. A revolt against imperialism becomes the only basis for the national democratic revolution.

This analysis, in our opinion, cannot fairly be criticized as being only 'economic analysis' and as being one-sided. The *Peking Review* article on which you relied for your Lome Convention criticism takes this broad view of these Conventions and the struggle for New Economic Order when it warns:

> The signing of the Lome Convention is a victory for the Third World. However, one must see that to thoroughly remould the old, extremely unequal international economic relations requires a protracted and arduous struggle ... So long as they persist in struggle, strengthen unity and unite with all forces that can be united with, the Third World Countries and their peoples are bound to win new and continuous victories' (p. 19).

This having regard to the audience for which it was intended, correctly puts the proletarian position to the 'national' and petty bourgeoisie of these countries – a line which the manuscript, as we have shown above, also takes on this issue.

Before concluding, we refer to a passage in your conclusion where the four fundamental contradictions as laid down in the *General Line* are outlined. You then state that, 'while all these fundamental contradictions exist today, the *principal* contradiction is that between the oppressed nations and imperialism'.

The above statement is then immediately followed by a purportedly supporting reference from another part of the *General Line*, wherein it is pointed out that 'the various types of contradictions in the contemporary world are concentrated' in the Third World, the most vulnerable areas under imperialist rule and the storm centres of world revolution dealing direct blows to imperialism'. The reader is given the impression that the *General Line* singles out this particular contradiction as the *principal* one. This is not the case and is very misleading on you part. In fact the *General Line* stops one from singling out any of these contradictions from the others. It states:

> These contradictions and the struggles to which they give rise are interrelated and influence each other. Nobody can obliterate any of these fundamental contradictions or subjectively substitute one for all the rest.

Quoting this passage on the very page where you single out one of the contradictions to be the *principal* one thus betrays a shallow understanding of the *General Line*, committing an offence against it, and also places you in one of the "deviationist" categories that you outline, namely, that of 'populist Third Worldists'. Thus although the *General Line* sees the countries of Asia, Africa and Latin America as 'storm centres', and points out that the outcome of the international proletarian revolution 'hinges on the outcome' of these struggles, it is at the same time careful to point out that:

> The national democratic revolutionary movement in these areas and the international socialist revolutionary movement are two great historical currents of our time. The national democratic revolution in these areas is an important component of the contemporary proletarian world revolution. (p. 13)

Our manuscript puts this same line:

> Thus in our conclusion the struggle against imperialism must be based on the correct strategy of the working class in the imperialist countries . . . In the colonial, semi-colonial and neo-colonial countries, a two-phased struggle historically offers the best chance of success. In this way the struggles of the working classes in the imperialist centre and the colonial, semi-colonial hinterland support one another. On this basis, the end of imperialism is assured and not otherwise.

Hence your accusation that the manuscript takes a 'Trotskyist line' which 'one-sidedly emphasizes the contradiction between capital and labour and substitutes it for the rest' is totally groundless and an out-and-out opportunistic slander. Your assertion that the conclusion in the manuscript regarding the necessity for a people's democratic revolution, correct as it is, 'doesn't follow from the argument in the manuscript' is therefore hollow. You do not comprehend the method of analysis adopted in the manuscript and, more importantly, you have not grasped Marx's laws of motion of capitalism. It is precisely because of this that you stick to the populist theory of 'unequal exchange', as we shall soon demonstrate.

2. NEW DEMOCRATIC REVOLUTION, CLASSES AND THE NEO-COLONY

Most of your criticisms on the new democratic revolution, classes, in the neo-colony and the politics of struggle are centred around one pivotal point: *national capital* and its contradiction with finance capital. You do not indicate the character of this contradiction. We begin from the proposition that finance capital dominates the petty bourgeoisie and exploits the working class and peasantry in the neo-colony and that because of this, there exists a <u>fundamental</u> antagonistic contradiction between imperialism (the rule of finance capital) and the oppressed <u>people</u> in the neo-colony. the contradiction between the petty-bourgeoisie (who have a portion of the finance capital) and the financial oligarchy is a basically non-antagonistic contradiction within the bourgeois class. Finance capital has fundamental and antagonistic contradiction with the neo-colony because it exploits the worker and the peasant there. Through exports of capital, it negates the development of a national capital and hence makes it impossible for the society in the neo-colony to be transformed. In the era of finance capital, this transformation of society is impossible under capitalism, hence Chairman Mao Tse-tung's correct characterization of the first phase of proletarian-led revolutions in colonies and semi-colonies after 1917 as 'New Democratic', leading not to capitalist development but to socialist reconstruction and transformation of society.

A. Unequal Exchange

Your wrong understanding of this contradiction between imperialism and the people leads you, as we have already indicated, to adopt a populist position on 'unequal exchange'. Our analysis adopts the correct position of Marx in *Capital* and Lenin on *Imperialism* which sees the major movement in capitalism as being determined by two antagonistic poles – labour and capital – on the basis of which unity in production is achieved in conditions of struggle between opposites. The general laws of capitalist development are worked out on this scientific basis which reflects reality. In other words, Marx demonstrates that with the rise of capital, a movement is established whereby all production is increasingly turned into commodity production and subjecting all labour – whether that of the worker or the peasant – to the exploitation of capital. It is within this framework that we analyse and demonstrate the correctness of Lenin's thesis which is based on Marx's analysis of capitalism. Thus colonial countries which were pre-capitalist in their social formation are brought increasingly under the exploitation of capital. In this connection Marx has pointed out:

> As capitalist production develops, it has a disintegrating, resolvent effect on all older forms of production, which, designed mostly to meet the direct needs of the producer, transform only the excess produced into commodities. Capitalist production makes the sale of products the main interest, at first apparently without affecting the mode of production itself. Such was for instance the first effect of capitalist world commerce on such nations as the Chinese, Indians, Arabs, etc. But, secondly, wherever it takes root capitalist production destroys all forms of commodity production which are based either on the self-employment of the producers, or merely on the sale of the excess product as commodities. Capitalist production first makes the production of commodities general and then, by degrees, transforms all commodity production into capitalist commodity production (*Capital*, Vol. II, p. 36)

The accusation you make that the manuscript 'confines itself to the exploitation of the worker but has not a word to say about the peasants exploitation's is populist and baseless. You do not understand Marx's use of the concept 'exploitation'. It is a scientific concept which is used solely in connection with the capital-labour relation. That is why he talks of the 'plunder, spoilation and entombment of aboriginal peoples' by merchant capital. He talks of 'exploitation' of labour by industrial capital. Your own use in this case of the word 'exploitation' is therefore, in this case, moralistic. Furthermore, your accusation is reminiscent of Luxemburg's slanders against Marx when, raising the same issue in a different context, she stated:

> As soon as he [Marx] comes to analyse the capitalist process of production

and circulation, he affirms the universal and exclusive domination of capitalist production.

Yet, as we have seen, capitalism in its full maturity also depends in all respects on non-capitalist strata and social organisations existing side-by-side with it. (*Accumulation of Capital*, p. 365)

As we demonstrated in the manuscript, Luxemburg did not comprehend Marx's scientific method and her theorizing on this issue gives fuel to most of today's neo-Trotskyist concepts of "unequal exchange" to which you subscribe.

Peasant exploitation by capital is not an issue for mystification. Marx and Engels were at pains to show how capital infiltrates, corrodes and brings to heel small-scale peasant production. in the *Peasant Question in France and Germany* and in the *Eighteenth Brumaire*, they unravelled this problem. In the *Peasant Question*, Engels points out its strategic importance to the proletarian struggle. He shows how by stages the peasant in France lost all the independence that he had before the rule of capital and concludes:

This small peasant, just like the small handicraftsman, is therefore a toiler who differs from the modern proletariat in what he still possesses his instruments of labour; hence a survival of a past mode of production . . . [Whereas in the past his unit of production was self-sufficient] capitalist production put an end to this by its money economy and large-scale industry.

Taxes, crop failures, divisions of inheritance and litigations drive one peasant after another into the arms of the usurer; their indebtedness becomes more and more general and steadily increases in amount in each case – in brief our small peasant, like every other survival of past mode of production, is hopelessly doomed. He is a future proletarian . . . The self-supporting small peasant is neither in the safe possession of his tiny patch of land nor is he free. He as well as his house, his farmstead and his few fields belong to the usurers. [*Selected Works*, Vol. 3 pp. 459–69]

Marx, in *Eighteenth Brumaire*, similarly points to this fact. He observes that smallholding property in Europe has been radically altered and this changed the relation of the peasant to the other classes. Its landmarks 'formed the natural fortifications of the bourgeoisie against any surprise attack on the part of its overlords'. He continues:

But in the course of the nineteenth century the feudal lords were replaced by urban usurers; the feudal obligation that went with the land was replaced by the mortgage, aristocratic landed property was replaced by bourgeois capital. The small holding of the peasant is now only the pretext that allows the capitalist to draw profits, interest and rent from the soil, while leaving it to the tiller of the soil himself to see how he can extract his wages. Smallholding property, in this enslavement by capital to which its development inevitably pushes forward, has transformed the mass of the French nation into troglodytes. (*Selected Works*, Vol. 1, p. 481)

In most of our countries, although the historical background is not the same, we observe that colonialism turns the peasant away from self-employment to commodity production for the market by the infiltration of the money economy. First by the tax, then by indebtedness that increases with each passing day, to the usurer and the village trader. These force him to produce capitalist commodities – and he cannot do this without putting aside part of the working day (labour power) for capitalist commodity production, so that although his smallholding is pre-capitalist in *form*, it is merely a shell which is highly corroded by capital. It is only pre-capitalist in name. And the so-called undervalued price of product is no more than a wage paid for his labour. He is exploited by capital in this manner. Regardless as to whether you see the peasant smallholding as 'a small capitalist enterprise', or as a class of labourers, the account of his unit – to the extent that the peasant engages directly in the labourprocess – will have to allocate him a wage. Whether you call this wage a profit through sale is of no consequence, for a portion of it must go to the reproduction of his labour-power which is consumed in the process of his being directly engaged in production. Our Third World peasant engaged in commodity production is therefore 'pre-capitalist' in form only. He is no longer self-employed. But although he is exploited by capital, he is not a proletariat. He remains scattered, and is tied to his piece of land 'by the deep rooted sense of property'. (Engels, op. cit., p. 460) But this is merely his illusion in the *First Outline – The Commune* which Marx refers to as a 'delusion'. 'What separates the peasant from the proletariat is, therefore, no longer his real interest but his delusive prejudice.' (p. 160)

Capital, in its infiltration of peasant production, seeks *surplus-value* and nothing else and, taking advantage of subsistence production for part of the working-day, the financial oligarchy pays a price for the peasant's products (nay, a wage) consistent with his subsistence needs. This is how a capital-labour relation exists at this level of articulation of the labour process. You illustrate confusion on this issue by talking of 'unequal exchange' explaining the 'exploitation of the petty commodity producer... not of the worker' and the exploitation of 'non-prletarian producers and not of countries.' This statement remains a mere assertion unless you grapple with the issue of exploitation of the peasant as above presented. Failure to do so means taking the peasant's illusion and delusion to be the fact!

You try to support your assertion about the nature of the unequal exchange with a *Peking Review* quote, the quote does not support what you are asserting. It talks of 'the present price relationships between primary products and finished goods in the international market', which, as you know, is between countries, for all primary producers in the world market are peasant producers. Here again the Chinese comrades' texts have been used opportunistically.

One further inference which follows from your concept of 'unequal exchange' is that all peasant production is owner-producer enterprise. You must surely know that capitalist production, wherever introduced on land, sets in motion a great differentiation among peasants, so that there are rich, middle and poor peasants. When a rich peasant employs a poor peasant, or a rural proletarian, he pays him a wage. There is nothing 'pre-capitalist' about this. This is a capital-labour relation within the peasantry. In producer-owner production the rule of capital is even more pronounced, since these producer-owners are increasingly thrown into the proletariat ranks. Your conclusion that the manuscript has 'not a word to say of peasants exploitation' is therefore unfounded, because the capital-labour relation would still apply. This is why Marx's analysis has stood the crude attacks of Luxemburg, who wanted to examine the capitalist-peasant relation as 'non-capitalist' which you unconsciously also suggest in your criticism. In a future work, in which accumulation process under finance capital will be demonstrated, we shall go deeper into this question; but we consider our analysis on this issue in the manuscript as adequate to repudiate the Emmanuel-Amin thesis. Your own thesis is completely in line with Luxemburg's which has been shown to be anti-Marxist.

B. Classes and the 'Semi-Colony'

We do not consider that your discussion of class relations which contains dogmas that could only be entertained by un-Marxist-Leninists follows from our analysis. To Marxist-Leninists the question of classes is a concrete question.

Although classes may be mentioned in their general relations in a major movement like imperialism, such treatment can only be meaningfully handled in a concrete way. Your dogmatic position is shown by such formulations as 'we must distinguish different sections – comprador and national'. The question is: where? when? A scientific formulation cannot be put in this dogmatic manner. The existence of a national bourgeoisie', comprador bourgeoisie or 'comprador industrial bourgeoisie' (sic) is not a general question (with which we were concerned) but a concrete question for a concrete situation. You yourselves remind us of this principle but then forget it as soon as it is stated.

It seems to us that you go against the Leninist principle of studying each situation concretely, by engaging in dogmatic generalities about classes. You commit the error which the Chinese comrades do not, and as Marxist-Leninists could not even attempt to suggest – of generalising the Chinese experience. You even suggest that our countries are 'semi-colonies', apparently because it is so suggested by Chairman Mao Tse-tung on *Contradictions*. This is incorrect. Chairman Mao Tse-tung here was referring to semi-colonies 'such as China' and in his *Chinese Revolution and the Chinese Communist Party*, in Chapter I where he treats the colonial, semi-colonial and semi-feudal society of China, he gives concrete periods, phases and characteristics of these questions and states at what periods a 'flabby national bourgeoisie' arose. His targets, motive forces and the character of the revolution are worked out on the basis of those concrete studies. A special feature of the semi-colony is that its relationship with the imperialists is based not on total occupation and colonisation, but on unequal treaties referred to in international law as capitulationist treaties. These treaties were signed with countries in which imperialist powers collectively wanted an open-door policy, allowing all monopolies free entry into these areas. Turkey, China and to some extent Leopold's Congo were such areas. In China the presence of the imperialist countries was established as spheres of influence at ports like Canton and Shanghai. Thus a basis was established for collaboration between the feudal ruling class in the hinterland and the financial oligarchy represented at the ports. In these circumstances, agents for monopolies at these ports were a necessary element of imperialist domination of China. The term 'comprador' originally meant a 'Chinese agent of a foreign business area at Canton' and represented this historic stage.

In a colony – particularly those which arose after 1880 – on the other hand, the imperialists established a colonial state structure to administer and protect the property interests (finance capital) of monopolies. Monopoly enterprises were set up and individual capitalists found their room within this arrangement. A comprador bourgeoisie therefore cannot strictly arise in the colony since monopolies have a free hand in the colony and are directly represented by companies and banks. Although one may speak of a comprador petty-bourgeoisie in the neo-colony in a very general way, one has to bear in mind these concrete historical facts.

Our views about a 'national bourgeisie' are quite clear. A 'national bourgeoisie' in India, Brazil, Egypt, etc. cannot be compared to a national bourgeoisie in, say, France. It is not that we do not recognise that imperialism, within limits established by it and within conditions prevailing internally in the colony, may allow a certain amount of growth. Indeed, the manuscript does recognise this (p. 505). But a national bourgeoisie cannot exist on mere 'aspirations', as you state, nor can their existence on the basis of 'national resources and national market' be clearly demarcated. The contradiction between the 'national bourgeoisie' and petty bourgeoisie lies in the domination by finance capital of production and distribution in the neo-colony by means of the centralisation and concentration of production and of the credit-system on a global scale and in each country; not on the assumed existence of 'national capital' which is (again assumed) in contradiction with finance capital. Our thesis on this question is based on Lenin's treatments of *Imperialism* and the *National Question*, and we would only emphasize that each country requires a concrete analysis in order to identify the actual existing classes on the basis of revolutionary struggle. that is why we refrain from laying down 'general principles', as you demand by which, given the context of the manuscript, can only mean the laying down of dogmatic positions. Rather than attempt to lay down general principles even in respect of the imperialist countries, apart from stating an obvious fact, we preferred to give concrete historical experiences of China and Vietnam and, on the basis of these, put forward the view that a two-phased struggle 'historically offers the best chance of success'. (p.). We leave it to the pure theorists to engage in abstractions of a general nature.

On the question of the petty-bourgeoisie, you again take a one-sided view of this class. Not all of them engage in the labour process as alleged. You one-sidedly see them as part of the 'revolutionary masses' and even seek the support of Lenin on this issue without quoting the source. We challenge you to indicate where he gives such a one-sided, unqualified view of this class. The Marxist-Leninist position takes a scientific view of this class. The *Manifesto* groups under this class – which it calls "the lower middle class" – small manufacturers, shopkeepers, artisans and peasants. Although it recognises their struggles against the bourgeoisie, it nevertheless sees them not wholly as a revolutionary class: "They are therefore not revolutionary, but conservative. Nay more, they are reactionary, for they try to roll back the wheel of history." (p. 19)

This class must not be seen in a static manner. It evolves each passing day and, with the rise of monopoly capitalism, gets more numbers added to it from upper ranks, while some of its own numbers are pushed to proletarian ranks. That is why we have to view them in motion, as they exist concretely, while finance capital reproduces itself globally. Marx, in his critique of Proudhon, clearly points to the vacillating nature of this class. In periods of prosperity, they are with the bourgeoisie and fight the proletariat; in periods of crisis, they increasingly join the proletarian ranks and support its struggles. They are unreliable. Without a proletarian leadership, even in periods of crisis, they cannot put up a fight against the bourgeoisie as Yash Tandon correctly points out in his commentary.

Comrade Chou Enlai, too, in his interview with Hinton pointed out that, "According to a Marxist point of view the petty-bourgeoisie belong to the bourgeoisie class and not to the working class or proletariat". It is for this reason that the petty-bourgeoisie, unless they have crossed the class line, or are under its strict leadership, have to be handled cautiously, giving them no chance to create confusion in proletarian ranks.

Your views on the semi-colony cannot be accepted. Indeed the very concept itself is not clearly defined by you. In some places you talk of neo-colony appearing to have the same sense for them both, as when you state that 'The transition from a colony to a semi-colony must be principally understood as a *political* transition in the form of the state'.

And again, 'central to the concept of the semi-colony is the intra-imperialist rivalry politically mediated through classes (or fractions of classes) within the semi-colony'. Elsewhere you talk of the 'neo-colonial state' in the same vein. As we have shown, Mao Tse-tung clearly explains what he means by a semi-colony. Your introduction of this term confuses the discussion. In the quote "the ruling class in semi-colonial countries capitulate to imperialism and the two form an alliance for the joint oppression of the masses of the people", Mao Tse-tung is referring to semi-colonies 'such as China', which he clearly defines. Thus you abstract from its historical context Mao Tse-tung's concept of semi-colony and apply it to a neo-colony, because Mao Tse-tung here talks of a 'ruling class in the semi-colony'; this was an attempt to give authoritative credence to your thesis of the 'national bourgeoisie' being the 'ruling class' at the 'political level' in the neo-colony. Your thesis is abstracted from history and the national question and, although you talk of the 'ruling class in a semi-(neo) colony [as having] a dependent relation to a particular imperialism', you do not show how this dependence arises. Is it an organic dependence? If so what does this mean concretely? Without the concept of finance capital you cannot in any convincing way demonstrate this dependence. Hence your formulations remain mere assertions conceived *a priori* to justify your faulty thesis on Uganda, in particular.

You seek the authority of Lenin where he referes to 'transitional forms of state dependence' almost to uphold the view that all countries, possibly with the exception of the superpowers, are 'transitional forms of state dependence . . . . enmeshed in the net of financial and diplomatic dependence, typical of this epoch'. The fact that Lenin in this case was speaking of the semi-colony and the informal colony such as Argentina and Portugal is mystified. (*Imperialism*, pp. 78–9 and pp. 82–8). If your line of reasoning is correct, then there would appear to be no qualitative difference in the dependencies of Britain, Italy, France, Portugal, India, and Uganda from say, the U.S.A., since these are all 'transitional forms of dependence'. This reasoning is in line with that of the Trotskyist Rohini Banaji's, who states:

'*All* capital is objectively dependent on other capitals, since no capital could exists without other capitals. At the same time *all* capital has an objective contradiction with other capital – one capitalist always kills many, as Marx says'.*

Here the notion is introduced that all capital is the same. The distinction between finance (monopoly) capital and non-monopoly capital is blurred. Similarly, all contradiction between the neo-colony and the imperialist Second World is blurred since they are all 'transitional forms of dependence'. This is further confirmed by the one-sided grouping of the Second World and Third World as 'oppressed nations', although you weakly add that the one 'partakes' in the exploitation of the other.

This thesis is intended to refute the view advanced 'by some comrades' that the ruling class in the semi-(neo-) colony is the 'international bourgeoisie'. You dispute this fact because, in your view, it gives the 'international bourgeoisie a political unity it does not possess' and this could not be, in the 'least, because there doesn't exist an international bourgeoisie state'.

The confusion on this issue arises because of failure to comprehend the whole question of finance capital and the neo-colonial state. Our position in the manuscript is clear. The national democratic revolution (which can only lead to socialist transformation) was anti-imperialist. It was led by the petty bourgeoisie (whom you call the ruling class at a political level) in its first phase. It was compromised because imperialism saw the danger in the struggle being 'exploited' by the international proletariat. It was halted with the neo-colony. In places where the struggle persisted, e.g. in Vietnam, it led to a socialist state. The struggle was

Ed's note: See pp. 301.

halted in other areas because the petty-bourgeoisie could not push it any further, since their class interest appeared to be met by the limited transition. But this petty-bourgeoisie in the colony is a creature of finance capital; it does not arise 'on the morrow of independence'. It accepts the class rule of the financial oligarchy, in this historical sense. But this class rule manifests itself in the state and to the extent that the neo-colony increasingly becomes integrated into the international production process of finance capital, there can be no doubt that the financial oligarchy, being 'the economically dominant class' on the world scale, exerts its rule (to appropriate surplus-values) through the state structure of the neo-colony. It is in this sense that we see the financial oligarchy as the ruling class on an international scale. It is mechanistic to imagine that this rule need be manifested in an 'international bourgeois state'. This is unnecessary and cannot happen historically since the bourgeoisies exist on the basis on nation-state. But since the financial oligarchy can only exist internationally it exploits and utilises the nation-state and neo-colonial state structures, which conform to the level of the productive forces. These state structures are themselves creations of the contradictory development of capitalism. This total unity of international (finance) capital does not rule out <u>particular</u> contradictions among them. Indeed this is the necessary law of the existence (competition) of capital.

Thus whilst recognising the significance of the state of political independence in the neo-colony as furthering the national democratic struggle, we at the same time take note of its incompleteness due to the rule of finance capital on a world scale. Here we see the neo-colonial state in its two-way, contradictory existence. It enables the continuation of the democratic struggle, now under the leadership of the proletariat, but at the same time it poses itself as the antithesis of this democratic struggle because of the existence of the financial oligarchy within the state. Thus the 'relative independence' of the petty-bourgeoisie in the neo-colonial state machine (which, by the way, is not peculiar to the neo-colony) reflects this basic contradiction. On the one hand the petty-bourgeoisie, because of the national question, want to demonstrate that they alone represent the 'national interest' (of the proletariat and peasantry, as well as their own), and on the other they have to please their masters – the financial oligarchies under multilateral imperialism – by opening up the neo-colony to capital exports, in which they partake, to exploit the working class and peasantry. The proletariat then arises as the only agent to bring to an end the neo-colonial state and establish a socialist state, putting an end to the class rule of the financial oligarchy and their agents.

CONCLUSION

We have shown that your positions are unscientific and therefore form no basis for spelling out the strategy for the new democratic revolution. You would have us contrive a united front not based on concrete class alliances; this we do not accept. The banalities about the internationalization of capital without contradiction is your own creation, not ours. The strategy we spell out comes from our analysis of imperialism and not outside it, as you allege. In short, you make no contradiction to the manuscript. We therefore reject your criticisms as wholly without foundation and adding nothing to its substance.

In view of the fact that we did not accede to your request to restrict the distribution of this discussion, and since you feel unable to agree to a wider audience, we have decided to reproduce your comments and distribute them alongside with this reply to a number of comrades and friends who have read the mansucript and whom you wished excluded. We find that no moral, ideological or legal obligation exists on our part to restrict the discussion. On the contrary, proletarian interest demands open debate. For this reason we have acted contrary to your wish, which can only be described as obscurantist and undemocratic.

D. Wadada Nabudere

10th August 1976

14

*ECHO** INTERVIEWS NABUDERE

Q Your critique of Ndugu Shivji's book Class Struggles in Tanzania *gave birth to what some members of this intellectual community have come to term as "The Great Debate". Inescapably some of us have failed to grasp the real issues at stake between the already apparent two schools of thought. Are the differences between you on one hand, and Shivji and the others on the other, concrete ideological, and thus class, differences?*

A I think the proper answer here is: read Shivji and read the *Critique*. You will then understand the issues. I think it is important to do this rather than to find out whether there are concrete ideological and class differences, for these would depend on our understanding of the issues involved. For, if Shivji's understanding of class is racial, then there is no basis for even raising the question. I will illustrate. According to Shivji (p. 88), by the mere fact that one occupies a senior position at this University, a parastatal organisation, and being a Tanzanian, such person *ipso facto* belongs to a 'class' called the 'bureaucratic bourgeoisie' in the sub-category 'economic', having 'detached' oneself away from one's 'class base' of the 'African petty-bourgeoisie' and emerged as a 'bourgeoisie' and member of the 'ruling class'. A Tanzanian Asian after Arusha, in the same position (for simplicity of analysis) would, according to Shivji (p. 45) fall somewhere between sub-stratum 1 or 2 of the 'Asian community', which *ipso facto* would place him in the 'class' of the 'commercial bourgeoisie', which includes all Asians whether industrialists, professionals, intellectuals, traders or workers. According to Shivji, therefore, these two people would belong to two separate 'classes' in bitter 'class struggles' with each other, after the Arusha Declaration. The question is: is this a Marxist-Leninist analysis of classes? Our critique clearly points out the Marxist-Leninist understanding of classes and the scientific method of analysing them, namely in relation to production. What do you say?

Q In light of your answer to the first question, do you still hold the view that these differences arise, among other cases, from the fact that your opponents were too contended with feeding themselves on neo-Marxist literature then available at our bookshop during its formative period? Or if there is a stronger factor which has contributed in impairing their analysis on imperialism, class, state and race, what, in your view, is this factor?

A I think this is clear from Shivji's own footnotes and the way he uses his sources. Mamdani, in a similar criticism of Shivji, points out the same weakness in Shivji's book, except that unconscious to him, he suffers from the same weakness on Uganda. I have pointed this out in the *Critique* and there is no point to elaborate further.

Q There are some of us who complain, behind the doors, that your critique on Shivji's book only manages to tear apart Shivji's analysis without putting across

*Organ of the former Dar es Salaam University Students Organization (DUSO).

the substitute which could be relied on. Could you please enlighten us on this issue, or was it not the intention of your Critique *to do that?*

A We have heard of this complaint on the sidelines but in our view it is as lame as the book itself. No wonder the complaint is being made 'behind the doors'. I did not set out to write *Class Struggles in Tanzania*. I wrote a critique of it. For me to succeed in doing this I had to demonstrate that the method used by Shivji was wrong, the evidence produced inadequate or unsuitable and that the thesis did not hold. I think I succeeded in doing this. Nay, I went further. I pointed the way to a proper study of Tanzania, or indeed for that matter of any imperialist-dominated country. I pointed to the need to understand the general (imperialism) before embarking on the concrete. In our view the critique as it is can enlighten those who would like to go further into the issue, and this is all we set out to achieve.

Q *Your attack on Shivji and Karim Hirji is not fundamentally different from another you made on Mamdani in your reply to Hirji. Having identified Shivji's areas and causes of their weaknesses, what can you say is the principal factor which causes damage to Mamdani's vision in trying to comprehend this all-important issue of imperialism, class, state and race?*

A I think part of the answer to this question can be gathered from our critique of Shivji. Mamdani shares the same weakness with Shivji. He has no concept of imperialism and of finance capital, since he sees 'Indian capital' competing against 'British capital' in Uganda in a period when India itself was a colony of Britain. His class categories are also racial. We intend to go a little further into this matter in a critique of Mamdani, at an appropriate moment.

Q *You seem to disapprove of the usage of 'bureaucratic bourgeoisie' as a term which scientifically applies to an identifiable class stratum. If we understand Shivji well, he argues that the term is intended to identify a particular characteristic of the petty-bourgeoisie stratum in Tanzania which is at the helm of political power; this characteristic is that it is bureaucratic. Thus the usage of petty-bourgeoisie, according to him, would seem to be too vague. What do you think is so unscientific about this coinage?*

A The class category petty-bourgeoisie has never been vague because it is understand to refer to a broad stratum of people. We can analyse the content of this class without creating a 'ruling class' out of it! This is what Shivji does. If we have to accept Shivji's analysis, we would also talk of a 'bureaucratic bourgeoisie' in France. For Shivji a bureaucracy is a 'ruling class', for us a bureaucracy is a 'governing class'. In Marxist literature the economically dominant class is the ruler. It rules because it controls the basic means of production, distribution and exchange. In order to rule, this class relies on a state machine. To the extent that finance capital rules internationally, it dominates the neo-colonial state machine, which it turns to its purposes through the operation of objective economic laws. This contradiction raises the national question to the fore. That is why imperialism becomes the principal enemy in an economically (and hence largely politically) dominated country.

Q *Some people have argued that from reading your works one is made to understand that the contradictions in the Third World seem to the oscillating solely between capital (of the financial oligarchy) and labour (of the toiling raw-material producers of the Third World.) Thus, the petty-bourgeoisie as a stratum with vested interests and serving a particular purpose, seems to be overlooked. Can you enlighten us on your view about this?*

A In analysing a major phenomenon like imperialism, we have to single out principal categories that represent the major movement. Under imperialism, where the principal element is export of capital, the categories finance capital and labour become absolutely basic in analysing the relationships that arise, because capital is exported for the purpose of extracting surplus-value. This surplus-value is created by labour, so you have finance capital (with its concentrating and centralising power) facing labour, its antithesis. This labour includes a proletariat and a poor peasantry. So you have the financial oligarchy and the proletariat (and peasantry) as the main forces opposed to each other – representing dead labour and living labour. For this proper understanding of imperialism it is important to analyse these basic relations. This is what Marx does in *Capital*. It does not follow that other classes e.g. the petty-bourgeoisie or feudalists, do not exist. Their rules are subsidiary and can be analysed within the major movement. We have pointed out that Luxemburg took the same position by accusing Marx of excluding from his analysis what she called 'the non-capitalist strata'. This was because she did not understand Marx's scientific method of analysis. We have argued this at length in the manuscript and we refer the reader to it. The petty-bourgeoisie have no concrete economic interests that are counterposed to monopoly economic interests. It is in the course of finance capital reproducing itself that the 'concrete economic interests' of the petty-bourgeoisie arise at all. For what indeed are these 'concrete interests'? According to Shivji and Mamdani, the petty-bourgeoisie in the neo-colonies are a 'dependent bourgeoisie' upon the 'metropolitan bourgeoisie'. Shivji states in his book: 'Tanzania's economy continues to be part of the international capitalist system. This is reflected in its internal structures and domestic class formations.' (p. 178 Whence then arises 'the concrete interest' of the petty-bourgeoisie that is so much magnified? Shivji and Mamdani's error in magnifying these interests has tended to be influenced by the role they attach to 'merchant capital'. They, like Kay and other neo-Trotskyists, think this capital is a producing capital and 'mediates' between 'industrial capital' and 'finance capital'. As we have also argued in the manuscript these gentlemen do this because they have no concept of finance capital, which according to Kay is a 'circulation capital' and which according to Mamdani and Shivji is non-existent. For Shivji, only industrial capital and commercial capital exist (p. 48). For Mamdani, 'metropolitan capital' is put at par with 'circulating capital' as 'dominating production' (see Mamdani's mimeo).

Q *There are writers and thinkers, at this University and in other parts of the Third World, who argue that finance capital can in fact develop the productive forces in the Third World, even though unintentionally. Do you think this is a convincing and thus scientific observation?*

A Those who have argued this point refer to a passage by Lenin in his pamphlet where he correctly observes that imperialist exports of capital into backward countries introduces capitalist development in those countries. They then one-sidedly proceed to demonstrate that imperialism in fact has left a level of development even though it has 'exploited' the colony. Others argue that Lenin's thesis that imperialism is parasitic is not true for the same reasons and go further to argue that in fact a 'national bourgeoisie' with its own 'national capital' is developing in many former colonial or semi-colonial countries. Those who have argued this include Bill Warren and Nicola Sawinson (on Kenya). Mamdani and Hirji would seem to subscribe to this view, although not Shivji, apparently.

All these arguments spring from the fact that these people read Lenin literally and ahistorically. It is true that imperailist capital exports introduce capitalism and develop it in these countries. But what type of development is this? Is it not because finance capital exploits as it further concentrates that we talk of our countries being enmeshed in a web of exploitative relationship; and is it not for the same reason that Lenin, Stalin and Mao speak of 'national exploitation, oppression and domination'? Is it not for the same reason that the national question is increasingly, ever-sharply so, brought to the fore by this imperialist exploitation and domination? Let us not make the error of falling into empiricist studies detached from the movement of history. This is what the Bill Warrens do. They have not shown us which country has developed into a fully fledged capitalist country under colonialism, semi colonialism or neo-colonialism . Elsewhere in his writings on the *National Question*, Lenin emphasizes the fact that, because the colonies (and we would add today, the neo-colonies) have no capital of their own, they have, under finance capital, in order to obtain it, to submit to political domination. In his discussion on this question he points out that political struggles, nevertheless, under these conditions can broaden the democratic rights of the people and thus help in consolidating their struggles against finance capital. These arguments of Lenin are described by the Bill Warrens as 'harmful'!

Q In a recent interview over Radio Tanzania, an American expert, in response to a question, said that it is wrong for the Third World to claim that the West, especially the U.S., was buying their raw materials at low prices and thus exploiting them. He said that the U.S. produces 48 per cent of all the raw materials needed in the world and is one of the greatest raw material exporters, so, he argued, the U.S., with so many raw materials could not fix low prices for these raw materials as it would be hurting itself in the first place, as well as the rest. Since our comrade of Radio Tanzania seemed contented with this arguement, can you put this issue straight for the benefit not only of our esteemed readers, but also specially for our bewildered comrade of Radio Tanzania?

A First, this so-called expert is an expert of the imperialists, who mystifies imperialism and makes it attractive. That is his job. If he were such an 'impartial expert' he would have known that the prices of raw materials produced in the imperialist countries never have the same problems as those produced in the Third World neo-colonial countries. Moreover, because of the superprofits the monopolies obtain in our countries, the imperialists are able to subsidise production of these agricultural products in their countries by means of taxes, in order to maintain production at satisfactory levels. Surely he must have heard of the U.S. Farm Programmes and the Common Agricultural Policy in the E.E.C.

It does not follow from all this that the U.S. and other imperialist countries are therefore not exploiting our peoples, for the real exploitation we are talking about is not in the market, but at the point of production, which the monopolies carry out through capital exports (packed together with skills, technology, etc.), in order to tie down raw material bases, outlets for capital exports and markets in our countries for their benefit.

Other 'experts' of the imperialists have argued that the level of capital exports to the Third World is very little compared to that between the imperialist countries *inter se*. These arguments ignore the organic composition of such capital, and the mechanisms of centralisation locally generated capital by finance capital, through the credit system, the company/corporation form and the international division of labour, which avails to the monopolies greater amounts of local capital for their production needs, and which results in turning such locally accumulated capital into a portion of finance-capital stock of the monopolies. Since many of our own academic 'experts' do not sometimes grasp this fact, it is not surprising that our interviewer would be so lost by such obscurantist arguments of the ideologies of imperialism.

Q As an accomplished student of imperialism, what strategy do you advocate for genuine and real economic development of the underdeveloped Third World countries?

A I cannot lay down a strategy in these few lines and I don't believe I am so 'accomplished' on these questions as you see to suggest. I would refer the reader to Lenin's *Imperialism, Critical Remarks on the National Question, A Caricature of Marxism* and *Economic Imperialism*, to Stalin on *Marxism and the National Question* and Mao Tse-tung on *New Democracy*. Until imperialism is completely smashed in our countries, thus solving the national question, removing all exploitation, national oppression and domination, there can be no genuine economic development; for all economic transformation is class struggle itself. It is a struggle in which the exploited take on the exploiters, thus transforming the relations to the productive forces. Only then can those forces be developed to the advantage of the exploited working people. No economic development programmes or plans can defeat the onverwhelming objective economic laws of monopoly capitalism in our countries. This is already clear. *A luta* must *Continua* against the monopolies.

Q 'Social Imperialism' is a very recent invention which remains elusive to many, and few Marxists really dwell on the merits an demerits of it. In his critique of your manuscript, 'The Political Economy of Imperialism', Mamdani touched on this issue and accused you of not attempting to say a word on it. What exactly are your views on 'social imperialism'?

A In my manuscript, 'The Political Economy of Imperialism', I set out to defend Lenin's thesis on *Imperialism, the Highest State of Capitalism* against anti-Marxist-Leninist ideologists, among whom the neo-Trotskyites abound. In order to do this I had to trace the development of capitalism in its three phases: mercantile, industrial and financial. Furthermore I had to locate Lenin's analysis in Marx's *Capital*, particularly in the Law of the Tendency of the Rate of Profit to Fall, which had been 'refuted' by Baran and Sweezy. I went further to argue that Lenin's analysis enabled us to comprehend contemporary multilateral imperialism and neo-colonialism. I did not set out to write a thesis on 'social-imperialism', and Mamdani has no business to tell me what I should have written about. Any criticism of the manuscript must be concerned with what I wrote and not with what I did not write about. Mamdani, or for that matter anybody else, is free to write us a thesis on 'social-imperialism'. There is no shortage of pen and paper. The latter part of the question does not therefore arise.

Q Having been in Tanzania for all this time, what do you think disables the Marxist intelligentsia camp in this country from organizing itself into a powerful force capable of forging a concrete alliance with the exploited class in a common struggle against the common enemy?

A I am not qualified to advise on how Tanzanians should organise themselves. they are better judges of the situation, which they have to analyse in a concrete way. Issa Shivji analyses class struggles in Tanzania, and this question should be addressed to him although, incidentally, nowhere in his books does he indicate what is to be done.

Q *The question of tackling the dominance of finance capital is too serious to lack ideological clarity. Genuine Marxists in this country would like a word of advice from you on this issue for the simple reason that there seems to be some difficulties in pinpointing the immediate enemy, that is, whether it is the intermediary petty-bourgeois class that should be tackled first in a concrete struggle to dislodge the dominance of finance capital, or whether the target should be imperialism first.*

A Those who raise the question in this way see imperialism as being <u>external</u> to our countries. To us imperialism is the <u>immediate</u> enemy. It is immediate precisely because it is the principal enemy. It is principal because it is the exploiter, through the *objectified power* of its finance capital, of the workers and peasants in our countries. It also oppresses and dominates our countries. The petty-bourgeoisie is a product of imperialist domination. It cannot be disjointed from it but at the same time it has a contradiction with imperialism because of this oppression and domination. That is why, the national democratic revolution encompasses a wide body of the population of our countries. By juxtaposing the so-called 'local ruling classes' to imperialism as the 'immediate enemy' which must be 'fought first', one is putting forward a manifesto for adventurism. A study of Mao's *New Democracy* has a lot of insights for us on this question. It should be read in this connection.

15

WHOSE CAPITAL AND WHOSE STATE?*

Yash Tandon

> If these gentlemen only knew that Marx thought his best things were still not good enough for the workers, and that he considered it a crime to offer the workers anything but the very best!... (Engels to Conrad Schmidt, Marx – Engels, *Selected Correspondence*, 1975 edition, p. 394)

For the working class, as Marx said, nothing is good enough but the very best. Those self-style Marxists who sulk with the slightest of criticism or take criticism as personal attack must reconsider their vocation, for they belong, despite their protestations, to the petty-bourgeois class ideologists, the 'neo-Marxist' liberals. The Marxist style is different. Personal attacks have no place in Marxist criticism. Criticism has a positive value. Self-criticism is even better. To the proletarian theorist, seeking collectively for the science of Marxist practice, *struggle and unity* is the only correct path. There is no other way.[1] ... Self-protection, self-pity, self-justification have no room in proletarian practice.

These words were necessary because sulking and refusal of self-criticism when under attack for wrong ideas, have become the hallmark of many who profess to represent the proletarian cause in the present struggle of the oppressed masses of East Africa against imperialism. This seems to be the dominant reaction to an earlier critique of the works of Shivji and Mahmood Mamdani by Dan W. Nabudere. This reaction has become a political fact of some significance in the struggle towards identifying a correct political strategy of the exploited and oppressed masses in East Africa. In the absence of self-criticism on the part of comrades, one must continue to battle against wrong ideas which lead to wrong practice. In the critique by Nabudere it was amply demonstrated that Shivji's and Mamdani's analyses of the East African situation are nothing short of a 'manifesto to adventurism'. They offer a strategy of struggle that, even before the struggle has begun in earnest, points to the direction of disaster. For this reason, no liberalism must be tolerated in subjecting their works to criticism. Bourgeois social scientists are always confounded when they see Marxists criticising one another even more harshly than they do the bourgeois social scientists. But then the latter will never understand criticism. For them criticism is an intellectual pastime. For the Marxists it is class struggle as intense in theory as in practice.[2]

Criticism of the three books is deserved for two reasons, one of which is purely circumstantial. The study of society in East Africa, at least as represented in writings for the consumption of secondary schools and universities, has hitherto been a virtual monopoly of bourgeois social scientists. The intensifying struggle against imperialism in the Third World, the struggle in Vietnam and the rest of

*A review article on: Issa G. Shivji, *Class Struggles in Tanzania*, New York: Monthly Review Press, 1976, p. 178; Colin Leys, *Under-development in Kenya*, London: Heinemann, 1975, p. 278; Mahmood Mamdani, *Politics and Class Formation in Uganda*; New York: Monthly Review Press, 1976.

South-east Asia, the virtual collapse of the credibility of bourgeois social sciences – all these culminated in the 1960s in the birth of a spate of writings in the Marxist tradition, at least self-professedly so. It was therefore not surprising that an intellectual readership, thirsting for an analysis that would make a better sense of the situation in East Africa than what bourgeois social sciences had to offer, took to the 'pioneering' works of Shivji, Leys and Mamdani as a thirsty man might clutch at a glass of water.[3] Where things began to go wrong was when these writings were absolutised by their readers (at least partly with the connivance of the authors, though Colin Leys has been more prepared to be self-critical[4]) as the final word on the question. That is why they must be criticised all the more relentlessly because where the authors are wrong, it could lead to a perpetuation of error a hundredfold by those emulating the same methods and the same theory.

The main reason for subjecting Shivji, Leys and Mamdani to criticism is, of course, for what they have said rather than for how they have been received. The source of their error is their misunderstanding of the method of dialectical materialism, a science of studying and apprehending nature and society whose method is dialectical (the law of contradiction), and whose theory is materialist (the primacy of matter over mind).

The metaphysical method, as opposed to the dialectical, is that which views phenomena in their separatedness, in their abstraction from the totality, not as part of a connected whole but as something that can be understood if taken by themselves. This is characteristically the method of bourgeois social sciences, especially that tendency which attempts to be 'scientistic' in the manner of experimental science by abstracting natural phenomena from their total environment in order to observe them more closely under laboratory conditions. Historical materialism is the very opposite of this method. Experimental science is impossible in the study of social relations.[5]

We have already said that Marxism is a very difficult science, especially for those coming to it like this reviewer himself, from the method of bourgeois social sciences, for metaphysical thinking creeps into the analysis of even the most wary. This is the most grievous error of both Shivji and Mamdani. While professing to apply dialectical materialism, they have defaulted on its very essence.

All major faults of Shivji and Mamdani stem from the fact that they have attempted to analyse Tanzania and Uganda, respectively, in abstraction from the totality of world imperialism, not as part of a connected whole but as something that can be understood in isolation of the totality. This criticism must come as a surprise to most readers, especially of *Class Struggles in Tanzania*, for did not Shivji conclude his analysis with the statement: "Thus Tanzania's economy continues to be part of the international capitalist system."[6] And did not Mamdani remind us, from time to time, that Uganda too was part of the international capitalist system, as when Amin discovered, after expelling the Asians, that the 'Asian' property was really not the property of the Asians, but that of British banks?[7]

Like any other phenomenon, a work of literature must also be viewed in its totality, and not in parts. Any careful reader will see that despite occasional affirmations to the contrary, either periodically, in the case of Mamdani, or as an appendix attached lamely at the end of the book, in the case of Shivji, both authors treat us to an analysis of Tanzania and Uganda as separate social formations or as 'territorial economies' in isolation from the world economy and imperialism. Their conception of classes, their conception of the state, and their understanding of the nature of contradictions accordingly suffer from a metaphysical analysis.

Take their understanding of the nature of contradictions in these 'peripheral' social formations. It is odd, to say the least, that in this day and age there should be people professing to be pursuing the proletarian line and recognising imperialism, even if only in the form of periodic revelations or as external appendages, who cannot see that the principal contradiction in the neo-colonies is between the workers and oppressed masses on the one side and the imperialist bourgeoisie who exploit and dominate them on the other.

No, it is not simply a matter of terminology. We are not fighting for words. We are struggling to identify the correct proletarian strategy in the era of imperialism. It is not simply a matter of substituting the word fundamental for the word principal, for there are people who might argue that the contradiction between imperialism and the broad masses is a fundamental contradiction, whereas the principal contradiction is something that changes every few years, which, as we shall show, is a false categorisation of contradictions in our epoch.

For Mamdani and Shivji the principal contradictions do indeed change every few years; some stay only for a few months, some get 'resolved' only to appear again. Let us illustrate with just one example from Mamdani. In the 1962 to 1971 period, we are told that, 'Unlike Kenya and Tanzania, Uganda did not emerge after Independence with one ruling petty-bourgeoisie . . . . Instead, two separate petty-bourgeoisies came forth, one Buganda and one non-Buganda . . . . Confronted by a successful organisation of the chiefs, the two petty-bourgeoisie formed a class coalition at independence'.

What, then, were the contradictions in Uganda at independence? There were two contradictions:

> . . . one within the petty bourgeois coalition, and one between the petty bourgeoisie as a whole and the Asian commercial bourgeoisie. Of these, the principal contradiction – the one that informed politics of the period under consideration – was the former. [i.e. tribal contradiction between Buganda petty bourgeoisie and non-Buganda petty bourgeoisie.] The struggles within the petty bourgeoisie . . . occupied the political stage until their resolution in the *coup detat* of 1971. Only then did the contradiction between the ruling petty bourgeoisie and the Indian commercial bourgeoisie assume principal significance.[8]

This understanding of the contradictions is confirmed when dealing with the situation after the coup.

> In the decade between independence and the coup, the contradiction between the petty bourgeoisie as a whole and Asian capital remained secondary, while the struggle within the petty bourgeoisie was resolved. . . . Its resolution was the coup. Then, after the state power had consolidated its state apparatus, the contradiction between the petty bourgeoisie and Asian capital (both the Asian petty and commercial bourgeoisies) emerged as the principal contradiction. Amin brought the same decisive resolution to this contradiction. . . these two classes were physically expelled.[9]

Since this 'principal' contradiction with 'Asian capital' did not really emerge until 'the state power had consolidated its state apparatus', and the Asians called to a conference by Amin in January 1972, following which they were expelled in August, this 'principal' contradiction had lasted for only eight months – such, according to Mamdani, is the duration of some 'principal' contradictions in the neo-colonies! They remain 'secondary' and dormant for a long time, and then suddenly come alive just before their 'resolution'!

On reading the intervening pages between p. 229 and 304, one finds that the 'principal' contradiction between the two petty-bourgeoisies, 'one Buganda and one non-Buganda' with which we started in 1962 did not, in fact, constitute the 'principal' contradiction throughout the period 1962-1971. As early as 1964, the Buganda petty bourgeoisie had begun to 'shed its tribal ideology' (p. 244), and in 1965 it had disbanded its separate party, the *Kabaka Yekka*, and had joined the Uganda Peoples' Congress. By 1966 it was crushed. 'The crisis was resolved when the central government used its armed might to physcially crush the Buganda state.' (p. 246)

Actually even before the Buganda 'state' was crushed, the 'principal' components of the 'principal' contradiction had already changed around 1965. 'Once the KY had disbanded and its members had joined the ranks of the UPC, the struggle between the "centre" and "right" factions – between the representatives of the governing bureaucracy at the centre and the petty-bourgeoisie proper (the small property-owning traders and kulaks, henceforth referred to as the petty-bourgeoisie) – came to the force.[10]

Hence the contradiction was now not between 'two petty-bourgeoisies', divided along tribal lines, but between the 'governing bureaucracy' and the 'petty bourgeoisie proper'. However, for a brief period between 1966-67 and 1969, a contradiction had arisen between the 'governing bureaucracy' on one side and monopoly capital and the 'Asian commercial bourgeoisie' on the other, leading, in 1969, to 'the crisis of accumulation'. The crisis was resolved, in the case of monopoly capital, on the one had by drawing Shs 38.4 million of Special Drawing Rights from the IMF (sic!) and on the other hand by nationalisations (pp 265-6); and in the case of the 'Asian commercial bourgeoisie', by postponing the contradiction with them and instead making an 'alliance' (sic) with them (pp 270–1). The governing bureaucracy had to do this because the petty bourgeoisie was seen as the real enemy, not monopoly capital or the Asian commercial bourgeoisie. The latter 'could never aspire to control the state . . . in contrast, the petty bourgeoisie was capable of organising peasant discontent . . . and aspired moreover to control the state apparatus in place of the governing bureaucracy. It was a clear and present *political* threat, which the Asian commercial bourgeoisie was not. Hence:

> . . . the only way the governing bureaucracy could resolve its political crisis was by taking the wind out of the mass discontent organised by the petty bourgeoisie. But to do this, the economy and with it prices, had to be stabilised, and it was this that dictated the relations of the governing bureaucracy to both international capital and the commercial bourgeoisie. Nationalisations were not contrary to the interests of either. In fact, there was a dramatic reversal in the attitude of the state to the commercial bourgeoisie: the contradiction between the two was resolved through an alliance. (emphasis added)[11]

Between 1969 and 1971, the contradiction between the governing bureaucracy and the petty bourgeoisie simmered unabated, until Brigadier Amin changed sides by joining the Uganda Muslim Community (UMC) rather than the National Association for the Advancement of Muslims (NAAM), thus bringing the army on the side of the petty bourgeoisie. Mamdani explains the 1971 coup in these terms. Imperialism played no part in it, or very minimal part in it: 'Behind the coup was also an external power, Israel, although its involvement was of secondary significance.' (p. 292). The contradiction between the governing bureaucracy and the petty bourgeoisie was finally resolved through murder and expulsion of the members of the governing bureaucracy.

This, according to Mamdani, is the saga of the rise and fall of 'principal' contradictions in Uganda. Throughout, the contradiction between the oppressed people of Uganda and imperialism remains 'secondary', remote, external and unimpeachable. Mamdani thus managed to reduce the theory of contradictions to a mere sophistry. The characters and conflicts remain the same as in any bourgeois analysis of Uganda, complete with their racial and tribal attire, only their labels change; that which at least made sense in bourgeois vocabulary, now appears as farcical tragi-comic drama.

In Marxist analysis the principal contradictions are not something that can be treated with such casualness. In every complex situation, there is only one principal contradiction, and every effort must be made to find out how this contradiction feeds itself on and determine the existence and development of other contradictions. Sure enough there are contradictions among the oppressed people themselves, even antagonistic contradictions, for example, between an oppressed national bourgeoisie in a neo-colony and the workers whom they exploit. But when compared with the principal contradiction with imperialism, the contradictions between the national bourgeoisie and the workers are secondary contradictions, contradictions among the people. They do not supersede the principal contradiction with imperialism.[12]

What, then, of Mao's argument, in his essay 'On Contradiction', that the principal and secondary contradictions sometimes replace each other, that there is nothing immutable about them?[13] That is true. He was here talking not about the contradictions among the people superseding the contradiction with imperialism, and so becoming principal in their turn. He was talking about how the contradictions the oppressed people have with imperialism on the one hand and with feudal oppressors on the other can change places under different circumstances; one may become principal at one time, and another at another time. In neither event do the contradictions among the oppressed people become principal contradictions for as long as either of the two principal enemies is still at bay. One cannot reduce Mao's argument to justify Mamdani's kind of analysis of contradictions in Uganda.[14] Having explained the difference between principal and secondary contradictions, Mao then underlined the importance of correctly identifying the principal contradiction.

> Hence, if in any process there are a number of contradictions, one of them must be the principal contradiction playing the leading and decisive role, while the rest occupy a secondary and subordinate position. Therefore, in studying any complex process in which there are two or more contradictions, we must devote every effort to finding its principal contradiction. Once this principal contradiction is grasped, all problems can be readily solved. This is the method Marx taught us in his study of capitalist society. Likewise Lenin and Stalin taught us this method when they studied imperialism and the general crisis of capitalism and when they studied the Soviet economy. There are thousands of scholars and men of action who do not understand it, and the result is that, lost in a fog, they are unable to get to the heart of a problem and naturally cannot find a way to resolve its contradictions.[15]

The theory of contradictions is the theory by which the proletariat in the present epoch identifies its principal enemy, and knows how to handle secondary contradictions among the people in such a way as to unite with all the classes among the oppressed people against the principal enemy. It does not serve the proletarian cause to poke fingers into the eyes of the 'bureaucratic bourgeoisie' (about which more later), as Shivji does in the case of Tanzania, or into the eyes of the 'nascent commercial bourgeoisie' as Mamdani does in the case of Uganda, because they have decided by their petty bourgeois analysis that these constitute the principal enemy of the workers and the oppressed masses. Nothing would please imperialism more than having the oppressed people fight amongst themselves as they observe from the pedestal. On the correct handling of contradictions among the people, Mao, speaking from practical experience, still has the best advice to offer:

> The contradiction between the national bourgeoisie and the working class is one between the exploiter and the exploited, and is therefore antagonistic in nature. But in the concrete conditions of China, this antagonistic class contradiction can, if properly handled, be transformed into a non-antagonistic one and be resolved by peaceful methods. However, it can change into a contradiction between ourselves and the enemy if we do not handle it properly and do not follow the policy of uniting with, criticizing and educating the national bourgeoisie, or if the national bourgeoisie does not accept this policy of ours. Since they are different in nature, the contradictions between ourselves and the enemy and the contradictions among the people must be resolved by different methods." (emphasis added).[16]

We submit that in Mamdani's analysis secondary contradictions among the oppressed people are magnified into 'principal' contradictions because Uganda is treated in isolation of its total world context, and its classes and contradictions analysed as if Uganda were abstracted from imperialism and placed in a huge social laboratory so that its 'local' movements could be observed under a microscope. It is no wonder that everything looms so large. 'Asian' capital suddenly becomes 'big' capital, the class that is supposed to have established its control over domestic capital accumulation. The 'governing bureaucracy', a bunch of bureaucrats of petty bourgeois background, suddenly become the 'ruling class', a ruling class which, however, has no basis in production (!) and therefore utilises its monopoly over the state apparatus to acquire control over the economy. 'The coup represented the failure of the governing bureaucracy to transform itself into a bureaucratic petty bourgeoisie' (p. 294); although later (on the same page and on p. 302), the author talks as if the bureaucratic petty bourgeoisie had already consolidated itself.

In all this, imperialism is placed outside the laboratory, as some kind of a polluting agent that would complicate the analysis of the social formation called 'Uganda'. 'Lost in a fog', Mamdani is 'unable to get at the heart of the problem', for the heart of the problem is that imperialism owned and controlled virtually all the capital that existed in Uganda; that the so-called 'big', "Asian", capital was neither big nor Asian; that the 'ruling class' consisted not of that bunch of 'governing bureaucracy' which was 'kicked out' as easily as mercilessly as the so-called 'big' Asian 'capitalists' a little later, but was comprised of the imperialist bourgeoisie itself which ruled Uganda through the agency at one time of direct colonial rule, at another time of sections of the Ugandan petty bourgeoisie, and yet another time of 'Field Marshall' Amin. 'Lost in a fog', Mamdani is unable to discover that the principal contradiction in Uganda, ever since finance capital stepped into it, has always been between the people of Uganda and imperialist bourgeoisie, and that this is the principal contradiction which has been behind the movement of Uganda's history all these years. For Mamdani the national question simply does not exist. This is as if Lenin never existed, as if it were not a fact that in the epoch of imperialism, the international bourgeoisie oppresses not only the workers of advanced capitalist countries but also entire nations that are brought under the heel of capital. This is as if the Leninist slogan for the imperialist epoch – 'Workers and oppressed nations of the world, unite!' – was a meaningless slogan. There are, of course, 'Marxists' who do repudiate Lenin on this. These are the followers of Rosa Luxemburg and Leon Trotsky and there are many of these at the University of Dar es Salaam. The struggling masses of the oppressed nations have nothing in common with them.

Mamdani has been taken as an example only because his is a more explicit and appears to be a 'better argued' and 'substantiated' piece of writing than Shivji's, although Shivji commits exactly the same errors. He too analyses the contradictions in Tanzania as if they had a movement of their own, independent of the principal contradiction between the people of Tanzania and imperialism. With him too the national question disappears with independence. The class struggle is now carried out purely within the territorial domain of Tanzania, with imperialism existing as something remote, external and untouchable. He admits that Tanzania is a neo-colony. But the Tanzanian state for him is not a neo-colonial state! It is a state of the 'bureaucratic bourgeoisie', which is a stratum of the petty bourgeoisie that is supposed to have consolidated itself into a separate class after the 1967 Arusha Declaration, and which as a result became the 'ruling class' in Tanzania. Imperialism is something with which Tanzania has a 'dependent' relationships; not something internal to Tanzania, integrated within the very class structure, and at the level of production itself. Of course he recognises imperialism, but the recognition is purely formal. It is not woven within the fabric of his analysis.

As for Colin Leys' *Underdevelopment in Kenya*, it is even more muddled and theoretically confused. Shivji and Mamdani misunderstand the method and theory of dialectical and historical materialism; Leys ignores it altogether. there is no sense of history or movement that emerges from the pages of Ley's books. There is not even the remotest notion of dialectics in his analysis. The homage to Marx is purely formal. The book is really a product of dependency school nurtured by the neo-Marxist followers of Paul Baran and Paul Sweezy, and grown hothouse fashion, detached from political practice, in some Latin American radical intellectual hideouts. All the mistakes of the dependency school are exemplified in Leys' analysis – a 'structural' analysis of the neo-colony without dialectics; classes without class struggle; eclectic borrowing from Marx and neo-Marxists who set out deliberately to repudiate Marx. 'Underdevelopment theory', Leys writes, 'is thus partly a correction and partly an expansion of Marx's interpretation of history'.[17]

Nevertheless, in his own structural fashion, Leys shows a little more clearly than do Shivji or Mamdani how finance capital dominates the economy in Kenya, and how the principal contradiction is between the masses of Kenya and imperialism, which he describes as 'foreign capital'. For him 'the central [meaning principal, no doubt] contradiction of neo-colonialism…[is]…a system of domination of the mass of population . . . by foreign capital, by means other than direct colonial rule'. (p. 271) This conclusion emerges in an empiricist fashion, almost accidentally as it were, for there is no proper theory of imperialism that informs the conclusion. Imperialism is simply 'foreign capital' and not that highest stage of capitalism 'at which the dominance of monopolies and finance capital is established; in which the export of capital has acquired pronounced importance; in which division of the world among the international trusts has begun; in which the division of all the territories of the world among the biggest capitalist powers has been completed'.[18]

Since Leys lacks the concept of a world economy, Kenya therefore appears to him as a territorial economy, in its own right, in a 'dependent' relationship with external, or 'foreign' capital, much as Uganda and Tanzania appear to Mamdani and Shivji. Hence, despite his conclusion about total domination by 'foreign' capital, the local characters in Kenya still loom large under his microscope, just as they do for Mamdani and Shivji. Thus the 'Asian merchant capitalists' are 'posed to become an indigenous industrial bourgeoisie of the classical type' (p. 38); 'the local Asian bourgeoisie' are made to appear even wealthier than 'foreign capital' (p. 120), 'owing' over two-thirds of the 'non-farm assets' in Kenya, not bothering to inquire whether these assets might have been mortgaged to British banks, and whether in the final analysis, these were not owned by finance capital itself; the African 'big farmers' are made to appear like really big fellows, with the world at their feet, while imperialist finance capital is made to look like the weaker partner waiting for 'African leaders' to 'allow them to stay in business'. (p. 42)

But why was it that 'the local Asian bourgeoisie' did not mature into an 'indigenous industrial bourgeoisie of the classical type'? That, Leys explains, was because of a more or less explicit conspiracy between the potential African 'auxilary' capitalists and 'foreign' capitalists.

> The logic of the pre-independence settlement was that Kenya should attract large amount of new private capital from abroad into the non-farm sectors of the economy. This was the more important, in that there was also a tacit decision not to allow the resident Asian commercial bourgeoisie to exchange their commercial dominance for dominance in manufacturing.[19]

So the 'big' Asian capitalists were not so big after all. What, then, of African capitalists? These turn out in the chapter on 'African Capitalism' (chapter 5) to be really small petty bourgeois elements (by no stretch of imagination describable as 'captains of industry') located in trade, transportation and construction, heavily indebted to bank or other institutional capital, and dependent for their survival on state protection. However, some of these, we are told, because of their political position, could become big capitalists, so big that they could now form an 'alliance' (presuming equal partnership) with 'foreign capital'.

> The effects of these forces thus seemed likely to be the consolidation of a firm alliance between foreign capital and the new African 'auxiliary bourgeoisie' operating under more and more heavily protected conditions.[20]

Thus what we have is eclecticism at its worst. Colin Leys is not sure which theory to support – that which argues that under imperialism no national bourgeoisie can emerge of the classical type in the neo-colonies, or that which argues that state power does provide a section of the local petty bourgeoisie to emerge as a national bourgeoisie. Hence he invents the concept the 'auxiliary' bourgeoisie which enters into an 'alliance' with 'foreign capital', and which 'allows them to stay in business'. With one stroke the whole movement of capital on a world-wide scale, the increasing centralisation of capital in the hands of finance capital, and with it the progressive elimination of the national bourgeoisie – all this is reduced to a purely empiricist observation about the rise of an 'auxiliary' bourgeoisie in Kenya in 'alliance' with 'foreign capital'. Leys thus keeps his options on both theories.

WHOSE CAPITAL AND WHOSE STATE?

Marx, in his *The Class Struggles in France*, talks about how the June 1848 insurrection by the workers was crushed by the Parisian petty bourgeoisie, and their armed force, the Mobile Guard, led by their strong-man, General Cavaignac.

> No one had fought more fanatically in the June days for the salvation of property and the restoration of credit than the Parisian petty bourgeois – keepers of cafes and restaurants, *marchands de vins*, small traders,

shopkeepers, handicraftsmen etc. The shopkeeper had pulled himself together and marched against the barricades in order to restore the traffic which leads from the street into the shops.[21]

But as soon as the barricades were clear, and property saved from the workers, the petty bourgeoisie found that the property they fought so hard to save was not their property after all. It was the property of the big bourgeoisie.

And when the barricades were thrown down and the workers were crushed and the shopkeepers, drunk with victory, rushed back to their shops, they found the entrance barred by a saviour of property, an official agent of credit, who presented them with threatening notices: Overdue promissory note! Overdue house rent! Doomed shop! Doomed shopkeeper!

And then Marx has this revealing passage on the real owner of the Parisian property, which the petty bourgeoisie tried to salvage from the workers.

Salvation of property! But the house in which they lived was not their property; the shop which they kept was not their property; the commodities in which they dealt were not their property. Neither their business, nor the plate from which they ate, nor the bed on which they slept belonged to them any longer. It was precisely from them that this property had to be saved – for the houseowner who let the house, for the banker who discounted the promissory note, for the capitalist who made advances in cash, for the manufacturer who entrusted the sale of his commodities to the retailers, for the wholesale dealer who had credited the raw materials to these handicraftsmen. Restoration of credit! But credit, having regained strength proved itself a vigorous and jealous god, for it turned the debtor who could not pay out of his four walls, together with wife and child, surrendered his sham property to capital, and threw the man into the debtors' prison....

The big bourgeoisie were quite happy to let the petty bourgeoisie fight battles on their behalf during the June insurrection, letting them cherish the illusion that what they were fighting for was 'their' property.

Their nominal property had been left unassailed as long as it was of consequence to drive them to the battlefield in the name of property. Now that the great issue with the proletariat had been settled, the small matter of the epicier could in turn be settled. In Paris the mass of overdue paper amounted to over 21,000,000 francs; in the provinces, to over 11,000,000. The proprietors of more than 7,000 Paris firms had not paid their rent since February.[22]

Marx was talking about an epoch when the 'big bourgeoisie' consisted of a bankocracy and an emerging industrial bourgeoisie still battling against the classes passed over from the feudal era, the landed gentry and merchant capital, in order to establish their control over the natural market. This was the period of competitive capital. Today the big bourgeoisie is of an entirely different order of magnitude and strength. The landed gentry and merchant capitalists have already been crushed and placed under the hegemony of industrial, then finance, capital. The monopoly bourgeoisies in the developed capitalist countries have not only established their total control over their national markets, but a section of the bourgeoisie have turned international through export capital. Capital has become internationalised; production and marketing have become internationalised; the world economy is integrated such that national boundaries do not make economic sense any longer, and this is the eve of the socialist revolution which alone can transform the objective internationality of the working class (growing hand-in-hand with the internationality of capital) into a political and organisational reality.

Whose capital is it that turns the wheels of the world capitalist economy? It is the capital of the big bourgeoisie of the present epoch, the 'international oligarchy', the monopoly corporations which have emerged through the merger of bank capital and industrial capital, and which control, directly or indirectly, all production in the world capitalist economy. Does it mean that there is no room for small production, for small property? Of course not. Small and middle property do continue all the time to generate themselves in the interstices of the capitalist world economy. But this property is not effectively the property of the small or middle bourgeoisie. It is only formally theirs. It plays a useful role in servicing the monopolies. If Lenin could say the following in 1916, it is hundred-times more true today:

> The enormous dimensions of finance capital concentrated in a few hands and creating an extraordinarily dense and widespread network of relationships and connections which subordinates not only the small and medium, but also the very small capitalists and small masters, on the one hand, and the increasingly intense struggle waged against their national state groups of financiers for the division of the world and domination over other countries, on the other hand, cause the propertied classes to go over entirely to the side of imperialism.[23]

Earlier, when talking about the 'Concentration of Production and Monopolies' he makes the same point even more emphatically:

> As we shall see, money capital and the banks make this superiority of a handful of the largest enterprises still more overwhelming, in the most literal sense of the word, i.e., millions of small, medium and even some big 'proprietors' are in fact in complete subjection to some hundreds of millionaire financiers.[24]

And later still:

> Here we no longer have competition between small and large, between technically developed and backward enterprises. We see here the monopolists throttling those who do not submit to them, to their yoke, to their dictation.[25]

The bitter truth to the petty bourgeoisie, the truth that the property they call 'theirs' is only formally theirs and, in effect, belongs to the big bourgeoisie, was brought home to the Parisian petty bourgeoisie after the days of the June insurrection. This bitter truth was brought home to 'Field Marshall' Amin in Uganda after he had expelled the Asians in 1972. Mamdani reports:

> In October 1972, when Asian businesses started closing down en masse, the main streets of Kampala were lined with signs saying: 'Property of Barclays Bank D.C.O.' or 'Property of Standard Bank'. Financial connections usually hidden in small print in the text of a contract or an agreement were now advertised for all to see. The fact was that the Indian commercial bourgeoisie was till a dependent class. Functionally, it lubricated the export-import economy; financially, it was heavily reliant on and subordinate to British banking capital.[26]

Of course, tragically for Mamdani's analysis, he too realised this quite late in the day, for having earlier built up the 'Asian commercial bourgeoisie' as 'big bourgeoisie', he now finds that what he supposed was 'their' property, was not theirs after all!

This bitter truth came home to the petty bourgeoisie in East Africa when the East African Airways collapsed in February 1977. For some thirty years, East Africans have been proudly advertising their 'national' airline, but when the airline collapsed, British capital moved in, sealed the V.C. 10s and proclaimed these as their property. The Airways was in debt to finance capital for almost everything it 'possessed'. Within days, Kenya floated a new airline called Kenya Airways, about which the only thing Kenyan was the airspace, if even that! – for we were told within days of Kenya Airways' formation, the British Midland Airways had wet-leased two aircrafts to Kenya and provided the management of the Kenya Airways, their sole 'property'. In an effort to recover the buses and mini-buses which had taken European and American tourists from Kenya into Tanzania, and which were now stranded in Tanzania on account of the latter's closure of the joint border, the Kenyan *nyang'aus* made a claim on these vehicles. Immediately, the British High Commission in Dar es Salaam stepped in: 'Don't touch these vehicles! These are British Property!'27

Such is the nature of the property 'owned' by the so-called 'big' capitalists in the neo-colonies. Lenin had warned us long ago, in his writings on the national question:

> In a commodity-producing society, no independent development, or development of any sort whatsoever, is possible without capital. In Europe the dependent nations have both their own capital and easy access to it on a wide range of terms. The colonies have no capital of their own, or none to speak of, and under finance capital no colony can obtain any except on terms of political submission.28

And do not forget that political submission in this case represents submission at the economic level! Those, such as Bill Warren, who argue that under imperialism, the neo-colonies are fast creating their own 'national' bourgeoisies, would want to reverse the process of history, much as Proudhon wanted to in his time. They are not only utopian; they are also reactionary, for the process of history cannot roll backwards. Instead of further concentration and centralisation of capital on a global scale, they 'see' deconcentration and decentralisation of capital, so that imperialism, through creating so many 'national' capitals against itself, is 'self-liquidating'. It is difficult for any but the most naive species of petty bourgeois apologists of imperialism to sink to such depths of ignorance of the movement of history. Even the full-blooded bourgeois apologists of imperialism can see the increasing concentration and centralisation of capital in the hands of monopolies on a global scale; only they see this as a healthy development for all humanity. The proletarian line is to recognise this movement of capital, and also to recognize its dialectical opposite, the anti-imperialist struggle of the workers of the world and the masses of the oppressed nations.

The struggle at the global level is thus a struggle against the international bourgeoisie. This universal contradiction particularises itself in every country subject to the rule of capital. And capital rules, at the politcal level, by means of every conceivable form of government of which one can think. In one country it may use a democratic republic ('the best possible political shell for capitalism' said Lenin); in another a monarchy; in yet another an out-and-out fascist dictatorship, etc. Capital is not particularly choosy about the form of government, though as far as possible it would prefer a democratic republic because it best disguises some of the more naked aspects of capitalist exploitation. And once capital has secured its power over a state, it does not lose it, no matter how persons, institutions or parties change, Lenin tells us. The denouement of the rule of capital comes only when the proletariat has captured state power and smashed the bourgeois state.

The neo-colonial state is still the state of the international bourgeoisie. The form of government has obviously changed from that of a colonial state. Then it was a government directly run from one of the metropolitan centres of imperialist power; and this was done either on behalf of just one imperialist bourgeoisie (as in Uganda, for example), or on behalf of the whole international bourgeoisie (as in the 'free state' of the Congo – now Zaire – and in the so-called 'Portuguese' territories). Now, in a neo-colonial state, it may be a government run by representatives of the local bourgeoisie or petty bourgeoisie, or a government of a one-man dictator, but it is still run on behalf of the international bourgeoisie. No amount of sophistry can alter this basic fact about neo-colonies. Engels had made this clear long ago:

> As the state arose from the need to hold class antagonism in check, but as it arose, at the same time, in the midst of conflict of these classes, it is, as a rule, the state of the most powerful economically dominant class, which through the medium of the state, becomes also the politically dominant class, and thus acquires new means of holding down and exploiting the oppressed class.[29] (emphasis added)

Lately a certain amount of petty bourgeois chauvinism about the state has crept into the writings of neo-Marxist scholars in the neo-colonies. They talk of the neo-colonies as 'their' states, the states of the 'bureaucratic bourgeoisie' (Shivji) or of the 'nascent commercial bourgeoisie' or personalised rule of one man (Mamdani) or of the 'auxiliary bourgeoisie' (Leys). This tendency is not unlike that which Lenin attacked on the eve of the October Revolution, a tendency that embraced the official socialist parties in Europe:

> This trend – socialism, in words and chauvinism in deeds . . . – is distinguished by the base, servile adaptation of the 'leaders of socialism' to the interest not only of 'their' national bourgeoisie, but precisely of 'their' state – for the majority of the so-called Great Powers have long been exploiting and enslaving a whole number of small and weak nationalities. And the imperialist war is precisely a war for a division and redivision of this kind of booty. The struggle for emancipation of the toiling masses from the influence of the bourgeoisie in general, and of the imperialist bourgeoisie in particular, is impossible without a struggle against opportunist prejudices concerning the 'state'.[30]

Once you abstract the neo-colonial state from imperialism and make it the 'property' of whoever is running the governments, you run down precipitously from Marxism to prediction and opportunism. All gates are now open to revisionism and reformism. Now that the state in the neo-colony is under the control of the 'local ruling class', what better instrument than the state for this 'ruling class' to acquire 'its' own capital, whether in the form of 'state capital' (as, according to Shivji, in Tanzania), or in the form of 'private capital' (as, according Leys, in Kenya), by simply nationalising 'foreign' capital? Listen, for comparison, to the reformist optimism of the revisionist non-capitalist readers about the role of the state in 'developing' countries:

> Relying on the state sector, these countries have great potential for establishing control over or nationalising foreign capital. Simultaneously, they restrict private capitalist activity and direct it into channels corresponding to national interests. When necessary, the state employs mixed companies in which national and foreign capital participate but the controlling blocks of shares and, hence, the management functions of such companies are in the hands of the state . . . the state sector has the important task of building up accumulation funds for the state to use them rationally for the country's economic development – first of all for industrialisation.[31]

Shivji saves himself from the reformist logic of his own argument about the Tanzanian state as being the state of the 'bureaucratic bourgeoisie' in virtue of the fact that at one level he electically <u>does</u> recognize the domination of imperialism over Tanzanian economy. But how can one class be dominant at one level, the economic level, and yet <u>another class</u> be dominant at another level, the political level? From Engels we learnt that 'as a general rule' the 'economically dominant class' also establishes itself 'through the medium of the state' as 'the politically dominant class'. Engels does admit, of course, exceptions to this general rule. But a careful reading of Engels (both in *Origin of the State, Family and Private Property* and the *Housing Question*) would show one that such exceptions arise when 'warring classes balance each other so nearly that the state power, as ostensible mediator, acquires, for the moment a certain degree of independence of both,[32] and secondly that, in any event, such a Bonapartist state continues to entrench the power of the class that is economically the more dominant. Neither Shivji nor Mamdani (to whom the argument equally applies) show which 'warring classes' had so nearly balanced each other in Tanzania or Uganda to warrant this exception from the general rule. Even if they were to show this, there would still be no justification for describing the classes whose political representatives run the apparatus of the state as the 'ruling classes' of the two states, for then they would have to show how these 'ruling classes' were using the state to acquire hegemony over all other contending classes, including, most importantly, over the imperialist bourgeoisie. Since so much is often made out of this argument based on the 'Bonapartist state', it is worth going a little further into this question.

Marx, in his *The Eighteenth Brumaire of Louis Bonaparte*, shows how a Bonapartist state actually arose in France in 1851. He describes the events leading to it in three periods. The first period, from 24 February to 4 May 1848, was the period of the provisional government. Although the bourgeoisie got the lion's share of power, nonetheless all classes, including social-democratic workers, were represented in the Parliament, and the workers got unexpected support from the petty bourgeoisie and the peasantry. The second period, from 4 May 1848 to 28 May 1849, was the period when the bourgeoisie achieved a crushing victory over the proletariat through isolating the proletariat, and uniting with all other classes to form the 'Party of Order'. Whereas formerly the bourgeoisie ruled in the name of the king as a bourgeois monarchy, now they ruled in the name of the people, as a bourgeois republic. The third period, from 28 May 1849 to 2 December, 1851, was the period of the Constitutional Republic and the Legislature National Assembly. The government, or the executive, was in the hands of the Party of Order, with Louis Napoleon Bonaparte acting as the President of the Republic, elected by the popular vote on 10 December 1848. But in the Parliament, the Party of Order, divided among its three factions (landed bourgeoisie, finance bourgeoisie and industrial bourgeoisie), found real opposition from the petty bourgeois *Montagne*. The petty bourgeoisie, having crushed the workers in the days of the June 1848 insurrection, and having found itself being crushed in turn by the big bourgeoisie, was now coming closer to the workers in forming a joint alliance against the Party of Order. The Party of Order was now increasingly realising that parliamentary democracy was a danger to its social power, and must be done away with.

> . . . the bourgeoisie confesses that its own interests dictate that it should be delivered from the danger of its <u>own rule;</u> that in order to restore tranquility in the country, its bourgeois parliament must, first of all, be given its quietus; that in order to preserve its social power intact, its political power must be broken . . . that in order to save its purse, it must forfeit the crown . . .[33]

From then on the Party of Order began to aid and abet every violation of the Constitution by the Executive, thus negating the power of the Parliament. The *coup d'etat* by Louis Napoleon, on 2 December 1851, was a logical outcome of this. As a Bohemian and 'Chief of the lumpenproletariat', Louis Napoleon Bonaparte raised himself on the strength of a private army consisting of, 10,000 rascally fellows', a drunken soldiery fed on 'liquor and sausages'. Who, then, was the 'ruling class' in the Bonapartist state? This 'class' of lumpenproletariat whose 'chief' Napoleon was? Or the 'poor peasantry' who put him in power way back in December 1848 as a Constitutional President? Or the big bourgeoisie? Marx answers:

> As the executive authority which had made itself an independent power, Bonaparte feels it to be his mission to safeguard 'bourgeois order'. But the strength of this bourgeois order lies in the middle class. He looks on himself, therefore, as the representative of the middle class and issues decrees in this sense. Nevertheless, he is somebody solely due to the fact that he has broken the political power of this middle class and daily breaks it anew. Consequently, he looks on himself as the adversary of the political and literary power of the middle class. But by protecting its material power, he generates its political power anew . . . As against the bourgeoisie, Bonaparte looks on himself, at the same time, as the representative of the peasants and of the people in general, who wants to make the lower classes of the people happy within the framework of bourgeois society . . . But, above all, Bonaparte looks on himself as the chief of the Society of December 10, as the representative of the lumpenproletariat to which he himself, his entourage, his government and his army belong, and whose prime consideration is to benefit itself and draw California lottery prizes from the state treasury. And he vindicates his position as chief of the Society of December 10 with decrees, without decrees, and despite decrees.[34] (emphasis added)

This, then, is the essence of the Bonapartist state. It came into existence through the decision of the bourgeoisie to strengthen the hands of the Executive, and to create an independent power of the state seemingly above classes, because parliamentary democracy had threatened to create social disorder. The 'grotesque mediocrity' who exercised final executive power, Louis Napoleon, had considerable sympathy for the peasants and the poor people, but his 'prime consideration' was simply to draw state funds for the consumption of himself and his entourage in the government and in the army, all of whom belonged to the *lumpenproletariat*. As for his relations with the bourgeoisie, he broke its political power daily, but 'by protecting its material power', he daily generated its 'political power anew'.

Thus even if Mamdani and Shivji were able to show that the model of the Bonapartist state applied to the situations in Uganda and Tanzania, as an exception to the general rule about the economically dominant class being at the same time the politically dominant class, they would be hard put to justify describing the classes whose political representatives run the state apparatuses in the two countries as their 'ruling classes'. The ruling class continues to remain that class, the international bourgeoisie, whose 'material power' is daily protected, and whose 'political power' is thus daily generated, by the governments which run the state apparatus in the neo-colonies.

And yet, above all, it would be incorrect to argue that a situation had arisen in the neo-colonies to make them exceptions to the general rule, making the Bonapartist states, however tempting the analogy might be. Shivji and Mamdani do not explicitly talk about the Bonapartist state, though their analysis implies it since they both take the position that Engels' general rule does not apply to the situations in

Tanzania and Uganda. Colin Leys, on the other hand, applies the analogy quite explicitly, although he adds the qualification that 'the parallel with Kenya is not exact'. (p. 208)

The neo-colonial state, we would argue, is a unique case. It is not a Bonapartist state. What has given rise to the neo-colonial state is the historically specific development of the contradiction between imperialism and the oppressed nations. It is a product, in other words, of the national question. The rise of nationalism in the colonies expressed itself in the demand for national self-determination. This demand, for the most part, has been articulated by the oppressed bourgeoisie and petty bourgeoisie who could carry with them the entire masses in their struggle against imperialism. Imperialism thus found it neccessary to make concessions, but the concessions amounted to no more than creating 'independent' governments in these countries run by the representatives of the local bourgeoisie and petty bourgeoisie. Nothing else changed. The masses of workers and peasants continue to be exploited and oppressed by imperialism just as before. Hence, the struggle against imperialism continues, only it is increasingly intensified.

This, in essence, is the character of the neo-colonial state. To describe it as a 'Bonapartist state' is to apply a false historical analogy, and to miss the specific features of the present epoch. The neo-colonial state remains the state of the international bourgeoisie, though, like all states, it enjoys a degree of relative autonomy from the direct control of the ruling classes, especially when the imperialist bourgeoisie is not a homogeneous united class, but one in which there is intense competition between rival monopoly bourgeoisies. This relative autonomy, plus the fact that even the most reactionary petty bourgeois regimes in the neo-colonies have to pay at least lip-service to the anti-imperialist demands of the exploited and oppressed masses explains why, at times, these states appear to take actions independently of the imperialist bourgeoisie. But twist and turn as they might, their actions only serve to protect the material power of the imperialist bourgeoisie, and with it, its political power. Not until a New Democratic Revolution is carried out against imperialism based on a common front of all the exploited and oppressed classes in the neo-colonies and led by a proletarian leadership and a proletarian ideology will the power of capital be broken, and with it the present class character of the neo-colonial state.

CONCLUSION

In this review we have concentrated on issues of theory rather than of detail because it is our contention that the theory that underlies the analyses of the three authors reviewed here is faulty, and therefore necessarily leads to faulty analysis; also because more detailed criticism of Shivji and Mamdani has already been carried out by D.W. Nabudere, with whose criticism I generally agree. We have also quoted extensively from Marxist texts because the authors adduce the authority of Marx to advance their false theories.

The key questions which have divided and which continue to divide Marxists in their analyses of 'Third World' countries are questions relating to the character of the state and the nature of the capital that arise in these countries. Whose state and whose capital? It is on the answers to these questions, based on a correct theory arrived at by the application of the method of dialectical materialism, that depend not only our understanding of these countries, but also the strategic implications for proletarian struggle. The importance of a correct theory cannot be underestimated. Facts interpreted empiricistically cannot yield a correct theory. Furthermore, theory is important and relevant only when it leads to correct practice. It is significant that none of the three authors reviewed have bothered to draw out the political implications for proletarian practice from their theoretical analysis.

When the questions of theory (whose state and whose capital) are exposed to the light of scientific inquiry of Marxism-Leninism and their practical implications fully drawn out, it becomes clear that the issues at stake here are not trivial. To maintain, as Shivji, Mamdani and Leys do, that the capital that exploits the workers and peasants in Tanzania, Uganda and Kenya is the capital of a local class which is only in a 'dependent' relationship with imperialist capital, is to take a theoretical position that is diametrically opposite to the position that that capital belongs to the imperialist bourgeoisie, and the local classes which employ that capital, while unquestionably appropriating a part of the surplus value, are objectively only servicing agents of imperialist capital. There are, no doubt, contradictions between the local classes and the imperialist bourgeoisie, but the character of these contradictions can be understood only if the ownership of capital is clearly determined. And on this there are two lines. The struggle therefore is between these two lines. No amount of sophistry that eclectically and idealistically attempts to combine the two lines, by maintaining on the one hand that the capital belongs to the local bourgeois classes and on the other hand that imperialist capital still continues to 'dominate' the local bourgeoisie, can invalidate the objective reality that that capital is the capital of the monopoly bourgeoisies. These bourgeoisies are in fierce competition with one another in the context of a continuous movement of capital toward its further concentration and centralisation, and to think that they would allow the rise of 'national' capitals in the neo-colonies is to misunderstand the very essence of the historical movement of capital, to misunderstand Marx himself.

As with capital, so with the state. To argue that these neo-colonial states are states of the local 'dependent' bourgeoisies is to compound the error at the superstructural level, having laid its roots at the economic level. The very concept of a separate 'ruling class' for every state in the world is a backward, reactionary concept. It is as if capitalism were not a world system, as if the world were divided into fragmented capitals, some large, some small, each in an interdependent relationship with the others. The reality of imperialism is thus bodily thrown outside the window. There is nothing scientific about this kind of analysis.

The strategy of proletarian struggle that follows this kind of analysis is a strategy foredoomed to failure. Though, as we said earlier, none of the three authors, like pure academicians, bother to draw out the strategic implications of their analyses, these are not far to seek. The anti-imperialist aspects in their analysis are given a purely formalistic treatment, and hence imperialism is for them only a formal enemy, remote and untouchable. The real enemy for them is the local bourgeoisie. It is against it that they would have the workers and peasants to take up their cudgels. This is so, also, because for them the state is the state of the local bourgeoisie, and insofar as the workers and peasants must battle against the state it is, as far as they are concerned, the local bourgeoisies against whom they would be fighting. Only when imperialism actually invades the country physically, one of them said,[35] does imperialism become the immediate enemy.

This is absolutely incorrect from beginning to end. Of course, the workers and peasants must arraign themselves against the state, the neo-colonial state, but this state is a state not of the local bourgeoisies but of imperialist capital. In fighting the neo-colonial state, including all its coercive and ideological apparatuses, the workers and peasants fight against imperialism itself. In this task the proletariat must not isolate themselves, but must build as broad in anti-imperialist front as possible. They must not be poking fingers into the eyes of the local bourgeoisie as the 'main enemy' driving them into the arms of imperialism itself. Many of these local bourgeoisie might well be reactionary and unredeemable, but a good number will come to the side of the exploited and oppressed masses, once the latter begin to show unity and strength. In trying to advocate a strategy of struggle which unites the local bourgeoisie and drive them into the ranks of imperialism, the neo-Trotskyites are issuing a clear 'manifesto to adventurism.'

NOTES

1. Or as Mao put it: 'This democratic method of resolving contradictions among the people was epitomized in 1942 in the formula "unity, criticism, unity". To elaborate, it means starting for the desire for unity, resolving contradictions through criticism or struggle and arriving at a new unity on a new basis'. *'On the Correct Handling of Contradictions Among the People', Four Essays on Philosophy,* Foreign Languages Press, Peking, 1968, p. 87.
2. In his essay 'Combat Liberalism', Mao writes:

> We stand for active ideological struggle because it is the weapon for ensuring unity within the Party and the revolutionary organizations in the interest of our fight. Every communist and revolutionary should take up this weapon.
> But liberalism rejects ideological struggle and stands for unprincipled peace, thus giving rise to a decadent, philistine attitude and bringing about political degeneration in certain units and individuals in the Party and revolutionary organisations. *Selected Works,* Vol. II, p. 31.

Mao then goes on to list eleven principal manifestations of liberalism, of which the first two are:

> To let things slide for the sake of peace and friendship when a person has clearly gone wrong, and refrain from principled argument because he is an old acquaintance... Or to touch on the matter lightly instead of thoroughly, so as to keep on good terms...
> To indulge in irresponsible criticism in private instead of actively putting forward one's suggestions to the organization. To say nothing to people to their faces but to gossip behind their backs, or to say nothing at a meeting but to gossip afterwards...

3. The title for "pioneering" Marxist analysis of Uganda must really be claimed by R. Mukherjee for his *Uganda: The Problem of Acculturation,* Berlin: Akademie-Verlag, 1956, a book much neglected for having appeared before the thirst for Marxist writing had fully developed.
4. See, for example, Colin Leys, 'The "Overdeveloped" Post-Colonial State: A Reevaluation', *Review of African Political Economy,* No. 5 (Jan.-Apr. 1976).
5. For a further elaboration of this see Engels, *Anti-Duhring,* 'Part 1: Philosophy'; and Mao Tse-tung, 'On Contradiction', *Selected Works,* Vol. 1.
6. I. Shivji, *Class Struggles in Tanzania,* Dar es Salaam and London: Tanzania Publishing House and Heinneman, 1975, p. 178.
7. Mamdani, *Politics and Class Formation in Uganda,* p. 307.
8. Ibid., p. 229.
9. Ibid., pp. 303-4.
10. Ibid., p. 245.
11. Ibid., p. 271.
12. Mao Tse-tung in analysing his own country, said the following:

> In our country, the contradiction between the working class and the national bourgeoisie belongs to the category of contradictions among the people. By and large, the class struggle between the two is a class struggle within the ranks of the people,

because the Chinese national bourgeoisie has a dual character. In the period of the bourgeois-democratic revolution, it had a revolutionary as well as a conciliatory side to its character. In the period of the socialist revolution, exploitation of the working class for profit constitutes one side of the character of the national bourgeoisie, while its support of the Constitution and its willingness to accept specialist transformation constitute the other.

'On the Correct Handling of Contradictions Among the People', *Four Essays on Philosophy,* p. 82.

13. Mao Tse-tuing, *Selected Works*, Vol. 1, Peking: Foreign Languages Press, p. 331.
14. M. Mamdani, *Maji Maji,* No. 29, Dar es Salaam: (1976).
15. Mao Tse-tung, *Selected Works,* op cit., p. 332.
16. Mao Tse-tung, *Four Essays on Philosophy,* p. 82.
17. C. Leys, *Underdevelopment in Kenya,* p. 7.
18. Lenin, 'Imperialism the Highest Stage of Capitalism', *Collected Works,* Vol. 22, Moscow: Progress Publishers, pp. 266-7.
19. C. Leys, op cit., p. 146.
20. Ibid., p. 169.
21. Marx and Engels, *Selected Works,* Vol. I, Moscow: Progress Publishers, p. 230.
22. Ibid., p. 231.
23. Lenin, op cit, pp. 104-5.
24. Ibid., p. 17.
25. Ibid., p. 26.
26. Mamdani, p. 307.
27. See *Daily News* (Dar es Salaam), February 1977.
28. Lenin, *Collected Works,* Vol. 22, Moscow: Progress Publishers, p. 538.
29. Marx and Engels, *Selected Works,* Vol. 3, Moscow: Progress Publishers, p. 328.
30. Lenin, *Collected Works,* Vol. 25, pp. 387-8.
31. From a study produced by a group of scholars led by V.F. Stanis, Rector of the Patrice Lumumba Friendship University, *The Role of the State in Socio-Economic Reforms in Developing Countries,* Moscow: Progress Publishers, 1976, p. 49.
32. Marx and Engels, *Selected Works,* Vol. 3, Moscow: Progress Publishers, p. 328.
33. Marx and Engles, *Selected Works,* Vol. 1, Moscow: Progress Publishers, p. 436.
34. Ibid., pp. 484-5.
35. Mamdani, *Maji Maji*, No. 29, Dar es Salaam, 1976.

16

THE STATE IN THE DOMINATED SOCIAL FORMATIONS OF AFRICA: SOME THEORETICAL ISSUES

Isaa G. Shivji

THE NATURE OF THE STATE

According to Marxist theory, the state is an instrument – an organ – of one class against another. It was born together with antagonistic classes in society. The state is an organ which expresses dominant class power in its most concentrated form. Although Marx and Engels used the term 'instrument' in describing the state, it is clear from their various writings that they did not have an 'instrumentalist' or mechanistic view of it. They saw the state as an organ, rather than simply a weapon of the oppressing class: it is its political power. And political power, as the *Communist Manifesto* put it, 'is merely the organized power of one class for oppressing another'.[1]

Thus, it is a fundamental principle of Marxist theory that the state is a class category and that state or political power always has a class character. For Lenin, therefore, the basic problem of every revolution was that of state power. And Marx's most important theoretical generalization, after the experience of the Paris Commune, was that the working class could not simply lay hold of the ready-made state machinery and wield it for its own purposes;[2] that the bureaucratic-military machine, i.e. the state, could not simply be transferred from one hand to another but that it had to be smashed and 'this is the preliminary condition for every real people's revolution on the Continent'.[3]

It is this very principle which lies at the base of the controversy on the nature of states in independent African countries. But before we deal with the different views on this, let us quickly recall two important recent events, both of which once again brought to the fore the theoretical question of the class character of the state.

One of the most significant points of difference between the Chinese Communist Party (CPC) and the Communist Party of the Soviet Union (CPSU), in their ideological split of the early 1960s, was the problem of characterization of the state in the Soveit Union. The 1961 Programme of the CPSU, adopted by the Twenty-second Party Congress, proclaimed:

> Having brought about the complete and final victory of socialism – the first phase of communism – and the transition of society to the full-scale construction of communism, the dictatorship of the proletariat has fulfilled its historic mission and has ceased to be indispensable in the USSR from the point of view of the tasks of internal development. The state, which arose as a state of the dictatorship of the proletariat, has in the new, contemporary stage, become a state of the entire people, an organ expressing the interests and will of the people as a whole.[4]

And further:

> The Party holds that the dictatorship of the working class will cease to be necessary before the state withers away. The state as an organization of the entire people will survive until the complete victory of communism.[5]

This was a declaration of a state without class character since it was a 'state of the entire people' and not a dictatorship of a particular class. The CPC, in its polemic, vigorously argued that the thesis of the 'state of the entire people' was fundamentally against the universal truth of Marxism-Leninism. It said:

> In the view of Marxist-Leninists, there is no such thing as a non-class or supra-class state. So long as the state remains a state, it must bear a class character; so long as the state exists, it cannot be a state of the 'whole people'. As soon as society becomes classless, there will no longer be a state.[6]

While between the CPC and CPSU this was essentially an ideological question, for the Indonesia Communist Party (PKI) the definition of the class character of the state had immediate practical implications. In attempting to define the character of the Indonesian state during Sukarno's time, the leadership of the PKI put forward, what has subsequently come to be called, the 'theory of two aspects in state power'.

This thesis argued that state power was characterized by two aspects: the anti-people aspect consisting of compradore, bureaucrat-capitalist and landlord classes on the one hand, and the pro-people aspect composed mainly of the national bourgeoisie and the proletariat.[7] D.N. Aidit, the then leader of the PKI, succinctly summarized the 'two-aspect theory' thus:

> The economic structure (basis) of the present Indonesian society is still colonial and semi-feudal. However, at the same time there is the struggle of the people against this economic system, the struggle for a national and democratic economy. . .
>
> The realities of the basis are also reflected in the superstructure, including in the state power, and especially in the cabinet. In the state power are reflected both the forces that are against the colonial and feudal economic system, and the forces that defend imperialism, the vestiges of feudalism, bureaucrat-capitalism and the compradores. . .
>
> The state power of the Republic of Indonesia, viewed as a contradiction, is a contradiction between two mutually opposing aspects. The first aspect is the aspect which represents the interests of the people (manifested by the progressive stand and policies of President Sukarno that are supported by the PKI and other groups of the people). The second aspect is the aspect that represents the enemies of the people (manifested by the stand and policies of the Right-wing forces or the diehards). The people aspect has become the main aspect and takes the leading role in the state power of the Republic of Indonesia.[8]

The 'two-aspect-in-state-power' theory had very little to do with the teachings of Marx and Lenin on the question of the class character of state power. However, it justified and rationalized the participation of the then leadership of the PKI in the state. It lent support to their reliance on and loyalty to the ideology of Sukarno, who was supposed to represent the 'pro-people' aspect in the state.

However, when the class battle came to a head, the state showed its true character. In the coup of September–October 1965, Sukarno's regime was practically overthrown and the party was banned. In the self-criticism[9] that followed, the PKI leadership that escaped annihilation bitterly criticized the two-aspect theory as in 'opportunist or revisionist deviation' because it denied the Marxist-Leninist teaching that 'the state is an organ of the rule of a definite class which cannot be reconciled with its antipode (the class opposite to it)'.[10] 'It is unthinkable that the Republic of Indonesia can be jointly ruled by the people and the enemies of the people.'[11]

If we have cited the Sino-Soviet debate and the PKI's theory at some length, it is because both of these have found echoes in the current debates in East Africa on the class character of the state.

The counterpart in Africa of the Soviet theory of the 'state of the entire people' is the theory of the 'non-capitalists state'. This tries to come to grips with those regimes which have adopted some form or other of socialism as their ideology. The states in these countries are defined as socialist-oriented: their class character is neither bourgeois nor proletarian. In other words, state power here has no definite class character but is said to be leaning towards socialism.[12] This type of state is a transitional type: not bourgeois (also not tendentially, though capitalist elements exist), not yet socialist.' The adherents of this theory see a special role for states, that of social transformation. 'These are countries where state power is used as an instrument of a social transformation, starting from predominantly pre-feudal and pre-capitalist, sometimes feudal or semi-feudal relations and aiming at socialist formation without passing through a capitalist formation'.[13] In one swoop, this thesis dismisses two fundamental propositions of the Marxist theory of the state: 'that state power is a concentrated expression of the rule of the oppressor class and that the transition from class to classless society (i.e. socialism) will inevitably pass through the dictatorship of the proletariat which is nothing but the proletariat organized as the ruling class'.[14] Lenin considered this second proposition so fundamental to Marxist theory, that, he said, it constituted 'the most profound distinction between the Marxist and the ordinary petty (as well as big) bourgeois'.[15]

There is a second school of 'independent' scholars which has also attempted to theorize on the nature of the state in Africa, particularly in those countries where the regimes have proclaimed some form of socialism. The two leading proponents are Roger Murray[16] and John Saul.[17] Their main focus has been Ghana under Nkrumah and the United Republic of Tanzania under Nyerere, respectively.

Succinctly, the main thesis of these writers may be summarized as follows. Their point of departure is that the social formations under discussion are essentially characterized by 'unformed' classes. This is especially true of that class – the petty bourgeoisie or Murray's 'political class' – which accedes to state power after independence. This, too, is an unformed class and therefore the class character of the post-colonial state is not only 'undetermined' but even opens up the possibility of sections of this class using state power to institute socialism.

"The essence of the matter is that the post-colonial state (the 'political kingdom') has simultaneously to be perceived as the actual instrument of a continuing anti-imperialist and socialist revolutionary."[18] Thus, these authors see a section of the petty bourgeoisie who are already in state power as 'committing suicide' and pursuing the 'historical alternative' of socialism. Whether they will do so or not is a 'political X' (to use Saul's phrase), i.e. an unknown in the equation.

It can be readily seen that this thesis comes very close to the two-aspect theory of Aidit. All along the line it is an outright denial of the fundamental propositions of Marx's theory. By introducing the concept of 'political class' and such notions as 'plasticity' of a class, it clearly departs from the Marxist understanding of a class as essentially defined in relation to its role in the social process of production. By positing the possibility of a petty-bourgeoisie opting for a socialist alternative, it completely negates the thesis of the hegemony of the proletariat. By propounding that the class character of the state is 'undetermined' and speculating on the possibility of state power carrying out socialist strategies, it denies the class character of the state and the neeed to smash the state machinery for revolutionary transformation. Since these authors claim to be applying the Marxist theory of the state to the concrete reality in Africa, it is important to emphasize these departures from the fundamental propositions of that theory: unless, of course, these authors argue that such propositions have been invalidated in Africa and develop an alternative theory of the state. Since they have done neither, their theses can only be evaluated in relation to Marxist theory as a whole.

Finally, there is another school of 'Marxist' theoreticians for whom the question of concretely determining the class character of state power does not arise at all.[19] We shall deal with their theses in greater detail in the next section. Suffice it to mention here that, for these scholars, state power in all the neo-colonies is in the hands of a global financial oligarchy, and local classes have no share in it. Members of local classes may man the state apparatus, but they have nothing to do with state power. They are only 'servicing agents' of the financial oligarchy. A few of these servicing agents may be reactionary and faithful agents of imperialism but a large number of them are 'innocent' and on the side of the people. the task of the revolution is to isolate these few elements and support the many against imperialism. thus the problem of both state power and revolution is solved these 'Marxists' by their overall analysis of global imperialism.

STATE AND RULING CLASS

The problem of which class or classes hold state power in the social formations dominated by imperialism has been at the centre of intense discussions in East Africa. As will be readily seen, this question is closely tied up with the change from colonial to neo-colonial state.

With differences of emphasis and formulations, it appears that most writers are agreed that, under colonialism, the ruling class was the metropolitan bourgeoisie. In other words the colonial state was part of the imperialist state. The question then arises: What change, if any, did independence bring? According to D.W. Nabudere and his associates, who have been most concerned with the issue, independence involved virtually no change in the class character of state power. They argue that the ruling class in all the neo-colonial states, as well as the imperialist state, is the financial oligarchy. With the rise of imperialism this financial oligarchy concentrated all capital in its hands at the global level; thus they control and dominate the economies of all the neo-colonies. Since the financial oligarchy is the economically dominant class, it also rules politically and is therefore the ruling class: the owners of capital are also the owners of the state.

Let us quote Nabudere at some length to get the flavour of his argument:

> We have already shown that when capitalism enters its monopoly phase it does so with the rise of a financial oligarchy which dispossesses other bourgeoisies and thus turns them into a petty-bourgeoisie. Colonialism, which arises with this phase, implies exports of finance capital.
> This capital produces a petty-bourgeoisie in the colonies. It could not reproduce a national bourgeoisie when, in the imperialist country itself, such a bourgeoisie is negated and destroyed, giving rise to a financial oligarchy. In colonies which arose before this phase any national bourgeoisie which might have sprouted was routed by finance capital and was increasingly turned into a petty-bourgeoisie. This petty-bourgeoisie is stratified according to its role

in the process of production and distribution. This to us must be the starting point in analysing classes in a particular country.[20]

Nabudere's starting-point is actually also his conclusion for he argues in the same article that 'in its old age a monopolist stratum within it dispossesses the other and increasingly turns it into a petty-bourgeoisie, and turns some of the petty-bourgeoisie into members of the proletariat while creating and reproducing a petty-bourgeoisie, proletariat and a commodity-producing peasantry on a world scale.[21] In this thesis we have a picture of global class formation which makes it almost unnecessary to attempt a class analysis of a concrete social formation. Since with the rise of imperialism, the financial oligarchy has 'dispossessed', 'routed', 'negated' and 'destroyed' all bourgeoisie, the only classes we can expect to find in the dominated formations are the petty bourgeoisie, the proletariat an the commodity-producing peasantry. And as with economics so with politics for, as Nabudere puts it rhetorically: 'Can there be any doubt that the economically dominant class in the neo-colony is the financial oligarchy of the imperialist countries and that politics must reflect the base?'[22]

Yash Tandon closely follows the footsteps of Nabudere. In his essay, significantly entitled 'Whose Capital and Whose State?', Tandon argues in the same vein except that, unlike Nabudere, he admits the existence of a local bourgeoisie. But he asserts that this local bourgeoisie has no capital of its own. All capital is owned by the imperialist bourgeoisie while the local classes only 'employ that capital'.[23] They are therefore nothing but the 'servicing agents' (Tandon's phrase) of imperialist capital. Whereas, for Nabudere, the only change at independence was that the personnel of the state apparatus was now recruited from the local petty bourgeoisie, for Tandon independence meant a change in the government, not the state.

Let us ignore the various inconsistencies and contradictions in these formulations and concentrate on the central theses. Those acquainted with the Marxist debates of the early part of this century would at once recognize the similarity between these theses and those advanced at different times by Kautsky and Kievsky. Both these theoreticians were answered by Lenin. Since Nabudere and his associates forcefully claim to derive their theses faithfully from Lenin, it is appropriate to recall very briefly Lenin's position in these early debates.

Kautsky speculated on the possibility of all national finance capitals uniting to form an internationaly united finance capital which would jointly exploit the world.[24] Nabudere's thesis of a world financial oligarchy comes very close to Kautsky's internationally united finance capital. Kautsky used his theory to justify presenting imperialism as peaceful. Lenin derided this view as opportunist, for

> It evades and obscures the very profound and fundamental contradictions of imperialism: the contradictions between monopoly and free competition which exists side by side with it, between the gigantic 'operations' (and gigantic profits) of finance capital and 'honest' trade in the free market, the contradiction between cartels and trusts, on the one hand, and non-cartelized industry, on the other, etc.[25]

Lenin argued that the various alliances between imperialist countries were simply temporary truces in periods between wars, and that monopoly capitalism did not do away with competition but rather intensified it among the rival finance capitals. It is this which is the source of imperialist wars. Thus Lenin could have never conceived of finance capital so united internationally that it could provide the basis of a world ruling class.

Kievsky, on the other hand, argued against the demand for national self-determination to be included in the party programme of the Bolsheviks on the grounds that in the 'era of finance capital' national self-determination was 'unachievable'. Not only that, but such a demand would be reactionary because the national state fetters the development of productive forces.[26] Lenin refuted this argument as a caricature of Marxism and an example of 'imperialist economism'. The demand for national self-determination, Lenin argued, was essentially a demand for political independence, for a right of the oppressed nation to establish a separate state. This did not mean that political independence would necessarily mean economic independence, for finance capital was capable of subordinating the economies of most sovereign, politically independent, countries. Nevertheless, the creation of separate, sovereign and politically independent states was possible and achievable. The right of the colonies and oppressed nations to secede and create independent states was a fundamental democratic right and should be supported by the proletariat.

In this polemic, Lenin's position on the question of the meaning of political independence is clear and may be summarized as follows:

Political independence or national self-determination means the establishment of a separate national state.

That under imperialism the establishment of such separate national state is possible and achievable.

That political independence does not mean that finance capital is unable to continue dominating independent countries.[27]

The question is: what could Lenin have meant by a 'separate national state' if not a state where power is in the hands of a local or classes? Or, could he, like Nabudere, have meant simply a state whose personnel is drawn from local classes? To ask these questions is really to answer them.

It is now clear that Nabudere's thesis has nothing in common with Lenin's theory on this important question of state and ruling class. Nor do writers like Saul provide us with an alternative, coherent theory in opposition to the theory of Marx and Lenin.

Finally, we must briefly discuss the thesis of another scholar, who has also written mainly on the United Republic of Tanzania. Freyhold has tried to escape Nabudere's conclusions derived from a formalistic application of 'economically dominant/politically ruling class' by creating a new term, 'governing class':

> One distinction which ought to be made is that between the ruling class and the governing class (Poulantzas). It is a normal feature of capitalism that the economically ruling class does not govern the state directly but leaves this to hierarchies of state functionaries and politicians who are conditioned and compelled in a number of ways to act according to the general interests of the ruling class. Unless the governing class actually determines the process of economic reproduction in the country it cannot be called a ruling class however large its formal powers may be.[28]

The governing class for Freyhold is made up of the top personnel ('i.e. the ministers, principal secretaries and directors of the administrative apparatus, the general managers of the larger parastatals, the heads of the appointed party bureaucracy at the different levels, the heads of the repressive apparatus[29]) of the state apparatus. They are the functionaries or top employees of the state but certainly not the holders of state power. Who then constitute the ruling class? 'The ruling class which determine the core functions of the state and the actual dynamics of the economy is the metropolitan bourgeoisie represented in Tanzania mainly by the World Bank, aid agencies of Nordic and other European countries and a variety of transnational corporations'.[30]

For Freyhold, as for Nabudere, there appears to be a single world ruling class which she calls 'metropolitan bourgeoisie' (Nabudere's 'financial oligarchy'). Whereas Kautsky logically extended the tendency towards economic concentration into the fact of a single world monopoly ('internationally united finance capital'), *a la Kievsky*, to create a 'fact' of a concentrated, single ruling class! All the arguments Lenin advanced against Kautsky and Kievsky, therefore, apply with even greater force to these writers. To uphold their thesis of a single ruling class at a global level, which exercises state power in all the imperialist and neo-colonial countries, Nabudere and Freyhold would have to show, first and foremost, that there exists such a single class at a world level. Since classes are 'large groups of people differing from each other by the place they occupy in the historically determined system of social production' (Lenin),[31] they would at least have to show the existence of a single system of social production at a world level. Certainly, neither Nabudere, much less Freyhold, would argue that there exists a single system of social production (a single social formation) at the global level.

The concept of 'governing class', too, presents many problems. First, it is not clear who constitutes the top personnel in the state apparatus as a class. they would constitute a class if it were shown that they occupy of a definite place in the system of social production, etc., which is not Freyhold's argument. Rather, she concentrates on the fact that are top functionaries of the state. Being employed by the state, however, does not make a social group into a class: if it did, then all the functionaries, from minister to messenger in the state apparatus, would be part of Freyhold's governing class.

Lastly, there is an irreconcilable contradiction between Freyhold's theoretical conception of the governing class and her description and analysis of the 'governing class' in the United Republic of Tanzania. In theory the governing class is supposed to have only formal power, while in practice the Tanzanian 'governing class', according to Freyhold, has exerted power and performed all those functions (through the state) that one would attribute to a ruling class.

According to Freyhold, the 'governing class' in the United Republic of Tanzania since independence has consolidated the state, established its supremacy and mobilized 'supportive' classes, in the process reconstructing the state in its own interests and in line with the interests of foreign investors. They have expanded the economic apparatuses of the state by nationalization and other measures, thus creating a public sector. There were two main reasons, Freyhold says, for the governing class to opt for state-capitalism.

> The option for a collective appropriation was dictated to the ruling class by its weakness *vis-a-vis* other social classes and the lack of resources for the state apparatus. Allowing its own members and African petty bourgeois outside the public sector to scramble individually for places in a newly opened up sector for African capitalism would have eroded the unity and discipline within the governing class and would have left it without the strength and the resources necessary to stabilise its position.

While consolidating its economic base through the economic apparatuses of the state, 'the governing class also transformed the old independence movement into a special ideological apparatus of the state capable of submerging any independent organization of peasants and workers and capable of providing an additional clientele for the governing class'. And finally the expansion of the repressive apparatus has gone on apace by the expansion of the army, the national service and the militia.

What is more, the 'governing class' has also developed its own ideology to justify this expansion, its extended power and to build up the support of intermediate classes.

> Seen over a longer period the socialism of the *nizers* [another terminological invention of Freyhold's, which means the same thing as her 'governing class'] was in practice a set of strategies which expanded their power *vis-a-vis* the submerged classes, gave them the means to build up an intermediate class which supports them and put them into a position that made them a viable partner to the metropolitan bourgeoisie.

It is thus that the 'governing class' has built up the 'post-colonial state' which 'enjoys more power and stability than it ever had before'. Of course, there are dangers to this stability which arise from the various 'contradictions internal to the Tanzanian type of state-capitalism which express themselves in the difficulty for the state to accumulate the capital which the governing class needs both in order to cooperate with the metropolitan bourgeoisie and order to maintain and expand its supporting class.'[32]

This interesting analysis of the Tanzania state probably comes quite close to reality but hardly justifies Freyhold's theoretical proposition that her 'governing class' has only 'formal power' and that it is different from a ruling class. We would suggest that Freyhold's own analysis shows that there is no conceptual difference between her 'governing class' and the concept of ruling class. In her concrete analysis she is describing the same phenomenon by a different term, which 'terminological' distinction is in any case hardly justified except to allow for opportunistic interpretations.

CONCLUSION

Here, we will attempt to gather together the main threads of the foregoing critique in the form of some broad theoretical propositions.

It must be emphasized that the concrete class character of any particular state is to be defined by a concrete analysis of the particular social formation under discussion. While general theoretical propositions are a guide, they cannot be a substitute for a concrete analysis. However, the issues raised above are of a sufficient general character to allow for theoretical treatment.

As we have seen, the main issues revolve around the nature and class character of the neo-colonial state. But this cannot be dealt with separately from the questions of the colonial state and political independence.

Although the term 'colonial state' has gained wide currency, it is clear that it does not constitute a separate category. With the colonization of a particular country, the imperialist power involved extends certain apparatuses of the imperialist state to its colony. The term 'colonial state' is a kind of short-hand to describe these local apparatuses of the imperialist state. The state power rests in the hands of the ruling class of the imperialist country. This does not, of course, preclude certain autonomy in decision-making on the part of those who run the local apparatuses. The point, however, is that the ruling class is that of the colonizing country, which makes the so-called 'colonial state' nothing but part of the imperialist state.

Many observers have noted the exaggerated prominence of the bureaucratic and military, as opposed to political (parliamentary institutions, etc.,) apparatuses in the 'colonial state'. This, we suggest, is one manifestation of the thoroughly anti-democratic nature of imperialism, for, as Lenin said, 'imperialism is . . . the "negation" of democracy in general, of all democracy'.[33] And this characteristic is to be seen not only in the 'colonial state' but also in the neo-colonial ones, where imperialism is allied with the most reactionary local ruling classes.

Political independence is an important step in the general struggle for national liberation. It is one of the democratic demands of the oppressed nation. It means the creation of a separate national state, but does not automatically bring the end of the economic domination of finance capital. It does mean, however, that state power is no longer directly controlled by the ruling class of the former colonizing power.

In a neo-colonial state, state power rests in the hands of a local class or classes which constitute the ruling class. This class or classes have their own class interests arising from the place they occupy in social production, which in the longer run coincide with the interests of imperialism as a whole.

In a neo-colonial situation, the inter-imperialist rivalries come to have a full weight because the various factions and classes in the local state power forge alliances with different imperialist powers in line with their own interests. Both the internal class contradictions and the inter-imperialist rivalries are reflected in the constant political turbulence and reorganization of the ruling blocs in these countries. Thus, power in the neo-colonial state is imbued with the crisis of hegemony, popularly interpreted as political instability.

The various neo-colonial ruling classes exhibit different degrees of independence from particular imperialist powers, in line with the conjuncture of class alliances and struggle at particular times.

Those who argue that political independence does not bring any change in the class character of state power are hard put to analyse the politics of neo-colonialism. They have to explain the local politics as a direct, crude reflection of inter-imperialist rivalries despite having first posited a monolithic, global financial oligarchy. On the other hand, their interpretation of local political struggle and alignments is reduced to islated conspiracies and intrigues since they deny the role of local classes in state power.

The force of the Marxist theory lies in its being able to explain concrete political movements, and thus become a guide to action. There must be something fundamentally wrong with the 'Marxist' theory of those who can repeat all the truisms but resort to subjectivist explanations of concrete political changes.

Notes

1. Karl Marx and Friendrich Engels, 'Manifesto of the Communist Party', in Marx and Engels, *Selected Works,* Vol. 1, p. 127, Moscow, Progress Publishers, 1969 (3 vols.).
2. Karl Marx, 'The Civil War in France', in Marx and Engels, *On the Paris Commune,* p. 68, Moscow, Progress Publishers. 1971, p. 357.
3. Karl Marx, 'Letter to Ludwig Kugelmann, April 12, 1871', ibid, p. 284.
4. 'The Communist Party of the Soviet Union: the New Communist Manifesto', D.N. Jacobs (ed.), *The New Communist Manifesto and Related Documents,* 3rd ed., p. 30, New York, Evanston/London, Harper & Row, 1965, p. 256. (Harper Torchbooks).
5. Ibid;, p. 31.
6. 'The Central Commitee of the Communist Party of China. Letter to the Central Committee of the Communist Party of the Soviet Union, June 14, 1963', in The Communist Party of China, *The Polemic on the General Line of the International Communist Movement,* p. 36, London, Red Star Press, 1976.
7. R. Mortimer, *Indonesian Communism under Sukarno, Ideology and Politics, 1959-1965,* p. 132-40, Ithaca and London, Cornell University Press, 1974.
8. Quoted in ibid., p. 134, taken from 'Build the PKI along the Marxist-Leninist Line to lead the People's Democratic Revolution in Indonesia (self-criticism of the Political Bureau of the CC PKI, September 1966)', *Five Important Documents of the Political Bureau of the CC PKI,* p. 50, London, Banner Books and Crafts Ltd., n.d.,p. 280.
9. The self-criticism is to be found in the booklet cited above. According to Mortimer, op.

cit., pp. 397-9, this self-criticism was put out by the Peking-based group of the PKI leadership, who disavowed Aidit's theories.

10. Ibid., p. 132. This quotation is from Lenin's 'The State and Revolution', *Collected Works*, Vol. 25.

11. Ibid.

12. See, for instance, G. Brehme: 'State and Law in Post-colonial Independent States', in Othman, Haroub (ed.), *The State in Tanzania*, Dar es Salaam, Institute of Development Studies, University of Dar es Salaam, July 1977 (mimeographed).

13. Ibid;, p. 6.

14. Karl Marx and Friedrich Engels, 'Manifesto of the Communist Party', op. cit., p. 126.

15. V.I. Lenin, 'The State and Revolution', *Collected Works*, Vol. 25, p. 417, Moscow, Progress Publishers, 1964.

16. R. Murray, 'Second Thoughts on Ghana', *New Left Review* (London), No. 42 March/April 1967.

17. John Saul's main relevant articles are 'The State in Post-Colonial Societies–Tanzania', *The Socialist Register* (London), 1974, 'The Unsteady State: Uganda, Obote and General Amin', *Review of African Political Economy* (London), No. 5, January-April 1976.

18. R. Murray, quoted in Saul, op. cit,. p. 352.

19. The main writers in this school are D.W. Nabudere and Y. Tandon. Their two articles summarize their position well: D.W. Nabudere, 'Imperialism, State, Class and Race' (A critique of Shivji's *Class Struggles in Tanzania*), *Utafiti* (Dar es Salaam, University of Dar es Salaam), Vol. II, No. 1 1977; Y. Tandon, 'Whose Capital and Whose State?', University of Dar es Salaam, March 1977 (mimeographed).

20. Nabudere, op. cit., p. 67-8.

21. Ibid., p. 65.

22. Ibid., p. 72.

23. Tandon, op. cit., p. 21.

24. The whole argument and Lenin's rebuttal are in V.I. Lenin, 'Imperialism, the Highest Stage of Capitalism', *Collected Works*, Vol. 22, p. 285-98.

25. Ibid., p. 293. In his Preface to N. Bukharin's pamphlet, 'Imperialism and the world economy', Lenin said: '*Abstract* theoretical reasoning may lead to the conclusion at which Kautsky has arrived in a somewhat different fashion but also by abandoning Marxism namely, that the time is not too far when these magnates of capital will unite on a world scale in a single world trust, substituting an internationally united finance capital for the competition and struggle between sums of finance capital nationally isolated. This conclusion is, however, just as abstract, simplified and incorrect as the similar conclusion drawn by our Struvists and Economists of the nineties. 'V.I. Lenin, *Collected Works*, Vol. 22, p. 105.

26. Kievsky's arguments and Lenin's rebuttal are in V.I. Lenin, 'A Caricature of Marxism and Imperialist Economism', *Collected Works*, Vol. 23 p. 28-75.

27. Ibid., p. 50-62.

28. Michaela von Freyhold, 'The Post-colonial State,' *Review of African Political Economy*, No. 8, January-April 1977, p. 76.

29. Ibid., p. 85.

30. Ibid., p. 86.

31. Lenin defined classes thus: Classes are large groups of people differing from each other by the place they occupy in a historically determined system of social production, by their relation (in most cases fixed and formulated in law) to the means of production, by their role in the social organization of labour and consequently, by the dimensions of the share of social wealth of which they dispose and the mode of acquiring it. Classes are groups of people one of which can appropriate the labour of another owing to the different places they occupy in a definite system of social economy'. (A Great Beginning', *Collected Works*, Vol. 29, p. 421.)

32. All the quotations are from Freyhold's article 'The Post-colonial State'. For a view different from both Nabudere and Freyhold, see Said Salum, 'The Tanzanian State: A Critique', *Monthly Review* (New York), vol. 28, January 1977, p. 51-7.

33. 'A Caricature of Marxism...', op. cit., p. 43.

17

ECHO INTERVIEWS SHIVJI*

> ... The African peasant is not an independent producer – a typical
> petty commodity producer ... (he) is in fact dominated and exploited
> by the capitalist mode of production ... He is therefore objectively the
> mainstay *not* of a bourgeois revolution, but of an anti-imperialist
> national democratic revolution, *provided* he is mobilised under the
> leadership of the working class...
>
> *Issa Shivji*

ECHO: *Ndugu, why did you 'baptise' your work 'Silent Class Struggle'?*
SHIVJI: Unlike the whimsical baptization of children by priests, the title of a book,
insofar as it reflects the contents at all, I suppose, reflects the ideological position of
the author. In the case of the *Silent Class Struggle* (SCS), I think, it reflected both
my own stage of ideological development at the time as well as the concrete
situation in Tanzania. The article, as you know, was written sometime in the first
half of 1970, i.e., just about three years after the Arusha Declaration. The Arusha
Declaration temporarily disrrupted the ideological coherence of the petty
bourgeoisie itself.

Hence, the situation *appeared* fluid, 'in flux', to use the phrase of the *Silent Class
Struggle*. Insofar as the SCS took the ideological appearance as reality, it could not
really discern the class struggle accurately. Thus you find that the SCS is in fact the
analysis of economic structures rather than that of class struggle. It is only in the last
section that the article just begins to talk about the class struggle. By the same
token, the SCS failed to analyse the form of the struggle thus ending up just
deciphering the superficial aspect – the *sound* of the struggle and found it to be
silent!!

Secondly, it required a concrete event – a practice, so to speak – like the workers'
post-*Mwongozo* struggles for the new ideological positions within the petty
bourgeoisie to coalesce, to precipitate. It was this crystallisaton of the positions
which cleared the ideological fog and brought forth the class struggle. In my *Class
Struggle in Tanzania*, I have attempted to analyse the actual course and forms of the
class struggle: I don't think the sound is important any more!
ECHO: *What motivated you to embark on such work? Was it out of ideological
drive or a mere analysis of the Tanzania situation?*
SHIVJI: No, it definitely wasn't *merely* to analyse the situation. Mere analysis is the
profession of the academies: even professionally I wasn't academic then.

If the motive was an 'ideological drive' (to your phrase), it could not have
dropped from heaven! It reflected some definite material situation. In the
Introduction to the SCS itself the motive was put thus: ". . . without a clear class
analysis, it is impossible to chart out a correct strategy and formulate appropriate
tactics. More important still it is impossible to make correct alliances. How can we
talk about a 'Tanzania Revolution' without even knowing the friends and the
enemies of such a revolution?"

*Issa Shivji is a Associate Professor in the Law Faculty. He is the author of *The Silent Class
Struggle in Tanzania*, Dar es Salaam, T.P.H., 1973. Ndugu Kimato, J.U.T. of *Echo*
interviews him on the subject.

ECHO: *To what extent was the struggle for Uhuru a class struggle and what legacies have been carried forward with it?*

SHIVJI: One talks about Uhuru as a class struggle at a very abstract level indeed at international level. Otherwise it was only a prelude to the internal class struggle insofar as it was aimed at removing formal colonialism which muted or suppressed the internal contradictions.

ECHO: *In your analysis, the workers – industrial or otherwise, tend to overshadow the peasantry (90% of labouring population) despite their small number. As a result you seem to strengthen Lenin's theory that the peasantry is hard to organise and lack revolutionary commitment.*

On the contrary Fanon puts his faith in the peasantry as a formidable force for Africa's revolution. Will you please enlighten us as regards your stand between Lenin and Fanon?

SHIVJI: The question of which class is an agency of the revolution requires a concrete analysis of a concrete situation. This is precisely what is lacking in most positions taken on this issue. Those who have attempted some analysis have completely confused the concept of 'revolutionary class'. For instance, there are those who have argued that in fact the working class in Africa is an ally of the multinational corporations because it is paid highly by them and get much more than an average peasant. In fact, according to these people, they form part of the 'labour aristocracy'. This is sheer confusion. These people confuse the analysis of economic structures (the policies of: the MNCs; wages; nature of employment etc.,) with that of class relations. Class relations are not based on employment situation but on the role a social group plays in a "historically determined system of social production," to use Lenin's words. It is precisely the failure to analyse the historically determined system of social production which results in labelling the whole working class as a 'labour aristocracy'. I have dealt in greater detail with this question in my *Class Struggles in Tanzania*. There I have tried to show that the working class objectively forms a revolutionary class but that it is incapable of carrying out a successful revolution without a thorough alliance with the peasantry.

On the other hand, there are those who simply dismiss the peasantry as if this peasantry was the nineteenth century European peasant who could only become the mainstay of the bourgeois revolutions. In fact, these people go so far as to argue that given the small working class and large peasantry it is impossible to have socialist revolution in the 'third world'. We should therefore wait until the European countries have made their revolution whose generosity would then help us to make ours! This is the Euro-centric view, fashionable among some 'leftist' circles.

The African peasant is not an independent producer – a typical petty commodity producer. He is a petty commodity producer only in the formal sense, though the importance of this formal sense, should not be minimised. The African peasant is in fact dominated and exploited by the capitalist mode of production, as an integral part of the international capitalist system. He is therefore objectively the mainstay not of a bourgeois revolution, but of an anti-imperialist national democratic revolution provided (and I emphasise this), he is mobilised under the leadership of the working class. Without this leadership he, at the most, becomes the social base of petty bourgeois populism which objectively only further integrates him in the international capitalist system. It is this objective situation of imperialist exploitation, aided by internal agent classes, which makes possible the worker-peasant alliance. Only this alliance can ensure the success of socialism in our countries.

Thus, if I were to summarise, I would say that the working class is the leading class while the peasantry is the main force. Of cource, the alliance itself and its

184

success are possible only under the guidance of the proletarian ideology.

Quite undertandably, Fanon is completely confused on these issues. Unlike Lenin he had neither a grasp of the scientific theory nor experience in working class struggle. His was essentially a very radical petty bourgeois populist position. For Fanon the analysis of the colonial situation is essentially at the level of individual psychology or at the level of masses – never at the level of class relations. No wonder therefore his social analysis is not at all grounded in political economy. He has no conception of the system of social production.

This is in fact the dilemma of all petty bourgeois populist positions. This position is essentially an ideological reflection of the material situation of an independent petty commodity producer. The greatest injustice for a petty commodity producer is unequal exchange, and therefore his greatest demand can only be equivalent exchange. This leads the most radical petty bourgeois to a kind of trade union consciousness, i.e., a demand for higher prices for his commodities.

For a proletarian, on the other hand, equivalent exchange only hides the appropriation of his labour. And this comes about not because commodities don't exchange at their value (unequal exchange) but because of the very system of commodity production. The worker requires the science of political economy to unravel the mystery of how, in spite of equivalent exchange, his labour is appropriated. Political Economy (Marxist) therefore becomes the kernel of the proletarian ideology. And because the peasant also in our case is dominated by capitalism his exploitation too comes very close to that of a proletarian – thus the petty bourgeois ideology to unravel the exploitation of the peasant as well. Thus it ends up being nothing but rhetoric.

I said the concrete experience of Fanon too was essentially petty bourgeois in nature. The Algerian struggle was a typical mass, popular struggle under the leadership of the petty bourgeoisie. Had Fanon lived to see the Algeria of today, he would have probably revised his theories or else declared "The Wretched of the Earth Betrayed"! But then the betrayal itself would have to come to grips with the scientific theory and proletarian practice.

All this is not to minimise Fanon's revolutionary commitment and his excellent exposé of certain aspects of the colonial and neo-colonial situations.

ECHO: *I think leadership is as indispensable as the revolutionary theory itself in any revolutionary struggle. What can you tell us about Tanzania's leadership in this light?*

SHIVJI: It is important to be clear what do we mean by leadership in the first place, for leadership can be analysed at several interconnected levels. First, there is class leadership. In any struggle where several classes are allied (i.e., mass struggle) it is important to know which class is providing the leadership. This class itself cannot provide leadership unless it is organised under a political party. So the class itself is guided and led by its political party. Thirdly, within the party there are individual leaders heading different organs.

In the case of working class parties, for instance, the revolurionary commitment and thorough grasp of the revolutionary theory by these individual leaders are very important and can even be crucial in certain situations. But in the final analysis, it is the Party which constitutes the seat of the revolutionary ideology and the custodian of the successful revolution. How far it is successful in carrying out these functions would of course depend on, among other things, the actual historical situation and the concrete struggles; and secondly on how far the Party is immersed in the working class in particular and the exploited masses generally.

It is in this light then any leadership and/or individual leaders have to be analysed.

ECHO: *Who do you think are the reliable people – carriers of Tanzania's revolutionary struggle, against oppression, exploitation and ignorance in present Tanzania?*

SHIVJI: The oppressed and the exploited themselves! They are the carriers of the revolution. For individual revolutionaries can be eliminated but you cannot eliminate revolutionary classes without eliminating oppression and exploitation. This is what the bourgeois and the petty bourgeois theories of 'trouble-shooters', 'ring-leaders', 'foreign elements', etc., as being responsible for resistance cannot grasp. That is why it is so important to analyse who are oppressed and the exploited at a particular time and therefore the carriers of the revolution. Here the importance of class analysis.

ECHO: *Recently Ndugu Awiti conducted a research in Iringa Region, Ismani area on several Ujamaa villages–more or less, on a similar approach as your 'Silent Class Struggle'. Do you see any correlation between your work and his work?*

SHIVJI: Awiti's analysis is very important because it attempts to analyse the peasantry concretely. We tend to generalise too much about the peasantry. It is important to have concrete analyses of different areas and regions of our country if we are to understand the peasantry as a force in the revolution.

ECHO: *What can be done to make sure that the people you address–workers and the peasants in particular, get your invaluable contribution so as to be on the forefront in the revolutionary construction of their destinies?*

SHIVJI: If our contribution is to be important it has to be in the *language* (both literally an ideologically speaking), which the people understand. That is the very important task of serious progressives.

ECHO: *Thank you very much Ndugu Shivji. Echo wishes you all the best. Meanwhile the struggle continues…*

18

WHO IS TO LEAD THE POPULAR ANTI-IMPERIALIST REVOLUTION IN AFRICA?

(In Refutation of Issa G. Shivji's Petty-Bourgeois Neo-Marxist Line)

Omwony-Ojwok

It is true that the small working class in Africa cannot be considered to be the same as the European proletariat or ipso facto revolutionary. (my emphasis)

Issa G. Shivji

Thus a large developed proletariat is not an essential condition for struggle against capitalism and the building of socialism. There exists in the African situation other strata – for example, lower sectors of the petty-bourgeoisie – with revolutionary potential (my emphasis) and these can be mobilised in alliance with the peasantry and the working class under the proletarian ideology.

Issa G. Shivji

INTRODUCTION

When in 1844 Karl Marx, then living in Paris, decided finally to break with Arnold Ruge, who was about to abandon the revolutionary struggle, Frederick Engels from Barmen (Germany) wrote to Marx, 'It is impossible to convince Jung and a multitude of others that a difference of principle exists between us and Ruge; they remain of the opinion that it is merely a personal squabble.'[1] (my emphasis).

In September 1937, at the heat of intense revolutionary struggle in China, Mao Tse-tung launched a bitter attack on liberalism. He warned that liberalism, by rejecting ideological struggle and sticking to unprincipled peace, endangers the movement by 'giving rise to a decadent, philistine attitude and bringing about political degeneration in certain units and individuals in the Party and the revolutionary organizations'.[2]

Mao's attack on liberalism and Marx's treatment of Ruge clearly demonstrate that both rejected a 'let-it-be' attitude towards erroneous views.

In East Africa within the last decade, an erroneous petty-bourgeois neo-Marxist line has developed, pretending to 'analyse' our society and to show the road to a 'correct revolutionary practice'.

Take the case of Issa G. Shivji and his analysis of Tanzania. In 1970, Shivji published an article in *Cheche* under the title *The Silent Class Struggle*.[3] A few years after that he wrote an unpublished piece, *Class Struggle Continues*. Then in 1976 appeared *Class Struggles in Tanzania*.[4]

When in his *Imperialism, State, Class and Race*, D.W. Nabudere showed concretely that Shivji is not a Marxist-Leninist but a neo-Marxist and a neo-Trotskyist, a number of people, including Karim Hirji and what he considers to be 'progressive circles' in Tanzania were shocked that Shivji's erroneous line had been uncovered and openly exposed. Since then, subsequent rejoinders have not only clarified some of those who had been genuinely confused by Shivji's neo-Marxism; they have also left the defenders of Shivji in the cold. That is why they have had to rush indoors to grumble there. Nevertheless Shivji's writings continue to circulate freely. And since he has not openly repudiated any of his falsifications of Marxism and the proletarian position, we reserve the right to attack these errors with a view to annihilating them politically from the ranks of the anti-imperialist movement, in Tanzania and East Africa.

We intend to show in this contribution that on the question of the leadership of the present stage of the revolution, Shivji greatly caricatures the ideology of the proletariat; that he puts into question the revolutionary role of the proletariat; that in this way he opens the door for other classes to pretend to lead the popular anti-imperialist struggle; that this is partly a result of failure to correctly analyse the present epoch, and therefore, to identify the principle enemy of the oppressed people of Africa; that this can only lead to an incorrect assessment of the friends of the proletariat and hence to a fundamental error on the nature of the alliance which must be forged in the struggle; that Shivji has not correctly grasped the essence of either the Guinean anti-colonial struggle or of the Chinese revolution. In the final analysis, our aim is to show that Shivji's relegation of the leading role of the proletariat to that of the 'leadership of the proletarian ideology' is counter-revolutionary; and that the leadership of any class other than the proletariat would be the doom of the struggle.

IMPERIALISM AND THE NATIONAL QUESTION WITH REGARD TO TANZANIA

The heart of Shivji's theoretical problem lies, really, in the fact that although he makes reference to it occasionally, he does not have a scientific conception of imperialism; and because of this, Lenin's and Stalin's as well as Mao's analyses of the national question completely escape him.

Tanzania as a country is a product of imperialism, arising during the colonial phase and remoulded and cemented during the neo-colonial phase. But what does this mean? It means that Tanzania was created when capitalism in Europe had already passed the stage of free competition, when monopolies had arisen, when industrial and bank capital had merged to form a new type of capital – finance capital. It arose, therefore, as part of the final division of the world by competing imperialist powers. These features of the period that led to the constitution of Tanzania mean that from the very beginning, the tendency developed towards the negation of any emergent national capital, since increasingly neither the constant part of the capital nor, quite often, a great part of variable capital could ever be acquired from within Tanzania. The financial oligarchy – that tiny section of what Shivji and other neo-Marxists call the 'metropolitan bourgeoisie', and who live by clipping coupons from the stock exchange – was already the economically dominant and politically ruling section of the bourgeoisie. The colonization of East Africa at the end of last century and the constitution of Tanganyika and Zanzibar were part of the struggle by the financial oligarchy against the tendency of the rate of profit to fall. It formed part of their struggle for sources of raw materials, for cheap labour, for a wider market and as a backyard for the export of capital. All these facts are clear from Lenin's theses on *imperialism*, but neo-Marxists either ignore them or do not see their importance. It is in this light that President Nyerere's often-quoted address to the Convocation of Ibadan University (November, 1976) cannot be quoted enough. In this speech, the Tanzanian President honestly and without reserve brought out the essence of neo-colonial imperialism. He said that when colonial oppression was liquidated, this was not the end of the road. Not only does the new government find itself greatly limited by the inherited institutions but if further discovers 'that it did not inherit effective power over economic developments in its own country'. And the reason is clear. For the neo-colonies:

> (T)here is no such thing as a national economy at all! Instead, there exist [in the neo-colonies] various economic activities which are owned by people outside its jurisdiction, which are directed at external needs, and which are run in the interests of external economic powers. Further, the Government's ability to secure positive action in these fields. . . depends entirely upon its ability to convince the effective decision makers [i.e. the imperialist countries] that their own interests will be served by what the Government wishes to have done.[5]

The President was rightly concerned about the seriousness of this situation, thus he put his finger at the heart of the problem of national oppression: 'Neo-colonialism is a very real, and very severe, limitation on national sovereignty'.[6]

But how does imperialism operate in the neo-colonies? It does so by identifying and promoting local agents. Here again Nyerere, as a patriot, showed a much deeper grasp of the inner workings of imperialism than 'Marxists' in East Africa who talk of the so-called 'bureaucratic bourgeoisie' as the enemy, rather than of imperialism operating through local comprador elements. He said:

> Some of our people identify their own personal interests with the existing neo-colonial situation. They are to be found among the local agents of foreign capitalists and among the local capitalists who have developed in the shadow of large foreign enterprises.[7]

Does this not constitute a correct identification of the enemy of the Tanzanian and East African people as a whole? We submit that it does. We further submit that any attempt to play into the hands of imperialism by weakening the ranks of the anti-imperialist struggle through talk about the 'bureaucratic bourgeoisie' or even of identifying all local bourgeois and petty-bourgeois elements (including small traders, handicraftsmen, rich farmers or capitalist farmers) as the 'immediate enemy', without concretely analyzing their links with foreign monopolies and therefore with imperialism, is neo-Marxist, unscientific and reactionary.[8] In this way it will be impossible for the proletariat to constitute around itself a broad anti-imperialist united front in struggle, since the analysis revels in dividing the ranks of the people and shielding the real enemy, i.e., imperialism operating through the local comprador class. The task of the Tanzanian Marxist-Leninists cannot be to invent imaginary 'enemies'; instead it is to concretely identify the compador elements in production as agents of the principle enemy of the Tanzanian people.

In this respect Shivji brings nothing but confusion, especially in Chapter Seven entitled 'Uhuru and After: the Rise of the "Bureaucratic Bourgeoisie",' and in Chapter Eight entitled 'Arusha and After: the "Bureaucratic Bourgeoisie Forges Ahead".' Shivji identifies this so-called 'bourgeoisie' with the top echelons of the state – Ministers, Principal Secretaries and Managers of parastatal enterprises, but even then leaves things very vague and confused. The confusion is so great that he completely ignores the basic Marxist position that classes arise, not from employment within the state, but in production. The confusion turns into chaos when on page 69, our 'Marxist' talks of the 'bureaucratic bourgeoisie' as 'the ruling sector of the petty-bourgeoisie'. And yet Shivji tells us that the various sections of the 'bureaucratic bourgeoisie' are 'self-explanatory'.

Shivji's confusion in the analysis of classes is compounded by his total neglect of the national question, and therefore of the character of the present anti-imperialist struggle in Tanzania.

In his analysis of Western Europe, Engels explained that nations emerged as part of the struggle by the bourgeoisie to liquidate feudalism and develop a national market in competition with the bourgeoisies of other countries. Whereas in primitive society, when classes had not yet emerged, social ties were founded on tribal links, thereby highlighting the language question, with the emergence of slave and feudal states, territory, not ethnic ties, became the basis of the development of the State and the elimination of the primitive democracy of tribal society. This is analyzed in detail by Engels in *The Origin of the Family, Private Property and the State*. With the rise of the bourgeoisie, however, as Lenin correctly explained in his refutation of Rosa Luxemburg and other erroneous positions in 'The Right of Nations to Self-Determination', a historically concrete presentation of the problem must distinguish two periods of capitalism, each of which has its specific features. First of all:

> there is the period of the collapse of feudalism and absolutism, the period when the national movements for the first time become mass movements and in one way or another draw all classes of the population into politics.[9]

During this phase there is:

> the awakening of national movements and the drawing of peasants, the most numerous and the most sluggish section of the population, into these movements, in connection with the struggle for political liberty in general and for the rights of the nation in particular.[10]

This is what led to the constitution in Western Europe of states which, with few exceptions like Ireland and Switzerland, were also single nations.

The next phase was the period of fully formed capitalist state with long-established constitutional regimes and a highly developed antagonism between the bourgeoisie and the proletariat, i.e. the rise of imperialism. In this period:

> developed capitalism, in bringing closer together nations that have already been fully drawn into commercial intercourse, and causing them to intermingle to an increasing degree, brings the antagonism between internationally united capital and the international working-class movement into the forefront.[11]

This epoch led to the constitution of multi-national states in Eastern Europe. It is also this imperialist phase of capitalism that led to the colonial expansion that brought the establishment of most of the states of Africa today, including Tanzania; and so it remains the epoch of the present: the neo-colonial phase of imperialist oppression.

J.V. Stalin not only developed Lenin's theses on the national question; he not only applied this analysis to the concrete situation of the Soviet Union (before the rise of modern revisionism), he further enriched Lenin's analysis of the national question as a colonial question and correctly summed up the tasks of revolutionaries in the oppressed countries in a number of brilliant expositions that are to be found in the collection *Marxism and the National and Colonial Question.*[12] If only Shivji had read and understood Stalin on this matter, he would have realized that when Mao Tse-tung advanced his thesis of the New Democratic Revolution as a stage in the anti-imperialist struggle and as part of the proletariat's revolutionary struggle to impose its dictatorship over the exploiters during the advance towards socialism, he was resolving a problem that Shivji's neo-Marxist analysis cannot solve, namely: what to do about the fact that Tanzania is a poor agrarian country greatly oppressed by imperialism. Mao Tse-tung showed the way out for all Marxists-Leninists in colonial, semi-colonial and neo-colonial countries in his *New Democracy.*[13] It was on the basis of this scientific presentation of the national question that, at the commemoration of the twenty-eighth anniversary of the Communist Party of China, Mao wrote 'On the People's Democratic Dictatorship' in which he summed up the experience of the Communist Party of China and the Chinese people as having been directed by the strategic aim of establishing 'the people's democratic dictatorship under the leadership of the working class (through the Communist Party) and based upon the alliance of workers and peasants'.[14]

Thus Shivji's lack of a correct position on the question of imperialism and his failure to realize that in none of the African countries has the national question been resolved (since it would require the leadership of the proletariat in a democratic, patriotic alliance to the exclusion only of the comprador class) lead him into blind and unprincipled attacks against important sections of the anti-imperialist united front which will have to be formed in struggle. It is further this error which makes Shivji stumble and fall in the face of the most heroic history of the Tanzanian working class and the anti-colonial national movement. We now turn to this.

DOWNGRADING THE ROLE OF THE TANZANIAN PROLETARIAT IN THE UHURU STRUGGLE

To begin with, Shivji's notion of the proletariat is extremely strange for someone who calls himself a Marxist. Throughout *Capital* Marx insisted, and went ahead to demonstrate, that the proletariat arise as a result of the capital-labour relation in production.

> As simple reproduction constantly reproduces the capital relation itself, i.e. the relation of capitalists on the one hand, and wage-workers on the other, so reproduction on a progressive scale, i.e. accumulation, reproduces the capital-relation on a progressive scale, more capitalists or larger capitalists at this pole, more wage-workers at that. The reproduction of a mass of labour-power, which must incessantly re-incorporate itself with capital for that capital's self-expansion; which cannot get free from capital, and whose enslavement to capital is only concealed by the variety of individual capitalists to whom it sells itself. This reproduction of labour-power forms, in fact, an essential part of the reproduction of capital itself.[15]

Marx concluded, 'Accumulation of Capital is, therefore, increase of the proletariat'.[16]

Instead of looking at the emergence of the proletariat in Africa and its increase in the process of capital accumulation, which is taking place all the time and has been so ever since capitalism was introduced into the continent after the imperialist division of Africa and its colonial subjugation, Shivji prefers a static 'classical' definition, namely: 'a large (sic!) group of wage-earners employed in large (sic!)

191

capitalist industry and constituting a substantial (sic!) proportion of the population'.[17]

Naturally, having presented us with this sort of artificial and static definition, he 'finds' that a proletariat 'did not develop' and 'could not' have developed under colonialism and today under neo-colonialism.[18]

Nevertheless Shivji tells us that a class of 'wage-earners' did develop; and he even calls them a 'working class' and identifies the sectors in which they emerged, namely, 'in the plantations, in the docks, in transport and commerce, and in construction, building, etc'.[18]

Shivji's subborn and blatant rejection of the proletarian character of the Tanzanian and African working class is, of course, not in the least surprising, for it is aimed at downgrading the working class's role in the anti-colonial revolutionary struggle and therefore at denying the necessity for its leadership in the present phase of the anti-imperialist struggle. The latter aspect of Shivji's reactionary deviation we shall see anon, but how does he downgrade the role of the Tanzanian proletariat during the anti-colonial struggle?

Shivji's argument in *Class Struggles in Tanzania* is that throughout most of the colonial period, the working class did not struggle against the colonial oppressor, did not fight for democratic rights and justice, and did not even organize, until after the Second Imperialist War when it allegedly succeeded to organize at long last. Moreover, argues our 'Marxist', the workers kept themselves out of the mainstream of the national anti-colonial movement until, in 1958, the 'alliance' between TANU and the Tanganyika Federation of Labour (TFL) was 'forged' when, according to Shivji, by that 'alliance', 'the workers had thrown their lot (sic!) with the nationalist movement'.[19]

Shivji goes further and tells us that the only contribution the workers 'probably' made to the independence struggle is when they organized strikes in 'strategic' sectors of the economy.

Thus, what is but a culmination of the long process which from the earliest opportunity gave to the working class a leading role in the anti-colonial movement, Shivji takes as the beginning of the proletariat's participation in the struggle! This is Shivji's 'dialectics' as applied to Tanzania's history.

Let us look at the naked facts.

Why was the TANU-TFL alliance formed? Precisely because of all the classes that stood foremost in opposition to (colonial) imperialism, the proletariat – for this is what they were although Shivji seeks to deny it – had actually proved to be the most uncompromising, the most ruthless, the most determined enemy of colonial oppression, and as that it was an essential component of the national movement. Shivji misunderstands Tanzania's history because he does not see the central fact that the anti-colonial movement (whether it took ethnic, religious, cultural or any other form) never really took off, never developed in a clear direction, never really threatened the colonial system, until the proletariat – however weak or embryonic it might have been – gave to it a solid national, consistently anti-imperialist and democratic stamp. And the failure of the peasants in the Maji Maji struggle (1905–07) is but one example. Shivji is writing about 'class struggles in Tanzania', but deals with workers in abstraction from the fact that without the proletariat, the nationalist struggle was doomed to failure. Once the TANU-TFL alliance was established, declares Shivji, 'The workers had thrown in their lot with the nationalist movement and the wave of strikes during the 1950's was probably [sic !] instrumental in bringing about independence.[20] And he adds –'Thus, despite their numerical smallness, the workers' contribution, given their strategic role in the economy, cannot be belittled'.[21]

Now these two sentences are once again a caricature of Tanzania's history. It is, of course, true that the proletariat did not assume the hegemonic leadership of the anti-colonial movement, because it failed to come out with its own party. Nevertheless the working class did not simply 'throw their lot' with the anti-imperialist struggle and certainly its contribution to the struggle was not just confined to the fact that they occupied a 'strategic' position within Tanzania's economy. They were the national movements most militantly consistent component as a class, whereas the other classes tended towards vacillation and compromise with the enemy. The proletariat did not lead the national movement through its own party, but instead got incorporated in an amorphous 'alliance' with the petty-bourgeosie; this was the cause of the present neo-colonial oppression of the country by imperialism, but it is a far cry from Shivji's underestimation of the working class's role.

As early as 1924, a strike of joiners at Kwiro Mission had shown the militant character of this 'dangerous' class, in the eyes of the colonialists. Throughout the 1930s there were workers' strikes on sisal estates and on other plantations. The wharf labourers' strike in Tanga (1937) clearly showed the developing militancy and consciousness of the proletariat when 250 workers left work for two days and aroused sympathy from broad sections of public opinion. Two years later, the colonialists witnessed a highly coordinated strike – not limited to Tanzania but linking workers at the docks of Dar es Salaam, Lindi and Mombasa. The workers were already beginning to see the international character of their struggle, right at the level of production, and therefore the need for solid internationalist links.

The working class struggle in Tanzania entered into the mainstream of the national anti-imperialist movement at least as far back as the 1930s, while Shivji imagines in his own head that it started with the TANU-TFL alliance!

The consistently democratic, patriotic and militant character of the Tanzania working class in the 1930s and the vacillations of the petty bourgeoisie are very well-illustrated by the political experience of a petty-bourgeois democrat and consistent patriot named Erica Fiah and an anti-imperialist democratic nationalist organization led by the petty-bourgeoisie called the *Tanganyika Africa Welfare and Commercial Association (TAWCA).*

In the mid-30s Fiah was a shopkeeper. He took to the promotion of the national movement very early in his life, and founded the patriotic paper, *KWETU,* as the mouth-piece of TAWCA. From the very beginning this Association did not hide its political aim:

> Since the Africans are not represented in the Legislative Council, [said the proposed by-laws of the Association] this Association, as the Central body, looking after the welfare of all Africans in Tanganyika Territory, would always watch carefully any laws proposed by the Government which may affect Africans and, after consideration, would make such representations to Government and Members of Legislative Council, as the Association considers proper in the interests of Africans... Every African is bound to obey the Association, whether he is contributing or not, just as he obeys the Government.[22]

The more the Association became militantly anti-imperialist, however, the more repressive the colonial staste became. The more the popular movement insisted on democratic rights and freedoms, the more the colonial state sharpened its carrot-and-stick policy. By 1936, Governor MacMichael reported to the Colonial Office:

> Here we have a shopkeeper of doubtful antecedents... from Uganda who puts up by-laws which reek of politics and bad digestion, conflict with liberty

of the individual and the responsibility of Government to the people and show signs of a desire to achieve influence and subscriptions.[23]

What happened to the Association and to its leader, Erica Fiah, is, however, instructive in showing whether the working class in Tanzania simply 'threw in their lot with the nationalist movement' through the TANU-TFL alliance on the eve of independence, as Shivji says, or whether all along they had championed and played in leading role in the struggle.

What happened from 1936 is that the more the colonial state put down its feet, the more the petty-bourgeois membership of the TAWCA wavered, vacillated and finally abandoned the Association. Those who remained now sought to water down its tone, to abandon the anti-imperialist, democratic and militant line by arguing that the Association 'must not' engage in 'politics'. Things became so disgusting to a consistent patriot like Erica Fiah that in 1939, he quit the Association. But to do what – to simply sit? Not at all. Fiah abandoned the petty bourgeoisie to help organise the working class in the docks of Dar es Salaam.

Did Fiah leave the TAWCA to go to dockworkers for sentimental reasons? Not at all. He did it because in practice, in the field of practical politics, he had discovered the true nature of the petty bourgeoisie and the militancy of the proletariat. Engels once said of the petty bourgeoisie: "They are extremely unreliable except after a victory has been won, when their shouting in the beer houses knows no bounds. Nevertheless, there are very good elements among them, who join the workers of their own accord."[24] Erica Fiah had discovered this fact that Engels had long talked about – but right in the field of practical action.

Shivji does not see that the working class did not 'go' onto the side of the national movement only in the 1950s but had championed the Uhuru struggle all along. Shivji does not realize that in their economic struggle the proletariat in Tanzania had long ago discovered – at least some 20 years before the TANU-TFL 'alliance' that imperialism was the principal enemy of not only themselves as a class, but of the entire Tanzanian people. While he tells us that the working class's role in the anti-colonial struggle 'cannot be belittled' because of its strategic role in the economy, Shivji precisely belittles the role of the proletariat in Tanzania's history. For it was not just the 'strategic role' of the workers in the economy that mattered. It was their position in production as suppliers of surplus value, their concentration in production (in comparison with other classes), their natural (i.e., inevitable) need to organizefor economic struggles, and their unflinching demands for democratic rights not only for themselves but for the broader masses of the population. These were the conditions that gave the working class their militancy, their uncompromising stand in opposition to imperialism, for self-determination and for democratic rights and freedoms. These were the factors that made the proletariat a major force in the independence movement, a fact which Shivji realizes only vaguely, and too late.

That the other classes later on – and at the last moment – usurped this leadership role has to be analyzed concretely in order to draw both positive and negative lessons from Tanzania's history. Shivji cannot do this important job because he does not seem to have seriously studied Tanzania's history either, and this because, according to him, it would have taken him 'too far afield'.[25]

This, then, is the basis of Shivji's caricature of Tanzania's history and of the consistently revolutionary history of the Tanzanian proletariat. He says of the Tanzanian working class, with a most derogatory tone:

> Notwithstanding the workers' role in the Uhuru struggle, TANU never came under the influence of proletarian ideology nor were the workers considered

[sic!] the leading force in the struggle. The trade union movement was basically structured on traditional (English) lines led by some elements from the petty bourgeoisie. If anything, the TANU ideology was essentially peasant-biased.[26]

The significance of this passage is to be found in the statement in which Shivji goes so far as to dismiss, or at least downgrade, the revolutionary character of the African proletariat. He says, 'It is true that the small working class in the African countries cannot be considered to be the same as the European proletariat [who says they are?] or *ipso facto* revolutionary'.[27]

These two passages alone would need a book, entitled *Anti-Shivji*, to refute point-by-point any pretensions this 'Marxist' may claim for being, in his own words, one of those who are 'imbued with proletarian ideology'. It is difficult to imagine what proletarian ideology can permit anyone to doubt the historically-tested and proven revolutionary character of the African working class and of the Tanzanian proletariat in particular. Indeed what 'Marxism' can ever lead anyone into doubting – even for a single second – the revolutionary character of the working class – wherever it may be? Only Shivji's Marxism. First of all, to say that TANU 'never came under the influence of proletarian ideology', or that the workers were not 'considered' the leading force in the struggle, prove nothing about the concrete, objective, reality which is independent of Shivji's will; but shows his subjective, idealist position which slanders the proletariat. If, during the anti-colonial phase of the struggle, the Tanzanian proletariat did not get to acquire and develop in a coherent manner their own ideology, i.e. Marxism-Leninism, this fact must be analyzed concretely, in order to expose the factors that hindered it. In doing so, what is certain is that sociological 'explanations', like those of Shivji, that ascribe everything to the smallness or migrant nature of the proletariat in Tanzanian will not do.

What Shivji does not seem to realize is that, whether or not the proletariat was 'considered' the leading anti-imperialist force by other classes is of absolutely no importance in regard to the role it actually played. What is important is, the reality, which is that, although it did not acquire leadership of the national movement, nevertheless it played a leading role, at least up to the period of the birth of TANU.

Due to the contradictions of material life in Tanzania, and Africa generally, since imperialism introduced capitalist relations in our societies, of all the classes that stood and continue to stand face-to-face with imperialism. The working class was and remains the most determined enemy of imperialism. The working class is the most uncompromisingly opposed to national oppression.

Shivji has not grasped this fact – and is forced to resort to eclecticism:

Even among the working class itself [he tells us] there are certain sections which tend to be more conscious than others. These small sections can form the nucleus to influence others. In each concrete situation, revolutionaries have to find, in Cabral's words 'our little proletariat'.[28]

We shall soon see that Shivji's references to Cabral border on opportunism because he has not at all understood this African patriot and because what Cabral says, far from proving his point, in fact, completely disproves it. For Cabral had an immense confidence, in the working class, whereas Shivji is unsure of its revolutionary capacity.

But what is difficult to understand from Shivji is how he can on the one hand say that there is no proletariat 'in the classical sense' in Africa,[29] and that the African working class is not, by its nature, revolutionary;[30] while on the other hand 'agreeing' with Cabral that we in Africa have to find 'our little proletariat'.

It is evident that Shivji is the very embodiment of contradictions. If there is any lesson to draw from eclecticism, it is that it can lead to Shivjism, i.e. the worst forms of confusion in 'analysing' a neo-colony.

The Author of *Class Struggles in Tanzania* has told us that a proletariat 'in the classical sense' did not develop in many African countries; he at least doubts the revolutionary character of the African working class; he has downgraded the revolutionary role of Tanzanian proletariat during the anti-colonial struggle and simply taken a vulgar sociological explanation of the difficulties the working class organization faced at the time.

We need now to see why Shivji is taking such an openly anti-proletarian line in the name of the 'proletarian ideology'.

Shivji informs us that while the working class was faced with all sorts of setbacks, 'In addition, different structures in the colonized countries have produced (!) their corresponding strata with revolutionary potential![31]

It is the first time we come across structures that are productive; indeed so productive that soon we see emerging from these structures 'corresponding strata', which have 'revolutionary potential'. This is Shivji's Marxism – a Marxism not of classes but of productive 'structures' and 'strata'!

Although it is difficult for Marxists to understand what our analyst means by the above sentence, he himself is quite clear in his own mind as to what he means. Thus from this muddle, he draws the conclusion that, 'Therefore, depending on actual conditions in the concrete situation of each country, various alliances are possible for revolutionary action'.[32]

And why this escape from the working class and hurried rush to the issue of alliances? Who is going to form this alliance and which class will lead it? Regardless of the question of the leadership of the working class itself in the Tanzanian struggle, 'What is important, says Shivji, 'is that such revolutionary strata are mobilized under the leadership [note!] of the proletarian ideology'.[33]

Clearly Shivji is determined to separate classes from their ideological positions; and we need to examine a bit more closely what this dualism means and to what it inevitably leads.

SEPARATING THE PROLETARIAT FROM ITS IDEOLOGY

To avoid confusion and misunderstanding, we need to point out that both Marx and Engels consistently stressed the importance of ideological and political education of the working class along the lines of a correct theory, if the proletarian struggle is to succeed.[34]

Following in the example of these great teachers of the proletariat, Lenin said in *What Is to Be Done?* that the importance of a correct ideological, theoretical line could not be overstressed because, first, the Russian Party was still young and had to settle 'accounts with other trends of revolutionary thought that threaten to divert the movement from the correct path'; secondly, that being an international movement, the proletarian organization and the revolutionary must make use of the experiences of other countries and do so critically in order 'to test them independently'; thirdly, because the tasks that confronted the Russian Party '(had) never confronted any other socialist party before'. It was in this connection that Lenin argued against the spontaneous theory of the Economists that 'the role of the vanguard fighter can be fulfilled only by a party that is guided by the most advanced theory',[35] (Lenin's stress). How relevant Lenin's position is to the present situaton in East Africa!

Shivji quotes a sentence from this most profound analysis of Lenin at the beginning of his book, but on reading the whole book one easily sees that his real teachers are not the Marxists-Leninists but Paul Baran, Paul Sweezy, Charles Bettelheim, Nicos Poulantzas, A.G. Frank, Stavenhagen and the host of 'independent' Marxists (and we appeal to the reader to check this for himself).

Shivji begins by separating the proletariat from the proletarian ideology and then absoluting the role of the latter.

Two situations need to be distinguished here. First, there is the proletarian leadership of the struggle with their own ideology, i.e. Marxism-Leninism, as its own ideological line. Secondly, there is the leadership of bourgeoisie or petty-bourgeoisie, camouflaged by slogans which pay lip-service to the 'proletarian ideology', but which can obviously be nothing but a mere masquerade of 'socialism'. Shivji does not distinguish between the two, and ends up telling us that it is possible for any other class to lead the present anti-imperialist struggle in Tanzania with success, provided that its party is 'imbued' with proletarian ideology. This naturally leads Shivji to sink into the deepest oblivion of idealism.

Marx and Engels were absolutely emphatic about the revolutionary role of the proletariat and in the *Manifesto of the Communist Party* they did not say that this revolutionary role is due to the proletarian ideology but to its place in capitalist production. 'Of all the classes that stand face-to-face with the bourgeoisie today', they wrote in 1847, 'the proletariat alone is a really revolutionary class'.[36]

Why is this so?

> The other classes decay and finally disappear in the face of modern industry; th proletariat is its special and essential product. The lower middle class, [not!] the peasant, all these fight the bourgeoisie, to save from extinction their existence as a fraction of the middle class. They are therefore not revolutionary, but conservative. Nay more, they are reactionary, for they try to roll back the wheel of history. If by chance they are revolutionary, they are so only in view of their impending transfer into the proletariat, thus they defend not their present, but their future interests, they desert their own standpoint to place themselves at that of the proletariat.[37]

Shivji starts off by denying the existence of a proletariat 'in the classical sense' (whatever that means) in Tanzania and Africa while at the same time saying a working class exists. He proceeds to say this working class is not necessarily revolutionary and then sinks into the ridiculous position of defending the proletarian ideology but not the proletariat itself. The writer of *Class Struggles in Tanzania* is so afraid of real class struggle that he fears we might miss his utopian doctrine of the leadership of the proletarian ideology; hence he repeats the doctrine over and over with amazing zeal. He starts to expound this doctrine in his appraisal of the Guinean anti-colonial struggle under PAIGC. Again while completely misrepresenting the Chinese revolution, as we shall see, he says, 'The important and decisive point is that the struggle was led by a party expounding proletarian ideology'.[38] In the next paragraph we are again told:

> As we have been emphasizing all along, class struggle is a political struggle for state power, and therefore what is important is that potential revolutionary classes and strata are organized for their political conflict under the leadership of the proletarian ideology'.[39]

In the next page, having for a second time quoted Cabral without understanding him, Shivji concludes:

Thus a large developed proletariat is not an essential condition for struggle against capitalism and the building of socialism. There exist in the African situation other strata – for example, lower sectors of the petty bourgeoisie [sic!] – with revolutionary potential, and these can be mobilized in alliance [note!] with the peasantry and the working class under the leadership of the proletarian ideology.[40]

Here Shivji totally fails to see the two phases of the struggle and dashes straight to 'the building of socialism'. Nevertheless Shivji's theme is clear on at least two points:

1. That in the struggle facing the African people today, the leadership of the proletariat is unnecessary; and,
2. That the leadership necessary is not of the working class itself, but only 'the leadership of the proletarian ideology'.

He even suggests specifically that 'other strata' which he claims 'have revolutionary potential' can be mobilized, with a view to establishing an 'alliance', through the ideology of the proletariat.

The question of alliances in class struggles is a vitally important one; for numerous liberation movements have seen success crumble at the very last minute precisely because of having failed to make a correct appreciation of the classes in struggle, their concrete positions vis-a-vis each other, the principal enemy of each given moment, and therefore the revolutionary alliance of all the classes and forces within the society that can be united in order to liquidate this principal enemy and advance the struggle a step further.

Marx and Engels' theory of class alliances in revolutionary struggle are most clearly brought out in *The Eighteenth Brumaire of Louis Bonaparte, The Peasant War in Germany, The Civil War in France*, the *Peasant Question in France and Germany, The Class Struggles in France, 1848 to 1850* and in their correspondence.

On the other hand, what Shivji has discovered – to the detriment of the African working class – is that during the present epoch of the most intense imperialist oppression, the working class must not lead the popular front. The workers, Shivji tells us, are too few, full of migrants and may not be revolutionary. Therefore they must be by-passed. First, 'potential revolutionary strata' must be mobilized (we are not told by whom) to the exclusion of the proletariat. Then, having done so, the peasants and workers can be brought in simply as tags, just to aid Shivji's 'revolutionary' classes and 'strata'.

Who are these 'revolutionary strata', these strata which are more revolutionary than the workers? Shivji does not enumerate them. But he gives us a clue when he suggests that, 'There exist in the African situation other strata – for example, lower sectors of the petty bourgeoisie – with revolutionary potential...'.[41] [Emphasis added]

There we see the modern petty bourgeois: Narcissus looking at and falling in love with his own image in a spring! What is not realized, of course, is that in the same way as Narcissus pined away and transformed himself into something else – in his case a flower – so does our 'Marxist' stand the risk of transforming himself into the ideologue of some other class: the petty-bourgeoisie! And in effect Shivji declares himself the ideologue of the 'lower sectors of the petty bourgeoisie' though in Marxist attire. Thus beginning as someone 'imbued with proletarian ideology' we get someone imbued with the ideology of the lower sections of the petty-bourgeosie masquerading as a Marxist-Leninist.

The working class in struggle will find its leaders. Nevertheless Shivji's caricature of Marxism and putting forth of the silent dreams of the 'lower sectors' of the petty bourgeoisie, and hence of the petty bourgeoisie as a class – dreams that are completely unrealizable under imperialist domination – makes it most important for such proletarian leaders to gain ideological clarity and spread the science of Marxism-Leninism among the masses of workers.

Having caricatured Marxism, slandered the African proletariat, and taken away all revolutionary content from the anti-imperialist struggle by considering it as a struggle 'under the leadership of the proletarian ideology' with the proletariat itself only as a tag, Shivji now turns around to 'defend' scientific socialism.

> Those who argue against the applicability of scientific socialism in Africa because the theory was based on a developed proletariat which does not exist in Africa are therefore expecting concrete conditions to conform to scriptures! This is not Marxism.[42]

What brilliant defence of Marxism! First of all he accepts the bourgeois nonsense that a proletariat does not exist in Africa. Then he turns round to say we must not expect these so-called 'concrete conditions' (i.e. absence of a proletariat,) 'to conform to scriptures' ! He then proceeds to dismiss his own reasoning as 'not Marxism'!

The point is this: If there is no proletariat in Africa, then the struggle in Africa is not a proletarian one. And if the struggle is not a proletarian one, then for what do we need the proletarian ideology, i.e. Marxism-Leninism? Here the non-Marxist petty bourgeoisie in Africa are far more consistent with themselves than the 'Marxist' Shivji. For they openly declare that there is no working class in Africa, and hence conclude that Marxism-Leninism is inapplicable to Africa.

Marx and other teachers of the working class again and again taught us that dialectical and historical materialism, i.e. the science of the proletariat, arose and can continue in existence only because the proletariat is there. Marxism is the ideology of the proletariat. No other class can consistently apply the proletarian ideology. Any attempt by anyone to divorce Marxism from the proletariat itself is reactionary because it seeks to present the struggle as being for but not by the proletariat itself. Shivji and those who agree with him ideologically must accept one of two things:

1. Either there is a proletariat in Africa, and therefore there is a proletarian ideology which is its arm against its enemies, or;
2. Either there is no proletariat in Africa, in which case let no one disturb the African people with the nonsense of being 'led' by the ideology of a class which is not there.

The existence of a proletariat is not a question of members. It is a question of relations established in production and the tendencies established therein. This is so regardless of the specific characteristics this proletariat possesses in each country.

Shivji has to accept another thing, namely, that for him to imagine that any other class can use the ideology of the proletariat, yet such an ideology to retain its proletarian content, is to sink into the depths of a utopian dream. The question as to where ideas, consciousness, knowledge – and therefore ideologies, philosophies and theories – come from is part of the ABC of Marxism. The fact that the petty bourgeoisie or any other class can claim to be 'led by the proletarian ideology' in any given situation does not – and cannot – mean that it is so. They are not to be judged by what they think of themselves. Nor can their class adopt the substance of the proletarian ideology. When the petty bourgeoisie talk of socialism, they mean a totally different thing from what the proletariat understand by socialism. Substance must be distinguished from form. Shivji's failure to grasp this point leads him into deep trouble.

MISUNDERSTANDING OF AMILCAR CABRAL OR THE LESSONS OF THE ANTI-COLONIAL ARMED STRUGGLE IN GUINEA BISSAU

Starting from the late 1950s the anti-imperialism revolutionary struggle in Africa advanced to the stage of popular and protracted resistance in a number of countries. In contradistinction to the earlier armed movements in which the working class did not play a leading role (including the Mau Mau resistance in Kenya), the new phase of the anti-colonial armed struggle started in Algeria. With the defeat of French colonial imperialism, the people rose up in arms against Portuguese colonial oppression in Mozambique, Angola and Guinea Bissau. This revolutionary wave is still rippling in the rest of southern Africa, while neo-colonial Africa is not far behind.

What was the character of this struggle?

First of all it was anti-imperialist; thus what was at issue was the solution of the national question. But it was not a struggle against imperialism in a general, unspecified manner. Thus, secondly, it was a struggle to resolve the national question as a colonial question.

This means that in the struggle to organize and advance the revolution and defeat the enemy, it was possible to unite a much broader section of the population, from a much wider political base, than it would be possible in a neo-colonial or even a semi-colonial situation.

Nevertheless, does it mean that the anti-colonial united front which emerged in these countries was an amorphous 'alliance' whose only uniting factor was 'the proletarian ideology?' Shivji thinks so and quotes Amilcar Cabral to support his case. He should read Cabral again! Let quote Cabral in full before showing our author's total misunderstanding, and therefore misrepresentation, of the Guinean revolutionary:

> One important group in the town [says Cabral], were the dockworkers; another group were the people working in the boats carrying merchandise, who mostly live in Bissao itself and travel up and down the rivers. Those people proved highly counscious of their position and of their economic importance and they took the initiative of launching strikes wihout any trade union leadership at all. We therefore decided to concentrate all our work on this group. This gave excellent results and this group soon came to form a kind of nucleus which influenced the attitudes of other wage-earning groups in towns – workers proper and drivers who form two other important groups. Moreover, if I may put it this way, we thus found our little proletariat.[43]

Amilcar Cabral is so clear!

Whom did the PAIGC rely to form the nucleus of the movement? Cabral tells us that at first they concentrated on: (a) dockworkers and (b) people working in the boats. He says that after the strikes they went to organise: (a) workers proper and (b) drivers.

Instead of taking the kernel of what Cabral tells us, namely that the working class played a leading role within the PAIGC movement, Shivji dashed out shouting: 'What is important is that such revolutionary classes and strata are more mobilised under the proletarian ideology'.

This is futile because Cabral is not simply speaking of the ideology of the Guinean struggle. He is more concrete than Shivji and specifically tells us that this ideology was not an empty slogan but based on recruitment from within the ranks of the workers.

Shivji, however, is not satisfied to misinterpret Cabral once; he does it a second time:

> [The leadership of the proletarian ideology] is truer still in the case of cadres who may have varied class origins. In fact, the leadership and the cadres [note!] may even come from bourgeois and petty bourgeois classes: provided they are imbued with proletarian consciousness [sic!] such traitors to their classes are only too common in history.[44]

Once again Shivji has confused two issues, namely, the need for the leadership of the proletariat as a class in revolutionary struggle; and the question of those individuals from other classes who – as a minute exception – join the working class party and may even – as a still greater exception – become good cadres and possibly occupy a leadership role therein. In either case, of course, one cannot have working class party without a proletarian ideology.

Moreover to Shivji the 'traitors to their classes' are not an exception but the rule. They are, indeed, so common that they must usurp the leadership of the proletarian struggle and make revolution on behalf of, and for, the proletariat. Once again in Shivji we see a 'proletarian theory' which in essence seems to tell the proletariat: 'Don't worry. You need not lead your own struggle as a class. There are many bourgeois and petty bourgeois traitors to their class who will come to lead you!'

This, then, is Shivji's dogma of 'proletarian ideology', aimed at emasculating the working class struggle and betraying it to the leadership of other classes. Instead of drawing correct lessons from the shortcomings of the past struggles of the African proletariat in order to fortify and develop proletarian militancy, the author of *Class Struggles in Tanzania* offers his services to the 'lower sectors of the petty bourgeoisie !'

The author's second quotation from Cabral actually comes from where Cabral is talking about the recruitment and formation of cadres.

> We are faced with another difficult problem: we realised that we needed to have people with a mentality which could transcend the context of the national liberation struggle, and so we prepared a number of cadres from the group I have just mentioned, some from the people employed in commerce and other wage earners, and even some peasants so that they could acquire what you might call a working-class mentality. You might think this is absurd – in any case it is very difficult; in order for there to be a working-class mentality, the material conditions for the working class should exist, a working class should exist. In fact, we managed to inculcate these ideas into a large number of people – the kind of ideas, that is, which there would be if there were a working class. We trained 1000 cadres at out party school in Conakry; in fact for about two years this was about all we did outside the country. When these cadres returned to the rural areas they inculcated a certain mentality into the peasants and it is among these cadres that we have chosen the people who are now leading the struggle.[45]

Again not only does this confirm that many proletarian elements played a leading role within PAIGC; but further, Cabral, who was not a member of a Communist or a Marxist-Leninist party, turns out to be concrete, to the point and consistent in his practice, where a self-styled Marxist preaches to the proletariat to accept the leadership of other classes through 'the proletarian ideology'.

MISREPRESENTING THE PROLETARIAN LEADERSHIP OF THE CHINESE REVOLUTION

We now go to Shivji's reference to the Chinese people's struggle against imperialist oppression and feudal exploitation which ended in the victory of 1949.

Having brought out his doctrine of the leadership of the proletarian ideology, Issa Shivji continues:

> Even the Chinese struggle was based [sic!] mainly on the peasants and not on the proletariat, though given the concrete conditions of China, the peasantry itself, objectively, had revolutionary capacity. The important and decisive point is that the struggle was led by a party expounding proletarian ideology.[46]

In this brief paragraph, the author has accumulated a mass of confusion, half-truths and downright nonsense; and it is evident that Shivji's doctrine of proletarian ideology has turned into an obsession.

First, confusion – what does Shivji mean by the phrase that the Chinese struggle was 'based' mainly on the peasants and not the proletariat? If he is speaking of political leadership by the peasants, this is downright contrary to facts, as we shall see. If he means numerically more peasants took part in the Chinese revolution than the workers, then that is evident. China, as Mao Tse-tung realized quite early, (despite the fact that 'left' opposition from within the Chinese Communist Party, made it difficult to see the significance of this fact, was a rural, agrarian country. Therefore most of the population consisted of peasants. How could the CPC lead the Chinese revolution to the end without fully allying the peasants to the working class? It could not. And this was precisely the heart of the struggle against the first left-opportunist line from August 1927 to the end of 1928.

Once this line was corrected, and especially once Mao's strategy of mobilizing the countryside to take the cities was accepted within the Party, the peasants became even more deeply involved in the struggle. Mao stressed again that the peasants and especially the poor peasants were the workers' most solid allies, the most powerful detachment against feudal oppression in the rural areas.

By not bringing out what he means by his declaration that the Chinese struggle was mainly 'based' on the peasants and not the proletariat, Shivji creates confusion which lends itself to the interpretation that the Chinese revolution was a peasant revolution. By saying that the peasants constituted the 'main force' of the Chinese struggle, Mao Tse-tung was not saying that this made the Chinese revolution a peasant revolution.

Secondly, to say that the peasantry in China 'objectively had revolutionary capacity' is to engage in a half-truth which arises from his abandonment of concrete and precise analysis. In his analysis of classes in Chinese society, and of the peasants in particular, Mao always stressed the fact this was a class in disintegration. There were rich peasants, middle peasants and poor peasants. The rich peasants were on the rise towards the class of capitalist farmers, i.e. in the process of becoming part of the bourgeoisie. The poor peasants on the other hand were in the decline, being constantly pushed to the ranks of the proletariat. The latter was revolutionary, the other was most often hesitant, if not worse. In this situation what scientific content can one give to Shivji's blank statement that the peasants in China were 'objectively. . . revolutionary?' Thirdly, Shivji is saying nonsense when he states that what was 'important' and 'decisive' in the Chinese struggle was that the CPC was 'a party expounding proletarian ideology'. Had this been the decisive thing in the Chinese Communist Party and not the actual proletarian composition and leadership within the Party, the revolution would have been doomed.

Chairman Mao specifically said that the revolutionary role of the Party could be undermined and the struggle compromised, by allowing too large a recruitment from other classes into the party, and especially into leadership position. He gave concrete examples to illustrate this fact.[47]

Mao confirmed from Chinese revolutionary experience that the working class's failure to exercise firm leadership through the Party in, for example, 1926–27, led to a major, though temporary, setback.

What was the Chinese Communist Party? It was, like all genuine and not bogus Communist parties, essentially a workers' party. You cannot flood a party with all sorts of elements with non-proletarian, non-poor peasant backgrounds and expect it to retain a proletarian ideology, as Shivji thinks. This is so even if this party continues to mout'. 'he most high-sounding vows that it is 'imbued' with the best of Marxism-Leninism. This is precisely one of the basic aims and results of revisionism – to change the class character of the party while paying lip-service to 'proletarian ideology', the bourgeoisie and other classes placing themselves in commanding positions of leadership, pushing away the core of the revolution, the working class.

In his *The Struggle in the Ching Kang Mountains*, Mao wrote in November 1928 to show the dangers of the other classes trying to take control of the struggle, even in such a body like the Red Army. Mao warned against the advisability of having too many lumpen-proletarians in the Red Army although, he pointed out, conditions then demanded that the struggle could not do without them altogether. For that matter, Mao explained, political training had to be intensified among the recruits from the other classes. He explained that the only way to rectify matters within the Red Army was to abolish the mercenary system, increase Party representation, and consistently practice democracy.

In the same article, Mao showed the dangers of the intermediate classes. He went on,

> In the early days the small landlords and rich peasants scrambled to get on to government committees. . . Wearing red ribbons and feigning enthusiasm, they wormed their way. . . by trickery and seized control of everything, relegating the poor peasant members to a minor role. They can be cleared out only when they are unmasked in the course of struggle and the poor peasants assert themselves.
>
> During the revolutionary upsurge [in June 1928] many careerists took advantage of the Party's open recruitment of members and sneaked into the Party. . . After September the Party carried out a drastic house cleaning and set strict class qualifications for membership.[48]

What all this clearly shows is that Shivji has 'drawn lessons' from the Chinese struggle without in the least studying it. This is most dangerous. It misleads those revolutionary intellectuals who really seek to serve the proletariat. Shivji gives to these elements the impression that they can constitute themselves into a Party, in isolation from the very best vanguard elements of the proletariat, and wage struggle – so long as they are imbued with 'proletarian ideology'. How often have we been told that socialism is nothing more than an 'idea'? Let someone tell us the difference between Shivjism and the modern, vulgar and naive 'socialism' of the petty bourgeoisie – besides, perhaps, a little tinge of adventurism hidden in the corner.

It is finally necessary to dispose of the idea – for it is nothing but Shivji's fertile idea – that the Chinese struggle was simply led by a 'party propounding proletarian ideology'.

In the very first article that appears in Mao Tse-tung's *Selected Works* we have the following statement: 'The leading force [note!] in our revolution is the industrial proletariat. Our closest friends are the entire semi-proletariat and petty bourgeoisie'.[49]

Thus Mao is absolutely clear about the leadership of the Chinese struggle, whereas Shivji wishes to reduce this leadership to that of an ideology.

One of the bitterest struggles the Chinese Communist Party had to wage war against an 'ultra-left' group that controlled the Southern Hunan Special Committee around March 1921. This group accused Mao and other revolutionaries of desertion. Why? Because the latter were uncompromisingly opposed to their adventurism, whose slogan was, 'turning the petty bourgeois into proletarians and then driving them into the revolution!'[50]

With this kind of Trotskyism – for that is what it was – of course the policy failed. But it was the CPC which had to pay its price. Those who think they have a role to play in the struggle of our people against imperialism must be extremely careful that they make correct, honest and serious analysis and not rush to the kind of Trotskyist conclusions to which Shivji leads us. Nobody has a right to mislead patriotic and democratic Africans into this kind of half-baked fascination with ideas, because this is not the proletariat's hobby.

In his bitter attack of the 'roving band theory' and 'strategy' that had developed within the CPC by the beginning of 1929, Chairman Mao had to send out a circular letter on behalf of the Front Committee of the CPC on 5 April, 1929. The letter said:

> Proletarian leadership is the sole [note!] key to victory in the revolution. Building a proletarian foundation for the Party and setting up Party branches in industrial enterprises in key districts are important organizational tasks for the Party at present. . . In the revolution in semi-colonial China, the peasant struggle must always fail if it does not have the leadership of the workers. . .[51]

CONCLUSION

Sometime during his exile, before 1899, V.I. Lenin wrote three articles intended for the newspaper *Rabochaya Gazeta* which had been adopted as the official organ of the Russian Social-Democratic Labour Party at its first congress. One of the three articles in question was entitled 'Our Programme'. In this concise and clear exposition of their programme and political line, Lenin wrote:

> We take our stand entirely on the Marxist theoretical position. Marxism was the first to transform socialism from a utopia into a science, to lay a firm foundation for this science, and to indicate the path that must be followed in further developing and elaborating it in all its parts. . . It made clear the real task of a revolutionary socialist party: not to draw up plans for refashioning society, not to preach to the capitalists and their hangers-on about improving the lot of the workers, not to hatch conspiracies, but to organize the class struggle of the proletariat and to lead this struggle, the ultimate aim of which is the conquest of political power by the proletariat and the organization of a socialist society.[52]

It shows the tasks of those non-proletarian elements who nevertheless consider that they take Marxism as the starting point of their theory and practice – which is to create the conditions that will enable the working class to take consciousness of themselves as a class so as to organize themselves and to lead the popular struggle upto the end.

This basic position of Marxism-Leninism is, however, most distasteful to the ideological representatives of non-proletarian classes. They cannot imagine *how* the working class can lead the revolution. They cannot fathom *how* they have to be led by such an 'uncultured', propertyless class; how they must take a lower place and how the classes they represent must accept the leadership of the proletariat. Such were the representatives in Russia of non-proletarian classes, organised as the Narodniks, the Socialist-Revolutionaries, and the Cadets. Such was the position of the ideological representatives of the landlord, the bureaucrat-capitalist, and – at the beginning of the revolution – of the petty bourgeoisie, including the peasants, in China. The trend has continued ever since, transforming itself from an isolated to a world-wide phenomenon.

Quite often, they even dare their anti-proletarian calumines against the proletariat in the name of the proletariat itself and in the name of Marxism-Leninism! These are ideologies of other classes within the emerging proletarian and anti-imperialist movement. However, precisely because they speak in the name of the proletariat, they fabricate the most dangerous 'theories', 'doctrines', 'political lines' and 'programmes'.

It is in this light that we must see Issa G. Shivji and his ideological followers. For they are part of the East African brand of the Neo-Marxist School – a school which historically emerged and developed in close association with the treacherous 'Marxism' of the Second International, flirted with modern revisionism and linked up with the various wings of the Trotskyist line.

We must resolutely reject and refute this petty bourgeois 'Marxism'.

NOTES

1. Frederick Engels, *Letters of the Young Engels*, 1838–1845, Moscow, 1976, pp. 205.
2. Mao Tsetung, 'Combat Liberalism', *Selected Works*, Peking, Vol. II. p. 31.
3. Issa G. Shivji, 'Silent Class Struggle', first appeared in *Cheche* in 1970. It was later published with comments by various persons by Tanzania Publishing House, 1973.
4. I.G. Shivji, *Class Struggles in Tanzania*, London and Dar es Salaam: Heinemann Tanzania Publishing House, 1976.
5. Excerpts of this speech were reproduced under the title 'Process of Liberation' in *New Outlook*, Dar es Salaam, No. 5 (Sept/Oct. 1977) p. 5.
6. Ibid., pp. 5–6.
7. Ibid., p. 6.
8. This glib talk about the 'immediate enemy' as a means of shielding the imperialist monopolies and dividing the ranks of classes and other forces that are oppressed by finance capital is neo-Marxist, as testified by the fact that it was imported by John Saul from A.G. Frank in a debate on Latin America. A. Gundar Frank, 'Who Is the Immediate Enemy?' In Cockroft, Frank and Johnson, *Dependence and Underdevelopment*, Penguin, Harmondsworth, 1972, pp. 429–430. Saul's reference is to be found in his 'Who is the Immediate Enemy?' in Cliffe and Saul, *Socialism in Tanzania*, Nairobi: East African Publishing House, 1973, pp. 354–57.
9. V.I. Lenin, 'The Rights of Nations to Self-Determination', *Collected Works*, Vol. 20, Moscow: Progress Publishers, 1972, pp. 395–454.
10. Ibid.
11. Ibid.
12. J.V. Stalin, 'Marxism and the National – Colonial Question'.
13. Mao Tsetung, On New Democracy, *Selected Works*, Peking, 1975, Vol. II. pp. 339–384. Mao Tsetung, 'On the People's Democratic Dictatorship, in *Selected Works*, Peking, Vol. IV, 1969, pp. 411–424.
14. Ibid., p. 422.
15. K. Marx, *Capital*, Vol. I, Moscow, 1972 ed. pp. 575–76.
16. Ibid., p. 576.
17. I.G. Shivji. op. cit., pp. 22–23.
18. See Shivji, pp. 23 and also pp.53.
19. Shivji, op. cit., p. 52.
20. Ibid.

21. Ibid.
22. 'The Proposed By-Laws of the Tanganyika African Welfare and Commercial Association', encl. in Fiah to Northeote, 16 March 1936, TNA SMP 22444/1/46-47 quoted in John Iliffe, 'The Age of Improvement and Differentiation' I.N. Kimambo and A.J. Temu, *A History of Tanzania*, Nairobi, East African Publishing House, 1969, pp. 148.
23. MacMichael, 26 June 1936, TNA SMP 22444/1/69, quoted by J. Iliffe, op. cit., p. 148.
24. F. Engels, Preface to *The Peasant War in Germany*, K. Marx and F. Engels, *Selected Works*, Moscow, 1975, p. 240.
25. I.G. Shivji.
26. I.G. Shivji, op. cit., p. 53.
27. Ibid.
28. Ibid.
29. Shivji, op. cit., pp. 22–23.
30. Shivji, op. cit., p. 53.
31. Shivji, op. cit., p. 23.
32. Ibid.
33. Ibid.
34. See, for example, Frederick Engels, 'Karl Marx'. 'A Contribution to the Critique of Political Economy', in Karl Marx, *A Contribution to the Critique of Political Economy*, Moscow, 1970., pp. 221.
35. V.I. Lenin, 'What Is to Be Done?', *Selected Works*, Vol. I, Moscow, 1970, p. 138.
36. Karl Marx and Frederick Engels, *Manifesto of the Communist Party*, Peking, 1972, p. 44. p. 44.
37. Ibid.
38. Shivji, op. cit., p. 23-4
39. Ibid.
40. Ibid.
41. Ibid.
42. Ibid.
43. A. Cabral, 'A Brief Analysis of the Social Structure in Guinea', *Revolution in Guinea, Stage I*, London, 1969, p. 54.
44. Shivji, op.cit., p. 23.
45. Cabral op. cit.,
46. Shivji, op. cit., p. 23.
47. See, for example, 'Why is it that Red Political Power Can Exist in China?'; *Selected Works*, Vol. I, Peking, 1975, p. 32.
48. Mao Tsetung, op. cit., pp. 92–95.
49. Op. cit., p. 19.
50. Op. cit., p. 98.
51. Op. cit, pp . 122–123.
52. V.I. Lenin, 'Our Programme' in *Collected Works*, Vol. 4 Moscow (1972) pp. 210–211.

19

A CRITIQUE OF NABUDERE'S THEORY OF MULTILATERAL IMPERIALISM*

Joakim Mwami

INTRODUCTION

The theory of Marx, Engels, Lenin and Stalin is universally applicable. We should regard it not as a dogma, but as a guide to action. Studying it is not merely a matter of learning terms or phrases but of learning Marxism-Leninism as a science of revolution. It is not just a matter of understanding the general laws derived by Marx, Engels, Lenin and Stalin from their extensive study of real life and revolutionary experience, but of studying their standpoint and method, in examining and resolving problems.

—Mao Tse-tung

Opportunistic trends and tendencies in Marxist movements and circles, as well as in the period of social crisis, are not a new phenomenon; in actual fact, they have emerged and will continue to emerge under various forms as long as their social base – the petty bourgeoisie – continues to exist. Whereas in revolutionary situations and under the guidance of a proletarian Party, and through revolutionary practice, the phenomenon may be easily detected and easily liquidated; in non-revolutionary circumstances, on the other hand, the case may be extremely difficult to handle.

This is so in East Africa today. In the Tanzanian situation, for example, where Marxist ideas are at an extremely embryonic stage, and where the only Marxist circle one can boast of is that one which is confined chiefly to a few Marxist academicians who, incidentally, happen to have no mass bases whatsoever, there is a great chance for opportunistic theories and tendencies among these academicians to emerge in one form or another, to flourish, to endure and even to pass unchecked. And we all know just too well the consequences of opportunism: reformist ideas take precedence over revolutionary ideas and hence non-revolutionary movements – as Lenin said, 'Without a revolutionary theory there can be no revolutionary movement'.[1] Exposing and combating such reformist ideas whenever they happen to emerge becomes not only necessary but also one of the most fundamental tasks of all progressive individuals.

It is from this perspective that I have taken up this topic and the critique that I am going to offer should not be regarded by the reader as simply an academic exercise but as a political piece. Throughout this paper my concern will be not only the exposure of the erroneous and un-Marxist theories of Professor Nabudere but also his political opportunism.

*Examination reply to the question 'Critically Evaluate Nabudere's Analysis of Multilateral Imperialism After the Second World War,' later published in Maji Maji No. 33 1977.

In the first place, it is my conviction that Nabudere's analysis of 'multilateral' imperialism is not something new; in actual fact, it is typical of all liberal academicians. The only difference is that he poses himself as a 'Marxist-Leninist by using quite profusely and indiscriminately Marxist jargons and phraseology. With this, therefore, he has managed to cause a lot of ideological confusion, particularly among a great number of Dar es Salaam University students, especially those who are just starting to learn the science of Marxism-Leninism. As far as I am concerned, therefore, unlike those who are easily taken in by new ideas, the importance of Professor Nabudere's works[2], i.e. his analysis of 'multilateral' imperialism and the corresponding political conclusions, lies not in his penchant for strong words instead of strong arguments; not in high-sounding phrases such as 'multilateralism', 'multilateral imperialist strategy', 'financial oligarchies of the imperialist countries', 'Multilateral imperialist arrangement', 'new-Marxists' and the like; but in the class interests such analysis objectively represents – regardless of whether or not the professor is subjectively aware of them.

Revealing the way in which Nabudere's analysis of 'multilateral' imperialism is metaphysically economistic, inconsistent and politically opportunistic is the task that I will attempt to tackle. Given the time constraint and academic 'terrorism', that beset an undergraduate student in this University, my critique should be taken as a modest attempt at unravelling Professor Nabudere's analysis and at no time should it be regarded as exhaustive.

'MULTILATERAL' IMPERIALISM

It is my considered opinion that any work on imperialism that claims to be scientific must, among other aspects, deal with analysis of class relations and also it must attempt to identify concrete contradictions of a given social formation. This means that imperialism must be concretely defined and analysed or else any talk of 'fighting against imperialism, imperialism is the enemy' and so forth loses its meaning. For it should be remembered that nowadays, it is quite fashionable for any one, be he Banda, Kaunda, Kenyatta, the Shah of Iran or Mobutu to regard imperialism as the enemy. So it is essential for anyone claiming to be a Marxist to present a class analysis of imperialism – and at no time should sloganeering substitute for analysis.

Unfortunately, what Nabudere presents to the world is not at all Marxist exposition of imperialism, as he claims. In the 'Introduction' to *The Political Economy of Imperialism*, Professor Nabudere tries to define what he calls 'multilateral' imperialism along the following lines:

> This is modern imperialism operating under conditions of narrowing horizons created by the emergence of the socialist system that was marked by the October Revolution. The Second World War worsened the contradictions between the imperialist countries, which led to a devastating destruction of the productive forces among vanquished and victors alike. The US which emerged as the strongest power, soon dictated a new redivision of the world based on the Open-Door policy. A system of multilateral institutions was worked out under US supervision to anchor this redivision. The dissolution of bilateral colonial markets marked this redivision. The monopolies could now compete in these open neo-colonial markets as long as US hegemony was assured. The rise of the transnational corporate strategy is the direct result of these developments.[3]

Elaborating more on this post-war strategy – one wonders how imperialism can be connected with a strategy! – the Professor singles out the US as the power behind it and whose rationale, we are told, it 'basically to get rid of imperial and colonial markets which its allies enjoyed to the detriment of the US'. He continues to say that

> the main culprit against whom US strategies were aimed was clearly Britain herself for she controlled the biggest empire. . .[4]

Reading through his manuscripts, one gets the impression that this 'multilateral' imperialism is a more or less conscious creation of the US. For example, he says 'The planning of a multilateral system of world production, trade and finance was therefore to be achieved by a three-pronged tactical approach; namely by creating trade, monetary, financial and political institutions'. And the objectives of this 'economic strategy' were

> aimed at creating fewer obstacles to movement of capital and payments on current transactions. Trade flows had to be influenced by relative price considerations rather than by artificial means to strike a bilateral balance. Purchases had to be made in cheapest markets and sales in the most lucrative. Such multilateral strategy, it was assumed, would promote the international division of labour under the monopoly capitalism of the post-war era and encourage each country to specialise in the production of those goods in which it enjoyed the 'greatest comparative advantage'. This would lead to the best allocation of resources on an international scale.[5]

Then we are finally told that

> this post-war imperialist arrangement, worked out at Bretton Woods and Havana, found its expression in the multilateral institutions which were created for this purpose,

and these institutions are the United Nations – which is a 'political institution'; the IMF 'through which monopoly capital in the post-war period tried to facilitate a currency and monetary policy to enable multilateral trade and finance to function'. Another is the IBRD (the World Bank) whose role was 'the mobilization of capital for construction and to stimulate the flow of private investment'. The last is the GATT, whose objective was 'the general elimination of quantitative restrictions'.

According to the Professor, the creation of these 'multilateral' institutions at Bretton Woods and Havana; the rise of what he calls transnational corporations, together with a shift in the pattern of investment in the 'Third World' countries – a shift from extractive imperialism. For him, without a clear understanding of these institutions and organs, it is 'impossible to comprehend' not only 'the contradictions that characterised Uganda's first ten years and the subsequent period under military dictatorship' but also, impliedly, the phenomenon of neo-colonialism.

One thing which strikes me from this analysis is that, first, 'multilateral' imperialism is regarded as a 'strategy', more or less as a 'policy' pursued by the US. This is manifested in his use of expressions such as 'planning', 'tactical approach' and so forth. Secondly, imperialism is identified or rather associated with countries, namely the US, Britain etc., and this will be clear when we look at what he considers as the immediate enemy of the Uganda revolution.

My objection to such type of analysis is twofold: first, it is un-Marxist to identify imperialism with 'strategy' or a 'policy' and with this regard, Nabudere's analysis comes very close to that of Kautsky against whom Lenin argued.

Secondly, Nabudere's analysis is very much economistic. For him, monopolies, the transnational corporations, the cartels, the multilateral institutions are everything. Actually, when he speaks about imperialism one gets the impression that he is speaking about these institutions. To be more precise, his analysis of 'multilateral' imperialism is essentially an <u>economic analysis</u> of the power of the transnational corporations and their expansion in the capitalist world.

But Marxism-Leninism teaches us that monopolies, parliaments, armies, schools, libraries, etc. are simply structures; that is, they are organizational forms of certain class interests, and that unless the class nature of these structures is analysed, one won't be able to comprehend social reality and its movement.

A hundred years ago, Marx defined capital in the following terms:

> ...capital is not a thing, but rather a definite social production relation, belonging to a definite historical formation of society, which is manifested in a thing and lends this thing a specific social character. Capital is not the sum of the material and produced means of production. Capital is rather the means of production transformed into capital, which in themselves are no more capital than gold or silver in itself is money. It is the means of production monopolised by a certain section of society, confronting living labour-power as products and working conditions rendered independent of this very labour-power, which are personified through this antithesis in capital.[6]

Likewise, finance capital, which is the basis of imperialism – the highest stage of capitalism – is a social relation of production and it is only pursuing a class analysis that it can be defined in concrete terms. But to talk of imperialism as 'intervening', sometimes as setting 'its foot on the soil of Uganda'; or as something that can be 'convinced', or 'scared' or that which can "pay heed" or "initiate" something clearly shows that the author does not understand what imperialism is. In actual fact, such conceptualisation only serves to cement the current view on imperialism – a view which regards imperialism as a monster residing somewhere in America or Western Europe; i.e. as a foreign entity located far away.

ON EXPLOITATION

Nabudere's shallowness in Marxism is also seen in the way he uses the concepts of exploitation and surplus-value. But let us first examine the former:

> The recent Lome Convention merely helped to bring together 46 African, Caribbean and Pacific countries (ACP) under new arrangement of the enlarged European Community, to continue the exploitation of these countries.[7]

Such formulations – of their countries being exploited by imperialist countries – are heard almost daily from the lips of exploiting classes in the Third World countries. It is therefore unpardonable for a 'Marxist-Leninist' to use the same language and meaning as the capitalists do. For one thing, to speak of the 'Third World' being exploited by imperialism not only reveals one's ignorance of what imperialism is, but also one's ignorance of the Marxist conception of exploitation. For it must be working people who can be exploited. Criticising Emmanuel for a similar error, Bettleheim had this to say:

> ... the concept of exploitation expresses a production relation, production of surplus labour and appropriation of this by a social class – it necessarily relates to <u>class relations</u> (and a relation between 'countries' is not and cannot be a relation between classes). This, too, is why a mere <u>transfer of surplus value from the capitalists</u> (or other exploiters) of the poor countries to the capitalists of the rich countries cannot be described as 'exploitation' in the strict sense of the word, since only <i>working people</i> can be exploited but not other exploiters.[8]

It is this misconception of 'exploitation' which leads the Professor to very queer and adventurist political conclusions, such as that in the neo-colony, a capitalist (capital) and a worker (labour) can embrace each other under the proletarian ideology and effect the national democratic revolution. How this can be done, given that the dominant ideology in these neo-colonies is bourgeois, is a question which can only be answered by the Professor himself.

My second quarrel with the Professor is his indiscriminate use of the concept of surplus-value. Throughout his works, the only form of surplus extraction that takes place in the neo-colonies is that of surplus-value. This, probably, is useful in his own analysis because he is more concerned with the exploitation of the 'Third World' countries by 'imperialism', rather than with the exploitation of the working people in these neo-colonies. For example, we hear that,

> Falling profitability compels monopolies to invest overseas in order to extract more surplus-value . . . Thus imperialist exploitation of weaker countries is a function of its contradictory development . . . [9]

This use of the category surplus-value is justified because, for him, all the neo-colonies are characterised by capitalist relations of production; that means, with the emergence of monopoly capital, only one single mode of production – the capitalist mode – is pervasive. In the case of Uganda, for example, we are told 'Thus the peasant is drawn into capitalist commodity production and capitalism – particularly under monopoly capitalism – turns him into a near-proletarian hand'. [my emphasis][10] And then he goes on to support his own erroneous view by quoting Engels out of context – for Engels was speaking under totally different socio-economic conditions to those obtaining now in neo-colonial Uganda where capitalism has not managed as yet to establish capitalist relations of production, as Nabudere asserts. He would be out to ask to prove that assertion of his. Moreover, if what he says is true, that is, the capitalist relations of production are pervasive (i.e., capitalists and workers), then he would not only be contradicting himself that the peasantry consists of 90%[11] of the total population in Uganda, but it would also be nonsensical to speak to the effect that, 'the new democratic revolution is in essence a peasant question with the working class as its leader. . . [12]

I would submit, therefore, that in the neo-colonial countries, Uganda included, there are many more modes of production than simply the capitalist mode – although the latter is in a dominant position. Hence, there are many more forms of surplus extraction besides surplus-value. Thus the categorisation of the various forms of surplus extraction from the producing classes in the neo-colonies is not a simple matter of generalisation (surplus-value only!!), but it calls for a concrete analysis of each social formation. Here, therefore, lies the usefulness of understanding the combination of modes of production. For it is only thus that one is able to characterise the various social classes in the rural areas rather than speak of the 'peasantry' in general, as if it were a homogeneous entity with no marked differentiation. Connected with this, therefore, are the phenomena of merchant capital and unequal exchange, which Nabudere repudiates. Although his criticisms against Emmanuel are well taken, nevertheless his repudiation of the concept altogether cannot be entertained. Again, what form does the surplus product which is extracted by the Tanzanian Authorities (coffee, tobacco, sisal, etc.) from the petty commodity producers in the rural areas take? Is it surplus-value, merchant profit or what?

CLASS, STATE AND NATION

> Marxism-Leninism consistently holds that the fundamental question in all revolutions is that of state power.
>
> —*The General Line*

Marxism maintains that any exploitative social system can only be sustained precisely because of the presence of the instrument (political) of oppression, namely the state. Furthermore, it also maintains that the state being the seat of political power and hence the focus of all class struggles, its seizure and its destruction by the rising (exploited) class become the chief objective. To talk of revolution, therefore, without speaking and specifying this chief objective is to betray one's opportunism. I shall come to this shortly.

At the level of structures, the state consists of the following organs: the repressive machinery, ideological instruments, the government and bureaucracy. But what is important as far as the state is concerned is not these structures, whose quantitative magnitudes can differ from one state to another. What is of important, and particularly for any Marxist, is the class nature of a particular state. For these structures are merely reflections of particular class interests in a given social formation. Furthermore, Marxism also maintains that there can never be a state without a corresponding ruling class. These are fundamental principles which can never compromised. This is my view.

It is, therefore, sheer opportunism for someone of Nabudere's calibre to state:

> Multilateral imperialism under neo-colonialism means that Uganda became a state of the total bourgeoisie of which the financial oligarchies of the imperialist countries is the ruling strata. The joint rule and joint exploitation of Uganda (sic!) [very similar to Kautsky's joint exploitation of the world by internationally united finance capital, which Lenin constantly repudiated] was to be on the basis of monopolistic (sic) competition of the monopolies of these countries, [emphasis mine][13]

Although this type of lifeless and abstract theorisation is essential for Nabudere's conclusions, such as 'a direct proletarian onslaught on the international bourgeois' – very close to Trostkyite propositions – it has nothing in common with Marxism and in particular with Marxist teaching on the theory of the state. From a Marxist point of view, the colonial, neo-colonial and imperialist states are all qualitatively different political organs and to regard the change from a colonial to a neo-colonial state as simply a 'change of persons, institutions' as the 'Marxist-Leninist' Professor Nabudere maintains, is, as far as I am concerned, the highest degree of opportunism.

Elsewhere, the Professor goes on to state the 'transformation from the colonial state to a neo-colonial state cannot change the rule of 'wealth' of finance capital, the rule of the financial oligarchy, the imperialist international bourgeoisie. . . Here again the Professor betrays his own ignorance of the dialectical relationship between the economic base and the political superstructure. He loses sight of the simple Marxist thesis which advances that though it is the economic base which gives rise to a given political superstructure, however, it is only through the latter that the former can be transformed. The professor cannot see the qualitative difference and change from colonial to neo-colonial state because he is deeply immersed in metaphysical economism.

As quoted in the prefatory note at the beginning of this essay, Mao emphasises the point that Marxism-Leninism is a science of revolution and hence 'we should regard it not as a dogma, but as a guide to action'. And that 'it is not just a matter of understanding the general laws derived by Marx, Engels, Lenin and Stalin from their extensive study of real life and revolutionary experience, but of studying their standpoint and method of examining and resolving problem'.[14]

But when we come to examine the way Professor Nabudere treats the national question, one is left with no doubt that the Professor is simply making a caricature of Marxism. The whole section is full of stereotyped definitions and quotations from the founders of Marxism. In his effort to raise himself to the level of Marx, Lenin and Mao, he has just managed to trivialise the science of Marxism-Leninism.

The premise which Nabudere uses as the foundation for the non-existence of nations in the present colonies is that of Stalin's definition of a nation as 'historical category belonging to a definite epoch of rising capitalism'. The Professor goes on to say that,

> on the basis of this definition these countries [meaning colonies and neo-colonies] are not nations. Like all colonial, semi-colonial and neo-colonial countries, they are 'oppressed' countries and not nations. Here the national question has never been resolved and, therefore, it still constitutes today's fundamental contradiction between these countries and imperialism.[15]

This is a typical example of prostituting Marxism and regarding it as a dogma. When 'classical' Marxist definitions do not fit into describing or analysing a given social phenomenon then the phenomenon does not exist. This sort of approach has nothing in common with Marxism-Leninism; it is a complete vulgarisation of it. It is also interesting and actually quite proposterous for Professor Nabudere to deny the existence of nations in the neo-colonies, when as early as 1900 Lenin was speaking of colonial people as nations: 'Europeans often forget that colonial people too are nations'.[16] Elsewhere, having outlined that in England, France, Germany etc., the national problem had been solved long ago, Lenin goes on to say that,

> The undeveloped countries are a different matter. They embrace the whole of Eastern Europe and all colonies and semi-colonies. . . In those areas, as a rule, there still exist oppressed and capitalistically underdeveloped nations. Objectively, these nations will have general tasks to accomplish, namely democratic tasks, the tasks of overthrowing foreign oppression.[17]

Had Professor Nabudere been consistent in his formulation, then that would have been another case. He denies one thing here, but then he acknowledges its existence some time later. The question is: How can Professor Nabudere speak so much about the 'new national democratic revolution' when there are no nations in these neo-colonies? Actually the entire Chapter XIV of his *Imperialism and Revolution in Uganda* is devoted to the whole issue of the national democratic revolution in Uganda. Moreover, if colonial Vietnam and semi-colonial China were not nations (under the rule of imperialism), how does Nabudere dare quote them as examples of where national liberation wars and national revolutions triumphed? In other words, if there are no nations in the neo-colonies, what then are his premises for the so-called national democratic revolutions? These are the questions which can better be answered by the Professor himself.

When it comes to specifying concretely (in Uganda) *who* is the immediate enemy today, Nabudere fails miserably to do this work; the reason for this failure is that the analysis is 'relatively difficult'. And instead, therefore we are just treated to the same sloganeering; imperialism again and again is the enemy:

> Thus the enemy of the people [who are the people? – no class analysis] of Uganda is imperialism in general. But since intra-imperialist rivalry within Uganda was introduced under neo-colonialism, it is important to determine

at each point in time which of the imperialist powers, during periods of acute rivalry amongst them, is the main supporter of local reaction. For the purposes of strengthening the struggle and uniting all the forces capable of being united, it is necessary to identify that imperialist power [one wonders whether imperialism can be identified with imperialist powers] as the immediate main enemy.[18]

He concludes by saying, 'Western imperialism therefore, for us, at this moment constitutes today's principal enemy in Uganda, with the British, French and US imperialists [sic] as the main ones'.[19]

So, at last, we are told (in a *Mwongozo*-type definition of imperialism) who is the immediate enemy today in Uganda.

CONCLUSION

There are a number of fundamental issues – such as Soviet social imperialism, of which Professor Nabudere does not say even a single word in spite of the fact that he is dealing with 'multilateral' imperialism – with which we have not dealt in this critique.

All in all, I find Nabudere's analysis of what he calls 'multilateral' imperialism, which is just a disguised version of Kautsky's 'ultra-imperialism', a hopeless piece of work full of sloganeering only, and abuses and insults of those whom he calls 'neo-Marxists'. But so far as advancing the Marxist analysis of the theory of imperialism is concerned, he has failed miserably. His works, therefore, can as well be placed in the museum of antiquity for posterity, so that future East African revolutionaries can judge for themselves what manner of man Professor Nabudere is and the objective class interests he represents.

NOTES

1. V.I. Lenin, *What Is to Be Done?*, Peking: Foreign Language Press, 1973, p. 28.
2. D.W. Nabudere, *The Political Economy of Imperialism*, and *Imperialism and Revolution in Uganda*. (manuscripts)
3. D.W. Nabudere, *The Political Economy of Imperialism*, (manuscript) pp. xx.
4. Ibid, p. 264.
5. Ibid., p. 265.
6. Karl Marx, *Capital*, Vol. III, Moscow: Progress Publishers, pp. 818–5.
7. D.W. Nabudere, *The Political Economy*, p. 395.
8. A. Emmanuel, *Unequal Exchange*, New York: Monthly Review Press, 1972, p. 301.
9. D.W. Nabudere, *The Political Economy*, p. 357.
10. D.W. Nabudere, *Imperialism and Revolution in Uganda*, p. 61.
11. Ibid., p. 363.
12. Ibid., p. 270.
13. Ibid., p. 200.
14. Ibid., p. 201.
15. *New Outlook* (Tanzania), Issue No. 5,
16. V.I. Lenin, *A Caricature of Marxism and Imperialist Economism*, Moscow: Progress Publishers.
17. Ibid., pp. 38–39.
18. D.W. Nabudere, *Imperialism and Revolution in Uganda*, p. 358.
19. Ibid., p. 358.

20

ON MULTINATIONAL IMPERIALISM AND OTHER RELATED ISSUES

(A Reply to a Petty-bourgeois Critic of Nabudere's *Political Economy of Imperialism*)

Takyiwaa Manuh and Sipula Kabanje

We have come across an essay circulating around the University campus by a Third-Year student of East African Society and Environment (EASE), to which we have decided to respond, since in our view it raises many erroneous points of theory and betrays remarkable confusion. As the writer did not dare put his name we shall simply for the sake of convenience refer to him as Ndugu EASE III.*

1. MULTILATERAL IMPERIALISM

> The facts show that differences between capitalist countries, e.g. in the matter of protection or free trade, only give rise to insignificant variations in the form of monopolies, or in the moment of their appearance; and that the rise of monopolies, as a result of the concentration of production, is a general and fundamental law of the present stage of development of capitalism.[1]

The above quote from Lenin needs to be borne in mind when discussing imperialism and trying to find out what is its essence. Thus monopoly is the essence of imperialism, and the transnational corporation in the era of multilateral imperialism is only one form.

Nabudere concretely discusses in his book the period of the rise of monopoly and the rise of modern imperialism.

An analysis of imperialism cannot but be an economic analysis, a preoccupation with its economic essence. Lenin stresses this point:

> I trust that this pamphlet will help the reader to understand the fundamental economic question viz., the question of the economic essence of imperialism, for unless this is studied, it will be impossible to understand and appraise modern war and modern politics[2] [our emphasis].

Therefore Ndugu EASE III's comment that Nabudere's analysis of multilateral imperialism is 'essentially an economistic analysis of the power of the transnational corporations and their expansion in the capitalist world' is not only meaningless and shows that he does not comprehend the essence of imperialism, but also opportunistic in so far as he quotes Marx's statement that capital is a social relation. From this, he jumps to the demand that Nabudere has to make a class analysis of the structures set up under multilateral imperialism in order for us to understand finance capital. Obviously Ndugu EASE III has not read Part III of Nabudere's book, dealing with the rise of the financial oligarchy. This financial oligarchy are a minority section of the bourgeoisie. It is the section which has monopolised

*The author of the essay, which appears in this volume on p. 206, is Joakim Mwami.

production and finance and divided the world among themselves. What further class analysis of these structure would the Ndugu want?

Lenin showed in his thesis on *Imperialism* that during the first phase of imperialism the financial oligarchy of the then major imperialist countries – Great Britain, United States, France and Germany – were able to subjugate the whole world by their capital. At that time Britain was the leading imperialist power. This ability of the financial oligarchy to impose its domination over the rest of the world is in no way denied under multilateral imperialism. The point that is made is that under the changed balance of forces, the U.S. financial oligarchy came out as the leader. The World Bank, for example, is an institution of the world financial oligarchy, but the control of each over this institution is determined by their respective command of finance capital. Reality happens to be that the U.S. financial oligarchy dominates in this institution not because the other imperialist countries want it that way but because the institution is an objective manifestation of the enormous power of U.S. finance capital. U.S. imperialism emerges as a leading power under conditions whereby the weakened imperialist powers were the majority shareholders of the colonial world.

Now the rearrangement of the then existing order entailed the reflection of this historic contradiction, that is the colossal power of the U.S., on the one hand, without a significant share of the world's colonies, and, on the other hand the possession of colonies by the European and British imperialist powers whose economic power had declined considerably. This meant that the U.S. had to strive for colonial markets to correspond with its new position in the world economy. And this was done. As Lenin put it '...the capitalists divide the world...and they divide it in proportion to capital, in proportion to strength, because there cannot be any other method of division under commodity production and capitalism. But strength varies with the degree of economic and political development'.[3] As we can see, the rearrangements that emerged – the World Bank, IMF, the GATT – were initiated by the U.S., though not without an amount of resistance from the other imperialist powers. In all these institutions the U.S. played the leading role, and this reflects the historic movement of the U.S. to the apex of world imperialism. It is a manifestation of the inherent law of uneven development in capitalism, implying that capitalist countries do not develop their productive forces at the same rate. This disparity in the development of the productive forces is reflected in political relations between countries. As Marx and Engels pointed out, 'The relations of different nations among themselves depend upon the extent to which each has developed its productive forces.'[4]

This is how we can see, for instance, that the era of competitive capitalism is more or less like the 'policies' of British imperialism, precisely because Britain had developed its productive forces to such an extent that it was christened the 'workshop of the world'. At the level of the superstructure the hegemony of the British appeared as if the execution of its policies were determined by the subjective whims of its policy-makers. In reality, this was determined by the triumphant industrial bourgeoisie of that country. So it is today that in the post-World War II period, the U.S. became the leading centre of finance capital within the world that had just emerged from a war for redivision of spheres of influence. Given that the U.S. financial oligarchy was the most powerful in the world, it had to pursue its own class interests taking into account the fact that the other imperialist powers were defeated but not destroyed, and taking into account the interest of the bourgeoisie as a whole in their struggle against communism and the national liberation struggle. The U.S. could not settle the issue of spheres of influence through war. This would have meant a further crisis for capitalism under conditions highly favourable for proletarian revolution. This is why we find that at this juncture multilateralism comes out as a most expedient form for the financial oligarchy as a whole. But this unity against communism and the forces of national liberation did not preclude inter-imperialist rivalry, and this explains the emergence of regional organisations such as the EEC to resist American dominance.

The power of U.S. imperialism is reflected in the establishment of the institutions we have mentioned. Ndugu EASE III, not comprehending the objective power of finance capital, states that 'one gets the impression that this "multilateral" imperialism is more or less, a conscious creation of the U.S.' To him the U.S. ruling class, which determines American policy, is abstracted from the financial oligarchy. He cannot link up what he reads about multilateral imperialism with what has been discussed before about finance capital. Capital does not operate in a vacuum, but under conditions created by the capitalists in struggle with the working class and other classes. He fails to see the functional role of the IBRD, the IMF and the GATT for the financial oligarchy in general and that of the U.S. in particular. This same error of not seeing the movement of finance capital under given historic conditions leads him to focus on the semantic aspect of the text and to abstract from the social reality described therein. This is why he 'wonders how imperialism can be connected with a strategy'.

He concludes that Nabudere's analysis comes very close to that of Kautsky. Perhaps we need to remind ourselves of the sense in which Lenin argued against Kautsky. For Kautsky, imperialism was the striving of every advanced industrial capitalist country to annex agrarian territory.[5] Lenin points out that in defining imperialism thus, Kautsky puts the role of the merchant in the forefront over the financier; secondly, he makes imperialism only a struggle for agrarian territory whereas in actual fact imperialism also strives to annex even highly industrialised regions. By positing imperialism as a 'policy preferred by finance capital', Lenin explains, Kautsky detaches the politics of imperialism from its economics. Now where does Nabudere do this in his book? Ndugu EASE III would be hard-put to point out where this occurs.

But isn't it interesting that Nabudere's analysis is Kautskyite, i.e. separating the politics of imperialism from its economics, and economistic at the same time? This is a riddle that only Ndugu EASE III, can solve.

2. ON EXPLOITATION

Ndugu EASE III criticises Nabudere when the latter refers to the Lome Convention, speaking about the control and continued exploitation by the monopolies of the countries of the Third World. As to the issue of countries being exploited by imperialism, let us recall what Lenin said about the export of capital providing '. . . a solid basis for the imperialist oppression and exploitation of most of the countries and nations of the world, for the capitalist parasitism of a handful of wealthy states.'[6] [our emphasis] Ndugu EASE III can go ahead and criticise Lenin for being 'ignorant' of the 'Marxist' conception of exploitation since, according to Ndugu, a country cannot be exploited, it is only the working people who can be exploited.

The concept of exploitation under capitalism refers to the capital-labour relationship, and nobody is saying that the petty-bourgeoisie are being exploited. It is significant that Lenin talks about imperialist oppression and exploitation because, as we shall show, the petty-bourgeoisie and 'national' bourgeoisie are oppressed by finance capital and as such have a contradiction with imperialism. Therefore the quotation from Bettelheim that Ndugu EASE III cites does not prove anything.

Bettelheim criticises Emmanuel for his concept of unequal exchange (exploitation taking place at the level of exchange). We have said that exploitation under capitalism involves the capital-labour relationship, i.e. it takes place at the level of production. Thus when we talk of exploitation we are talking of the appropriation of surplus value at the level of production and not a mere transfer of surplus value, which is just merchant profit. In our neo-colonies the monopolies are engaged directly in production. Thus in the Lome Convention, one of the compulsory conditions under which a neo-colony qualifies for loans under the European Development Fund is that it must allow only firms from the EEC member countries to carry out the projects to which such funds are devoted. Thus the main reason for setting up the Lome Convention was to 'consolidate the EEC's economic footing in these countries, both for the community as a whole and for the individual members, and to tie Africa to the economy of the EEC.'[7]

On the so-called absolutisation of the capital-labour relationship by Nabudere, and the consequent conclusion that surplus value is the only form of extraction of surplus, we need to make a preliminary point. On the one hand, we are told that Nabudere does not understand what exploitation is, i.e. that he does not understand the capital-labour relationship, namely the appropriation of surplus value. On the other hand, Nabudere manages to absolutise the capital-labour relationship. Are these two positions not contradictory?

Ndugu EASE III would have us believe that capitalist relations have not yet been established in our neo-colonies. If he accepts that capitalist production exists in our countries, will he accuse us of quoting 'out of context' the general law Marx laid down that:

> wherever capitalist production takes root it destroys all forms of commodity production which are based either on the self-employment of the producers, or merely on the sale of the excess product as commodities. Capitalist production first makes the production of commodities general, and then by degrees transforms all commodity production into capitalist commodity production.[8]

Thus, as we see, the peasants in the neo-colony start producing tea, sisal, coffee, cocoa and other cash crops. The monopolies set up plant and soil research institutions, credit institutions and marketing organisations to make sure that production takes place in an orderly way. Thus under the International Coffee Agreement of 1962, there is a coffee fund which is for the advancement of credit facilities to the producers and for research. This fund is directly linked to the World Bank, so that ultimately the coffee producer is supervised by finance capital at a multilateral level. Nabudere shows concretely in his manuscript on Uganda the control by finance capital of production itself. There is no contradiction between the fact that capitalist relations of production are *pervasive* and the fact that 90% of the total population of Uganda consists of the peasantry. The issue is their exploitation by finance capital, which determines in advance in terms of what to produce, how and when to produce, and at what price the peasantry will sell.

The neo-colony is a source of raw materials and markets for the products of the financial oligarchy and is consequently prevented from developing its productive forces; thus capitalist relations are predominant. But since in the colonies, semi-colonies and neo-colonies these relations are the historic creations of the financial oligarchy and not due to the internal development of the productive forces, we find co-existing obsolete relations of production which become denuded of their essence, and remain pre-capitalist only in form. For example, even the products that the merchant circulates are products of the financial oligarchy.

Indeed we should like to know what modes of production the Ndugu is referring to when he seems to speak of other modes of production independent of capitalist development! It is not the combination of modes of production which helps us to understand the various social classes within the peasantry, as is suggested. When we see a poor peasant working for a kulak and receiving a wage, we recognise it as a capital-labour relationship. Lack of dialectics, however, prevents our Ndugu from grasping the fundamental movement in the neo-colonies, from comprehending the various social classes and making out the principal ones from secondary.

He fails to do so since he cannot see surplus value as a form of surplus product which takes predominance in society under the capitalist order. The same lack of particularity in history comes out when he talks about merchant capital. There was, sometime in the past, merchant capital within the womb of feudalism, under industrial capital, and to some extent even under finance capital. However, these forms of merchant capital have played different roles under different social-economic conditions. What does our anonymous writer mean by a merchant? Does he mean the petty trader who gets credits from the banks? Under finance capital the small capitalist must rely heavily on the banks to survive.

The very fact that other forms of extraction of surplus that exist beside the dominant mode of appropriation of surplus value are remnants of the past shows that capitalism in our countries has not developed as a revolutionary force that dissolves all archaic relations. This means that imperialism does not develop capitalism on behalf of the neo-colonies! The days of the revolutionary bourgeoisie are done and gone. As Lenin stressed, imperialism is parasitic, decaying and moribund capitalism. When the Chinese communists were preparing for an assault on the financial oligarchy they knew who the principal enemy was. They did not bother themselves with the various modes of production in order to comprehend the facts that people were being exploited also by other classes other than the imperialists.

When Nabudere attacked the centre-periphery ideologists – Emmanuel, Amin and others – he showed very clearly that these petty-bourgeois ideologues confuse issues of production relations and exploitation with the question of prices. This formula inevitably leads to reformist conclusions objectively, regardless of the wishes of the proponents.

Nabudere points out,

> The whole centre-periphery ideology plays into the hands of, the populist 'national bourgeoisie' and petty bougeoisie. The populists who have for years been making noises in the GATT, the UNCTAD and the UNO that they are being cheated as Third World countries in international markets find their ideology ready-made for them by the Emmanuels and Amins. The struggle of the neo-colonial peoples is directed towards trade councils, and negotiations on 'terms of trade' and 'exchange rates', and away from class struggle.[9]

It was the major contribution of Marx in political economy to prove that the enrichment of the capitalist class does take place on the exchange of equivalents and *not* on cheating by hiking up prices. Whatever exceptions may be found with regard to specific enterprises under specific conditions, these cannot be elevated to the pinnacle of a 'new' law. To waver from this is to abandon Marxist political economy and hence to sink into the depth of obscurantism, a state which will in no way enable us to explain imperialism and its exploitation and oppression of our countries and peoples.

3. CLASS, STATE AND NATION

Ndugu EASE III starts his attack on Nabudere's conception of the state by quoting from the *General Line* that, 'Marxism-Leninism constituently holds that the fundamental question in all revolutions is that of state power.' Fine. Then he tells us that 'from a Marxist point of view, the colonial, neo-colonial and imperialist states are all qualitatively different political organs'.

How is a colonial state qualitatively different from an imperialist state? Let us sum up the Marxist thesis on the state. Engels says that,

> The state arose from the need to hold class antagonisms in check, but because it arose, at the same time, in the midst of the conflict, of these classes, it is, as a rule [note!] the state of the most powerful, economically dominant class, which, through the medium of the state, becomes also the politically dominant class and thus acquires new means of holding down and exploiting the oppressed class.[10]

Further on, Engels points out that the highest form (as it then was), the democratic republic, was an institution of the propertied class, the bourgeoisie. In this time, he noted, wealth exercised power over the state partly through the corruption of government officials but mainly through an alliance between government and the stock exchange.

But under imperialism every bank is a stock exchange,[11] Lenin tells us. Banks now become powerful monopolies having at their command almost the whole of the money capitalists and small businessmen and also the larger part of the means of production and sources of raw materials in any one country and in a number of countries. The huge banks merged or coalesced with industry at the beginning of the 20th century and gave rise to the financial oligarchy. The financial oligarchy becomes the ruler of the world by virtue of its economic power. Noting this, Lenin quoted a bourgeois author who had correctly referred to France as 'a nation of the financial oligarchy; it is the complete domination of the financial oligarchy; the latter dominates over the press and government'.[12]

What was said of France applied to all other imperialist states. Just to complement the remarks on France, Lenin cited another bourgeois author who, in referring to Germany, had this to say: 'the economic liberty guaranteed by the German constitution has become in many departments of economic life a meaningless phrase', said that under the rule of the plutocracy 'even the widest political liberty cannot save us from being converted into a nation of unfree people'.[13]

Lenin stated:

> Colonial possession alone gives the monopolies complete guarantee against all contingencies in the struggle with competitors, including the contingency that the latter will defend themselves by means of a law establishing a state monopoly. The more capitalism is developed the more the shortage of raw materials is felt, the more intense the competition and the hunt for sources of raw materials throughout the whole world, the more desperate is the struggle for the acquisition of colonies.[14]

Thus clearly the colony formed part of the imperialist state. The colonial state cannot be seen outside the context of the imperialist state. Now then, how can it be said that the colonial state is qualitatively different from the imperialist state? When we talk about a qualitative change in the state we refer to a change in the relation between the classes. The class character of the state is our index in judging change in the state apparatus. The imperialist and colonial states are states of the dictatorship of the bourgeoisie, of the financial oligarchy. But the rule of the financial oligarchy cannot be restricted by political (legal) change. Lenin pointed this out:

> Finance capital is such a great, it may be said such a decisive force, in all economic and in all international relations, that it is capable of subjecting and actually does subject to itself even states enjoying the fullest political independence.[15]

In his polemics with Rosa Luxembourg on 'The Right of Nations to Self-Determination', Lenin pointed out that the political self-determination of nations and their independence as states in bourgeois society had nothing to do with their independence from finance capital.[16] Hence, according to Lenin, the question of freedom from finance capital demanded a social revolution, whereas the question of self-determination was within the sphere of the broad struggle for democracy. By-the-by – a ruling class is not the same thing as 'ruling individuals'. Ruling class represents a social power whose interests are maintained by the state.

Now whose interests are maintained by the neo-colonial state? Surely it cannot be in the interests of the workers and peasants, since these are exploited. Nor can it be in the interests of the patriotic elements of the petty-bourgeoisie, since these are still crying for a New Economic Order. Nor, further, can it be to promote the 'national bourgeoisie', who are oppressed. Or is the neo-colony exploiting itself? Our Ndugu was wise enough to have noted earlier on that capital is a social relation of production. It follows that under imperialism the existing relations of production are geared to the exploitation of the neo-colony. We have argued above that the exploiter in our countries is the financial oligarchy and therefore the state operates in the interest of this class. The financial oligarchy rules in the neo-colony because it monopolises capital and industry while turning the neo-colonies into sources of raw material. The financial oligarchy is the exploiter of the proletariat and peasantry in the neo-colony as well as oppressor of the petty-bourgeoisie and the national bourgeoisie.

4.   THE NATIONAL QUESTION

It would have been useful if our Ndugu had read through the whole of Lenin's pamphlet *A Caricature of Marxism and Imperialist Economism*. Then he would have understood what Lenin meant when he spoke of colonial peoples as nations.

As we have noted earlier, Lenin speaks of countries and nations when talking of exploitation and oppression. Now Lenin distinguishes three different types of countries when dealing with self-determination:

> First type: the advanced countries of western Europe (and America) where the national movement is a thing of the past. Second Type: Eastern Europe where it is a thing of the present. Third type: semi-colonies and colonies, where it is largely a thing of the future.[17]

Now what does Lenin mean by the national problem and its solution? In talking of Eastern Europe Lenin says that:

> only a Martian dreamer could deny that the national movement has not yet been consumated there, that the awakening of the masses to the full use of their mother tongue and literature (and this is an absolute condition and concomitant of the full development of capitalism, of the full penetration of exchange to the very last peasant family) is still going on there . . . [18]

Further he says 'in the semi-colonies and colonies the national movement is, historically still younger than in Eastern Europe ' [our emphasis]. From this, our Ndugu cannot abstract the statement that 'colonial peoples too are nations' to conclude that therefore the national question does not exist in the colonies and neo-colonies. Lenin here was using nations in a formal sense. When he talks of the general democratic tasks which the colonies (and now neo-colonies) have to solve he is actually talking about the solution of the national question, because he shows that national self-determination belongs to the realm of politics, and he cites the case of Norway's secession from Sweden as an example. As he puts it, this example 'prove(s) again and again . . . that Norway's "self-determination" and secession did not halt either the development of finance capital generally or the expansion of its operation in particular, or the buying up of Norway by the English!'[19]

The solution of the national question involves the tasks of overthrowing foreign oppression and creating conditions for the full development of capitalism. That is why the petty bourgeoisie and 'national' bourgeoisie are very interested in the solution of the national question. Historically this is what the solution of the national question has involved – the throwing off of the feudal yoke and restrictions, and the creation of national states for the full development of capitalism. However, as Mao points out, it is not possible for us to tread the path taken by western capitalism, in the era of imperialism. That is why the solution of the national question now is not for the establishment of bourgeois democratic republics. As Mao says:

> In this era any revolution in a colony or semi-colony (and we may add neo-colony) that is directed against imperialism, i.e. against the international bourgeoisie or international capitalism, no longer comes within the old category of the bourgeois-democratic revolution, but is part of the new world revolution, the proletarian socialist world revolution.[20] [our emphasis].

When Lenin talks of the colonial peoples as nations he does not mean that they have already formed national states but that colonial peoples are nationalities and therefore entitled to form national states. Thus once again 'nation' here is used in its formal sense and not as a historical category in the sense used by Stalin. Both Lenin and Stalin stressed that the rise of imperialism linked the struggle for national self-determination in Europe to the struggles of the oppressed peoples in Asia and Africa against colonial domination. Stalin noted that:

> Formerly the national question was usually confined to a narrow circle of questions, concerning primarily 'civilised' nationalities. The Irish, the Hungarians, the Poles, the Finns, the Serbs and several other European nationalities – that was the circle of unequal peoples in whose destinies the leaders of the Second International were interested. The scores and hundreds of millions of Asian and African peoples who are suffering national oppression in its most savage and cruel form usually remained outside of their field of vision. They hesitated to put white and black, 'civilised' and 'uncivilised' on the same plane . . .[21] [our emphasis]

Ndugu EASE III should therefore not get emotional about Nabudere's statement that our neo-colonies are not nations because, as we have shown historically, they have not fulfilled the conditions for the establishment of nations.

We need not bog ourselves down over why there should be a new national democratic revolution in the neo-colonies when there are no nations. We have shown that there are nationalities in the neo-colonies. Now Lenin cites Hilferding's statement that:

> capitalism itself gradually provides the subjugated with the means and

resources for their emancipation, and they set out to achieve the goal which once seemed highest to the European nations: the creation of a united nation-state as a means to economic and cultural freedom. This movement for national independence threatens European capital in its most promising fields of exploitation, and European capital can maintain its domination only by continually increasing its military forces.[22] [our emphasis].

Mao Tse-tung explains why this movement is different from that experienced in Western Europe and characterises it as 'New Democracy'.

It is from an examination of the concrete reality in the neo-colonies, i.e. who exploits whom and oppresses whom, that the demand for the new national democratic revolution is formulated. It is new because it differs from the old bourgeois demand; it is national because it embraces all sections of the population except the comprador bourgeoisie; and it is democratic because it seeks the widest possible area for the participation of all patriotic classes in national life, and for an end to national oppression.

The conclusion that imperialism, the rule of finance capital, is the principal enemy in the neo-colonies does not arise from any mental gymnastics or pious wishes, but from concrete analysis of concrete situations. It is facile and serves the interests of imperialism to divide the national front against imperialism and the local comprador forces, to regard our petty bourgeois leaders in general as 'the enemy'.

5.   ON SOVIET SOCIAL IMPERIALISM

Since the Ndugu himself does not go into this issue we shall not take this matter any further than to say that the Introduction to Nabudere's book, in it is stated that the Professor's aim was to link up Lenin's thesis on *Imperialism* with Marx's *Capital*, in order to explain modern monopoly capitalism. It is thus not surprising that social imperialism does not feature in such a study.

CONCLUSION

We have tried to show that we cannot understand modern politics without understanding the question of the economic essence of imperialism. Thus the U.S.' rise to predominance after the Second World War due to the great development of her productive forces and her lack of colonies on the one had, and the fact of the weakened position of the other imperialist powers coupled with their possession of large numbers of colonies, on the other, explain why imperialism operated in the form it did after the war. We have shown why peaceful rearrangement was imperative given the narrowing horizons for imperialism created by the growing advance of socialism in Europe and the forces of national liberation in Africa, Asia and Latin America. It is only when we understand the fundamental economic question of imperialism and grasp the movement of finance capital under given historic conditions that we shall avoid falling into the trap of abstraction by regarding multilateralism as a 'more or less conscious creation of the U.S.' Multilateral imperialism today is the reality of the power of the U.S. financial oligarchy reflected in the institutions that are set up under their initiative.

It is the multilateral strategy of finance capital which creates conditions leading to neo-colonial control, to ensure that these oppressed countries remain firmly under the domination of finance capital to serve as out-posts for capital exports and sources of raw materials. The neo-colonial state is in every way an appendage of the imperialist state and is a state of the financial oligarchy because the latter dominate all production and industry and finance and appropriate surplus value from the workers and peasants in the neo-colony. It is this fact of imperialist domination, exploitation and oppression which leads to the necessity for the new national democratic revolution in which the workers and peasants seek to end their exploitation by finance capital, and the petty-bourgeoisie and 'national bourgeoisie' seek also to end imperialist oppression. This therefore makes possible a broad alliance of all democratic and patriotic forces within the neo-colony in the struggle against imperialism in order to resolve the national question.

We should like to make one or two additional points before we end. The first concerns the opportunistic use by the anonymous writer, of the Albanian comrades' position on the *Theory of the Three Worlds*, by lumping together Banda, Kaunda, Kenyatta, the Shah of Iran and Mobutu. This is, in our view, just an attempt to trivialise the argument in order to sound ultra-revolutionary. We need to point out that, in the end, both 'left' and 'right' opportunism serve the cause of reaction. The writer demands a concrete analysis of class relations within a society and yet he fails to make one himself. Why this double standard? Ndugu EASE III may accuse us of political opportunism, but if he cannot see the difference between patriotic elements and out-and-out agents of imperialism – for example, the difference between Nkrumah and Busia, between Kaunda and Kenyatta, between Lumumba and Mobutu, between Nyerere and the Shah of Iran, then he really has a lot to learn. It is not just 'fashionable' for our petty-bourgeois leaders to cry against imperialism – they also do have contradictions with imperialism. This constitutes the dual character of the petty bourgeoisie.

Secondly, it is very strange that Ndugu EASE III should have got the impression that Nabudere regards imperialism as residing somewhere in America or Western Europe. This is because Nabudere, especially in his manuscript on Uganda, shows how finance capital operating within Uganda and controlling the economy though the comprador-bourgeoisie who are their local agents has subjugated, exploited and oppressed that country for the last 80 years. It is the 'penchant' for abstraction again which makes the Ndugu fix on words like 'intervening', 'convinced', 'scared' etc., and makes it difficult for him to comprehend the reality that is being presented, namely the reality of the dominance of finance capital in our countries.

NOTES

1. Lenin, *Imperialism, the Highest Stage of Capitalism*, Peking: 1975, p. 18.
2. Op. cit. Preface, p. 1.
3. Op. cit. pp. 88–89.
4. Marx & Engels, *The German Ideology*, Moscow: Progress Publishers, 1976. p. 36.
5. Lenin, op. cit., pp. 108–110.
6. Lenin, op. cit. p. 75.
7. *Neo-colonialism: Methods and Manoeuvres*, Moscow: Pro'gress Publishers, 1973.
8. Marx, *Capital*, Moscow: Progress Publishers, 1977, Vol. II, p. 36.
9. Nabudere, *The Political Economy of Imperialism*, Dar es Salaam: TPH., 1977, p. 238.
10. F. Engels, 'Origin of the Family, Private Property and the State' in Marx & Engels, *Selected Works in One Volume*, Moscow: Progress Publishers, 1975, pp. 577–8.
11. Lenin, op. cit., p. 42.
12. Ibid., p. 63.
13. Ibid., p. 68.
14. Ibid., p. 98.
15. Ibid., p. 97.

224

16. Lenin, 'The Right of Nations to Self-Determination', *Selected Works*, Moscow: Progress Publishers, 1976. Vol. 1, p. 570.
17. Ibid.
18. Lenin, *A Caricature of Marxism and Imperialist Economism*, Moscow: Progress Publishers, 1974, p. 17.
19. Lenin, op. cit., p. 18.
20. Mao Tse-tung, *On New Democracy*, Peking, 1967, p. 7.
21. Stalin, *Problems of Leninism*, Peking: 1967, p. 67.
22. Lenin, *Imperialism, the Highest Stage of Capitalism*, p. 147.

21

INSTRUMENT OF POSITIVE IDEALISM

Obeid Mkama

I read with great interest Omwony-Ojwok's "review" of Professor Nabudere's *Political Economy of Imperialism.*

Omwony-Ojwok applauds the appearance of his fellow academician's book as an event of major historical significance for the people in East Africa and the Third World. One wonders why, if the book is so historical, the people of the rest of the world should not revel in its greatness. Or is the reviewer an unwitting centre-peripherist?

But that is only in passing. Lenin linked his thesis on imperialism with Marx's analysis of the laws of motion of capital and Lenin's was indeed an epoch-making contribution. What Professor Nabudere has done is to restate Lenin's thesis in a language which is far more inferior. Yet the reviewer says the professor's book has made history.

But let us credit the professor with having summarised a fair amount of secondary historical material revolving around Lenin's main thesis on imperialism. Unfortunately for the professor, Lenin ceased to write in 1924 and Stalin in 1953. Mao's four volumes, too, were published soon after Stalin's death.

How does the professor fare as soon as he leaves the safe province of quotations from the works of these thinkers? Well, of course, we get the theory of "multilateral imperialism." What is "multilateral imperialism"? Let the reviewer tell us: Nabudere's is an analysis of the "transnational corporate strategy" of US imperialism.

In the beginning the professor sets out to write a political economy of imperialism in general, that is "multilateral imperialism". What does he end up with? - a political economy of US imperialism.

All conscious people of "East Africa and the Third World" witness everyday a sharp rivalry between the two superpowers, for instance, in Angola, in the Middle-East, in South-East Asia, etc. But in a book of major historical significance they are being told that this rivalry does not exist at all. For according to the professor, there is only one superpower – the US.

And did I say the professor ends up with a political economy of US Imperialism? I was wrong. What transpires is that he does not give us any political economy at all.

Political economy is the science of the production relations of any given mode of production. All social-economic formations, the capital-dominated one included, are self-moving entities which exist and develop independently of anybody's will or knowledge.

It is the taks of the political economy of capitalism (imperialism) to lay bare the objective laws which govern the phenomena which together constitute imperialism.

This is the materialist standpoint, the materialist conception of history. It is not the consciousness of men that determine their being, but, on the contrary, it is their being, their production activities, their struggle, that determines their consciousness.

In a work of major historic significance, on the contrary, we are told that "multilateral imperialism" is a "strategy" or a "policy" of the US monopolists and their state.

In other words, imperialism is nothing but the conscious work of the US. In what way is this different from subjective sociology? Thus, far from being a materialist approach, Nabudere's work is an instrument of positive idealism.

It would be undialectical to suggest that the conscious element is not important, since social science is about the laws governing social production, laws of which exist whether we are conscious of them or not. Thus far is Professor Nabudere's main contribution.

Now for its secondary wares, or should we call them commodities? Omwony-Ojwok tells us that the book "refutes the 'centre-perifery' ideology of the unequal exchange school." Be that as it may.

However, every conscious peasant and worker knows that the power of the monopolist is reflected in his objective ability to hike the price of his commodity above and to keep those of others below the price which competition would otherwise establish. This is how the monopolist secures an extra profit in each case. Lenin calls it super-profit.

The professor, says the reviewer, has refuted in theory what the exploited people experience in practice everywhere. How does the reviewer conclude this? Here it is useful to note that the reviewer unwittingly disagrees with his mentor, unless there is some intellectual dishonesty somewhere.

The reviewer identifies the main enemy as "imperialism in league with the comprador forces in each oppressed country." Although he is fawning and is sycophantic towards the professor, he must know that, according to the professor, the main enemy is no more and no less imperialism.

Imperialism, says the professor, has no local class allies, but only individuals acting as agents. The professor proves this by means of a false dichotomy. He says the enemy must be either the local bourgeoisie or imperialism. To identify the local bourgeoisie as the main enemy of the people would be tantamount to adventurism. Therefore, imperialism is the main enemy!

A fine argument! An argument worthy only of Katheder socialists. For there is no such dichotomy. The two classes are not mutually exclusive. To fail to see this is to fail to see the local base of imperialism. And there is no use trying to hide behind the bogey of adventurism. Only opportunists can parade this kind of liberalism as Marxism-Leninism. That is why such "Marxist-Leninists" are darlings of any Shah or Sheikh. Any local despot can simply cry "imperialism" and the people are his for exploiting.

There are some absurd conclusions which one can draw from this *Political Economy of Imperialism*.

Marx says that the importance of interpreting the world is so that we can use the interpretation to change the world for our benefit. How do we change our word using the professor's interpretation, since "imperialism" is the enemy of our people, and since it has no local class allies, there is no ruling class here but only "imperialism."

So since the class struggle – which is mentioned by the professor only in vague terms is always about state power, it is difficult to see against whom our working people should fight to free themselves. Should they take up arms, hire a few ships, and march upon Washington, D.C.? Is this not one way of telling the working people to lay down their arms? Is this not liberalism pure and simple?

22

AFRICA LARGELY IGNORED

Ole Parsalaw

Let me comment on the review of Professor Nabudere's book, *The Political Economy of Imperialism*, which appeared in the *Daily News* of January 28, 1978, entitled, "A Mechanistic Approach."

To begin with, Professor Nabudere's book is not a particularly easy book to read because it is addressed to a particular category of people of Nabudere's calibre – his opponents, the neo-Marxists.

I thus totally disagree with your correspondent's assertion that the book "will serve well to orientate students awash in the sea of often conflicting development theories"; unless by students your correspondent means people like Paul Baran, Paul Sweezy, Samir Amin, etc., to mention just a few.

Professor Nabudere points out quite clearly in the introduction to his thesis that his is a refutation of the 'neo-Marxist centre-periphery ideology which treats the relationship between the 'centre' and the periphery as based on 'unequal exchange' (Introduction). You definitely must have read Baran, Sweezy, Samir Amir, Trotsky, etc. in order to comprehend this "Mechanistic Approach" to the study of this vital subject of imperialism.

Enmeshed in the refutation of his opponents' views, Professor Nabudere finds no time at all to say anything "on the contributions of African theorists on the anti-imperialist struggle", for example, Cabral, Nkrumah, etc. I have already pointed out that the Professor was writing with his opponents in mind rather than Africa's problems.

What is more, the Professor laments the wasted 'weak moments' in France in 1968, and the incapability of the bourgeoisie to rule in Italy thus creating another weak link that was also wasted. For Portugal, the Professor says that, "revisionism and Trotskyism have clearly shown how links can be lost to the proletarian cause through adventurism and capitulationism" (p. 278).

He also points out that "Spain, one of the weakest of the link's is crying for a proletarian revolution. Surprisingly the Professor does not say anything about Africa specifically.

If Professor Nabudere has signed out France, Italy, Portugal and Spain from the "centre", why not Africa from the periphery? Why not the lost chance in South Africa in 1976, for example, during the Soweto uprisings? Can't the Professor see that never before had the objective conditions been so ripe for the launching of an armed struggle in South Africa as during that period? Doesn't that amount to a wasted "weak moment" in South Africa mainly due to lack of an organized United Front to lead the Soweto parents against the apartheid regime?

Furthermore, talking about writers, the late Mao once pointed out that, "since many writers and artisans stand aloof from the masses and lead empty lives, naturally, they are unfamiliar with the language of the people. Accordingly their works are not only insipid in language but often contain nondescript expressions of their own coining which run counter to popular usage" (Vol. 3, p. 72).

228

If therefore, Professor Nabudere is expressing the views of "a class", as he asserts, isn't it essential that those views are expressed in the language of that class?

Finally, one of the biggest quarrels between African intellectuals and the great Professor Ali Mazrui is that the latter displays a remarkable absence of concern for the African masses in his numerous works. I am therefore worried that to engage in the exposure of "efforts by neo-Marxist revisers to create confusion in the Marxist-Leninist thesis on imperialism," and forget to say the effects of that confusion vis-a-vis those struggling against imperialism and all its machinations so that they can be on guard, is truly to get very close to the Mazruian camp.

23

ACADEMIC ATTEMPT TO MAKE HISTORY

F.L.N. Lupa

It is not very often that events of major historical significance find their way into the publishing world of East Africa and the Third World. It was with great satisfaction, therefore, that I read Dr. Omwony-Ojwok's review (*Daily News*, 11/2/78) of Professor Nabudere's book, announcing its publication. He said that this was an "event of major historical significance for the people in East Africa and the Third World." Presumably, the second "event of major historical significance for the people in East Africa and the Third World" must be the publication of Omwony-Ojwok's review itself.

Generally speaking, the academics of the metropolitan world never thought that the peoples of the Third World had any role to play in history and therefore they took it upon themselves to decide what was of great historical significance for them. We can now see that this fine tradition is being carried over by the academics of the Third World itself. So, while the people of the Third World carry the heavy burden of oppression, its academics carry the equally heavy burden of deciding which of their publications is of major historical significance.

It is a neat division of labour where the people are put in their right place. No doubt, this neatness will continue until such time when the people themselves will decide what events are of major historical significance for them.

That time has yet to come, and then, probably the gratuitous services of Professor Nabudere and his fellow academics would become redundant.

24

FROM UTOPIANS TO NABUDERE

Sipula Kabanje

In contradistinction to the critics of Nabudere's *The Political Economy of Imperialism* ('*Daily News*,' February18, 1978), to us this book inaugurates the period of ideological offensive by the ideologists of the African working class and all its people. So far, the only theoreticians that we have had are the utopians of all hues. These are not a very serious danger because social practice has since exposed the limitations of their idealistic horizons.

The most dangerous enemies of the working class in the realm of theory are the petty-bourgeois elements posing as Marxist-Leninists. In Africa they are represented by Samir Amin, who is a partisan of the centre-periphery school. Together with the neo-Marxists of the West these scholars have suddenly "discovered" new theories of capitalist development. What are these new theories? Among them we have unequal exchange!

Instead of analysing the domination of our countries by the financial oligarchy through the export of capital, the whole analysis is shifted to the so-called "imperialism of trade." Lenin's thesis that the banks in the era of monopoly capitalism centralise all capital and all revenues, and transform "thousands and thousands of scattered economic enerprises into a single national capitalist, and then into a world capitalist economy" has been brushed aside. Apparently Lenin's theory is taken as outdated, the tyranny of the World Bank, nothwithstanding!

The new discoveries of these "Marxists" are to repudiate Marixism-Leninism. This comes out in sharp relief in their conception of unequal exchange. Both Marx and Lenin's contribution to political economy no longer found any place in this theory. Marx's law of the appropriation of surplus value by the bourgeoisie from the proletariat on the basis of exchange of equivalent is implicitly denounced.

Yet, as Engels pointed out, exploitation under capitalism takes place in a purely economic way excluding all cheating. And this was Marx's most epoch-making achievement where bourgeois political economists had tottered and fallen. Scientific socialism was born with the discovery of surplus value. This is Nabudere's central thesis in defence of Marxist-Leninist political economy against the centre periphery ideologist. This polemic is concentrated in Chapter XX. The point is that unequal exchange is not a theory that advances proletarian politics. On the contrary, it mystifies and distorts the issue of exploitation. Supposing there was unequal exchange and this was "ended" through trade negotiations, would imperialism come to an end? Nabudere hammers the point home when he observes that "the whole centre-periphery ideology plays into the hands of the populist national bourgeoisie and petty-bourgeoisie."

The populists who have for years been making noises in the GATT, UNCTAD, and the UN that they are being cheated as Third World countries in international markets find their ideology ready made for them by the Emmanuels and Amins.

"The struggle of the neo-colonial peoples is directed by this ideology towards trade councils and negotiations on terms of trade and 'exchange rates' and away from class struggle (p. 238). With the publication of *The Political Economy of Imperialism*, the militant class character of Marxist-Leninist political economy has been restored for the purpose of solving the political question of the proletariat. This is, namely, that of socialism in Western Europe where the national question has been solved long ago; and that of people's new democracy in the neo-colonies where the national question is an immediate topic.

It is not surprising that the book has attracted savage attacks from the petty-bourgeoisie who have no faith in the capacity of the working class and its principal ally, the poor peasantry, to lead the struggle against imperialism to its logical conclusion.

Unlike the unequal exchange theories who look forward to UN conferences for better terms of trade, Professor Nabudere looks towards the exploited classes' struggle as the only solution.

For this "the role of proletarian ideology and the struggle for political power becomes the only item on the agenda for the proletariat and those exploited by imperialist domination." (p. 279).

25

ARGUE, DON'T SHOUT!

A Student of the Professor

I fully agree with Ndugu Mkama's excellent criticism of Professor Nabudere's book, *The Political Economy of Imperialism* (*Daily News*, February 18, 1978). He is absolutely correct in pointing out the professor's lack of originality. The professor only regurgitates the writings of Marx, Lenin and Mao without understanding them concretely.

When it comes to dealing with concrete contemporary issues the Professor fumbles and abounds in contradictions and inconsistencies, not to mention the basically reactionary political positions that he takes. Let us take two important issues.

Nabudere sees imperialism as a monolithic force without fundamental internal contradictions. He is so overawed by the power and wealth of the multinational corporations etc. that he fails to see that imperialism is torn by internal contradictions and rivalries and that its united face is only temporary.

Undoubtedly, such contradictions strengthen the struggles of the exploited and oppressed peoples to overthrow imperialism. Witness the successes of the socialist revolutions following the First and Second World Wars when the imperialist bourgeoisie were at each other's throats.

Secondly, the Professor is incapable of analysing concretely the internal contradictions in the societies dominated by imperialism. According to some of his writings, with the rise of imperialism, all the bourgeoisie have been routed and reduced to petty bourgeoisie while it is the financial oligarchy which rules the whole world.

Thus the Tatas and Birlas of India or the Madhvanis and Mehtas of East Africa who own iron steel textile and other mills employing thousands of workers are nothing but petty bourgeoisie!

It is elementary Marxism that the category "petty bourgeoisie" refers to small property owners who live off (mainly) their own labour without exploiting others. But our great "Marxist" professor fails to understand this and this failure has serious political consequences. It allows the professor to lump everyone in the camp of "the people" except for "a few agents" who represent imperialism. And this becomes a substitute for analysing concretely the nature of the local bourgeoisie which is allied with imperialism.

Objectively the professor's views in this respect represent the standpoint of the bourgeoisie. Its effect would be to disarm the working class ideologically and make it the tail of the bourgeoisie. There is absolutely nothing revolutionary about such a position and the professor cannot stop any one from pointing this out by calling them names and using abusive language to cover his weak arguments.

In his self-glorified attempt to make a global analysis, the professor has only succeeded in landing himself in the quagmire of global errors.

26

HE DEALS IN ABSOLUTES

H. Saliwawa

The publication of Professor Nabudere's long-awaited book, *The Political Economy of Imperialism* is a welcome occasion to bring to the attention of the general public the "debate" on vital questions affecting the oppressed masses of the world that has been simmering at the University.

While this opportunity of debate beyond the barricaded confines of the "Hill" should be welcome, it will nevertheless continue to be restricted to a narrow circle of the educated elite of the country. This is because of the language in which the book is written, but also, more importantly because the oppressed masses will not find in it a clue to their liberation. For genuine liberation a correct analysis of the concrete conditions under which the masses find themselves in a particular historical epoch is absolutely essential. We can agree with the professor that imperialism did not come to an end at midnight with the raising of the colourful flags.

Indeed with Vietnam fresh in our minds and with the continuing inter-imperialist rivalry between the US and the Soviet social imperialists in Angola and the Middle East in front of our eyes, we would hardly need such a reminder. That is, were it not for the amazing existence, even in the oppressed countries, of groups which are only too eager to announce to the oppressed masses that imperialism is dead and buried. Such groups will be hard put to explain to the masses the sudden appearance of the US Sixth Fleet or the Soviet Migs in support of the regimes against whom they alone had been directing their attacks.

However while the so-called revolutionary groups reduce all the present contradictions to a single one, the one between the oppressed masses and the local bourgeoisie, Professor Nabudere absolutises the other extreme reducing all contradictions to the one between imperialism and the oppressed countries. The Chinese and Vietnamese experiences, to which the Professor constantly pays lip-service, should teach us that these two contradictions in the era of imperialism are not mutually exclusive. In fact they have always coexisted, the external exploiters finding a congenial host among the local exploiters.

Even Nabudere is forced to recognise that "the chief targets and enemies in the first phase of the Chinese revolution were imperialism and feudalism – the bourgeoisie of the imperialist countries and the landlord class in China. He moreover adds that "the landlords were enemies, being the main social base for imperialist rule in China" (p. 275).

However, when it comes to discussing the other oppressed countries the two contradictions are collapsed into one, and simultaneously, apparently, imperialism ceases to need a social base within these countries except for a few "agents".

This allows the professor to call for an orgy of class collaboration between the exploited masses and the exploiting local ruling classes tied by a thousand strings to the imperialists.

Such an ideology will give a new lease of life not only to the local ruling class but also to its protector, imperialism, providing a convenient camouflage to both. The politically conscious workers and peasants will not need such an obscene demonstration.

27

A MECHANISTIC APPROACH

The Political Economy of Imperialism is a valuable historical account of the rise of imperialism to its present form analysed from a Marxist-Leninist fundamentalist standpoint.

It is a development in 300 pages of two themes: Marx's theory concerning the tendency of the rate of profit to fall; and Lenin's work on imperialism. These, Nabudere defends in vigorous polemic against various "neo-Marxists."

It is not a particularly easy book to read, but as a statement from one clear-out political stance it will serve well to orientate students awash in the sea of often conflicting development theories. Though it deals with its subject from the period of mercantilism the present day situation is of particular interest.

Nabudere characterises imperialism today as "multilateral". After the Second World War, the US set about a redivision of the world on the basis of an open door policy with multilateral systems to anchor this redivision; organisations such as the World Bank on the International Monetary Fund saw the light of day, and closed colonial markets were replaced by neo-colonies in which monopolies could compete under US hegemony.

Imperialism relates, of course, not only to Western-Third World links, the EEC. Nabudere believes it was formed by European capital in response to the activities of the US transnationals.

The EEC has of late sought closer economic ties with former colonies through various agreements and latterly through the Lome Convention.

The main idea for these linkups, he writes, "is to maintain by such inducements as 'aid and technical assistance' and 'trade preferences' the neo-colonial ties by which Europe is assured of raw material supplies and markets as well as markets for capital exports." This is true as far as it goes, but he pays too little attention in his critique of imperialism to the significance of the day-to-day economic and political struggles of Third World countries like those linked to the EEC.

Imperialism will not be demolished within these forums, but it is simplistic to believe that the countries fighting for better terms of trade and a restructuring of the capitalist world economy are merely dancing to the tune of the imperialist powers. There is a conventional bourgeois wisdom that Western investment in the Third World is at least getting some development going where previously there was only peasant production. But Nabudere demonstrates, "imperialism cannot allow the complete transformation of precapitalist societies, but on the contrary, exists on the basis of hindering their transformation and thus subjects them to the needs of monopoly capitalism."

It does not, as some "neo-Marxists" have it, develop capitalism in a country in such a way as to ensure its own automatic demise. Another myth is that the transnationals develop the Third World by injecting capital. Nabudere concludes: "The neo-colonial state is of course a real outpost of the transnational and the 'economic plans' are nothing but field activities which conform to the transnationals' global strategy and not vice versa."

Again this is too simplistic a statement and one which development planners in many countries of the Third World will find hard to swallow. The line between "neo-colony" and "independent Third World State" is blurred. So what does a development plan need to aim for to successfully fight imperialism? It is a relevant question Nabudere pays little attention to.

What he does pay attention to is the straying of "neo-Marxists", the most influential of whom are the so called centre-peripherists (such as Samir Amin, Arghiri Emmanuel and Gundar Frank) and the "centrist neo-Marxists", Baran and Sweezy, who, Nabudere says, "ignore any role of the class struggle and the labour process in the centre on the apparent ground that the class struggle has been 'internationalised' to the periphery."

It has not been, as Nabudere correctly stresses while adding that in the Third World, still under the domination of imperialism a different strategy and tactics are needed from those applied in the imperialist countries. Concrete revolutionary situations have to be studied. "Pure theory will not do," he emphasises.

Yet, in considering the struggles within the imperialist countries, it is precisely this error he falls into. How is this for "pure theory?" France "is still a weak link, but what do we get from the 'vanguard' of the French proletariat? We have recently a 'new thesis' which abandons the dictatorship of the proletariat as the aim and creates a 'national party' out of the original vanguard party, thus favourably responding to the national-chauvinism of the French bourgeoisie... Spain, one of the weakest of the links, is crying out after Franco's death for proletarian revolution."

It is disappointing, too, that a book produced at Dar es Salaam University and published also by Tanzania Publishing House should have so little to say on the contributions of African theorists to the anti-imperialist struggle.

Amilcar Cabral, for instance, who led Guinea-Bissau to liberation has put a special emphasis on the development of culture. "We see national liberation essentially as an act of culture, in the same way that cultural oppression is a vital necessity to imperialist domination," he wrote.

It is a useful counterweight to Nabudere's somewhat mechanistic approach.

28

THEORIES OF UNDERDEVELOPMENT AND IMPERIALISM

Charles Bettelheim or the Comedy of Errors

J. Shao

Charles Bettelheim has the misfortune of standing above most theoreticians of the dependency school, as one of its better representatives, if not the best representative, on the question of the theory of underdevelopment as it is currently expounded by the "New Left" or the so-called "Neo-Marxists". In his "Theoretical Comments to Arghiri Emmanuel's Unequal Exchange",* he puts forward the basic premises and theoretical framework which have guided most theoreticians of the dependency school in their investigations into the nature and causes of economic and social backwardness in the ex-colonial and semi-colonial countries on the one hand, and in their theoretical battles against the bourgeois view in the interpretation of the questions of imperialism and underdevelopment on the other.

These battles are theoretical in two ways. In the first place they are battles on questions of theory, real battles fought by the pen with zeal and passion, proclaiming hostilities and belligerence against the bourgeois and all other views contradict theirs, formulating indictments against the bourgeois of the ex-colonial and semi-colonial countries, shouting out his subservience, dependence and impotence from the towers of universities of the world and whispering in his ears sinister prophesies of his inevitable and forthcoming doom. In the second place, these battles are theoretical or fictitious because the practical results of their views and theories are to befuddle the theories of the working class revolution and tranquilise the struggle of the proletariat for political supremacy while they do not materially affect the entrenchment of bourgeois rule. On the grounds that the bourgeoisie of the Third World is impotent, is not really bourgeois or cannot become really bourgeois, this bourgeosie is given the way clear and left to pursue its policies and to implement its view. "What ever they do they do not get anywhere. Let them try and see that our words are time." That is their view of the Third World bourgeoisie. In practice, therefore, they provide a cloak over and protection for the bourgeoisie while shakling the proletariat to erroneous tactics. The alleged impotence of the Third World bourgeoisie becomes a real impotence for the proletariat. This factor alone would make critical remarks on the theories of underdevelopment and imperialism not only justifiable but an all out war against such views absolutely imperative.

Charles Bettelheim's "Theoretical Comments", because it is short and theoretical, provides one of the best and concise expositions of the basic premises

---

*Theoretical Comments to Arghiri Emmanuel's Unequal Exchange, Monthly Review Press, New York, 1972, Appendix I, pp. 271-332.

and theoretical postulates of the Dependency School on the question of underdevelopment and imperialism and its influence on the petty bourgeois "Marxists" is deep and wide. It constitutes the main strand of "Marxist" thought on this question at the University of Dar es Salaam.[2] Since his basic views are generally common to the "Neo-Marxists" and are contained in a more or less covert form in all their writings on this question, our critical remarks on Bettelheim are intended to be at the same time a criticism of the dependency theoreticians as a whole.[3]

The argument of "Unequal Exchange" as put forward by Arghiri Emmanuel or Charles Bettelheim's specific comments on it do not concern us here, our concern being confined solely to Bettelheim's general views on underdevelopment and his idea of "blocking" the productive forces in the ex-colonial and semi-colonial countries.

On page 288, Bettelheim defines what he calls the "objective basis" of the poverty of the Third World countries. This objective basis, he says, is the nature and specific combination of the productive forces and production relations in the poor countries under the aegis of worldwide capitalist relations. It hinders the development of the productive forces. The constituent elements of this "hindering" or "blocking" of the productive forces are quite clear.

The essential element is the domination of the world by the capitalist mode of production. This domination makes necessary (entails) an international division of labour "which renders inevitable a polarised development of the world's productive forces", with one pole in the advanced, dominant countries and the other pole in the backward, dominated countries. Relatively rapid development of the productive forces takes place in the advanced, dominant countries and relatively slow development of the productive forces in the dominated backward countries leading to expanded reproduction of economic inequalities. This is because the international division of labour resulting from the domination of the world by the capitalist production relations is unfavourable to the development of the productive forces of the poor countries. The material basis of this international division of labour is grounded in the conditions that lead to rapid development of the productive forces associated with machine production in the countries first to industrialise. These conditions (he quotes Marx) are the demand for (machinery's) raw materials and markets, which demands arise from the rapid development of industry in these countries. These countries then transform "the rest of the world" into fields for supply of the requisite raw materials and presumably markets for the "superfluous" produce of the metropolitan industries. . .

Before we proceed any further, let us go back and look more closely at Bettelheim's logic. We grant him his gratuitous premises. Points, we have: (1) The domination of the world by the capitalist mode of production; (2) This domination makes necessary a certain international division of labour; (3) This international division of labour "renders inevitable" a polarised development of the world's productive forces with one pole in the advanced countries. . . etc. and (4) The material basis of this international division of labour is grounded in the conditions that led to rapid development of the productive forces associated with machine production in the countries first to industrialise, their demand for raw materials etc.

Obviously here we have a serious contradiction. In the first place we have the international division of labour being necessitated by the domination of the world by the capitalist mode of production. The mere existence of this domination, not of one country or of one region but of the capitalist mode of production engenders this international division of labour. On the other hand, this same division of labour is brought about, not by the domination of the world by the same capitalist mode of production but by the requirements and demands of rapid industrialisation in one country or a number of countries. Either this international division of labour is brought about or necessitated by the domination of the world by the capitalist mode of production *per se* or it is brought forth by the demands and requirements of rapid industrialisation in one part of the world. Bettelheim does not even notice this contradiction and therefore makes no attempt to resolve it but trudges on trying to reconcile it. He could have resolved this contradiction only by assuming a premise and then a derivative. Let us help him.

To be consistent, he should have argued that the requirements of rapid industrialisation in one part of the globe led to this international division of labour which in turn, has engendered the hegemony or domination of the world by the capitalist mode of production.

Having resolved this contradiction and thus, as it were, "legalised" the birth of the international division of labour, we are left with the basic characteristics of this international division of labour which, under the conditions according to Bettelheim, renders inevitable a polarised development of the world's productive forces. As we said to support his postulation he makes the following observations "from" Marx: "(Marx) showed that in those countries where modern industry was first established, production acquires an elasticity, a capacity for sudden extension by leaps and bounds that contrasts with the conditions of the production in the other countries whose industry is thus easily overwhelmed. These other countries are transformed into fields for the supply of (machinery's) raw material. . . A new and international division of labour, a division suited to the requirements of the chief centres of modern industry springs up and converts one part of the globe into a chiefly agricultural field of production for supplying the other part which remains a chiefly industrial field".

What conclusion does Bettelheim draw from this observation? From this observation he draws the conclusion that polarised development of the world's productive forces follows. In other words, this division of labour springs up and remains so, unchanging and immutable in the one pole relative to the other pole. That is the conclusion Bettelheim draws and it forms the hub of his subsequent constructs on polarised development. But does it follow? In the way the observation stands, Bettelheim has successfully turned Marx into a petty bourgeois philistine who thinks that systems or processes spring up and remain so, unchanging and immutable. Congratulations.

First of all, in the passage from which Bettelheim quotes, Marx says clearly that he is referring to some actually existing relations, so that Bettelheim should have the advantage of this empirical evidence to support his theory. But how does Marx's actual observation stand in relations to Bettelheim's theory? Let us make a more or less full quotation of the passage from which Bettelheim made the quotation and see what Marx actually observes. It reads:

"So soon, however, as the factory system has gained a certain breadth of footing, and a definite degree of maturity, and, especially, so soon as its technical basis, machinery, is itself produced by machinery; so soon as coal mining and iron mining, the metal industries, and the means of transport have been revolutionised; so soon, in short, as the general conditions requisite for production by the modern industrial system have been established, this mode of production acquires an elasticity, a capacity for sudden extension by leaps and bounds that find no hindrance except in the supply of raw material and in the disposal of the produce. On the one hand, the immediate effect of machinery is to increase the supply of raw material in the same way, for example, as the cotton gin augmented the production of cotton. On the other hand, the cheapness of the articles produced by machinery, and the improved means of transport and communication furnish the weapon for conquering foreign markets. By ruining handicraft production in other countries, machinery forcibly converts them into fields for the supply of its raw material. In this way East India was compelled to produce cotton, wool, hemp, jute and indigo for Great Britain. By constantly making a part of the hands "supernumerary", modern industry, in all countries where it has taken root, gives a spur to emigration and to the colonisation of foreign lands, which are thereby converted into settlements for growing the raw material of the mother country; just as Australia, for example, was converted into a colony for growing wool. A new and international division of labour, a division suited to the requirements of the chief centres of modern industry springs up, and converts one part of the globe into a chiefly agricultural field of production, for supplying the other part which remains a chiefly industrial field. This revolution hangs together with radical changes in agriculture..."[4]

Now for our observations:-

First observation: The industry of the other countries is thus easily overwhelmed. This sentence, as it stands in Bettelheim's work, gives the impression that this industry of these other countries which is easily overwhelmed is industry in the same sense or similar connotation as the modern industry of the countries producing by machines and the factory system that it is desirable and its destruction is thus a charitable act etc.

This impression becomes an actual statement when in Note 12, page 318, he says, ". . . this may even involve a setback to, or the collapse of production in certain countries (in India, for example the ruin of the industry that was beginning to arise at the time when British domination began, and the ruin of the country's formerly prosperous agriculture)". Was Indian industry capitalist by any stretch of the imagination? Not at all. Bettelheim knows as well as any one else that Indian industry as well as agriculture were slumbering in Asiatic despotism, fettered and strangled until British capitalism "annihilated old Asiatic society and laid the material foundations of Western society in Asia".[5] Thus it is handicraft production, backward industry, pre-capitalist industry that is overwhelmed, and in exchange for this, the material foundations of modern industry are laid. The present condition of India with its heavy industrial production and pursuit for foreign raw materials as well as markets proves Marx's observations absolutely right and how little Bettelheim has understood either Marx or capitalist society – its nature, the preconditions for its genesis, or its historical tasks.

Second observation: According to Bettelheim, it is production that acquires elasticity and capacity for sudden extension by leaps and bounds. From this premise, production *can* acquire this sudden expansion on the basis of existing extent of production relations, that is, with more or less the same number of workers and capitalists, acquiring only its requisite materials from other modes of production or from societies with different production relations whose social structure however it can leave unscathed or little transformed. From this to polarised development or socio-economic poles consisting of different modes of production and "articulated" or tied together in indissoluble unity is a very short step indeed. Bettelheim takes this short step. Having made a first false step there is nothing he can do but to take the second, third, etc. subsequent steps.

What is Marx's observation? According to Marx, it is not production but the mode of production (i.e. production by the modern industrial system) that acquires an elasticity, a capacity for sudden extension etc. What does this mean? This means and can only mean the extension of machine production and production by the modern industrial system to areas and branches where before, production was by the old system or systems, the dissolution and supercession of handicrafts and manufactures (proper), the further proletarianisation of the petty commodity producers, the destruction of the old production relations and their replacement by capitalist production relations on an extending scale. This view is irreconcilable with the view of polarised development as propounded by Bettelheim. The history of the past 100 years, and for the Third World, especially since the Second World War, again proves Marx absolutely right and Bettelheim absolutely wrong, and his self-professed Marxism a farce. Bettelheim's materialism is, in reality, camouflaged metaphysics.

Third observation: In the passage, Marx clearly refers to the two types of colonisation, the colonies with indigenous population whose production is converted to production of industrial raw material, and the colonies of new settlements whose production is *also* geared to production of raw materials. As far as Bettelheim is concerned only the first type of colonies exist and he avoids reference to the second type of colonies.[6] Why he does this we shall soon see. What is important to note is that both types of colonies at this point in time, i.e. at the time when production by the modern industrial system first becomes established, both types of colonies are suppliers of raw materials for the machinery of Europe, especially Great Britain, so that we have the international division of labour so beloved to Bettelheim and so fundamental to his theory of polarised development in full operation.

In footnote to the passage quoted above, Marx gives the following data. (extracts):

EXPORTS TO GREAT BRITAIN

	INDIA		CAPE		AUSTRALIA		USA	
YEAR	1846	1865	1846	1865	1846	1865	1846	1865
COTTON '000 lbs.	34540	445948					401949	1115.89
WOOL '000 lbs.	4571	20679	2958	29921	21789	109,734		
YEAR							1850	1862
GRAIN '000 cwt.							35366	74083

What the above data proves incontrovertibly is that these countries were converted into fields for the supply of raw materials to Britain. Marx proves it and Bettelheim affirms it, or rather affirms half of it and omits the other half. But are we justified in any way to draw the conclusion that these countries remain in time suppliers of raw materials, that we have therefore polarised development? Bettelheim saw the untenability of such an argument in the face of facts which stare him in the face and that is why he deleted the example of the second type of colonies. The USA, Australia, South Africa etc. were turned in to suppliers of raw materials for British industry no less than were India, Kenya, Tanzania etc. If this international division of labour brings forth polarised development in the fashion of Bettelheim and Co., then it ought to apply not only to the Third World, but also to USA, South Africa, Canada etc. The laws of development of society are not scared or cowed by the race or colour of any society. On the contrary, it is people like Charles Bettelheim and the theoreticians of the dependency school who are scared of these laws.

Rather than review his theory in the light of facts proving the contrary, Bettelheim sacrifices the facts at his altar of "theory", turning and twisting them to suit his preconceived views. In another footnote to the passage quoted, Marx and Engels noted: "The economic development of the United States is itself a product of European, more especially of English modern industry. In their present form (1866) the States must be considered still a European colony. (Added in the 4th German edition, 1890, by Engels: 'Since then they have developed into country, whose industry holds second place in the world, without on that account entirely losing their colonial character).

It is this comment which Bettelheim suppressed and which flies in the face of his theory and makes any claim that the theory of polarised development is Marxist a figment of Bettelheim's excessively fertile imagination. Colonialism, the domination of the world by the capitalist mode of production, the international division of labour and development of the productive forces in the colonies are not incompatible. On the contrary, they provide conditions for the rapid development of the productive forces on a world scale. A view of an international division of labour which is immutable and unchanging has nothing in common with Marxism.

Let us go back and resume Bettelheim's theoretical strands. He says that polarised development is subsequently re-inforced by the political and ideological domination wielded by the dominant countries. This political and ideological domination consolidates within the dominated countries the domination of social classes, linked with the interests of the big industrial countries (dominant countries), that cannot play an active role in the advance of these countries' productive forces. Thus the blocking of the productive forces of the dominated countries constitutes both the results of a condition for the capitalist mode of production. It ensures the expanded reproduction of capitalist production relations on a world scale. He concludes: "It is, therefore, imperialist domination and the incapacity of the dominant. . . classes of the poor countries to free themselves from this domination . . . that accounts for the stagnation of the poor countries. . . (This domination favours) the maintenance (and in some cases the development) in the dominated countries of production relations and political and ideological relations that have 'blocked' the development of the productive forces".

First observation: When we began our critical remarks on Bettelheim's views on the international divisional of labour and polarised development we granted him his assumptions. Now it is clear we cannot proceed without looking into his basic assumptions. From his article, it is clear that his basic premise, his starting point for the investigation of underdevelopment is the capitalist world economy. He states this point in numerous places in his articles in various phrases. Let us take a few examples: ". . . domination of the world by capitalist production relations . . . gives rise to a certain international division of labour . . ." (p. 289). "The economic inequalities between countries are rooted in the complex combination of productive forces and production relations that is characteristic of the different countries and of the structure of capitalist world economy". (p. 292). Criticising Emmanuel's thesis that the law of value operates the same way on the capitalist world market as it does inside each social formation, he argues that the formulation is unsatisfactory and that we "cannot grasp why (that is so) unless we see that the structure of the capitalist world market is much more complex than that of a particular social formation and that one of the effects of this more complex structure manifests itself in the form of a profound transformation of the working of the law of value. . . " (p. 293).

Thus Bettelheim takes the capitalist world economy as his starting point and from here he makes his inroads and investigations into its manifestations in various countries or parts or halves or poles of the capitalist world economy. It is not national capitalism which grows into world capitalism. Oh No! On the contrary, it is world capitalism which fractions itself, bends itself over backwards into national or regional capitalism. World capitalism is not an image of national capitalism but national capitalism is the reflection of the former. The wood do not make the forest; on the contrary, the forest makes the wood. World capitalism is a specific and integral system. It is the independent variable while national capitalism is the dependent variable.

This way of looking at things is shared by the vast majority of the current "Marxist" theoreticians of underdevelopment. The exception is Bill Warren in his brilliant article, "Imperialism and Capitalist Industrialisation".* Bill Warren's critics, for example, demand that Warren should view world capitalism as a global system, "an international economic complex that operates from the imperial metropoles, through various centres. . . "⁸ Andre Gundar Frank, Jairus Banaji, Samir Amin and their mentors share the same view. It cannot therefore be an accident that this view is totally in agreement with Trotsky's view which forms a pillar of his theory of Permanent Revolution. Since Trotsky advanced this view, at least in printed form, in 1903 (possibly earlier), he has the copyright. Bettelheim should make the acknowledgement. Selling the old merchandise under new wrapping? Well, you cannot fool everybody.

According to Trotsky, "Marxism takes its point of departure from world economy, not as a sum of national parts but as a mighty and independent reality which has been created by the international division of labour and the world market, and which in our epoch, imperiously dominates the national markets. The productive forces of capitalist society have long ago outgrown the national boundaries".* From this to the banishment of all national liberation movements or refusal to recognise them as progressive is only one step. All nationalism must be reactionary. Proletarian revolutions are possible only on a world scale, etc. These are the logical and consistent conclusions that have to be drawn from this view of things. Trotskyites have long ago outgrown the proletarian revolution. The greatness of Trotskyism lies in the fact that since its inception in 1903, it has not organised a revolution anywhere, on any scale, world scale or national scale or even a village scale. On the contrary it has always been a heavy grinding stone on the necks of the proletariat. "Sabotage the proletarian revolution", that has consistently been its motto. Every successful proletarian revolution has had to be carried out in bitter opposition to it. The Trotskyite conception is one sided. It does not see the dynamic elements in the "parts" of the world economy, sees the forest but not the wood, runs ahead of history and is therefore adventurist and bankrupt. It has nothing in common with Marxism. Bankrupt practice is the surest proof of erroneous theories. Bettelheim's Trotskyite premises fully deserve this dictum.

Second observation: The domination within the poor countries, of social classes that cannot play an active role in the advance of the productive forces of these countries. "It is the specific combination of internal production relations and political and ideological relations on the world scale that engenders what is meant by the 'blocking' of the productive forces in the dominated countries". (p. 290) Wherein lies the impotence of these social classes? Bettelheim does not distinguish

---

*New Left Review, No. 81, September-October 1973.
*Leon Trotsky, The Permanent Revolution and Results and Prospects, New Park Publications, London, 1962, p. 22.

the different types of the dominant classes and lumps together classes of the *ancien regime* and elements of the rising bourgeoisies. Why does he do this?

Under conditions of transition to capitalism or capitalist relations the forces of the pre-capitalist regime, the *ancien regime*, are impotent and reactionary while the forces of capitalism are revolutionary. Marx paid tribute to the bourgeoisie on this respect and wrote a eulogy in praise particularly of their revolutionary role in developing the productive forces and in dismantling the pre-capitalist relations and the *ancien regime*. On the other hand, with respect to the proletarian revolution, the forces of capitalism are reactionary and the bourgeoisie becomes so many fetters on the development of the revolution and the productive forces.

The bourgeoisie mount the rostrum of history with nationalism on their banners. National liberation is the form of the struggle of the elements of national bourgeoisie and forces of capitalism held down and fettered by a foreign regime. The experience of these struggles over the Third World since World War II amply prove this and Bettelheim ought to know as he was in India in the early fifties. If the proletariat can take over the leadership of the national liberation struggle and turn it to its own account, it is only because present world conditions are favourable and make this leadership possible. But no proletarian leadership of the national liberation movement can succeed if at any moment it loses sight of the democratic tasks of the national liberation struggle, that is its bourgeois aspects. Trotsky is famous or infamous for having lost sight of this fact, or rather, for never having conceived it as early as in 1905, in spite of his later protestations, when he advocated the dictatorship of the proletariat <u>without</u> the peasantry. Since the forces of capitalism have long outgrown the national boundaries, all nationalism is reactionary. Thus to Bettelheim, the forces of capitalism cannot play an active role in the advance of the production forces of these countries. On the contrary, they block them.

As the reader may know, Marxists use the term "fetter" rather than "block" to describe the effect of backward and decadent production relations with their corresponding social superstructure on the development of the productive forces. Bettelheim uses the term "block" rather than "fetter" partly because he thinks he is so clever and he has found something new, but mostly, because he is not so clever and he understands Marx so little. This we shall prove as we proceed.

In the course of their development, the productive forces of society outgrow the existing production relations and the corresponding social superstructure which then becomes so many fetters on the development of the productive forces. Bettelheim's argument therefore must mean – don't laugh – that the productive forces in the Third World have outgrown capitalist production relations. This view completely loses sight of the fact that in most of the Third World Countries, the forces of capitalism are just developing and far from outgrowing the national boundaries, capitalism has yet to get hold of all or most of production within these countries. You want truth? Look around you. Once more to his theoretical stands.

From Bettelheim's postulations, we must make a third observation, that concerning his conception of the capitalist mode of production and capitalist production relations. To make this observation more comprehensive, however, we must proceed a little further with his postulations. According to him, there are two tendencies characteristic of the capitalist mode of production.

(1) Within the "national entity", the tendency of the reproduction of the productive forces and production relations, i.e. the development of the national market as the basic "geographical framework" of the capitalist mode of production and what is implied by the socialisation of labour within this framework, and thus the repercussion within the social formation of the variations affecting the material

conditions of the labour process in <u>one or other of its sections.</u>

(2) On the international scale, the tendency for the reproduction of inequalities, of unequal relations between the national entities. This latter form of reproduction tends to break up the former, a process that is described by the expression "tendency of the capitalist mode of production to become worldwide".

What Bettelheim is trying to say in this contorted language of his is the following:

(a) Capitalism is considered at two levels, the national level and the world level. At the national level, within the nation or the national entity, there are two poles, a capitalist pole, and a non-capitalist pole. The capitalist mode of production here consists of the "articulation" of the capitalist and the non-capitalist poles. The capitalist production relations consist of the relations between the capitalist and the non-capitalist poles as an essential element. The tendency to reproduction of the productive forces and production relations is nothing more than a tendency to maintain the two poles in perpetual coexistence. (What about <u>within</u> the capitalist pole, Mr. Bettelheim? What are the relations of production here? If the relations are not capitalist then why do you call it a capitalist pole?)

(b) At the world level, there are also two poles, or rather a tendency to polarise into two poles on a world scale. This tendency also has the tendency to overwhelm and break up the tendency to reproduction of the poles on a national scale i.e. to overwhelm and break up the coexistence of the capitalist and non-capitalist poles within the national entity, so that the end result is a polarisation of the world into a dominant, advanced homogeneous capitalist (as we understand it) half, and a dominated, backward, homogenous non-capitalist (as we understand it) half. These two halves together are the worldwide capitalist mode of production, (that is, of course, how Bettelheim understands it) and the relations between them are the worldwide capitalist production relations, again, as Bettelheim understands it. God help the intellect of professors. Obviously, with a conception like this, it is impossible to be consistent.

The problem of calling a social system or set up consisting of a capitalist pole and a non-capitalist pole "capitalist mode of production" is apparent to Professor Bettelheim and he tries to extricate himself from it <u>once in a while</u> by calling a "social formation".[9] But he cannot do this consistently because if he did he would have to concede the fact that the capitalist "pole" or sector does exactly this, that it overwhelms, undermines, destroys and swallows up the non-capitalist "pole" or sector and in the last analysis, the capitalist mode of production permiates practically the whole of production. He cannot be consistent because his conception of the capitalist mode of production consists in precisely the opposite of this, i.e. in the coexistence of the capitalist and the non-capitalist sectors. Let us present Bettelheim's conception in a diagrammatic form:

	ON A NATIONAL SCALE		ON A WORLD SCALE
ADVANCED COUNTRIES	Capitalist	Non-Capitalist	Advanced Countries (Capitalist)
BACKWARD COUNTRIES	Capitalist	Non-Capitalist	Backward Countries (Non-Capitalist)

Bettelheim constantly thinks he can cheat the world by clothing and camouflaging old and bankrupt arguments in different phraseology. The only thing we can agree with Bettelheim's entire exposition is that it is in complete accord with the old arguments of the Russian Narodniks in the 1890's about the impossibility of capitalism in Russia. Why did the Narodniks say that capitalism was impossible in Russia? How did they argue their case? The Narodniks divided the economy into a capitalist sector and a non-capitalist sector (direct producers) and argued that the capitalist sector developed through exchange between the capitalist sector and the non-capitalist sector. As the purchasing power of the non-capitalist sector was "saturated" by the commodities of the capitalist sector that was the end! In the long run, capitalism could not develop further. In other words, capitalism develops and expands only if it co-exists with a non-capitalist sector. So long as exchange is carried out between a capitalist and a non-capitalist sector, capitalism can develop and expand, but, of course, only in the capitalist sector itself.

That is how the Narodniks saw it towards the end of last century. What Bettelheim and Co. argue is that the development of capitalism in the non-capitalist sector is impossible because of the "requirements of expanded reproduction at the (capitalist pole)." In other words, for capitalism to develop and expand at the capitalist pole, the non-capitalist pole must remain non-capitalist. Is there any difference between the Bettelheimians and the Narodniks? In our view, there is none whatsoever. Bettelheim's argument is totally in agreement with the argument of the Narodniks. Both the Narodniks and Bettelheim arrived at this view because they regard capitalism as something isolated from the "peoples' system", as extraneous etc., and not as a historical mode of production, arising from the bowels of old society itself and destined to encompass and supercede the whole of old society.

Lenin first criticised the theoretical mistakes of the Narodniks in his article "On the So-called Market Question" (1893) and later proved their practical fallacies in his "The Development of Capitalism in Russia" (1899). In order to bring out clearly the connection between the Narodniks and our present-day dependency theoreticians and their errors, let us recapitulate in brief the relevant points in the Narodnik exposition as put forward in Lenin's article and later, Lenin's criticism of it. How did the Narodniks conceive capitalist accumulation or capitalist reproduction on an expanded scale? In his lecture on "The Market Question", G.B. Krasin gave the following exposition:

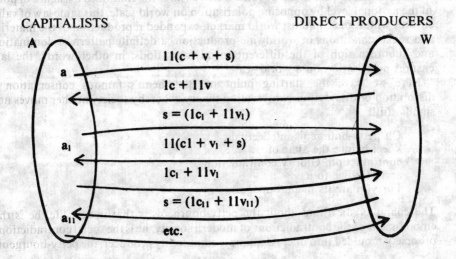

CAPITALISTS   DIRECT PRODUCERS

A   W

$$11(c + v + s)$$
$$1c + 11v$$
$$s = (1c_1 + 11v_1)$$
$$11(c1 + v_1 + s)$$
$$1c_1 + 11v_1$$
$$s = (1c_{11} + 11v_{11})$$

etc.

a, a$_1$, a$_{11}$,-*capitalist enterprises. The arrows show the movement of the commodities exchanged.*
c, v, s,-component parts of the value of commodities. s is surplus value.
1, 11,-commodities in their natural form: 1-means of production; 11-means of consumption.

The capitalists in "A" expand production by investing their surplus value whereas in "W" the direct producers consume their surplus value (the value of the product over and above the means of production and necessary means of consumption). Now let us see how the requirements of expanded reproduction in the dominant mode are "fulfilled" or how the two poles are "articulated". The product of capitalist enterprise a, goes to the direct producers; in exchange for it the direct producers return the constant capital (c) in the form of means of production and the variable capital (v) in the form of means of consumption, and the surplus value (s) in the form of the elements of additional productive capital (c$_1$+v$_1$). This capital serves as the basis of the new capitalist enterprise (a$_1$) which in exactly the same way sends its product to the direct producers and so on. From this schema, it is obvious that there is a very close dependence between capitalist production or expanded reproduction and the relations between "A" and "W". Every new enterprise or expansion of an old one is calculated to cater for a new round of consumers in "W" so that as soon as all producers in "W" have become commodity producers and exchanged their commodities with the commodities of "A", expanded reproduction will come to an end. As we can see, the only difference between Bettelheim and G.B. Krasin is, unlike Charles Bettelheim, Krasin followed the logic of polarised development to its absurd conclusion. Our contemporary Narodniks are more dishonest than the classical Narodniks.

Back to Bettleheim.

If we follow Bettelheim further, we see two forces which are opposed to the second tendency we mentioned above, i.e. the tendency of the capitalist mode to become worldwide. (1) The State which ensures the defence of the internal and external conditions of existence of these unities, that maintains the two poles in perpetual co-existence. (2) The law of value which ensures within each "capitalist social formation" i.e. within each nation, expanded reproduction of the material and social conditions of production characteristic of this "social formation". But at the same time, this same law of value which ensures the continued existence of poles at the national level by opposing polarisation on world scale, this same law of value ensures within the capitalist world market, expanded reproduction of the material and social conditions of worldwide production, a definite pattern of domination and subordination of the different social formations; in other words, the law ensures polarisation on a world scale!

Here we have the starting point of Bettelheim's famous conservation – dissolution or dissolution-conservation theory, whereby society neither moves nor stands still!!

> Oh petty-bourgeois intellectuals,
> kneel before the altar of
> contradiction, Glorify contradiction
> and sacrifice to it,
> For you are its mental image.

The characteristic thing about the petty-bourgeois is that in real life, he is the embodiment of the contradictions of modern society, he is the social contradictions of society moulded into one. As a simple commodity producer, the petty-bourgeois is both a worker and an owner of his means of production, a proletarian at the same time a bourgeois. The contradictions of modern society, therefore, find a ready and material receptacle in him. The petty-bourgeois intellectual "is himself nothing but social contradictions in action. He must justify in theory what he is in practice. . ."[10]

But, historically, the petty-bourgeoisie is a disintegrating class. A class of commodity producers selling in the same market, competition sorts them out so that the stronger, a minority, triumphs, while the weak, the vast majority, becomes ruined as petty commodity producers. The minority becomes bourgeois while the majority becomes proletarian is that the historical destiny of a petty-bourgeois society is to become bourgeois. A petty-bourgeois struggle, therefore in so far as it tries to retain the conditions of existence of petty-bourgeois society, to perpetuate petty commodity production against the forces of *bourgeoisification*, tries to oppose its own dissolution and disintegration. It is a reactionary struggle because it is opposed to the historical trend, it tries to move the wheel of history anti-clockwise. Ideologically, the conception of dissolution-conservation or conservation-dissolution is nothing but the theoretical articulation of this condition and desire of the petty-bourgeoisie by its political and intellectual representatives. To see the fallacy of this way of looking at things, let us look at Lenin's criticism of G.B. Krasin's schema of capitalist expanded reproduction.

We will recall that Krasin's schema postulates two poles in the economy, a capitalist pole and a non-capitalist pole (direct producers). The capitalist pole which consumes its surplus productively first of all carries out exchange with the non-capitalist pole; secondly it expands by investing its surplus. All these, allegedly, leave the non-capitalist pole, i.e. the "peoples' production" intact.

First observation: It is obvious that since exchange takes place between the two poles, commodity production also takes place in the non-capitalist sector. As commodity production and exchange become no longer incidental or occasional but general, the division of labour develops more and more and the process of differentiation of the petty-commodity producers accentuates as competition sorts them out so that in time we have poor producers on one side and rich producers on the other leading up to a proletariat and a bourgeoisie.

Second observation: It is equally obvious that to establish the additional enterprises a_1, a_{11}, etc. additional workers are needed, as evidenced by v_1, v_{11}, etc; and these come from nowhere else than from the direct producers. For the direct producers to become workers, their conditions of production, the means of production and existence must have been expropriated from them, that is, they must lose them somehow.

Third observation: Even for the first enterprise a, both the means of production and workers must be at hand. If the direct producers are a non-dissoluble entity then the question of the origin of these workers, and therefore, the origin of capitalism as a whole remains inexplicable. Therefore, it is impossible to maintain expanded capitalist reproduction or even the genesis of capitalism itself while at the same time maintaining the integrity or indissoluble integrity of the direct producers. Incidentally, it follows from the above three observations that the proper indices for gauging the development of capitalism are *not* per capita output as the critics of Warren think, or whether the goods produced are mass consumption or luxury consumption goods as Samir Amin thinks, or the presence of a capital goods sector as Dos Santos and Banaji think, or any other vulgar criterion, but. . . (1) the degree and extent to which commodity production has developed and is developing; (2) the extent and intensity of the social division of labour; (3) the growth of the industrial and commercial population relative to the agricultural population and; (4) the extent and degree of differentiation of the small commodity producers, the <u>ruination</u> of the poor and the <u>bourgeoisification</u> of the rich producers. Some would – be Marxists forget the simple but fundamental fact that <u>capitalism is social relations.</u>

In the Footsteps of Historical Materialism

Bettelheim has not only tried to turn Marx into a petty-bourgeois philistine, he is trying to turn his petty-bourgeois conception into Marxism by claiming, for example, that his dissolution conservation theory is consistent with historical materialism! How does Bettelheim understand historical materialism? Let us look at his two tendencies in the capitalist world economy (p. 297).

(1) Inside the social formation (he is back to social formation!) in which the capitalist mode of production is predominant (first half). Here, "this domination mainly tends to expand reproduction of the capitalist mode of production, i.e. to dissolution of the other modes of production and their subsumption to capitalist production relations". But, this is only the main tendency, the predominant tendency. This tendency is combined with another, a secondary tendency, that of conservation – dissolution, that is before the non-capitalist forms of production appear, they are "restructured" (partly resolved), and subordinated to the predominant capitalist relations and so <u>conserved</u>. (This is what Mahmood Mamdani swallowed bait, hook and line, and tried to use it as a theoretical framework – in the face of contrary historical movement – in his study of Uganda.)[11] But Bettelheim surrenders. However, in the last analysis, they are dissolved. He resigns with a sigh. If rape is inevitable, lie down and enjoy it! Bettelheim confesses that he does not understand why the predominant tendency here is dissolution and not conservation-dissolution, and yet he claims he is treading in the footsteps of historical materialism. The problem is not so much in his brain as in his heart, that is, not his failure to understand so much as the reasons for this failure – his pious petty-bourgeois wish to conserve the non-capitalist mode although history has already passed the death sentence on it.

(2) Inside social formations in which the capitalist mode of production is not directly predominant (second half). Here the main tendency is not dissolution of the non-capitalist modes of production but to their conservation-dissolution. This, not surprisingly, Bettelheim understands!

Is Bettelheim so ignorant of Marx, Engels and Lenin that he is unaware of the numerous passages scattered all over their works which prove incontrovertibly that capitalism, wherever it goes, creates the conditions for its own development, dissolve the pre-capitalist modes and transforms them into the capitalist mode? A few examples taken more or less at "random" from Marx will illustrate this point.

In *Capital*, Volume II, p. 36, Marx says, "(On the other hand), the same conditions which give rise to the basic condition of capitalist production, the existence of a class of wage workers, facilitates the transition of all commodity production to capitalist commodity production. As capitalist production develops, it has a disintegrating, resolvent effect on all older forms of production, which, designed mostly to meet the direct needs of the producers, transform only the excess produced into commodities. Capitalist production makes the sale of products the main interest, at first apparently without affecting the mode of production itself. Such was for instance the first effect of capitalist world commerce on such nations as the Chinese, Indians, Arabs, etc. But secondly, wherever it takes root, capitalist production destroys all forms of commodity production which are based either on the self employment of the producers on merely on the sale of the excess product as commodities. Capitalist production first makes the production of commodities general and then by degrees, transforms all commodity production into capitalist commodity production." Clear, one would think!

In *Capital*, Volume III, pp. 331-2, he says, "The development of commerce and merchant's capital gives rise everywhere to the tendency towards production of exchange-values, increases its volume, multiplies it, makes it cosmopolitan and develops money into world money. Commerce, therefore, has a more or less dissolving influence everywhere on the producing organisation, which it finds at hand and whose different forms are mainly carried on with a view to use-value. To what extent it brings about a dissolution of the old mode of production depends on its solidity and internal structure".[12] And whither will this process of dissolution lead? "In the modern world, it results in the capitalist mode of production".

In *Capital*, Volume II p. 113, he says, "(But) it is the tendency of the capitalist mode of production to transform all production as much as possible into commodity production. The mainspring by which this is accomplished is precisely the involvement of all production into the capitalist circulation process."

No, we cannot accuse Bettelheim of being "unacquainted" with Marxism. The failure of the Bettelheimians does not lie in this. Their failure lies in reading Marx from the standpoint of "the people", i.e., from the standpoint of the petty-bourgeois, while Marxism is written from the viewpoint of the proletariat. Failure to understand the class base or class standpoint of a doctrine – a proof, in itself sufficient, that one has not grasped the fundamentals of materialism – will inevitably lead to errors of conception. That is how matters stand with regard to Bettelheim and the theory of polarized development in general.

Erroneous theories inevitably lead to problems in analysis and in view of Bettelheim's theory of underdevelopment, we should expect it to land him in problems of theoretical consistency and conformity with reality. He lands squarely into this mess when he approaches the question of exploitation of the poor countries by the rich ones. He says: "The capitalists of the industrial countries have (also) an 'International basis' of exploitation ensured by the enlarged reproduction of the international production relations specific to capitalism which enable these capitalists to exploit the working people of the dominated countries, by buying products they supply at prices that ensure expanded reproduction of economic inequalities . . ."

In his effort to explain this exploitation, Bettelheim is forced to concede the serious shortcomings of the whole of his previous theoretical edifice. He discovers, to his chagrin, that his theory is not conforming to reality. How does he extricate himself from this mess? Without compunction and with impunity, he abandons his edifice and substitutes in the place of polarized regions, class structure! He says the structure of the world economy, viewed from the standpoint of polarized regions is heterogeneous in appearance only, the heterogeneity being according or because of the different levels of development of the productive forces. (Such vulgarity, such common banality! To take appearances and try to construct a theory of political economy around it, this is the last word in the abrogation of political economy as a science!). Therefore we must substitute for this apparrent heterogeneity, the *real* heterogeneity of classes. Homogeneous "units" at one pole (of exploiters) or the other pole (of exploited) is illusory. We quote him:

"Hence-forth it is necessary to think of each 'country' as constituting a social formation with a specific structure . . . no longer consisting of different modes of production, one dominant and another dominated but. . . of classes with contradictory interests." About turn! So after all, capitalist exploitation is a class relation and not a regional relation. "Capitalist relations of exploitation" he concedes, ". . . are constituted by relations between workers, on the one hand, and owners of the means of production and exchange on the other," and not at the level of exchange but at the level of production. But so soon as he "strays" into this correct path does he quickly make another about turn and revert to his old dreary road and smuggle in his old arguments again. He says, "But the relations between the capitalists of the advanced countries and the workers of the backward countries are not direct. Most commonly it is not a matter of buying the labour power of the workers but of buying products from local exploiters – landlords, merchants, usurers, traders, capitalists etc." Therefore to expand the "exploitation of the working people of these countries requires an expansion of banking and commercial capital". As the reader will see, Mr. Bettelheim is properly confused.

Bettelheim cannot show that there is exploitation in the relations between the dominating and dominated countries as such so that, his postulation that it is the "maintenance of this exploitation" that "blocks" the development of the productive forces in the dominated countries cannot follow. The exploitation he could argue of is that of direct, that is, in production, involving the capitalists or the capital of the advanced countries and the workers of the backward countries. And this type of exploitation, he cannot argue with the slightest bit of logic, of "blocking" the development of the productive forces of these countries. . .

That is how matters stand with regard to Bettelheim's and the current "Marxist" theory of underdevelopment in general. Judge for yourselves.

NOTES

1. The argument for confining the "Dependency School" to Latin America is, in my view, superficial since the basic premises of this school of thought are found throughout the world, and as I prove in this paper, at different periods within the epoch of capitalism. Although they may differ here and there on the secondary points, fundamentally they agree in their world outlook and therefore their basic premises. It is this characteristic more than anything else, certainly more than their geograpahical location, that stamps them as members of the same school of thought.
2. See for example Mahmood Mamdani, *Politics and Class Formation in Uganda*, Heinemann, Nairobi, 1976, Michaela von Freyhold: "The Rise and Fall of Colonial Modes of Production," IFM (Mimeo); Issa Shivji: "Peasants and Class Alliances" in *Review of African Political Economy*, No. 3, May–October, 1975.
3. Those who share the views criticized in this paper to a larger or lesser extent are numerous but among the best known we may include: Paul A. Baran, Andre Gundar Frank, Samir Amin, Ernesto Laclau, F.H. Cardoso, T. Dos Santos, Jairus Banaji, Rhodes, and of course, Charles Bettelheim.
4. Karl Marx, *Capital*, Vol. 1, Progress Publishers, Moscow, pp. 424–25.
5. Karl Marx: "The Future Results of British Rule in India".
6. For a distinction between the two types of colonies, see note 11.
7. It is the credit of H. Cardoso to have noticed that dependency does not necessarily negate economic development. "Strictly speaking, if we consider the purely economic indicators it is not difficult to show that development and monopoly penetration in the industrial sectors of dependent economies are not incompatible. The idea that there occurs a kind of development of underdevelopment, apart from the play of words, is not helpful. In fact, dependency, monopoly capitalism and development are not contradictory terms: there occurs a kind of dependent capitalist development in the sectors of the Third World integrated into the new forms of monopolistic expansion" —H. Cardoso, "Dependency and Development in Latin America".
8. ". . . Warren does not see any inconsistency between his image of world capitalism as a collection of distinct national economies rather than as a global system, and his assertion that world capitalism is nevertheless characterized by changing hierarchies

of uneven development. He unfortunately does not go to consider the possibility (sic!) that world capitaiism is an international economic complex that operates from the imperial metropoles of North America, Western Europe and Japan through various centres (financial, sub-imperial, military, commercial)" pp. 94. And earlier: "analysis at the level of the national unit disintegrated the structure of international capitalism, and therefore assumes away the very totality whose character determines the social relations of production and uneven sectoral configuration within each Third World country". P. 86. In: Philip McMichael, James Petras, Robert Rhodes: The Warren Critics: "Imperialism and the Contradictions of Development", *New Left Review*.

9. Michaela von Freyhold tries to make a clean breast of the theory of polarized development by bringing the two poles under a social formation. She defines a socio-economic formation as follows: "Several modes of production form a socio-economic formation." Without stopping to criticize this definition, let us proceed and see what she understands by the colonial socio-economic formation. According to her, these socio-economic formations are composed of two parts, "...dominant capitalist modes of production at the centre and dependent pre-capitalist modes of production at the periphery. While the former developed according to their own intrinsic laws, the latter were shaped and determined by the demands of the centre." Before this she had said: "The fundamental difference between a developed and an underdeveloped society is, however, that in the latter the historical laws which would determine the progress of that society were suspended by the intrusion of dominant outsiders". (my emphasis). M. von Freyhold: "The Rise and Fall of Colonial Modes of Production". IFM (mimeo), Dar es Salaam.

10. "In an advanced society the petty-bourgeois is necessarily from his very position a socialist on the one side and an economist on the other; that is to say, he is dazed by the magnificence of the big bourgeoisie and has sympathy for the sufferings of the people. Deep down in his heart he flatters himself that he is impartial and has found the right equilibrium, which he claims to be something different from mediocrity. A petty-bourgeois of this type glorifies contradiction because contradiction is the basis of his existence. He is himself nothing but social contradictions in action. He must justify in theory what he is in practice, and (M. Proudhon) has the merit of being the scientific interpreter of the (French) petty-bourgeoisie – a genuine merit, because the petty-bourgeoisie will form an integral part of all the impending social revolutions". K. Marx, *The Poverty of Philosophy*, Progress Publishers, 1973, pp. 167. It is, therefore, the misfortune of Bettelheim rather than his fault that he is the theoretical representative of today's petty-bourgeoisie.

11. "Capitalism implanted its own mode of production in those territories that it *populated*, in the territories that it dominated, however, capitalism did not simply destroy the pre-existing modes by appropriating the producers and making them wage labourers. The process on the other hand was more complex. The pre-colonial modes of production were partially destroyed, restructured and then incorporated into the world capitalist system as subordinate to the capitalist mode internationally. The tendency here, as was pointed out by Charles Bettelheim, was dual; towards both the dissolution and the conservation of the pre-capitalist modes. Their movement was henceforth not autonomous but derived from their dependent relation to what was the dominant mode in the international capitalist system". Mahmood Mamdani, ibid: ch. 5. The distinction between the territories capitalism populated and those it dominated, Mamdani attributed to Jairus Banaji.

12. Bill Warren therefore scores another point when he writes: "... empirical observations suggest that the prospects for successful capitalist economic development (implying industrialization) of a significant number of major underdeveloped countries are quite good; that substantial progress in capitalist industrialization has already been achieved; that the period since the Second World War has been marked by a major upsurge in capitalist social relations and productive forces (especially industrialization) in the Third World; that in so far as there are obstacles to this development, they originate not in current imperialist – Third World relationships, but almost entirely from the internal contradictions of the Third World itself; that the imperialist countries' policies and their overall impact on the Third World actually favour its industrialization;" ... (my emphasis). Bill Warren, ibid.

29

IS IMPERIALISM PROGRESSIVE?

D. Wadada Nabudere

1. INTRODUCTORY REMARKS

The recent 'uproar' – as the Editor called it – in the *Daily News* over the reviews of the *Political Economy of Imperialism*[1], gives us an opportunity to revert to the whole question of imperialism which was raised in earlier debates over the same issue. Readers of the *Daily News* might have not appreciated the subtleties of the arguments which were advanced by the critics of the book, since they may not have been aware of these earlier discussions.

With the appearance of the book, new outcries by the same people but now who feigned a grasp of imperialism have come to the fore. Yet these were precisely those same forces that denied imperialism as having anything to do with "the internal contradictions" of our societies! Expressing profound shock about the book, they unleashed their banalities. 'It is an instrument of positive idealism'!!, declared Obeid Mkama – a well-known crony of the 'bureaucratic bourgeois' school. 'It is an academic attempt to make history', declared someone from Iringa! 'Argue, don't shout;' shouted 'a student of the professor'. 'He deals in absolutes' retorted a Saliwawa of Dar es Salaam. All these empty 'attacks' on the book, which the Editor correctly called an 'uproar', were then closed by the same Editor who reminded us that it was no lesser a 'thinker' than Marx who said: 'Philosophers have only interpreted the world in various ways; the point, however, is to change it.' With these wise words we were apparently reminded that we were talking too much, whereas the point in issue was to change the world; but how, we were not told.

Be that as it may, the criticism of the book at least revealed that despite efforts by the Shivjis, the Mamdanis and the Hirjis, taking vicarious cover under the names of these critics, their bankrupt 'theories' were becoming more and more banal. Instead of trying to read and understand the book as a whole they were picking on single words like 'multilateral imperialism', 'agent', etc., to argue in circles. All these disputations failed to raise any slightest cloud which would have concealed their erroneous views about imperialism. From being opponents of imperialist theory, they now wanted the world to believe that they were the strongest supporters of 'correct' imperialist theory! This dualism suited them very well, at least their own ego; something to talk about. If this had been all, matters would have been let to lie. But not yet! This is because there has emerged another school of thought which arose at the University of Dar es Salaam with the coming of another trend of Trotskyism whose advance guard was David Rosenberg. This Trotskyism has a following of people such as Bill Warren, Kay, Cowan and others who have been pushing the devious theory that imperialism is a progressive force in the world because Marx and Lenin said so.

Despite their denunciation of Lenin on major issues of his theory of imperialism, they nevertheless seek his theoretical support on this question, upon which they tack all manner of empty empiricist material to come to the conclusion that imperialism is a progressive force, 'developing the productive forces' of the 'ex-colonies'. These arguments are put in very sharp focus by a paper which has recently come to our notice written by J. Shao of the University of Dar es Salaam, Economics Department, who is the local spokesman of this school. In his paper entitled 'Theories of Underdevelopment and Imperialism', he sets out to argue against Charles Bettelheim's 'Theoretical Comments' on Arghiri Emmanuel's book, *Unequal Exchange*, as well as against what Shao called the University 'Marxists', who he accused of supporting Bettelheim's theory.

In his attack, Shao's main concern was not to delve deep into the arguments and counter-arguements of Emmanuel and Bettelheim. His aim was rather limited to an attack on Bettelheim's view on underdevelopment and of imperialism 'blocking' the productive forces in the 'ex-colonial' and semi-colonial countries. Thus we have an utterly limited objective which, one might say, ignores the real issues between Emmanuel and Bettelheim, and instead focusses on an issue that is not of concern to the two. The issue between Emmanuel and Bettelheim was whether the relationships between the imperialist countries and Third World countries could be reduced to mere trade relationship as such – a relationship in which the stronger had the advantage over the weaker through 'unequal exchange' – or whether there were other things more basic than this. Bettelheim's central criticism of Emmanuel, that these relationships must be viewed as production relationships in which the exploitation of the workers at both ends of the system must be analysed in the context of exchange of equivalents, is thus obscured by Shao's effort to sidetrack these issues and concentrate on a singular issue not raised between Emmanuel and Bettelheim. It is not suggested here that such isolation of an issue for specific treatment is not acceptable. All we say here is that the real issues of contention in the earlier discussion between Emmanuel and Bettelheim should have been brought out, if only in summary form, and an opinion expressed on them by Shao before embarking on what he regarded as other important issues, requiring singular attention, which arose out of the discussion. Such an approach would have enabled us to know where Shao stood as regards the whole debate, a fact that would have given Shao's readers his particular views on Emmanuel's thesis. This requirement will be demonstrated to be of real importance about Shao's own treatment of imperialism.

For the moment, however, it is enough for us to declare out attitudes to this debate between Emmanuel and Bettelheim. Our attack on Emmanuel has already been argued.

We need only say a word or two on Bettelheim's criticism of Emmanuel. On the whole we think that Bettelheim's general criticism of Emmanuel is justified on the central issue of exchange. Bettelheim's characterization of the relationship between the imperialist countries and Third World countries as being determined by imperialist exploitation and domination is also correct on the whole. Bettelheim's only failure, in our view, arises out of his incapability to follow up his main thesis with a demonstration of how this exploitation takes place in actual life. His failure to demonstrate this fact theoretically leads him to re-establish a dualism between the centre and the periphery, with the paradoxical result that he himself is later convinced to accept the theoretical arguments of Emmanuel! This situation arises because, although Bettelheim singled out imperialism as the central contradiction in the labour-capital relation, his reading of Lenin's *Imperialism: The Highest Stage of Capitalism* was inadequate, with the result that he did not have a clear, scientific understanding of Lenin's concept of *finance capital*, and of its present day mechanisms. This alone would have enabled him to establish a monist view of the international system of exploitation consistent with his correct characterization of imperialism as the exploiter and dominator of the peoples of the colonies and neo-colonies.

This demonstration would have vindicated Marx's scientific observation, based on his analysis of the capitalist mode of production, that exploitation of labour under this mode is only possible on the basis of exchange of equivalents, in which labour-power as a commodity (expressing the level of the needs of subsistence and reproduction of the worker and his family), is paid for at its price. In this connection Marx stated:

> To explain the general nature of profits, you must start from the theorem that, on average, commodities are sold at their value. If you cannot explain profit upon this supposition, you cannot explain it at all.[2]

This scientific position of Marx does not imply that unequal exchange cannot take place between particular countries or individuals. But such occurrence of isolated exchanges away from the general relations cannot constitute the rule for a general theory of exchange. Such unequal exchange must be empirically demonstrated on the basic theory of value. This means that the general theoretical outfit for analysing exchange of equivalents is again the starting point for empirically demonstrating unequal exchange in those particular cases. These points on Bettelheim, in our view, constitute his strengths and weaknesses against Emmanuel's wholly erroneous theory of international relations in the contemporary world. Emmanuel's erroneous and reactionary theory arises, moreover, because of his hostility to the Marxist-Leninist thesis on imperialism. And as we pointed out earlier, Shao's attempt to obscure Emmanuel's hostility to Lenin's thesis on imperialism forms the cornerstone of Shao's own pro-imperialist views. Emmanuel, before posting his thesis on unequal exchange, had preceded it with an attack on Lenin's thesis. In an article in *New Left Review*, (No. 73), Emmanuel argued that Lenin's theory of finance imperialism, which 'is supposed to be different from mercantilist imperialism', had been 'put to a severe trial' by the break-up, 'without proportionate violence and without any marked impoverishment of the great imperial states or any reduction in their capacity to exploit the rest of the world', of colonial empires which had taken centuries to build. For him colonialism had been destroyed, the national question consummated and any talk of 'neo-colonialism' was 'unsatisfactory', no more than a coined word, 'devised for arguement's sake, in the face of an unexpected situation'. Lenin's work on *Imperialism* was underrated by Emmanuel as a 'marginal work which never had any scientific pretensions, and which was written rapidly (sic!) in the difficult conditions of exile with no other documentary at hand but the Berne library'.[3] This 'demolition' work by Emmanuel became the point of departure for his 'new' and 'scientific' thesis on *Unequal Exchange*, which he sub-titled, *The Imperialism of Trade*.[4]

Thus for Emmanuel, the imperialism of the era of collapsing empires just as that of mercantilism, is the imperialism of trade and not the imperialism of finance capital with which Lenin was concerned. There are independent countries at the centre and at the periphery, each having relations with one another on the basis of exchange of commodities – the one cheating the other through unequal exchange, the result of unequal prices reflecting inequality in wages between the two poles. Thus 'a country with lower wages – regardless of the technical composition of capital – loses in exchange'. It is the exchange of these unequal exports that gives rise to a large part of the surplus of the poor countries going to rich countries. Capital accumulation in the centre, which deprives the periphery of these surpluses through trade, is the result of this relationship. Thus in the periphery a narrow, stagnant market is inevitable and because of this capital is discouraged and forced to flee.

The real bottleneck for these Third World countries is, therefore, the internal structures which tend to perpetuate this situation. Therefore, Emmanuel advises these countries to tax exports and 'transfer this excess surplus value to the (neo-colonial) state, and diversify production from export sectors to replace import sectors'. Emmanuel is probably not aware that this itself is a neo-colonial strategy of import substitution, about which many neo-colonial states need no theoretical constructs from him, since many of them have considerable experience in this field with its record of failure manifesting itself in today's demand for a new international economic order!

All this recounting is necessary, although perhaps somewhat boring, because one needs to show the groundings of Shao's aberrations on imperialism. It is not by accident that Shao talks of our countries as being 'ex-colonies' instead of 'neo-colonies'. This is because, like Emmanuel, he sees the national question as having been consummated and the tasks for capitalist development as having been passed to the 'national bourgeoisies of our countries. Therefore, to talk of imperialist domination of these bourgeoisies by the imperialist financial oligarchy is to hide these bourgeoisies from 'responsibility' for what is going on in these countries. We can see here the similarity in conclusions with the Trotskyists of the 'left' – the Shivjis and Mamdanis who have argued in the same vein. Thus for Shao, what we have today in the imperialist world is the capitalist mode of production on a world scale. Each of the countries in this world is a unit which is inter-connected with other units through capitalist relations because all capitals are 'interdependent'. Here we have neither dominated nor dominating countries. This is what Henry Bernstein told us also on the debate on imperialism and the world market in Nkrumah Hall last month.[5] To talk of imperialist domination, according to Shao, also is to engage in a generality and populist claptrap against the working class!

These views are not isolated and for Shao they come from a very illuminating intellectual source, richer in content than those of the 'University Marxists', whom, by the way, he tells us are Shivji, Mamdani and Freyhold! Shao's intellectual source is specifically Bill Warren, whom Shao tells us is 'brilliant'. Before we turn to the real content of Shao's pro-imperialist arguements, we must trace them, as science requires us to do, to their real intellectual roots. In this way we expose the trend rather than merely the individual.

2. IMPERIALIST ECONOMISM OF TODAY

In this section we try to show the link between Shao and Bill Warren. Just as we have done with Arghiri Emmanuel, we shall first argue that the real theoretical and ideological starting point for Warren is his anti-Leninist standpoint. A transcript report of the talk Warren gave in 1974 at a public meeting at Belco Hall, London, on Lenin's *Imperialism*, gives us a deeper understanding of the ideological basis for his earlier theoretical piece published in the *New Left Review*. In this talk, Warren tries to convince us that Lenin's *Imperialism* was 'in many respects, self-contradictory factually incorrect, and consequently it has had harmful effects – at least, it is now having harmful effects – on the working class movement, both in the developed and in the under-developed world'. In this rather incoherent fashion we are encouraged to believe that Lenin's 'primary task' in writing the pamphlet was to explain the causes of World War I and why 'large sections' of the working class fought patriotically on the side of their imperialist bourgeoisie, leading to a split in the international movement:

And as far as Lenin was concerned it seems to be the case that he was above all most concerned to explain this split in the working class movement and the opportunism of the western working class... He related both a imperialism. [p. 1–2].

As can again be seen, Warren is incoherent as to Lenin's real aim in writing his thesis, but this apparently considered explanation has its aim too, as we shall soon see. But to turn to Lenin himself, there can be no doubt as to what his aim was in writing *Imperialism*:

> The main purpose of the book was, and remains, to the present, on the basis of the summarised returns of irrefutable bourgeois statistics, and the admissions of bourgeois scholars of all countries, is [to show] a composite picture of the world capitalist system in its international relationships at the beginning of the twentieth century – on the eve of the first world imperialists war.[6]

Clearly Lenin's main aim in the pamphlet was to give 'a composite picture of the world capitalist system' at the turn of the century. In order to prove Lenin wrong, Warren had, therefore, to present a coherently argued case that, in fact, that was not so; and in order to prove him harmful he had also to convincingly demonstrate what "harm", in historical and concrete terms, Lenin did by his analysis. Warren fails miserably to do so! He gives us disjointed arguments on investments, profits, capital exports, to argue that imperialism was not behind all these happenings. We have argues and made rebuttals to these banalities and the reader is referred to that polemic. We would only bring out here Bill Warren's arguments about Lenin's harmfulness, resulting from the latter's observation that under imperialism capitalism was overripe in the imperialist countries. Warren's central attack on Lenin is concentrated only in this statement:

> What I want to deal with mainly is the whole conception of the overripeness of capitalism, and in this conception the idea of capital export is crucial. It is first crucial because it is taken by Lenin to be the main evidence in some respects of the idea that capitalism is overripe. [p. 4]

This initial attack is important because, as we shall see, Warren is going to argue that export of capital to backward countries developed the productive forces; the initial attack is also Warren's further basis for castigating Lenin as not being clear enough on this point. The attack is also central because territorial redivision is associated with it. Warren argues that in fact territorial division in the period 1870–1914 was not associated with overripeness of capitalism; on the contrary, the U.S., Germany, and small imperialist states ('if you could call them imperialist') were themselves importers of capital. So naturally, for Bill Warren, that was proof that capitalism was not so ripe in these countries as to overflow to the colonies as such. This banal argument associates Lenin with the idea that capital exports which were due to the overripeness of capitalism in the imperialist countries was a centre-periphery affair alone. As we know, Lenin's arguments were more detailed than that. Lenin gave figures in a table showing capital invested abroad for Britain, France and Germany for the period 1862–1914. These figures showed that British investments rose from 3.6 billion francs in 1862 to 100 billion in 1914, and for France from 10 billion francs in 1869 to 60 billion in 1914, while for Germany these rose from 12.5 in 1902 to 44 billion in 1914. In another table he broke down these investments and their distribution in different parts of the globe in 1910. This showed that

The principal sphere of investment of British capital are the British colonies, which were very large also in America (for example, Canada), not to mention Asia, etc. In this case, enormous exports of capital are bound up most closely with vast colonies, of the importance of which we shall speak more later. In the case of France the situation is different. French capital exports are invested maily in Europe, primarily in Russia (at least ten thousand million francs). This is mainly loan capital, government loans, and not capital invested in industrial capital undertakings. Unlike British colonial imperialism, French imperialism might be termed usury imperialism. In case of Germany, we have a third type; colonies are inconsiderable, and German capital invested abroad is divided most evenly between Europe and America.[7]

Thus we have a clear answer from Lenin as to the types of capital exports in this period, as against Warren's incoherencies on the same issue. Moreover, Lenin is clear as to each type of capital exported and does not leave us in generalities about capital exports. With him we have the types and the directions of each, as well as the countries from and to which it went. Warren, however, is not satisfied with this clarity. He goes further to assert that capital exports before 1870 grew faster than after, the reason for advancing such argument being that capital exports are not a characteristic of modern imperialism as such! Here again our imperialist economist cannot explain to himself – for we do not need his explanations to understand the point – what capital he is talking about, loan or finance, and from whom. If he had cared to dig further, he would have found that capital exports in this earlier period were not finance capital. They were loan capital, raised through brokers, going to governments in South America for military equipment and supplies: and mainly from Britain to Europe, also to governments, to build railways. These capital exports were not controlled by banks and the oligarchy. Only later do financial houses come into the picture after the joint-stock company has become a legal entity. Moreover, Warren cannot explain to himself why there was a decline in investment in relative terms after 1870, say, for England, with which he should be more familiar. If he had done so, he would have found that, even if they declined absolutely, this would not be an argument against Lenin's overripeness of capitalism, for Lenin's concept of overripeness is related to the profitability of particular lines of production and not money capitals. He would have found that Britain's relative decline in investment between 1870 and 1914 was caused by the profitability crisis of the 1870s, itself a sign of overripeness, leading to a serious decline of prices – the result of the second industrial and technological revolution of the 1860s, with the result that export values fell, while export quantities could only increase with difficulty because of the US and German challenge in the world market. He would have found that Britain had in the meantime to buy more food, more copper, and more iron and wool for which she had to pay. Thus whereas her total investments abroad in 1874 stood at 15 million pounds, this had within three years been withdrawn. Jenks, a bourgeois economist not of the exceedinlgy obscurantist type like that of the Bill Warrens, pointed out:

In 1876 and 1877, Great Britain collected income from her foreign property [note Warren!] for home consumption. She was at the end of the era. The balance of industry and agriculture at home had been destroyed. She could scarcely balance her requirements of food and raw materials with the manufactures she could export and the freight her merchant marine could collect. The export of surplus capital was over. Her further investments were to come for a generation from the accruing profits of those which had already been made. They had to consist of what a German writer has termed the 'secondary export of capital'.[8]

This, we should have thought, would explain Bill Warren's problem if he had read bourgeois economists instead of rushing to judgements about Lenin. Warren's banalities are what he calls 'points' against Lenin's concept of overripeness of capitalism under imperialism, for Warren states:

> Now, if you add all these points together, ... the export of capital, from a fairly early stage of industrialisation, the faster export of capital in the period before 1870, the fact that major imperialist powers were actually net importers of capital, the fact that domination by monopolies and a financial oligarchy was not characteristic of the major imperialist countries, all of these when you add them together have one thing in common. Each of them serves quite seriously to weaken the idea that capitalism was overripe and that capital export was the result of this overrippeness. And therefore it serves to weaken the whole theory of imperialism as being based on the overripeness of the capitalist economies. [p. 6]

All these so-called points when 'added together' on the contrary, go to weaken any idea that Bill Warren had any faintest 'idea' about Lenin's concept of overripeness of monopoly capitalism nor any faintest understanding of the theory of imperialism. This is even made more abundantly clear by Warren's further conclusions drawn from all these 'points', for he states:

> It is quite possible that, for example, trade or market reasons, which are quite irrespective of overripeness, that the major imperialist countries will reach a stage when they begin to divide the world among them quite irrespective of whether or not they are internally mature (what an illusion, when in fact they are already mature and 'overripe' for overthrow!), or internally overripe (in fact they are externally, too!) [p. 6].

I thought I smelt a Kautskyite rat but that will come later. But this is only one eclectic 'hand'. There is another 'hand', for Warren continues:

> On the other hand, it is quite possible that they will become internally overripe before the world has reached the stage that it becomes completely divided a [what a mess, the world was completely divided by 1914!]. In fact, as I have actually been arguing there is good reason to suppose that the overripeness of major capitalist economics and the redivision of the world were not coincidental and in fact I am not entirely clear in what sense one can really talk about the overripeness of the capitalist economy, but I will touch on that later! [p. 6].

Such confusion, and incoherencies, and banalities are suggested by Bill Warren to be a challenge to Lenin's scientific thesis on imperialism. Warren is not sure in what sense he himself can 'talk' of overripeness yet he feels competent to challenge those who have a scientific sense of overripeness! He lulls us into 'possibilities' of 'new division', not *redivisions*, for trade reasons of which he is also not sure! He gives us no 'example' for this 'irrespective of overripeness'. He engages us into illusions about a future 'overipeness' before the capitalist world had disappeared, when in fact it is disappearing! We would have concluded with Bill Warren and left Shao to lick his wounds if there were nothing more to him. But we still have a 'point' with him, and that concerns the general conclusion drawn from all this that what was in issue in the scramble for territory and export of capital was not imperialism as defined by Lenin, but trade rivalries resulting from earlier British supremacy in the world market.

In the period 1870-1914, the period with which Lenin is concerned, according to Warren, Britain was being 'menaced in all its main markets', including its own home market, by the US and Germany. He does not tell us what was behind this 'menacing'. He seems to suggest that this was due to 'consciousness' of the competitors, yet it is not quite clear what brought about this 'consciousness'. Even if we were to grant Warren every possible benefit of the doubt, it would still not be clear how someone who claims to be a Marxist can separate trade and the market from finance and production itself, which creates the market, as well as from the historical conditions under which all these circumstances arise dialectically. This eclectic analysis leads him into the same position as Emmanuel in concluding that what Lenin mistook for imperialism of finance capital export was nothing but an imperialism of trade:

> Therefore from both the negative and positive evidence it is strongly suggested that the economic rivalries underlying the imperialist competition of this period were fundamentally trade rivalry. Insofar as [they were – Ed.] trade rivalries, then we have to again knock a prop from under the idea that capitalism was overripe. [p. 9]

Although Warren does not tell us what the situation would be 'insofar as' export of capital, which he admits took place, he glosses over this issue because he is going to say that such capital exports 'developed the productive forces'. This is the very basis for denying that there are any specific stages through which capitalism has passed, one vigorous and youthful and the other overripe, moribund and parasitic, for he asks:

> Can we say that imperialism is the last [sic!] stage of capitalism? Does the experience after 1914 [what about before 1914 but after 1870?] support the thesis that imperialism is the last stage of capitalism? Well, bearing in mind of the difficulties of what is imperialism [sic! not even trade imperialism!?], for example if we define it as monopoly capitalism there are signs [!] that monopoly capitalism is here to stay until socialism comes.

Although this later contention would then prove that in fact imperialist is the highest stage of capitalism... for it has been overthrown in nearly one-half of the world... Warren sticks to the dogmatic idea that 'hopefully' that would not in fact be so, for he then comes to his central thesis that capitalism has never been anything but progressive. It is for this reason that Warren opposes Lenin's overripeness theory, from which theory Lenin concluded that monopoly capitalism is parasitic, coupon clipping and 'robbery' of Third World countries by the imperialist ones. At this stage Bill Warren's true class role as spokesman of the imperialist bourgeoisie comes out so clearly. Although he admits 'a sense' in which it could be said that robbery does take place, namely in the sense that 'all exploitation is robbery', yet he is able to defend this too on the ground that Britain maintained an 'imports surplus'. Speaking in the name of his imperialist masters, with whom he identifies himself, he tells us:

> We imported more goods than we were selling abroad. We financed this to a large degree by the profits we earned from our earlier investments abroad. It is not correct to characterise these profits as being robbery; these profits were the necessary condition for the British investments in the first place [who would assert otherwise, except that in fact they were superprofits and not mere average profits?], and these investments abroad were on the whole highly productive and tended to create much more advanced economic systems. [p. 10]

Bill Warren then continues his case for the financial oligarchy by pointing out that, when capital extracts a profit in those circumstances it is because it has 'created' a surplus, for nothing can be taken from nothing:

> So whenever one sees references in left-wing literature to a surplus being drained from underdeveloped countries, it ought to be borne in mind that before this surplus can be drained, it has to be created. In the course of its creation permanent assets are left behind in the country concerned. [p. 11]

This is why Lenin's view on imperialism 'in some respects' had progressive effects 'in giving vigour and rationale to the anti-imperialist movement', 'but in the period after the Second World War it is undoubtedly having, it has had and is still having to my mind a profoundly harmful effect in the development of socialist politics both in the developed and the underdeveloped countries' [pp. 12-13]. In brief, we are presented with dubious and very harmful anti-Leninist views in Warren's talk. Warren is so lost in the obscure niceties of his case that he does not bother about the fact that 'left-wing literature' does not condemn the draining of profits as such but the draining of superprofits which are only obtainable in the Third World countries by the monopolies. Moreover, such superprofits are obtainable by these monopolies because of national oppression in the colonies and former colonies. Warren reminds us of Kautsky's concept of imperialism without contradictions, its analysis at economic level without its politics. For how does capitalism develop without its politics, the politics of national oppression? Warren, moreover, gives illusions of the 'possibility' of redivision in the future, without the 'harmful' elements of the real imperialism of finance, but under an imperialism of trade.

Bill Warren exhibits a sorry understanding of the literature on capitalist development when he tries to make us believe that it is Lenin who introduced the issue of parasitism of capitalism. Yet it was no less a person than Marx himself who scientifically explains this phenomenon. In his Capital, Vol. III, in the chapter on the role of credit in capitalist development, Marx draws attention to the phenomenon of the increasing transformation of 'the actual functioning capitalist into a mere manager' of other people's capital, and of the owner of capital into a mere money capitalist now earning a mere interest for the application of his capital by the manager. It is this transformation which is accompanied by the creation of stock companies, 'a necessary transitional phase towards the reconversion of capital into the property of producers', that is towards socialism. In other words, Marx is telling us that capitalism develops and rules itself out, but in phases. One of these phases is a phase of parasitism, a phase characterized by 'monopoly in certain spheres and thereby requiring state interference' to sustain it:

> It produces a new financial aristocracy, a new variety of parasites in the shape of promoters, speculators and simply nominal directors; a whole system of swindling and cheating by means of corporation promotion, stock insurance, and stock speculation. It is private production without the control of private property.[9]

Nor did Marx conjure up the idea of these speculators from the 'fantasies' of his proletarian 'wickedness'. He obtained his evidence from the working of the capitalist system itself and from the evidence cited by the bourgeoisie itself. We have referred to a bourgeois economist, Jenks, who wrote about the migration of British capital of this period. Jenks says in his analysis that, with the rise of the stock company, there also arose 'democratization' in the money market, as many people could now buy shares in the new properties. But he continues to observe that such widening of participation in the profits of business did not mean its democratic control. On the contrary:

> There came a divorce of proprietorship from control. Not even boards of

directors were adequate to the latter function. To manage both business and its nominal organs of control there developed in a shadowy from financial and promoting groups, centering now about and indispensable banker such as George Car Glyn, now about a flashy organiser such as George Hudson, and again about the personality of a great contractor and railway builder. The interests of such groups in many instances dominated the policy [i.e., of the company].[10]

Is this not what Lenin refers to in the era of intensified speculation, not through the stock exchange, but through the monopoly banks and monopoly industry which have merged or coalesced, giving rise to the financial oligarchy which Marx referred to as the financial aristocracy in his time? It is this oligarchy, that engages in this ever-increasing swindling and cheating, and in clipping of coupons the world over, which Bill Warren tries to mystify under the general label 'capitalist development'. Is this not what Lenin analyses at some length in section III of his pamphlet, in which he shows this parasitic clique, through the holding company, is able to engage 'with impunity' in all sorts of 'shady and dirty tricks to cheat the public' and, through balance-sheet 'juggling', to engage in all manner of speculative robberies? Lenin's words reproduced below are a clear summing-up of the experience in capitalist development and decay since Marx wrote. He observed thus:

> Finance capital, concentrated in a few hands and exercising a virtual monopoly, exacts enormous and ever-increasing profits from the floating of companies, issue of stock, state loans, etc., strengthens the domination of the financial oligarchy and levies tribute upon the whole society for the benefit of monopolists.[11]

It is this parasitic clique of speculators, not only levying tribute on society as a whole in the imperialist country but also clipping coupons all over the world, that Lenin talks about. Such is the era of monopoly capitalism, the era of modern imperialism. We leave Warren's other article on industrialization to be handled in the next section.

3. IMPERIALISM AS A DEVELOPER OF THE PRODUCTIVE FORCES-THE CASE OF SHAO

Having shown the roots of Shao's inclinations in Warren, we now turn to him in his dialogue with Bettelheim. We have shown his weaknesses in handling the issue. We are able to see his shallowness in swallowing root and branch all the imperialist economism that goes against the anti-imperialist struggles of our people and their determination to continue the struggle until the domination of our countries by finance capital is wholly destroyed and the fetters that imperialism places over the development of our countries' productive forces removed. Anybody who calls himself a Marxist but ignores these facts is a fraud. There can be no doubt that the history of the post-Second World War period shows that imperialism is a real threat to the further development of our countries. The reality that neo-colonialism imposes on our societies is so obvious that many honest leaders of Africa, despite their role in it, see it very clearly. President Nyerere in his Ibadan speech observed that the reality of neo-colonialism becomes obvious when a new African government tries to act to advance the economic interests of its people:

> For such a government immediately discovers that it inherited the power to make laws, to treat with foreign governments, and so on, but that it did not inherit effective power over economic developments in its own country.

Indeed, it often discovers that there is no such thing as a national economy at all! Instead, there exists in its land various economic activities which are owned by people [i.e. monopolies – D.W.N.] outside its jurisdiction, which are directed at external needs, and which are run in the interest of outside economic powers.[12]

These economic powers which the President refers to are monopoly interests vested in the neo-colony by the export of finance capital, which then ties down local resources to its needs. What President Nyerere says here represents the democratic sentiments of the oppressed peoples of the Third World. It represents the reality of the fact that lathough the right to self-determination and independence was achieved at the political level, the domination of imperialist finance capital continues its grip on our countries. This is the same thing as saying that there was only a partial resolution of the national question, implying that the struggle against imperialism must continue. But this is precisely the issue upon which the whole edifice of the Bill Warren/Shao vulgarisms must stumble and fall.

To be sure, although Warren argues on the one hand that imperialist exploitation, as Lenin analysed it, does not exist, yet in his article on industrialization he seems to agree that it exists, but not entirely! He sees neo-colonialism as a 'term' intended to designate the view that formal, political, independence, 'has not substantially modified the relations of domination and exploitation by the developed capitalist imperialist countries over the Third World', and hence also (which in our view does not follow) that 'formal independence has not significantly improved the prospects of industrialization in the periphery'. Thus, although in our view national independence and the continued struggle against imperialist exploitation and domination are not irreconcilable with a significant increase in industrialization as such, for Warren and Shao they are: that is their thesis. That is why Warren continues that 'even if inequality [what has inequality got to do with it?] – persists unabated' – which according to him is not the case – 'the character of inequality must have been significantly, and not marginally, altered by the industrialization achieved since the war' [emphasis added]. It is for this reason that:

> The term 'neo-colonialism', although, possessing certain merits (sic!) in stressing the continuation of imperialist domination and exploitation, is thus misleading in so far as it obscures the new and dynamic elements in the situation, both as to causes… and as to effects.

In other words, although imperialist domination continues unabated 'to some extent', its harmful 'effects' are counter-balanced by a significant rate of industrialization! But in order to prove that industrialization has taken place, we must start from the dogmatic proposition that independence 'must have' significantly altered the chances for industrialisation! Although the Warrens deny capitalism's parasitism and its capability of draining without creating, they can still (dualistically) talk of imperialism as a term having merit in stressing the 'continued' exploitation and domination – which they are not sure takes place! This is the economism that Shao swallows root and branch, because for him even colonialism, and not neo-colonialism, would have done! He says:

> It is this comment which Bettelheim suppressed [i.e. from Marx on industry in the US on the English model] and which flies in the face of this theory and makes any claim that the theory of polarised development is Marxist a figment of Bettelheim's excessively fertile imagination. Colonialism, the domination of the world by the capitalist mode of production, the international division of labour and development of the productive forces in

the colonies are not incompatible. On the countrary. They provide the conditions for the rapid development of the productive forces on world scale. [Emphasis is in original – Ed.]

We shall see that Shao's concept of the development of the productive forces is exactly the same as that of Warren's about industrialization. Since this is the major attack by Shao on Bettelheim, it will be necessary for us, at this stage, to disentangle the issue between him and Bettelheim in order to make sense of what Shao is up to. We have already argued the weaknesses of Bettelheim in his disputations with Bill Warren, which Shao does not do in his paper. Bettelheim's weaknesses, nevertheless, are not the issue with Shao for we have already indicated that Shao takes on Bettelheim on an issue which is not in question between Emmanuel and Bettelheim. But the issue of 'polarized development' that Shao now singles out for attack proves 'fertile' for Shao in his own struggle to assert imperialist economism.

To begin with, Shao's disagreement with Bettelheim is over whether capitalism in its development, in its introducing a certain divison of labour on a world scale, leads to polarized development and blocking of the productive forces at one pole, in which the essential element is the domination of the world by the capitalist mode of production. Shao sets out to disprove this, but instead of posing the issues arising out of this rather incoherent framing of the relations between imperialism and the Third World, he leads the discussion into narrow focus in order to assert his own narrow compradorial position. It is quite clear here that the issues of whether capitalism develops the productive forces (or rather fetters them, as Shao would have preferred) or not is an issue that must be tackled historically and in relation to the whole issue of imperialism. Instead Shao argues about capitalist development in general and the capitalist mode of production on a world scale in general, thus obscuring the real relations between imperialist exploitation and oppression of nations, countries and peoples. Bettelheim, although not too clear in his own theoretical arguments – because of his lack of grasp of the concept of finance capital – nevertheless is generally on the right track in saying that the blocking or fettering of the productive forces in the Third World was brought about principally by imperialist exploitation and domination. Instead of curing the theoretical weaknesses of Bettelheim, Shao, on the contrary, takes advantage of them; or, because of them, he manages to drag the debate back in terms of history to talking about capitalist development in general, out of historical context.

As we have seen, Shao argues that colonialism is not inconsistent with the development of the productive forces in the backward countries. Once capitalism has been introduced by imperialism, capitalist development takes root where none could have taken place and begins to 'develop the productive forces'. In this he takes the authority – to no avail, in our view – to support his thesis from Marx. His attack on the concept of the 'two poles' springs from this authority:

> What conclusion does Bettelheim draw from this observation? From this observation he draws the conclusion that polarised development of the world's productive forces follows. In other words, this division of labour springs up and remains so, unchanging and immutable in the one pole relative to the other pole. That is the conclusion Bettelheim draws and forms the hub of his subsequent constructs on polarised development.

Shao then goes on to quote Marx that, once the factory system has taken root and achieved a breadth of footing, and 'a definite degree of maturity'(emphasis added), particularly in mining iron metals had been achieved, and transport has been revolutionised, 'this mode of production acquires an elasticity, a capacity for sudden extension by leaps and bounds that find no hindrance except in the supply of raw materials and in the disposal of the produce'. This, according to Marx and contrary to Shao's caricature, goes to increase the production of raw materials, and the cheapness of the manufactures, with the new means of transport leading to increasing conquering of foreign markets: 'By ruining handicraft production in other countries, machinery forcibly converts them into fields for the supply of raw materials'. This is how East India produced cotton, wool, hemp, jute and indigo for Great Britain. Marx then points out that this development leads to movement of population in new lands like Australia, thus creating a new division of labour, 'a division suited to the requirements of the chief centres of modern industry', and converting one part of the globe into a chiefly agricultural field of production for supplying the other part, which remains a chiefly industrial field.[13] From these profound observations of Marx, Shao draws very historical 'observations' of his own, which lead him into misusing Marx's authority. First, he 'observes' that contrary to Bettelheim, Marx (correctly) meant that the industry that was destroyed in the backward areas was of the Asiatic despotic type and not capitalist industry which laid the material foundation for modern industry. But then Shao draws a one-sided conclusion:

> The present condition of India, with its heavy industrial production and pursuit for foreign raw materials as well as markets, proves Marx's observations absolutely right and how little Bettelheim has understood Marx or capitalist society - its nature, the preconditions for its genesis, or its historic tasks.

Actually Marx's observation 'proves' Shao 'absolutely' wrong. Marx here was talking of an industry that was developing in the conditions of early European and particularly British capitalism and not in India; but, on the contrary, precisely under historical and material conditions in which Britain could call India, Australia and many other countries into the production of raw materials which limited their expansion, under conditions when Britain could remain mainly an industrial field and India and other countries mainly agricultural fields. The conditions under which India engaged in industrialization are not the same, to the extent that India today cannot call any country into production of raw materials for her industry except it be as an adjunct of existing monopolistic control of the world's fields of raw materials and markets, the division of which was long completed. In this division India finds herself as one such field and market in a highly intricate system of imperialist exploitation and domination, which only the imperialist economists of the 'left' are capable of mystifying as an independent capitalist development. Shao – just as does his intellectual mentor, Warren – argues very eclectically that (and this is his so-called second observation) the record of the last 100 years and particularly that after the Second World War, 'again proves Marx absolutely right and Bettelheim absolutely wrong, and his self-professed Marxism a farce'; namely, that 'successful industrialisation has taken place in India'.

The ahistoricism that forms the cornerstone of Shao's mystifications leads him into deeper waters from which he cannot retreat without drowning, for in his third observation he tries to enlighten us as to Marx's real intention in drawing attention to two types of colonies, India and Australia (which would include the U.S.A. and South Africa). Shao's reason for doing this is to show that raw material production was not the sole specialization in all the colonies, in order to disprove Bettelheim's thesis of polarized development:

> The laws of development of society are not scared [sic!] or cowed by the race or colour of any society. On the contrary, it is people like Charles Bettelheim and the theoreticians of the dependency school who are scared of these laws.

Shao then goes on to argue on the authority of Marx and Engles that the economic development of the U.S.A. was itself a product of European development, although it remained a European colony. Quoting Engles as saying the 'since 1866, the United States had by 1890 developed an industry which holds second place in the world, without on that account entirely losing their colonial character' Shao now argues to make the general observation quoted above that colonialism is not inconsistent with the development of the productive forces.

Although Shao is very keen to quote the authority of Marx to support his arguments, he does a lot of injustice to his case by using one side of Marx in order to prove the other side of the same Marx wrong! Thus although he uses these quotes to say that India was industrialized and therefore developing her productive forces, he does not tell us that Marx does not say that in absolute terms. Marx states the contrary! In his article on 'British Rule in India', Marx emphatically points to lack of overall development for India under British colonialism. He said:

> There cannot, however, remain any doubt but that the misery inflicted by the British on Hindostan is of an essentially different and infinitely more extensive kind than all Hindostan had to suffer before... England has broken down the entire framework of Indian society, without any symptoms of reconstitution yet appearing. This loss of his world, with no gain of a new one, imparts a particular kind of melancholy to the present misery of the Hindoo, and separates Hindostan, ruled by Britain, from its ancient traditions, and from the whole of its past history.[14]

This was 1853. In the same year Marx reverted to the issue in his article on the 'Future Results of British Rule in India', where he pointed out that this misery laid the necessary material conditions for future development of India under conditions of national independence in India or of socialism in England:

> All the English bourgeoisie may be forced to do will neither emancipate nor materially mend the social condition of the mass of the people [please not our imperialist economist!], depending not only on the development of the productive powers, but their appropriation by the people. But what they will do is to lay down the material premises for both. Has the bourgeoisie ever done more? Has it ever effected a progress without dragging individuals and peoples through blood and dirt, through misery and degradation? The Indians will not reap the fruits of the new elements of society scattered among them by the British bourgeoisie, till in Great Britain itself the now ruling classes shall have been supplanted by the industrial proletariat, or the Hindoos themselves shall have grown strong enough to throw off the English (i.e. colonial) yoke.[15] [Emphasis added].

Shao and his imperialist economist friends should note that this was a period of competitive capitalism, a period when capitalism was still strong and rejuvenating other parts of Europe and America, when prices of primary commodities and manufactures were still fixed primarily by the free market that it was possible under favourable historical and technological conditions for a colony like the US to develop faster. But this was not possible for a colony like India without the strength of the bourgeoisie to mobilize all the classes in India for national liberation. It should also be noted that Marx was not a vulgar economist who detached the economics of capitalist development from politics like our modern economists do. And yet again Marx was writing this at a time when new productive forces had been introduced in India. Despite this fact Marx did not get drunk with these economic developments in order to ignore the real social conditions and political dimensions that these implied for the Indian people. Can the truth of these observations and predictions of Marx not be confirmed by the fact that despite the gigantic development in the productive forces that the concentration of capital have brought about in India, India's partial resolution of the national question has not as yet released India from the grip of imperialist finance capital and national oppression. Is the misery of the Indian people in India today not proof beyond doubt that Shao and his imperialist economist friends are the biggest enemies of the people who grovel before statistics of inflation and imperialist domination and call them national development of the "productive forces", shutting their eyes to, and glossing over, one of the most fundamental contradictions of our times, namely, that between imperialism and the people of the oppressed countries.

Yet Shao's wrong position equips him with the necessary wrath to attack what appears to us to be a reasonable conclusion of Bettelheim which is consistent with the above position of Marx. For, Shao now quotes Bettelheim as follows:

> It is therefore imperialist domination and the incapacity of the dominant classes of the poor countries... that accounts for the stagnation of the poor countries... (this domination favours) the maintenance or in some cases the development in the dominated countries of production relations and ideological relations that have blocked the development of the productive forces.

Having quoted Bettelheim thus, Shao then proceeds to attack him. But attack him over what? Over the fact that Bettelheim is here suggesting that capitalist relations in the imperialist world cannot be viewed on a national scale, but essentially on a world scale; for he continues·

> Thus Bettelheim takes the capitalist world economy as his starting point and from here he makes his inroads and investigations into parts or halves or poles of the capitalist world economy. It is not national capitalism which grows into world capitalism. Oh no! On the contrary. It is world capitalism which fractions itself, bends itself over backwards into national or regional capitalism. World capitalism is not an image of national capitalism but national capitalism is the reflection of the former. The wood do not make the forest; on the contrary, the forest makes the wood. World capitalism is a specific and integral system. It is the independent variable while national capitalism is the dependent variable.

This play of words that merely confuses issues is here meant to destabilize Bettelheim on his pedestal ready for demolition through a manipulated association with Trotsky's "Permanent Revolution". For having said this he then states that this way of looking at things is shared by the 'vast majority of the current "Marxist" theoreticians of underdevelopment' as well as Trotsky. But this does not include the Great Bill Warren:

> The exception I knew of is Bill Warren in his brilliant article, 'Imperialism and Capitalist Industrialisation' (New Left Review, No. 81, September-October 1973). Bill Warren's critics, for example, demand that Warren should view world capitalism as a global system, 'an international economic complex that operates from imperial metropoles, through various centres'... It cannot therefore be an accident that this view is totally in agreement with Trotsky's view which forms a pillar of his theory of permanent revolution.

We will later see in what context Shao agrees with Warren, but the whole point that Shao is at pains to make here boils down to denying the internationality of capitalism. Bettelheim's view of today's capitalism just as that of the earlier period as an international system is a correct one. Trotsky's view on the same issue is also a correct one. The only thing that is wrong with Trotsky is that he absolutizes this internationality to the exclusion of the national question. This is what formed the "pillar" of Lenin's disagreements with Trotsky as with Rosa Luxemburg. These differences which are clearly debated in the literature on imperialism and the national question between Lenin, Kievsky, Trotsky and Luxemburg are there for all to see. This global economistic view of the world of Trotsky led him, as Shao correctly points out, to deny the importance of national liberation. But Shao is blind to the fact that his own "national" economistic view of this question also leads him into denying and, in fact, into condemning, the national movement. For surely if Shao must be taken seriously in his own arguments, he must understood to mean that since colonialism develops capitalism *per se*, which according to him is a "revolutionary" thing inasmuch as it demolishes the pre-capitalist *ancien regime*, and if neo-colonialism does the same, any "interference"with the activities of these national bourgeoisies in "competition" with each other to advance their interests and therefore the interest of the whole "national" society, must be seen as hindering the development of the productive forces.

In this way the national movement, since it is viewed in such narrow focus, becomes reactionary, with the result that Shao must logically take the rostrum of these bourgeoisies and call for *laissez faire* (let us alone). This call itself turns out to be reactionary since it ignores that today's capitalism is monopoly capitalism which ruled out free competition. It further ignores the fact that today's monopoly capitalism has reached the highest levels of concentration and centralization on a world scale, that it becomes illusionary to call for national capital under imperialism, and of multilateral imperialism in particular. This fact is so obvious as to be absurd to emphasize it! A US Assistant Secretary of State, Henry Grady, a spokesman of US monopolies, declared in 1946 at the height of the working out of the US multilateral strategy which reflected US hegemony in its demand for redivision of the colonies on the new basis thus: "The capitalist system is essentially an international system. If it cannot function internationally, it will break down completely." Shao should learn a bit from that, for all monopoly literature on the transnational corporation emphasize the internationality of the monopoly firm.

It must be clear that Shao's line leads to narrow nationalism itself, for how, indeed, can the proletariat be a leading force when the national bourgeoisie can still mount the rostrum of nationalism to advance the development of the productive forces. Clearly the working class must wait while this national bourgeoisie completes this revolutionary role. Thus according to Shao, to say that imperialism has led capitalism to outgrow its national boundaries under it is to deny the relevance of national capital which is still dynamic in its historical mission, for he states:

> This view of things completely loses sight of the fact that in most Third World countries, the forces of capitalism are just developing and far from outgrowing the national boundaries, capitalism has yet to get hold of all or most of production within these countries. You want truth? Look around you.

Thus national capital is not defeated and relegated to a minor role by monopoly capital and imperialism. Imperialism only scratched the top soil of national development and with "ex-colonialism" underway, imperialism has been rolled back leaving tremendous room for national capital to grow and capture most if not all production. All this is possible under "ex-colonialism". If this is not illusory fantasy, what is it? Shao thus turns the era of proletarian led revolutions into the era of national movements of western Europe and all this in the name of Marx and

Lenin! He has already opportunistically had recourse to Marx on India and the United States. He now quotes Lenin to the effect that exports of capital under imperialism accelerate capitalist development to those countries to which it is exported. Since this passage in Lenin has been put to use by opportunists of all hues, it is necessary for us to quote it here in full and to try to analyse its content against other passages in Lenin's works in order to get its true meaning. Lenin states:

> The export of capital influences and greatly accelerates the development of capitalism in those countries to which it is exported. While, therefore, the export of capital may tend to a certain extent to arrest development in the capital exporting countries, it can only do so by expanding and deepening further development of capitalism throughout the world.[16]

From this contextually sound position of Lenin, Shao and Emmanuel, draw an imperialist economistic conclusion that colonialism develops the productive forces in a rather absolute sense. The above passage of Lenin is to be found in the part where Lenin showed the distribution of foreign capital in the different parts of the globe by Britain, France, and Germany for the period 1910. These showed that Britain's capital exports went mainly to the colonies and the U.S.A., those of France mainly to Europe and particularly Russia, and those of Germany mainly to Europe and America. Of the capital exported by Britain to her colonies the bulk of it went to areas of white settlement like South Africa, Australia and New Zealand. Thus while it is true that capital exports accelerate capitalist development in these colonies it did not do so in equal measure in all the colonies all the time. Moreover it did not bring about the same developments in all the colonies all the time. This is why Marx's distinction between the two types of colonies is important in this respect and Bettelheim's silence on the second type of colony in the present era is correct since, on the whole, capitalist development had greatly been accelerated on the pattern of European development in the second type of colony, and the reasons for these are quite obvious.

Therefore to use the authority of Lenin on this issue in the abstract is to betray a high sense of onesidedness. Nowhere does Lenin say that these developments were revolutionary and "progressive", for the Shaos and Warrens to then use this statement in Lenin to conclude that imperialism is "progressive". It also enables Shao to quote Marx "at random" in "scattered" passages to the effect that wherever capitalism takes root it dissolves all old modes, transforming all commodity production into capitalist production; that the development of commerce and merchant capital gives rise "everywhere" to the production of values. We are are also treated to the extent to which capitalism is able to dissolve these old bonds depends on the solidity of the internal structures and how, in the modern world, this leads to the capitalist mode of production on a world scale. Shao tries to prove his case from these scattered quotes, without caring about historical materialism, for which ignorance he castigates Bettelheim.

If Shao had cared to quote the full context of Lenin, he would have found no support in him for his economism. In *Imperialism...* Lenin makes it clear that this exported capital that accelerates this capitalist development is at the same time moribund and parasitic, and it is for this reason that he condemns Cunow for suggesting that imperialism is progressive. Lenin states:

> Kautsky who enters into controversy with the German apologist of imperialist and annexations, Cunow, who clumsily and cynically argues that imperialism is present day capitalism; that the development of capitalism is inevitable and progressive; therefore imperialism is progressive; therefore we

should grovel before it and glorify it. This is something like the caricature of the Russian Marxists which the Narodniks drew in 1894-95. They argued: if Marxists believe that capitalism is inevitable in Russia, that it is progressive, then they ought to open a tavern and begin to implant capitalism![17]

This, in fact, is what Shao tells us to do. Since today's imperialism is present-day capitalism and since all capitalism is progressive and since it has not outgrown its limits, but is still in its initial stages nationally, and able to take most if not all aspects of national development, then we must grovel ourselves before it and open a tavern in Tanzania for it to grow! Such are today's Cunows and Tanzania Narodniks who have claimed the garb of Marxism. It is not Bettelheim, despite his theoretical weaknesses, who is a Narodnik as Shao argues, and in circles at that, but Shao himself. This is because he does not understand Lenin's aim in analysing capitalist development in Russia in his famous book, the *Development of Capitalism in Russia* and his refutation of Krasin *On the So-called Market Question*, to which Shao makes reference with a view to proving his economism about today's capitallism playing a progressive and révolutionary role in our countries.

But why does Lenin, while saying that capitalism accelerates the development of capitalism, at the same time condemn it? He does so because Lenin knows fully well, as we have said, that monopoly capital that is exported is moribund and parasitic, and because of it, politically oppressive. This is why in his article on Imperialism and Split in Socialism he states:

> Imperialism is monopoly capitalism. Every cartel, trust, syndicate, every giant bank is a monopoly. Superprofits have not disappeared; they still remain. The exploitation of all the other countries by one privileged, financially wealthy country remains and has become more intense. A handful of wealthy countries – there are only four of them, if we mean independent, really gigantic, 'modern' wealth: England, France, the United States and Germany – have developed monopoly to vast proportions; they obtain superprofits running into hundreds, if not thousands, of millions, they 'ride on the backs' of hundreds and hundreds of millions of people in other countries and fight among themselves for the division of the particularly rich, particularly fat and particularly easy spoils.[18]

The nature of this imperialism has not changed in our time despite what the (new) opportunists and revisionists of the new age may say. Concentration of capital continues unabated, increasingly ruling out national capitalist development on a world scale. Under the new conditions of US-led multilateral imperialism, Japan has joined the former big four among the big powers that ride roughshod on the backs of the neo-colonial and colonial world for fat spoils. There has been a shift in the balance of power among the imperialist powers, with new superpowers coming into the picture, but the fact of imperialist exploitation continues. This is because, as we shall learn from Lenin later, the achievement of the right to self-determination by people oppressed by imperialism does not by any stretch of imagination remove the power of finance capital that imperialism has imposed on them. Yet Shao and his intellectual mentors would like the workers and other classes in our countries to believe that the power of finance capital over these countries has been vanquished and a basis has been laid for national capital to thrive if it were not for the "internal structures".

We have already seen that for Bill Warren neo-colonialism is a "term" which obscures the fact that "imperialism declines as (national) capitalism grows". This is, in his words, because "the international system of inequality and exploitation called imperialism created the conditions for the destruction this system by the spread of capitalist social relations and productive forces throughout the non-capitalist world". In short, imperialist exploitation through capitalist development in the non-capitalist world destroyed imperialist exploitation within imperialism itself! It is for this reason that after colonialism new conditions were created which "permitted" industrial development to advance in these countries. After giving us figures upon figures of industrial growth in these countries since the Second World War, he concluded, and this is what Shao calls "brilliant" about Warren's imperialist economism, that this development has been substantial:

> It will be the burden of this article that empirical observations suggest that the prospects for successful capitalist economic development (implying industrialisation) of a significant number of countries are quite good; that substantial progress in capitalist industrialisation has already been achieved; that the period since the Second World War has been marked by a major upsurge in capitalist social relations and productive forces (especially industrialisation) in the Third World; that in so far as there are obstacles to this development, they originate not in current imperialist Third World relationships, but almost entirely from the internal contradictions of the Third World itself; that the imperialist countries' policies and their overall impact on the Third World actually favour its industrialisation; and that the ties of dependence binding the Third World to the imperialist countries have been and are being loosened, with the consequence that the distribution of power within the capitalist world is becoming less uneven! (*New Left Review*, No. 81, pp. 4–5)

This is the celebrated "Bill Warren Thesis" that puts the case of imperialist economism so well. It is not our purpose here to go into the analysis of his economics, for economic analyses alone cannot answer Warren. In our view he puts the interpretation of his data upside down. Where the evidence proves that monopoly control has been intensified, Warren sees this as proof of independent development of Third World countries which imperialism has enabled and brought about. Unable to comprehend capitalist developments in its totality, denying the development of capitalism itself as leading to a new stage based on monopoly and to imperialism, but admitting capitalist development in its competitiveness only; taking the partial resolution of the national question for its complete resolution; analysing capitalist contradictions not in their dialectical relationship and development but eclectically; denying the scientificity of Marx's and Lenin's analyses of capitalism; Warren like Shao finds himself back on the hooks of imperialist ideology. Whereas all bourgeois research up to date confirms Marx's scientific thesis about the internationality of capitalism, and Lenin's thesis about imperialism, our new "Marxists", sunk deep into imperialist economism of the new era of multilateral imperialism, ride roughshod over abundant facts which are there for all to see. To Bill Warren, joint ventures, technological licensing and "transfers", a dominated home market based on imperialist dictated "import substitution", centralisation by finance capital of local capital which Warren acknowledges but regards as a "considerable leverage" for dealing with foreign firms; all these, the manifestation of imperialist control and domination, are the flowering of national capital.

Bill Warren who claims to be a Marxist analyst should listen to the bourgeois economist Dymsza and draw a lesson from him to dispel his illusions about "national capital". For Dymsza, who has done a study on the transnational corporation, local resources are what finance capital goes out to tap to its advantage and not to advance it. He states:

The multinational company transmits its basic resources — management, other personal, technology, business know-how, and funds — across national frontiers in the process of undertaking various types of business, including exporting, importing, licensing, contract manufacturing, sales of technology and services, management contracts, and international production to make profits and to grow. The principal transmission is of skills — managerial, technological, business, and entrepreneurial. However, the multinational company does more than transmit skills and other resources. It also mobilises and combines available resources with available local resources [i.e. local capital which Warren and Shao would call 'national capital' – D.W.N.] in the process of international productioin, marketing, and management. It combines transmitted scarce resources with available local and international resources in producing, distributing, and marketing goods and services.[19]

The above if synthesized makes good reading about the power of today's finance capital to centralise (i.e. 'combine' and 'mobilise') all national capitals and resources for its employment in order to make superprofits and grow (i.e. concentrate even further). Concerning the superprofits which today's transnational monopoly goes out to make and grow which Warren obscures under his narrow economism, Kindleberger has this to say:

It will be seen that earnings (i.e. profits) are higher on foreign investments and on foreign sales than in the United States, whether for Ortis Elevator, Du Pont, Gillette, Corn Products Refining, Standard Oil Company of New Jersey, or whatever. This trend would be much greater were it not for the existence of defensive investments in which the return is less than the average at home.[20]

Thus, for the open right wing spokesmen of big monopoly capital, there is no mystification regarding the internationalily of capital in its exploitative activities throughout the globe. Indeed these spokesmen of big capital go out to describe any talk about national capital as "instinctive reactions" to the reality of international capital. We quote below Kindleberger at length to get the point:

It is only a slight exaggeration to suggest that the normal individual has certain instincts which come into play in discussing foreign investment, irrational instincts which the study of economics is perhaps designed to eradicate. Social man tends to some considerable degree to be a PEASANT with a territorial instinct which leads him to object to foreign ownership of national natural resources; a POPULIST which makes him suspicious of banks; a MERCANTILIST, which makes him favour exports over imports; a XENOPHOBE, which leads him to fear those from outside the tribe; a MONOPOLIST who reacts strongly against competition; and an infant, to the extent that he WANTS TO EAT HIS CAKE AND HAVE IT TOO. It is over-stating the case to suggest that these instincts, which we recognise as on the whole unworthy of rational man, are at the basis of three quarters of the objections to foreign investments, but the proportion cannot be much below two thirds, or five eighths, or three fifths.
The PEASANT INSTINCT appears more clearly in the reaction to foreign ownership of our land, or natural resources. The thought is that Nature or God gave the land to "us" and intended us to have it. It is all right, perhaps, for foreigners to build factories within our borders, but it goes contrary to nature to have them own our mines, forests, waterfalls, petroleum reserves, farms, or grazing land. To an economist [i.e. imperialist economist – D.W.N.] this is an example of the fallacy of misplaced concreteness. Natural resources, like man-made plant and equipment, are

capital assets. If the asset is worth more to a foreigner than to a citizen of the country, it adds to natural wealth and income for the citizen to sell the natural resources to the foreigner and use the financial capital gained from the sale in lines of greater productivity. There is no difference between natural and man-made capital in this regard. Some natural resources, like farmland and forests, are not replaceable. These are exactly like man-made capital. Where they are not replaceable, as in the case of mines, the capital values can be maintained through depletion allowances which are invested in exploration and discovery of new natural resources, or maintained as other kinds of productive capital, earning an equivalent income. . .

But the main objections to foreign bankers is the instinct of POPULISM which has such a stronghold in the south and west of the United States. Fear of Wall Street and its malign schemes is endemic among farmers, small merchants, and such informed Populists as Representative Wright Patman and former President Lyndon B. Johnson. That Populism merges into simple *xenophobia* or dislike of foreigners was indicated when the Canadian Government decided against the First National City Bank's application to buy the Mercantile Bank on the ground that it was opposed to foreign ownership of banks, only to discover that the Mercantile Bank was already foreign owned – by Dutch interests. As in Australia, where British-owned banks are tolerated but American attempts to acquire ownership of banks is resisted, it may be less the fact of foreign ownership than the nationality of it. . .

To a considerable degree host countries object primarily to having foreigners control their enterprises. This NATIONALIST sentiment is understandable and normal, but it is noneconomic. The economist has no basis for objecting if a country chooses to exclude foreign exterprise on the ground that it wants to preserve its national identity, or worries about being overwhelmed by goods made to foreign designs and specifications. Nationalism can be regarded as a public good, like national parks, paid for not by taxation but through foregoing opportunities for increases in national income. All the economist can rightly do is to ask the decision makers to recognise that nationalism has a cost, and they should be prepared to decide how much they want at what cost.[21]

That is Kindleberger. What about Bill Warren? For him too resistance to foreign investment is "backward" and reactionary, for he states:

In fact vulgarised versions of Lenin's *Imperialism* occur all throughout the underdeveloped world among nationalist radical and so-called socialist organisations, movements, publications and so on, a characteristic example of which is the quite backward and reactionary opposition to foreign investment which many left wingers urge on underdeveloped countries. [Belco talk, p. 16].

Well! Well! At last Kindleberger and Bill Warren, and in equal measure Shao, are all on fours as imperialist economists. All see imperialism as progressive, all condemn nationalism as reactionary in as much as it is opposed to foreign capital; and all defend the right of monopolies to make superprofits in the Third World. The only difference is that Kindleberger does not claim the garb of Marxism, whereas Warren and Shao do so. Despite this difference all oppose the national movement which is opposed to imperialist exploitation and national oppression.

4. IMPERIALISM AND THE NATIONAL QUESTION

We have seen above that despite their pretensions Warren and Shao and all imperialist sportsmen oppose the national movement in the era of the general crisis of capitalism. Yet for all Marxist-Leninists the question of capitalist development is dialectically linked to the national question. Just as it is always said that the economics of capitalism must be analysed in the context of bourgeois politics and that of other classes, capitalist development too must always be analysed in the context of the national question. This is the Marxist method of dialectical and historical materialism. Yet our imperialist economists of today, just like their forefathers the Russian Narodniks and Second International, imperialist economists in the garb of Marxism separate the economics of imperialism from its politics, with the result that what we are presented with are lifeless abstractions that are so much detached from the real movement of the totality.

Marxism drew a distinction between three periods of capitalist development in its dialectical link with the national movements. These three periods are the very history of capitalist development in advancing the interests of all classes (i.e. society) in the first period; the development of capitalism alongside national oppression in the second phase; and the period of generalised oppression of colonial and other weaker peoples in the third period. These periods constitute the era of capitalism within the feudal womb, of capitalism itself, and capitalism in the era of imperialism – the era of transition to the socialist revolution. In the first period capitalism is young, virile and liberating; in the next it is virile but dominating, while in the third it is entirely dominating and oppressive, negating democracy in production and in politics. These are the fundamental differences in the development of capitalism that Warren, Emmanuel and Gundar Frank wish to obscure in their effort to generalise imperialism, thereby losing all the essential characteristics between them and their effort to deny stages in capitalism and thus seeing, capitalism as wholly ossified, unchangeable and immutable, something that Shao blames Bettelhiem for not doing without understanding what he is talking about!

Capitalism in its youth in Western Europe plays a very important role in developing the productive forces and liberating western Europe from all the vestiges of feudal backwardness. Here capitalism released the potentiality of the entire people whose energy had been fettered and arrested by feudal restrictions, protectionism and feudal monopoly. Here capitalism developed to the full and to a stage that Marx called a stage of "maturity". But this development was achieved on the basis of feudal enslavement of aboriginal peoples, colonisation of backward societies and their consequent plunder as well as the "entombment" of the Mexicans and Peruvians in the mercantilist imperialist quest for silver and gold, not to talk of the internal colonialism and expropriation of the European peasantry in its infancy. Nevertheless, the developments that followed were on the whole beneficial to society, and this is what marks this era of capitalism as dynamic and virile. It consolidated the nation against Rome and built the home market. developed production, advanced education and the general cultural development of the people. As a result it developed European language in the West at the expense of an alien (Latin) tongue. With the development of the languages, there also developed communication among the European peoples which was improved on by firmer liberal democracy that was the fruit of the bourgeois revolution. Capitalism here brought with it greater liberty for the people resulting in the institution of universal suffrage, doing away with discrimination against women, and creating conditions for greater revolutionary struggles by the people against the decadent capitalism of the next phase.

In Eastern Europe, on the other hand, where capitalism was late in developing, the forces of development were distorted, with the result that the despotic rule of feudalism continued in the major part of the region. In those countries where capitalism managed to take root, the dominant nationalities took it upon theselves to bring together into single states other smaller nationalities. Capitalism had not yet taken root vigorously with the result that there, unlike in the West, multinational states, dominated by the bourgeoisies of the dominant nationalities became the rule, rather than the exception, as had been the case in the West (England and Ireland). This special method of state formation took place where feudalism had not been eliminated, where capitalism was feebly developed, where the dominated nationalities had not yet formed themselves into economically integrated units (nations). This had fateful consequences for these countries, for as soon as capitalist development began here, the bourgeoisies of the dominant nationalities, "swiftly" moved in to quel any competition to them from the emergent bourgeoisies in the dominated nationalities. Restrictive measures were imposed on them, repression of their culture including language and religion were made the rule. Schools of the smaller nationalities were closed, franchise restrictions imposed on them etc., to arrest their development. It is no wonder then that Lenin and Stalin characterised the multinational states of Eastern Europe as backward for, instead of freeing peoples from feudal restrictions, it was subjecting them to domination by bigger nationalities. It was not surprising, therefore, that the dominated bourgeoisies began to organise the peoples of the dominated nationalities into a national movement opposed to foreign domination.

Here Lenin argued, and Trotsky and Luxemburg opposed, like the Bill Warrens and Shaos of today would have done, the view that the proletariat of the dominated nationalities as well as those of the dominating nationalities should support the national movement of these nationalities. As these nationalities gained strength, a few were able to cut themselves off into separate nation–states thus removing the restrictions imposed on the development of the productive forces and the development of the full potential of the people and their culture and social life. Others, which could not win national independence as those in the Russian multinational state, were caught with their pants down for the proletariat of the dominant nationalities and some elements in the dominated nationalities took the leadership in the struggle against the Tsarist autocracy and overthrew it, giving an opportunity to these dominated nationalities to opt out of the multinational state and form nation–states of their own. But this clearly was too late since this was the era of imperialism and these dominated nationalities could not have built capitalism in their own countries without accepting domination of the imperialist bourgeoisie. Thus for these countries, instead of opting out, they remained in a multinational state of a new type, in which capitalism was quickly to be replaced with socialism.

The matter was even more different for the colonised peoples which were brought under imperialist domination in the era of finance capital, 1880–1914, which phase of capitalism the Bill Warrens and the Emmanuels deny. In this phase, monopoly capital in the capitalist countries had become moribund, parasitic and decadent. It could only continue to survive by extracting superprofits from the colonies which now became very vital to all the capitalist states which now vied with each other in the division and redivision of the whole world among themselves for the export of capital by the financial oligarchy that now emerged to form the monopoly bourgeoisie. "These were the magnates of capital" or the "financial aristocrats" who now controlled all major industries and banks in all the capitalist states, and with this power of capital controlled with the support of the state the whole world for themselves on the basis of cartels, trusts and syndicates, riding roughshod on the backs of the people in the oppressed countries as parasites, clipping coupons, and fettering instead of advancing the development of the productive forces and national potential further. Because of the decadence of capitalism at home the capital that was now exported only accelerated capitalist development on the basis of great parastism. It extracted great superprofits on the basis which profitability was maintained at home for the capitalist firm which was increasingly outgrowing its competitive size in a situation of general crisis. And with the superprofits they bribed a whole line of opportunists among the working class movement at both the political and economic level in order to quieten the working class to accept an imperialist policy under the banner of "defence of the fatherland".

In the colonies where new relations of production were introduced, the old backward conditions (economic, social, cultural and political) were swept away slowly giving way to new conditions, but these new conditions did not signify the advancement of a new life in favour of the people. In a country like India, as we have seen in Marx's analysis, the condition of the people increasingly deteriorated in a situation of total misery and deprivation. India is a good case in point because of her having gone through all the phases of capitalist domination. This national oppression only unleased great antagonism in the colonies and with new elements of capitalist development that had arisen, elements of the bourgeoisie and petty bourgeoisie who had emerged within the womb of imperialism, began to challenge this oppression and slowly built up a national movement of all classes to challenge this foreign oppression that imposed a new terror upon the people; a national oppression that deprived them of their culture but substituted no new national culture. And because no independent national economy was possible, it provided no new political system giving greater freedoms to the people.

But such struggle of the people was led by a bourgeoisie that had at the same time strong economic and class links with the oppressing bourgeoisie. Moreover, it was not fighting feudalism but capitalism which they themselves wanted to build. For this and other related reasons this class was not resolute and thorough in its prosecution of the national revolt against foreign domination. Because of its economic and social (class) position it began to waver and vaccilate whenever the national movement made great strides, giving greater strength to the working class and poor peasantry. And because of its fear of these two classes, the national bourgeoisie began to compromise with imperialism and sometimes struck dirty deals behind the back of the people, only trying to advance its interest to the exclusion of that of the working class and poor peasantry.

But what did this national movement stand for? Did it stand for the total elimination of foreign economic domination or did it only seek a change in the political sphere? This question was a central point of contention between Lenin and Luxemburg, Trotsky and Kievsky, as we have already noted. The Luxemburgists argued that since in the era of finance capital the omnipotence of finance capital could not be eradicated except by proletarian revolution, any political struggles in the political sphere which did not challenge the economic power of finance capital were pointless. On the contrary, it was argued, it would go to advance bourgeois nationalism which was reactionary and which tended to weaken the working class politically. These economistic views were combated by Lenin who argued that all struggles in the sphere of democracy to which the struggle for self-determination belonged, were as a matter of fact in the political sphere. But this did not imply that all political struggles on this issue could not be supported by the proletariat because of their "impracticability". To the extent that democracy was a freer, wider and clearer form of class struggle, such a transformation would enable the proletariat to develop its struggle for fundamental democratic rights, in the struggle for socialism. Luxemburg's argument of the "impossibility" and "impracticability, in the economic sense, of one of the demands of poliical democracy under capitalism were therefore, according to Lenin, reduced to a theoretically incorrect definition of the general and basic relationships of capitalism and political democracy as a whole. He emphasized that all demands for self-determination were only partially "practicable" under imperialism. Not until the proletariat had organised itself and rallied the peasanrty onto its side for the struggle for socialism could the power of finance capital be finally challenged at its roots with the proletarian onslaught to expropriate the bourgeoisie. Lenin's thesis gives us a clear understanding of the political programme of the proletariat in its different phases as a leader of the national movement, taking into account the interests of the different classes oppressed by imperialism in the era of the proletarian revolution.

5. THE NEW DEMOCRATIC REVOLUTION

Lenin's thesis was further developed by Mao Tse-tung in relation to the revolutionary struggles of the exploited and oppressed peoples of the colonial and semi-colonial (and today of the neo-colonial) countries. Mao Tse-tung pointed out that in order to succeed, the proletariat had to lead the new democratic revolution until the proletarian expropriation of the imperialist bourgeoisie was completed. Therefore the working class had to put forward a political and economic programme that could mobilise the people against the enemy in its different forms of development, first for the "New Democracy" and second for socialism.

(i) The Political Programme of "New Democracy"

The political programme of "New Democracy" is anti-imperialist and anti-local reaction. Mao explained that it was "new" because, unlike the old bourgeois revolution which led to the development of capitalism, the new democratic revolution led not to the building of capitalism as such (although this was its aim in a restricted way in the first phase of the revolution) but to the building of socialism as its aim, and eventually to communism. But in saying this, Mao did not deny that the penetration of foreign capital had hastened capitalist commodity production in China. He argued that feudal economy in old China had developed a certain level of commodity production which carried the roots of capitalism:

> Penetration of foreign capital accelerated all this. Foreign capital played an important part in the disintegration of China's social economy; on the other hand, it undermined the foundations of her self-sufficient natural economy and wrecked the handicraft industries both in the cities and in the peasants' homes, and on the other, it hastened the growth of a commodity economy in town and country.[22]

But did Mao and the Chinese Communist Party grovel before this foreign capital and open a tavern for it to flourish in China in order to "develop the productive forces"? On the contrary, Mao and his comrades correctly pointed out that although foreign capital accelerated capitalist development yet, and because of it, China was being turned into a semi-colony of the imperialists:

> It is certainly not the purpose of the imperialist powers invading China to transform feudal China into capitalist China. On the contrary, their purpose is to transform China into their own semi-colony. To this end the imperialist powers have used and continue to use military, political, economic and cultural means of oppression, so that China has gradually become a semi-colony and colony.[23]

It was this domination of China and the exploitation of its people and resources that constituted the principal contradiction in China and the political programme of the party was to organise and combine all national forces to combat the enemy and establish new democracy in China that would lead to the joint dictatorship of all revolutionary forces in its first phase.

What were these forces that could be combined? Mao emphasized that the proletariat in China together with the poor peasantry in alliance constituted the motive force of the Chinese revolution. Apart from these classes, the non-peasant petty-bourgeoisie could also be mobilised on the side of the revolution. The national bourgeoisie, despite the wavering and vacccilating relationship it had with imperialism, could be united with the struggle against it. The only exception was the comprador bourgeoisie whose economic interest were linked directly with imperialism. These constituted along with imperialism the targets of the Chinese revolution.

The significance of this class analysis is that it took into account all the national forces having contradiction with imperialism from the biggest to the smallest and put them on the side of the revolution against imperialism and feudal vestiges. The significance of this analysis goes to disprove anarchic half statements of the Warrens and the Shaos as well as the Shivjis and Mamdanis as to the breadth of national forces that can be mobilised on an anti-imperialist platform. Shao, for instance, shows great confusion in the positions of the bourgeoisie and the proletariat in the national movement. On the one hand he sees their role and that of nationalism – as reactionary under all conditions, while on the other he seems to castigate Bettelheim for suggesting that they are. As for the proletariat its leadership is viewed in absolutist terms. When it comes to the petty-bourgeoisie Shao takes an ultra "proletarian" line in seeing their struggle as "reactionary" in as much as it "tries to retain the conditions of the existence of the petty-bourgeois society" in historical terms. But that view of the petty-bourgeois becomes so one-sided as to be unhopeful in concrete situations of struggle.

In analysing what the petty-bourgeoisie oppose, it is important at specific instances to identify the content of their struggle and where possible to channel that struggle into constructive and revolutionary ways. If the petty-bourgeoisie are fighting big capital in anti-imperialist situations, particularly where the national question is involved, it is all the more incumbent upon the proletariat which, of course, is thoroughly anti-imperialist, to analyse their struggles and incorporate them into the general democratic programme of all national forces. This is what Marx (and Lenin) teach us despite the statement in the *Manifesto* that the petty-bourgeoisie are reactionary when they fight the big bourgeoisie to save themselves from extinction as a middle class. Yet in concrete struggles Marx tells us to channel their struggles against big capital for revolutionary purposes. As far back as 1848 Marx, in a criticism of one Kriege, a German co-worker of Marx who had gone to the US to organise the working class but who at a certain stage, instead organised the peasantry into a movement of social reform on land put this issue very squarely.

At that time capitalist development on land was not as yet a reality, but conditions were being created for its development. In accordance with the law of capitalist ground rent, all land was becoming increasingly monopolised in the hands of a few landlords. Kriege, instead of understanding the current that was underway, engaged in illusions about the "general redistribution" of land to the producers in opposition to its concentration, a fact that Shao would today call reactionary *per se*. He said: "If this immense area (the 1,400,000,000 acres of North American public domain) is withdrawn from commerce and is secured in restricted amounts for labour, and end will be put to poverty in America at one stroke. . ." This was illusionary and utopian and Marx was constrained to remark with sarcasm: "One would have expected him to understand that legislators have no power to decree that the evolution of the patriarchal system, which Kriege desires, into an industrial system to checked, or that the industrial and commercial states of the East coast be thrown back to patriarchal barbarism".

But what attitude did Marx take of this movement despite its utopian, illusory weakness? This is an important question for the weak proletariat that had emerged within industrial society of the US at the time. He did not take a narrow view of this reform movement, on the contrary he drew materialist conclusions that took into account the progressive content of the movement. As Lenin commented:

> Marx does not simply 'repudiate' this petty-bourgeois movement, he does not dogmatically ignore it, he does not fear to spoil his hands by contact with the movement of the revolutionary petty-bourgeois democrats – a fear that is characteristic of many doctrinaires. While mercilessly ridiculing the absurd ideological trappings of the movement, Marx strives in a sober materialist manner to determine its real historical content, the consequences that must inevitably follow from it because of the objective conditions, regardless of the will and consciousness, the dreams and the theories, of the various individuals. Marx, therefore, does not condemn, but fully approves a communist point, i.e., examining the movement from every aspect, taking into account both the past and the future, Marx notes the revolutionary aspect on the attack on private property in land.[24]

Why did Marx take this position? He did so because he realised the potential of this movement in terms of the long term struggle against capital. Thus although the evil these petty-bourgeois reformers feared was in its unfolding going to destroy the very illusions these reformers yearned to instal, Marx reminded them that such a development was going to accelerate social development in the long run, bringing with it higher forms of the communist movement. Lenin argued:

> A blow struck at landed property will facilitate the inevitable further blows at property in general. The revolutionary action of the lower class for change that will temporarily provide a restricted prosperity, and by no means for all, will facilitate the inevitable further revolutionary action of the very lowest class for change that will really ensure complete human happiness for all toilers.[25]

But this was 1848, three years after the *Manifesto*. In the 1930s the demands of the petty bourgeoisie in the oppressed countries constituted one of the elements of the national movement against finance capital. And this is what Mao took into account in framing the programme for the new democratic revolution, and went a long way to refute anarchist "revolutionary" phrasemongering that is characteristic of academic "Marxism" that turns out to be no more than imperialist economism.

What were the main political tasks that the movement for New Democracy stood for? It stood for the elimination of imperialism and local reaction. It opposed monopoly capitalism, but not capitalism in general. The reason for this difference will become obvious in a moment. It stood for the establishment of the new democratic state at first but with a double task of linking it to the socialist revolution in its second phase. In its first phase it put forward Sun Yat-sen's Three Peoples Principles, thus showing the historic link between the bourgeois revolution that never consolidated and the new democratic revolution that was being led by proletarian forces that emerged within it. To smash imperialism and feudal vestiges was to smash the power that enchained China to the needs of imperialism, to unleash the full potential of the Chinese nation, to develop her national economy and advance a new culture, "a national scientific and mass culture—such is the anti-imperialist and anti-feudal culture of the people, the culture of New Democracy, a New culture of the Chinese nation".[26]

Thus it can be seen that the politics of the people in the colonies, semi-colonies and neo-colonies, the politics of New Democracy have nothing in common with those of the imperialist economists who grovel before imperialism, build taverns for imperialism to continue its exploitative and oppressive "investments" which are presumed to develop the productive forces of the oppressed countries. We shall see that the economic programme of New Democracy further refutes once and for all the erroneous views of the imperialist economists of the Shao type.

(ii) The Economics of "New Democracy"

As pointed out above the new democratic revolution was not opposed to capitalism in general. It opposed monopoly capitalism in particular. It did not oppose Chinese national capital that had emerged around the 1870s and in particular around 1917-19 due to favourable conditions created by the war. Such capitalism, although dominated by foreign capital, had begun to play a considerable part in China's political and cultural life. But because of foreign domination China's economic, political and cultural development was very uneven and her national economy could not thrive. The economic programme of the new democratic revolution, therefore, aimed at taking over big banks and big industrial and commercial enterprises, whether Chinese-owned or foreign-owned, so that private capital might not "dominate the lives of the people". Mao, nevertheless, emphasized that the new republic would not confiscate or forbid private capitalist enterprises which did not "dominate the lives of the people". In the countryside although certain steps were taken to confiscate the land of the landlords and distribute it to those poor peasants who did not have any land or who had very little, the rich peasantry were not expropriated. This was the policy of "equalisation of land". Socialist agriculture was not encouraged at this stage. Mao emphasized:

> China's economy must develop along the path of 'the regulation of capital' and the 'equalisation of land ownership', and must never be 'privately owned by the few'; we must never permit the few capitalists and landlords to 'dominate the lives of the people'; we must never establish a capitalist society of the European – American type or allow the old semi-feudal society to survive. Whoever dares to go counter to this line of advance will certainly not succeed but will run into a brick wall… Such is the economy of New Democracy. And the politics of New Democracy are the concentrated expression of the economy of the New Democracy.[27]

This economic policy of New Democracy was given concrete expression by a directive of the seventh central committee of the party on 5 March 1949 to be applied in liberated zones; and this was to form the cornerstone of the economic policy after the first phase of the revolution. It was directed that in order to develop the economy in the cities the party must "rely on the working class". It was also emphasized that in order to restore production and advance it further, state capital, would come first, then private capital and lastly handicraft industry. It was observed that China's modern industry constituted a minute 10 per cent of the economy, while agriculture still held away over the other 90 per cent. It was, nevertheless, pointed out that, minute as it was, modern industry was "extremely concentrated", with the largest part concentrated in imperialist hands and their lackeys. It is this which was to be confiscated and transferred to the peoples' republic, to constitute the socialist sector within the economy of New Democracy, and to develop as the main lever of the economy. Private capitalist industry on the contrary had been oppressed and hemmed in by imperialism, feudalism and bureaucrat capitalism. Furthermore, because of this oppression, the Chinese national bourgeoisie had taken part in the new democratic revolution:

For this reason and because China's economy is still backwards, there will be need, for a fairly long period after the victory of the revolution, to make use of the positive qualities of urban and rural private capitalism as far as possible, in the interest of developing the national economy. In this period all capitalist elements in the cities and countryside which are not harmful but beneficial to the national economy should be allowed to exist and expand. This is not only unavoidable but economically necessary. But the development of capitalism in China will not be unrestricted and uncurbed as in the capitalist countries... However in the interest of the whole national economy and in the present and future interest of the working class and all labouring people, we must not restrict (it) too much or too rigidly, but must leave room for it to exist and develop within the framework of the economic policy and planning of the peoples republic.[28]

What is the significance of this economic policy of New Democracy? It is necessary to answer this question in order to refute imperialist economists like Shao. The economic policy line explained above refutes once and for all the idea that imperialist investment far from advancing and developing national industry on the contrary hinders it and only advances imperialist dominated and controlled production. It goes to prove that this hindering and hemming in of national industry constitutes one of the elements of the contradiction between the people and imperialism and that the new democratic revolutions which have been and will continue to be waged in the "ex-colonies" and semi-colonies are a necessary phase in the elimination of this hindering, blocking and fettering of the national productive forces. The illusion that imperialism must be praised to the skies for developing "the productive forces" in general is a 'misguided concreteness' on very dangerous generalities. The economic programme of New Democracy in China which we use as an illustration above goes to show that the struggle of the people of the "ex-colonies" and semi-colonies are real and concrete struggles against a real and concrete enemy. They are not contrived and conspiratorial struggles against a legitimate power, but open, legitimate and just struggles against an illegitimate power over the people, a power that advances its interests with "blood and iron". To ignore this is to ignore the most obvious and naked contradictions of our time.

The New Democracy economic policy lays down the broad policy for application in eliminating foreign monopoly-control and exploitation of the people and national resources. After doing so, it removes the fetters which have all along bound national capital. It does not eliminate this national capital. On the contrary it gives it a new lease to develop and expand in a freer atmosphere without foreign domination. But its expansion is made possible only within the national plan in which it plays apart. Within that plan Chinese private capital acquired a whole national market in the areas of their specialisation in production, a fact the Chinese national bourgeoisie would never have dreamt of with their national market dominated by imperialist investment. New Democracy was giving a new lease of life to Chinese capitalism. But this new lease did not imply that China's development was to proceed on the lines of the Old Democracy of Western Europe and to some extent of Eastern Europe. As we have seen, capitalism led to monopoly capitalism and to imperialism. This resulted in the complete division of the world among the powerful capitalist states in which China together with all the countries of the Third World found themselves enchained to the demands of foreign capital. To embark on the road of Old Democracy, China and other Third World countries would have to recreate a situation where they too would divide the world among themselves after arriving at the stage of monopoly of their own (a greater illusion still such as the "fertile" petty-bourgeois mind is capable of entertaining!). But where in the corner of the world are there new territories reserved for such countries?

It is for this reason that an economic programme of New Democracy puts forward a new policy for the development of capitalism of a new type. It is released from monopoly fetters of private (and foreign) monopolists. It is restricted to operate within the plan in which state capital of a new type plays the leading role. This new state capital did not exist "chiefly to make profits for the capitalists but to meet the needs of the people and the state". Although a share of the profits went to the capitalists (about a quarter), the remaining three quarters were produced for the workers, for the state and for the expansion of productive capacity:

> Therefore, this state-capitalist economy of a new type takes on a socialist character to a very great extent and benefits the workers and the state.[29]

The table below shows how under New Democracy —the joint dictatorship of all revolutionary classes—the national product of state capital was distributed:

Income tax	34.5%
Welfare fund	15.0%
Accumulated fund	30.0%
Dividends to capitalists	20.5%
Total	100.0%

Thus under this policy as state capitalism consolidated itself, it increasingly became the dominant sector, and private capital the minor sector; and in this way capitalism was being replaced by socialism on the basis of developing capitalism of a new type—one state and one private—ruling out the road of the Old Revolution in Europe, America and Japan. It was on the basis of this approach that China and the Chinese nation *"Stood Up"*. And we may add, that is how the people of the neo-colonial world, now still exploited and dominated by imperialism, will Stand Up!

FOOTNOTES

1. D.W. Nabudere, *The Political Economy of Imperialism*, Zed Press/Tanzania Publishing House, 1977, p. 239.
2. K. Marx, *Value, Price and Profit*, Moscow: Progress Publishers.
3. A. Emmanuel, "White-settler Colonialism and the Myth of Investment Imperialism", *New Left Review*, No. 73, p. 34. See also *Unequal Exchange*, London: New Left Books, 1972, pp. 184-192.
4. *Ibid, Unequal Exchange, op. cit.*
5. Panel discussion on Imperialism and the World Market organised by the University Economics Association.
6. V.I. Lenin, *Imperialism, the Highest Stage of Capitalism*, Preface.
7. V.I. Lenin, *Imperialism, Op. cit.*, pp. 62-68.
8. Jenks, *Migration of British Capital to 1875*, pp. 332-333.
9. K. Marx, *Capital*, Vol. III, pp. 436-8.
10. Jenks, *op.cit.*, p. 133.
11. V.I. Lenin, *Imperialism*, p. 48.
12. J.K. Nyerere, "The Process of Liberation", *Daily News*, 18 November 1976.
13. K. Marx, *Capital*, Vol. I, pp. 425-6.
14. Marx & Engels, *Articles on Britain*, pp. 168-69
15. *Ibid;*, pp. 201-2.
16. V.I. Lenin, *Imperialism*, p. 63.
17. *Ibid.*, pp. 89-90.
18. V.I. Lenin, *Collected Works*, Vol. 23, p. 115.

282

19. W.A. Dymsza, *Multinational Business Strategy,* 1972, McGraw-Hill, p. 12 (Emphasis added.)
20. C.P. Kindleberger, *International Economics,* 1973, p. 254.
21. *Ibid.,* pp. 263-267.
22. Mao Tse-tung, "Chinese Revolution and the Chinese Communist Party" in *Selected Works,* Vol. II, p. 309.
23. *Ibid.,* p. 15.
24. V.I. Lenin, *On the United States,* p. 14.
25. *Ibid.,* p. 15.
26. Mao Tse-tung, "On New Democracy", *Selected Works,* Vol. II, p. 382.
27. *Ibid.,* p. 353.
28. Mao Tse-tung, *Selected Works,* Vol. IV, p. 367.
29. Mao Tse-tung, *"On State Capitalism",* *Selected Works,* Vol. V, p. 101.

30

REVIEW OF THE DEBATE ON IMPERIALISM, STATE, CLASS AND THE NATIONAL QUESTION

Omwony-Ojwok

The 1976 debate in Dar es Salaam over imperialism, state, class and the national question deserves a review and comment. This is so because this debate raised many theoretical issues of proletarian ideology which have direct bearing on the revolutionary struggle of the working class and oppressed peoples of Africa and the world. In the process of the debate many issues were clarified. Once we understand that without revolutionary theory there is no revolutionary movement, we shall be able to appreciate and to understand the importance of this debate.

Of the numerous issues that were raised, the most important were: imperialism and the national question, the relationship between the economic base and the superstructure, the neo-colonial state and classes in the neo-colonies. It also dealt with the strategy and tactics of revolution in the neo-colonies, that is to say, problems of the new democratic revolution. Other issues included exploitation of the peasantry in the neo-colonies and methods of ideological struggle within revolutionary organisations.

The debate opened in London between May and June 1976 when Mahmood Mamdani and Harko Bhagat, among others, decided to open a discussion and write critical comments on the manuscripts of Issa Shivji and D.W. Nabudere. The comments actually arrived in Dar es Salaam the first week of July. The comments were not openly circulated, but at least one of them, the critique on Nabudere's manuscript, was appended to Nabudere's reply to it. Almost about the same time there appeared Nabudere's own critique of Shivji's *Class Struggles in Tanzania*.

1. NABUDERE'S CRITIQUE OF SHIVJI

In his *Imperialism, State, Class and Race*, Nabudere presented his critique of I.G. Shivji's *Class Struggles in Tanzania*. He explains that this was the latest of Shivji's attempts to analyse Tanzania. He pointed out that the book however "fails to deal with the problem scientifically and therefore raises more questions than it purports to answer". That it continues Shivji's past theoretical errors which other earlier critics had tended to compound, especially John Saul who, in asking the question "Who is the immediate enemy?", fell in line with Debray, Gundar Frank and other neo-Trotskyist theoreticians. Nabudere argued that all these errors of Shivji must be viewed within the context of how Marxism came to East Africa as part of the neo-Marxist and neo-Trotskyist school, through academics imported from Western Europe.

Nabudere summed up the Marxist-Leninist thesis on imperialism as the stage of capitalism in which *finance capital* and the financial oligarchy "acquires control over *basic* industries and the credit system, and, on the basis of this control, exports finance capital for the exploitation of cheap labour and other resources in the backward countries". Capital, and finance capital in particular, develops and survives because the bougeoisie control not only the means of production but also the instruments of suppression of the opposing classes. But under capitalism, such class suppression, it must be borne in mind, continues on the basis of inter-capitalist competition and the reproduction of the working class. Nabudere pointed out that Shivji lacked the theoretical basis for examining the historical movement in Tanzania, namely the theory of imperialism. Thus Shivji, taking the Latin American neo-Marxist anaysis, spoke of underdevelopment being an integral part of the world capitalist system and that "the historically determined production system is the system of underdevelopment". Nabudere demonstrated Shivji's inconsistencies and contradictory positions even within the neo-Marxist framework, quoting from Shivji himself on the so-called "Colonial (Economic) Structures" and on the nature of the relationship between the "nationalised" industries in Tanzania and "foreign" capital. Making reference to Shivji's eclectic quotations and the tagging into the Appendix the very material that should have been analysed and synthesised, Nabudere shows that "(these) positions of Shivji should prove to us that he has no concept of imperialism as analysed by Lenin".

On "Class and Race" Nabudere stressed that once the financial oligarchy had taken a dominant position in imperialist countries, it negated the basis for a national bourgeoisie in the oppressed countries. He quoted Shivji's preface to show how the latter starts from an abstraction and creates a dualism in his analysis of class and race. Nabudere strongly attacked Shivji's view that the "development of classes and class struggles can only be talked about tendentially", showing that this is the modern equivalent of Kant's idealism and Plato's great gimmick of transubstantiation". This, said Nabudere, led Shivji into a static, ethnographic "analysis" of class in his Chapter 5. Quoting from pages 42 and 45-46 of Shivji's book, Nabudere showed how Shivji looked at classes in racial terms and added "We must conclude that the thesis is not a Marxist-Leninist scientific method of analysing classes on his own admissions and accordingly must be dismissed as petty-bourgeois". He continued to further elucidate this in his critique of Shivji's Part Three where Shivji treated "the kulaks", "Yeoman farmers", "the bureaucratic bourgeoisie", "cultural exclusivism" as aspects of class struggles in Tanzania.

Nabudere pointed out that because of major theoretical errors, Shivji's occasionally correct observations on *Ujamaa Vijijini* and workers strike actions go astray within the general treatment. For he "has no concept of class and state" a fact which leads him to abandon Marxism-Leninism. He concluded that Shivji's book was "very bad", put Marxism-Leninism in extremely bad light and, indeed, could not be accepted as a Marxist-Leninist thesis on class struggles in Tanzania.

2. MAHMOOD MAMDANI AND HARKO BHAGAT ON NABUDERE'S MANUSCRIPT ON IMPERIALISM

In their critique of Nabudere, Mamdani and Bhagat raised the question of imperialism, holding that any political analysis of modern imperialism must reveal the various contradictions of imperialism "in both their particular importance and interrelations". They went on to categorise these contradictions as:

(a) Contradiction among the superpowers.
(b) Contradictions within the bourgeoisie of the imperialist countries.
(c) Contradictions among the superpowers and the second world.
(d) Contradictions among the imperialists.

They concluded that the <u>principal</u> contradiction was that between imperialism and the oppressed nations, quoting the authority of "the Proposal on the General Line of the International Communist Movement". Their criticisms of Nabudere's manuscript were:

i.   (a) That it abstracted from all contradictions except that between labour and capital and this was possible because the manuscript absolutized the concept of centralisation of capital arriving at a concept of world finance capital, thereby emphasising its unity in a one-sided manner and thus coming "perilously" close to taking the Kautskyite stand of ultra-imperialism.

       (b) That the manuscript did not analyse social imperialism.

       (c) That the manuscript suggested that the financial oligarchy was the 'entire' bourgeoisie of the imperialist countries.

       (d) That the manuscript did not analyse the contradictions between the first and the second world, and thus could not explain Gaullism in France and the significance of the Lome convention.

       (e) That its analysis of nationalisations in the third world was static.

       (f) That it denied that the peasants in the third world were exploited through unequal exchange.

       (g) That this allegedly one-sided emphasis on the contradiction between "labour and capital" is a Trotskyite deviation.

ii.   (a) That the manuscript has nothing to say on the principles of the peoples democratic revolution in the "semi-colonies".

       (b) That the manuscript gives an incorrect analysis of classes in the neo-colonies holding that a section of the bourgeoisie which does not partake in production cannot be called petty-bourgeoisie and that the petty-bourgeoisie partakes in the labour process and is "part of the working masses".

iii   (a) That the manuscript has little to say on the "semi-colonial state".

       (b) That the manuscript takes the position that politics obediently follow economics; and finally that

       (c) The financial oligarchy is not the ruling class in a semi-colony, because, "The principal flaw in conceptualising the international bourgeoisie as the ruling class in a semi-colony is that it abstracts from intra-imperialist rivalry".

The first person to comment on the Bhagat-Mamdani critiques was Yash Tandon.

3. YASH TANDON'S COMMENT ON MAMDANI AND BHAGAT

In his comments, Yash Tandon dealt with the questions of classes and the state in a "neo- or semi-colony" and finally the question of unequal exchange. He pointed out that Mamdani's and Bhagat's critique of Shivji was opportunistic. They had criticised Shivji for having failed to establish the emergence of bureaucrat capital and thus of the bureaucratic bourgeoise because he could not establish that the social group that emerged in control of the state after the Arusha Declaration "exercises control over the means of production" and not simply managerial or legal control. The evidence in the Appendix to Shivji's book showed that it was the multinationals that "exercised control" over the means of production after the Arusha Declaration.

Yet Mamdani and Bhagat after criticising Shivji went on to conclude: "In this scientific sense, then, we can identify the emergence of bureaucratic bourgeoisie in Tanzania after the nationalisations accompanying the Arusha Declaration". But they had not shown that "bureaucratic capital" had emerged after Arusha. Nor had they shown that the bureaucrats owned the means of production! Like Shivji they had no evidence of the emergence of bureaucratic capital and thus a bureaucratic bourgeoisie. As such Mamdani and Bhagat, who had set out to criticise Shivji, ended up being Shivjist themselves!

Tandon also criticised Mamdani and Bhagat for not providing evidence for the existence of a national bourgoisie which the latter claimed existed in Tanzania and vindicated the Nabudere case of putting national bourgeoisie in inverted comma's because any such bourgeoisie that exists in the neo-colony in the epoch of imperialism will never accomplish the national democratic bourgeois revolution due to the dominance of monopoly capitalism that has divided the world. Thus this "bourgeoisie" cannot be genuinely called national.

Tandon criticised Mamdani further for one-sidedly emphasizing that the petty-bourgeoisie is part of the working masses and belongs to the camp of the people in the democratic revolution. He pointed out that the petty bourgeoisie joins the camp of the people when it knows that its fate is to be determined by the proletariat. He further pointed out that it joins the revolution under the leadership of the proletariat, only with correct proletarian practice. Otherwise the petty-bourgeoisie can and does take a reactionary and anti-revolutionary stand. Is it not the petty-bourgeoisie that fought the proletariat during the Paris Commune? Is it not the petty-bourgeoisie that removed their barricades from the streets of Paris thus paving the way for the bourgeoisie to return from their 'exile' in Marseilles? Tandon said that Mamdani and Bhagat should realise the nature of the petty bourgeoisie from the contrasting cases of Chile and Vietnam where under different practices the petty-bourgeoisie reacted differently to the revolution.

On the question of ruling classes in the neo- or semi-colony, Tandon criticised the 'critiques' for creating a rupture between the political and the economic which is un-Marxist. In their critique of Nabudere, Mamdani and Bhagat held that "in the case of a semi-colony there is a radical rupture between economic exploitation and political oppression. The state, the apparatus of oppression, is now managed by a class situated within the semi-colony; on the other hand imperialist exploitation continues". Here Tandon argued that Mamdani and Bhagat adopted a purely managerial concept of class for which they had earlier criticised Issa Shivji.

Mamdani and Bhagat held against Shivji that: "The analysis of imperialism must be integral to that of classes in the neo-colony". Yet in their 'criticism' of Nabudere, while purporting to understand the meaning of imperialism, they failed to give an integrated analysis of classes under imperialism. While Mamdani and Bhagat accused Shivji of making "a class analysis (which) is often abstracted from imperialism" they did exactly the same thing in their own critique of Nabudere.

Tandon pointed out that general theories should not be formulated for classes in neo-colonial states, but specific analyses that correspond to the reality of each neo-colonial state should be made. He further said that it is false to hold that a ruling class must be internal, and that it is possible for a ruling class or at least a section of it to be external. The dictatorship of the financial oligarchy over the neo-colonies proves this fact. The financial oligarchy rules in the neo-colony because it monopolises capital, turning the neo-colonies into markets for export of finance capital and manufactured goods as well as turning them into sources of raw materials. The financial oligarchy is the exploiter of the proletariat and peasantry in the neo-colony. It makes it possible for the "national bourgeoisie" to accumulate capital and complete the bourgeois revolution, since finance capital has divided the market, the whole neo-colonial world, which it reserves for its own capital and commodities. Lenin long ago pointed out:

> In a commodity-producing society, no independent development, or development of any sort whatsoever, is possible without capital. In Europe the dependent nations have both their own capital any easy access to it on a wide range of terms. The colonies [and today we can say the neo–colonies, if we take into account, as Lenin further pointed out, that self-determination of colonial countries belongs to the *political* sphere—Reviewers], have no capital of their own, or none to speak of, and under finance capital no colony [or neo-colony today] can obtain any except on terms of political submission. [Lenin, *Collected Works*, Vol. 22, p. 339].

If the financial oligarchy economically exploits a neo-colony and politically subdues it, then how can we say it is not ruling in the neo-colony? Can it then be argued that the ruling class in the neo-colony *must* be found within the neo-colony, creating the impermissible rupture of the dialectical link between the economic and the political?

Finally, Tandon querried Mamdani's and Bhagat's proposition that the peasant is exploited at the level of exchange while the worker is exploited at the level of production. He challenged them to show why the law of equivalents will not apply to commodities produced by a peasant as well as a worker. He pointed out that the law of equivalents (exchange of commodities at their values or exchange of commodities of equal value at their values) does not always operate in practice i.e. that prices deviate from their values, and continued:

> It is this deviation that brings about unequal exchange, i.e. an exchange of unequal values at the level of the market where prices, not values, rule. And this can happen as easily with the products of workers as with the products of the petty-commodity producers, and it can happen in exchange between the products of capitalist countries themselves as in the exchanges between the products of a capitalist country and those of a neo-colony.

He concluded that exploitation, appropriation of surplus value, takes place at the level of production. Exploitation cannot be explained by unequal exchange.

4. NABUDERE'S REPLY TO MAMDANI AND BHAGAT'S "COMMENTS" ON HIS MANUSCRIPT

Around the second half of July 1976, Nabudere replied to Bhagat's and Mamdani's "criticism". He pointed out that Mamdani's criticism of Shivji had pointed out that Shivji had failed to comprehend his task. Yet, he had concluded: ". . . We consider the book a step forward representing a stage in the development of Marxist-Leninist thought in our countries . . ." Nabudere pointed out that Mamdani was able to reach such a conclusion because although he disagreed in *form,* he was in agreement in *substance* with Shivji. In addition, he argued that Mamdani's insistence that his (Nabudere's) critiques of Issa Shivji's *Class Struggles in Tanzania* be restricted to a small circle of arbitrarily selected "comrades" was a clear betrayal of his effort to conceal errors of theory and ideology which had already beed disseminated in book form.

Thus Mamdani's half-hearted critique of Shivji, being opportunist, was unacceptable. Nabudere concluded that for Mahmood to repudiate Issa, therefore, he must first repudiate himself".

Turning to their comments on his manuscript, Nabudere pointed out that they were "left" only in form but "right" in essence. He said that the use of Chinese comrades references exhibited a certain amount of petty-bourgeois dogmatism and stereotyped analysis which amounted to opportunism. Nabudere then went on to expose the substance of the criticisms.

Imperialism and Contradictions

In this section Nabudere pointed out that the claim attributed to him of setting out to "analyse imperialism in its totality" was false because he had made no such claim. He added that anybody who had read the manuscript as a whole would not have failed to see its scope and purpose, namely – to defend Lenin's thesis: *Imperialism the Highest Stage of Capitalism,* and to try in a theoretical manner to connect it with Marx's *Capital.* The accomplishment of this task was acknowledged by Bhagat and Mamdani in their critique in these words: "The manuscript, particularly the relation it underlines between Marx's analysis of *Capital* and Lenin's *Theory of Imperialism* we consider to be a scientific contribution to the development of Marxist-Leninist ideology of our time". For this comment, Nabudere concluded thus: "Thank you. We never undertook to do more nor have we claimed to have done any more than that".

It followed, Nabudere argued, that the criticisms of Mamdani and Bhagat were drawn from outside the manuscript and that they tried to join issues on thesis he had not advanced. On the point advanced by Bhagat and Mamdani that he absolutizes the centralisation of capital and is oblivious of the intensifying contradiction within the camp of American imperialism since the Second World War, Nabudere challenged them to show where he denied this contradiction in the manuscript. He asserted that any casual reading of Part IV of the manuscript would reveal that the criticism had no foundation.

On the criticism that Nabudere "abstracts" centralisation of capital into a "world finance capital" he held that there was no such abstraction, and that world finance capital is the total capital of the financial oligarchies in their unity aimed at exploiting the total working class of the world under their hegemony. That this is the *reality* that Lenin analyses. He further said that this does not rule out contradictions among the financial oligarchies as is shown in Part III of the manuscript.

On the issue where Mamdani and Bhagat pointed out that Nabudere comes 'perilously' close to Kautsky and where they use a quote from Lenin to prove this, Nabudere pointed out that they quote Lenin incorrectly, and from a source where he does not even discuss the issue of Kautsky. He said that in *Imperialism,* where Lenin discusses Kautsky, he was refuting obscurantists like Mamdani and Bhagat who separated the political from the economic and that he, Nabudere, had nowhere in the manuscript faild to take into account the "political dimension", or said that "politics obediently follow economics". Nabudere also denied that he obscures the contradictions within the bourgeoisie. He pointed out that these critics had not bothered to look at Part III of the manuscript, where the rise of the financial oligarchy is treated historically and there was no need here for Mamdani and Bhagat to quote Mao Tse-tung's *On Contradiction.* In his entire analysis, he said, he put emphasis on the financial oligarchy since this is the bourgeoisie involved directly in imperialism.

Contradictions Between the Superpowers and the Second World and Relationship with the Third World

To the accusation that he had failed to analyse contradictions between the superpowers and the "Second World" as intermediate zones which are also "oppressed", Nabudere replied that this "oppression" was one-sidedly absolutized by his critics to the point where they saw no unity between these and the superpowers as exploiters of the Third World. He pointed out that he had shown that contradiction exists between monopolies whether immediate or otherwise this contradiction is over who should have the upper hand in exploiting labour both in the Second and Third World.

> This contradiction, generally non-antagonistic as it is within the same class— the bourgeoisie–for a greater share of the oppressed third world, at times breaks out in open war. You state that if we do not "grasp" this contradiction we cannot understand the formation of Euratom, Gaullism, etc. But we had shown that by grasping the "fundamental contradiction" among imperialist countries, we have also grasped the contradiction between the superpowers, among imperialist countries and among monopoly capitalist groups. All these stem from this fundamental contradiction.

On the point that Nabudere one-sidedly concludes that the Lome Convention is a victory for the monopolies of the U.S.A. and Japan he replied that the critics misunderstood the context because they didn't know the history of these conventions. If they had known they would have found that the ACP countries fought tooth and nail to remove preferential treatment formerly given by them to E.E.C. countries, insisting that their markets should be open to other countries. Since trade between third world countries with the socialist countries is almost non-existent, this meant the entry of U.S.A. and Japan in a big way – i.e. open door neo-colonialism, at least in the short run. It is in this sense that the multilateralisation of neo-colonialism in the Lome Convention was a victory for US and Japanese monopolies. Nabudere rapped the critics for not showing how the Convention was a "limited victory for the Third World" and for quoting *Peking Review* out of context on the issue, which he concluded, amounted to an opportunistic use of the source. *The Peking Review* position was that since the oppressed "national" or petty-bourgeoisie in the neo-colonies have a contradiction with imperialism, the proletariat has the greatest interest in deepening this contradiction in order to be able to generalise and popularise its case against imperialism on a broader front.

The question of nationalisation must also be viewed as part of this broader struggle. Mamdani and Bhagat had used the authority of Mao Tsetung to argue: "Nevertheless, these are anti-imperialist struggles and as such objectively form part of the world socialist revolution, as Mao Tsetung pointed out in *New Democracy*". This, Nabudere pointed out, was clearly a one-sided treatment of the question, because it implied that the petty bourgeoisie was capable of waging this struggle against imperialism. This view of nationalisations and the struggle for the "New Economic Order" coming "perilously" to the revisionist "non-capitalist" road, Nabudere pointed out further that Comrade Mao's authority was misused because he was describing the character of the two democratic revolutions, old and new, in *New Demoracy*. He was nowhere discussing nationalisations and the "New Economic Order".

On the accusation that he attempted only an economic analysis of imperialism, Nabudere pointed out that the critics contradicted themselves when in a similar comment on Shivji's book they stated the other one-sided view thus: "That property under concrete historical circumstances assume another legal form, in this case a public form, should not blind Marxist-Leninists to the fact that it still remains private (class) property". And concluding, Nabudere pointed out that the critics had not successfully shown that the Manuscript bears the faults they had purported to show. He further said that the manuscript contained a political appreciation of these forms of struggle in spite of the fact that change in legal form does not change property relations. The manuscript acknowledged these measures to be "important developments". The accusation that it makes only an "economic analysis" was thus rendered false and baseless. Nabudere further criticized the "critics" for undimensionally holding that, of all the fundamental contradictions, the principal contradiction was that between imperialism and the oppressed nations and quoting the *Proposal on the General Line of the International Communist Movement*, while the same *General Line* points out that:

> These contradictions [which it describes] and the struggles which they give rise to, are inter-related and influence each other. Nobody can obliterate any of these fundamental contradictions or subjectively substitute one for all the rest.

Finally, he pointed out that the criticism that the strategy against imperialism as expounded in the manuscript took a Trotskyist line is one-sidedly emphasizing the contradiction between capital and labour and substituting it for the rest, was groundless. He further said that this analysis on strategy is in line with the *General Line* on "The national democratic revolutionary movement . . ."

The New Democratic Revolution and the Neo-Colony

Here Nabudere pointed out that most of the criticisms of Mamdani and Bhagat on the new democratic revolution, classes in the neo-colony and the politics of struggle were centred around one pivotal-point–national capital and its contradiction with finance capital. However, the critics did not indicate the character of this contradiction under imperialist domination of the neo-colonies. Is it antagonistic or not? Nabudere held that the petty-bourgeoisie belong to the bourgeois class and thus their contradiction is basically no-antagonistic. Finance capital has an antagonistic contradiction with a neo-colony because it exploits the working class and peasantry there.

Unequal Exchange

Nabudere pointed out here that the wrong understanding of the contradiction between imperialism and the people led Mamdani and Bhagat to the populist position of unequal exchange. This position, he said, was that of Marx, which was that with the rise of capital, a movement is established where all production is increasingly turned into commodity production (i.e. for exchange in the market) and subjecting all labour-power, whether that of the worker or peasant, to the exploitation of capital. In this context, Marx pointed out:

> ...Wherever it takes root capitalist production destroys all forms of commodity production which are based either on the self-employment of the producer, or merely on the sale of excess product as commodities. Capitalist production first makes the production of commodities general and then, by degrees, transforms all commodity production into capitalist commodity production (*Capital*, Vol. II, p. 36).

Thus the accusation that nothing is said of the exploitation of the peasantry in the manuscript was baseless and populist. Exploitation is a scientific concept used in a capital-labour relation. That is why Marx talks of the "plunder, spoilation, entombment of aboriginal peoples" by merchant capital and of the 'exploitation' of labour by industrial capital. *In The Peasant Question*, Engels points out that:

This small peasant, just like the small handicraftsman, is therefore a toiler who differs from the modern proletariat in that he still possesses his instruments of labour; hence a survival of the past mode of production...

Whereas in the past his unit of production was self-sufficient), capitalist production put an end to this by its money economy and large-scale industry [*Selected Works*, Vol. 3, pp. 459-60].

Thus the cheap talk that the manuscript does not talk of the exploitation of the labour of the peasantry because it does not take the "unequal exchange" position is totally baseless.

Classes and the "Semi-Colony"

Here Nabudere pointed out that the question of classes is a concrete question. That although classes may be mentioned in their general relations in a major movement like imperialism, such treatment can only be meaningfully handled in a concrete way. Thus the question of the existence of "national bourgeoisie", "comprador bourgeoisie" or whatever other bourgeoisie in a neo-colony is not a general question but a concrete question for a concrete situation, a question of concrete class analysis of a particular neo-colony and not a generalisation of class analysis in all neo-colonies. This is what Comrade Mao Tse tung did for Chinese society. Nabudere also criticised his critics for confusing *neo-colonies* with semi-colonies and reducing these concepts to mere word-juggling.

A semi-colony, as the word suggests, is a country which has not been wholly or totally occupied by imperialism; its relationship with imperialism is based not on total occupation and colonisation but on unequal capitulationisttreaties. Turkey and China were such areas. 'Neo-colony' on the other hand refers to those countries which were brought under colonial rule and were totally occupied by imperialism but have achieved self-determination which, as Lenin emphasized, belongs to the political sphere. The new form of domination after self-determination is what is referred to as neo-colonialism. There was no need for "Marxist-Leninists" to confuse these concepts.

It was again pointed out that not all petty-bourgeoisie take part in production, i.e. in the labour process, and thus the critics take a one-sided view of this class which leads them to the conclusion that they are part of the "revolutionary masses". The *Communist Manifesto* was to show that this class, which is called "the lower middle class" in the Manifesto, includes: small manufacturers, shopkeepers, artisans and peasants. The *Manifesto,* although recognising their struggle against the bourgeoisie, does not see them one-sidedly as "part of the revolutionary masses". The *Manifesto* says of this class: "They are therefore not revolutionary, but conservative. Nay more, they are reactionary, for they try to roll back the wheel of history". The petty-bourgeoisie, Nabudere pointed out, is a vacillating class. In periods of prosperity, they gang up with the bourgeoisie and fight the proletariat. In periods of crisis, they increasingly join proletarian ranks and support its struggle. Even in times of crisis they join the struggles under proletarian leadership. Moreover, Nabudere added, Comrade Chou Enlai in his interview with Hinton pointed out: "According to a Marxist point of view the petty bourgeoisie belong to the bourgeois class and not to the working class or proletariat." In the last paragraphs Nabudere analysed forms of state dependence and criticised Mamdani and Bhagat for taking a dogmatic position when they talk as if all forms of state dependence are the same. He further exposed their confusion where they held that the international bougeoisie cannot rule because there is no international state. This same question was raised by Hirji and we shall deal with it later.

In conclusion, Nabudere pointed out these criticisms were a jumble of confusion. "We therefore reject your criticism as wholly without foundation and adding nothing to its substance!" He also pointed out that he could not accept that the debate be closed and some comrades be excluded. He said that proletarian interests demand open debate so that issues and errors could be brought to light and not be kept in the dark.

There were then murmurings behind the scenes that an open debate among the left was not healthy because it would "split the left". This criticism was groundless, since Shivji's book had already come out in print, and Mamdani's and Nabudere's manuscripts were freely circulating on the campus.

The demand that an open debate be scotched because it tends to "split the left" is usually the demand of those who have something to hide about the weakness of their positions. Lenin, when confronted with such petty-bourgeois demands, was merciless. In a letter written to Appolinaria Yakubova in 1900, he wrote, *inter alia*:

> I am not in the least ashamed to fight – seeing that things have gone so far that the disagreements have concerned fundamental issues, that an atmosphere has been created of mutual non-comprehension, mutual distrust and complete discordance of views... To get rid of this oppressive atmosphere, even a furious thunderstorm, and not merely a literary polemic, can (and should) be welcomed.

Lenin continued:

> And there is no reason to be so much afraid of a struggle: a struggle may cause annoyance to some *individuals,* but it will clear the air, define attitudes in a precise and straightforward manner, define which differences are important and which unimportant, define where people stand – those who are taking a completely different path and those party comrades who differ only on minor points.

And further:

> Without struggle there cannot be a sorting out, and without a sorting out there cannot be any successful advance, nor can there be any *lasting unity*. And those who are beginning the struggle at the present time are by no means *destroying* unity. There is no longer any unity, it has already been destroyed all along the lines... an open frank struggle is one of the essential conditions for *restoring* unity... Yes, *restoring!* The kind of "unity"... that makes us resent the publication of statements revealing what views are being propagated under the guise of ... (Marxism)... Such "unity" is sheer cant, it can only aggravate the disease and make it assume a chronic, malignant form. That an open, frank and honest struggle will cure this disease and create a really united, vigorous and strong... movement I do not for a moment doubt.

And Lenin concluded:

> Of course struggle in the press will cause more ill-feeling and give us a good many hard knocks, but we are not so thin skinned as to fear knocks! [Emphasis added]. To wish for struggle without knocks, differences without

struggle, would be the height of naivete, and if the struggle is waged *openly* it will be a hundred times better... and will lead, I repeat, a hundred times faster to lasting *unity*.

Mao Tsetung on the Need to Combat Liberalism

Mao Tse-tung's "Combat Liberalism" is a further indictment of those who prefer to hide behind conspiratorial murmurings behind doors rather than an open debate, and who preach an unprincipled unity with "friends" rather than establishing unity on the basis of the formula *unity-struggle-unity*. We quote some relevant passages, but the whole essay of Mao's is worth reading.

> We stand for active ideological struggle because it is the weapon for ensuring unity within... the revolutionary organisations in the interest of our fight... But liberalism rejects ideological struggle and stands for unprincipled peace, thus giving rise to a decadent, philistine attitude and bringing about political degeneration in certain units and individuals in the Party and the revolutionary organizations...
> To let things slide for the sake of peace and friendship when a person has clearly gone wrong, and refrain from principled argument because he is on old acquaintance, ... Or to touch on the matter lightly instead of going into it thoroughly, so as to keep on good terms. The result is that both the organization and the individual are harmed. This is one type of liberalism. To indulge in irresponsible criticism in private instead of actively putting forward one's suggestions to the organization. To say nothing to people to their faces but to gossip behind their backs... To show no regard for collective life but to follow one's own inclination. This is a second type.

As such how could an open debate on the general issues raised be prevented? These behind-the-scene grumblings and gossips continued until Karim Hirji's "Criticism" came in around 22 August 1976.

5. KARIM HIRJI'S REJOINDER AGAINST NABUDERE

Karim Hirji raised nothing new in his criticism and therefore we can treat it briefly here. He raised issues of class, state, ruling class and Kautskyism of which Nabudere was again accused. At the same time he was accused of economism. According to Karim, as to Mamdani and Bhagat, the financial oligarchy cannot rule because there is no international state, and since according to them a separate state implies a separate ruling class, Hirji compared Nabudere to Kievsky whom Lenin had criticised for economism. The question of transitional forms of state dependence was raised again as well as the qestion of contradictions within imperialism. Karim Hirji accused Nabudere for allegedly seeing the financial oligarchy as the only bourgeoisie – an accusation also levelled by Mamdani and Bhagat. Hirji asserted that under certain conditions politics determine the base, and suggested that this is the case in the neo-colonies.

The first people to reply to Hirji's comments were Sam Magara and A. Kayonga around the end of August 1976.

6. S. MAGARA AND A. KAYONGA'S DEFENCE OF NABUDERE AGAINST HIRJI'S ATTACKS

They pointed out that although Hirji said "progressive circles" were surprised to learn that Shivji's book was neo-Trotskyite, idealist, etc. he did not say a word in defence of Shivji's thesis. They also deplored the fact that Karim Hirji had used slanderous language. While the use of scientific categories such as "petty-bourgeoisie", "neo-Marxist", "neo-Trotskyist", or "eclectic" was permissible, as scientific concepts, there was no need to use petty slandering as a substitute for argument.

On Classes

Magara and Kayonga defended Nabudere's thesis showing the falseness of Hirji's accusation when he said that Nabudere saw the financial oligarchy as the sole bourgeoisie. One had only to read Nabudere's manuscript to discover that this was not so. They pointed out further that it is not a "fundamental break" with Marxism to state that the petty-bourgeoisie is a portion of the bourgeois class. Morever Nabudere had shown on the authority of Marx and Chou Enlai that the petty bourgeoisie belong to the bourgeois class.

If Hirji had depended on Mao's authority, namely that under certain conditions politics determine the base, to argue that the financial oligarchy, although the economically dominant was not a ruling class in the neo-colony, then it was incumbent upon Hirji to show whether the "certain condition" of which Chairman Mao was talking included the neo-colonial state. He was challenged to show that a neo-colony is an exception to the general rule that the economic base determines the superstructure, the politics, and that the ruling class is as a rule the economically dominant class. Hirji was challenged to show how the politics of neo-colonial states determines the economic base. Magara and Kayonga also showed that Hirji's accusation of Nabudere as being Kautskyite was baseless. Nabudere's views had nothing in common with those of Kautsky. Kautsky defined imperialism not as a phase of capitalism but as a policy "preferred" by finance capital. Nabudere set out in his manuscript to defend Lenin's *Imperialism, the Highest Stage of Capitalism* clearly showing that imperialism is a phase of capitalism. Nabudere also showed that amalgamation and concentration of capital led to monopoly thus he did not regard imperialism as a policy 'preferred' by finance capital. Nabudere had also refuted in his manuscript Kautsky's position that imperialism is a tendency of "industrial" countries to annex agrarian countries. Nabudere points out that imperialism is the rule of finance capital which strives to dominate the whole world. Thus Hirji's accusations were shown to be baseless.

7. NABUDERE'S 81-PAGE REPLY TO KARIM HIRJI

Around 10 September 1976, Nabudere released his 81-page reply to Karim Hirji. We shall only summarise the main points. In this reply, Nabudere showed the idealist positions of Hirji for holding that a separate state implies a separate ruling class. He pointed out that this method of transubstantiating reality into ideas and presenting ideas as reality springs from the idealism of Plato which was perfected by Kant. And it manifests itself in the neo-Kantianism of Rikert Dilthey on which Durkheim and Weber based their bourgeois theories while claiming to be materialist.

Economisms and the National Question

Under this readings, Nabudere reviewed Lenin's struggle against Kautsky, Kievsky and Rosa Luxemburg. We have already dealt with Kautsky. We shall here restrict outselves to the review of Kievsky and Luxemburg.

Nabudere pointed out what Lenin meant when he accused people of the Kievsky type of economism and struggled against them in his famous: *What Is To Be Done, Critical Remarks on the National Question*: and in "Caricature of Marxism and Imperialist Economism". He showed further that economism was an opportunist trend in the Russian Social Democratic Party whereby the Russian Economists argues that because of the level of capitalist development in Russia, political struggles of the proletariat were "impossible" and that therefore the working class should restrict itself to economic struggles for better working conditions, higher wages, etc.

Other deviationists, particularly Rosa Luxemburg, sought to implement a similar line on the national question holding that political self-determination of oppressed nations under imperialism is unachievable, and that political struggles for political independence are "illusory" and impracticable. Since history has proved this theory bankrupt we shall not go further into it. The point here is that the "economism" that Hirji accused of Nabudere is not the economism that Lenin meant. On the contrary, petty bourgeois theorists, who see Marxist analysis as 'economism' or at other times as "economic determinism" had long levelled this accusation against Marx. Among the first of such petty-bourgeois theorists to accuse Marx of economism was Proudhon who was followed by Durkheim and Weber. This "economism" or what the bourgeois and petty bourgeois see as "economism" has nothing in common with the Leninist understanding of economism. Thus Hirji was gravely mistaken and distorting Lenin when he quoted him to support his case of "economism" which as we have shown is a petty bourgeois distortion of Marxism.

Hirji, however, being eclectic landed in a contradiction. Having accused Nabudere of "economism" he then goes ahead to call him a Kautskyite, alleging that he sees imperialism as a "policy". This would mean that, as Lenin pointed out, he separates the politics of imperialism from its economics in which case he would be accused of 'politicism'. Now isn't it absurd to accuse one, as Hirji does, of 'economism' and 'politicism' at the same time!.

Nabudere showed further that Hirji's conception of economism is that of the bourgeois and petty bourgeois types who deny the materialist conception of history which holds that the production of real life is the basis of all ideas. Hirji does this to create room for his idealist theorising that it would be "economistic" to deny a "new ruling class" which must come into being with a "separate stage" in the neo-colony. Since Mao Tse-tung "asserts" that under "certain conditions" politics determine the base Hirji then concludes that it is "implied" (sic) that a ruling class, upon the rise of a separate state, would emerge. Hirji, however, does not indicate what "certain conditions" Chairman Mao meant. Chairman Mao has never said that politics in a neo-colony determine the economic base. Moreover, since self-determination belongs to the political sphere, then Hirji's capitalist ruling class rises "non-economically". Now certainly this is not "economism" but probably "politicism". Such are the a priori idealist assertions of Hirji which deny the dominant place of the economic base vis-a-vis the superstructure. Moreover, as we pointed out, the petty bourgeoisie belong to the bourgeois class according to Marxism. It is therefore unacceptable for Hirji to disjoin them from the economically dominant stratum, namely the financial oligarchy. It is a very well known fact that under imperialism the petty bourgeoisie may man the bourgeois state, while effective political power is exercised by the financial oligarchy precisely because of its economic power.

We repeat that the neo-colonies have no capital of their own, or non to speak of, and under finance capital no neo-colony can obtain any except on terms of political submission. This is the source of the whole outcry on "The New International Economic Order, "Transfer of Resources", "Transfer of Technology" etc. Hirji does not understand this, because according to him the financial oligarchy cannot rule as no international state exists. If that is so why this outcry and "begging", we ask our dear Hirji.

In his conclusion Nabudere criticised Mahmood Mamdani according to whom imperialism is "external" to Uganda and the 'enemy' 'principally' is the nascent commercial bourgeoisie. (See *Maji Maji,* No. II, August 1976). Now one wonders whose commerce this nascent commercial bourgeoisie carries on. Whose commodities to they circulate? And can this class survive without the producers of the commodities? And whose capital is involved in the production of these commodities, if it is not of finance capital?

Again who principally exploits labour in Uganda? Is it the nascent commercial bourgeoisie or finance capital? If finance capital has reduced Uganda to its market allowing only a commercial bourgeoisie, and if again it is finance capital that exploits the labour of Ugandan proletariat, how then can Mamdani hold that imperialism is external and that so long as imperialism does not invade, the enemy remains principally internal? We would like to tell Mamdani that imperialism invaded long ago and has never left. Mamdani should tell us when it did. If it did, then what do we mean when we say Uganda is a neo-colony? What does Mamdani think the neo-colonial state is – a people's state?

Mamdani holds that if we say the enemy is imperialism we are disarming the working class ideologically and sheltering what he calls the "ruling class" (the nascent commercial bourgeoisie) in the camp of the people. We hold that in the struggle against imperialism during the new democratic revolution and under correct proletarian practice, this "commercial bourgeoisie" being oppressed by imperialism has the chance to join the popular united front. Or at least a major part of it can be won to the proletarian side. This is what we mean by united front or broad alliances against imperialism, as Chairman Mao has pointed out. Does broad alliance in a united front mean *"sheltering"* the ruling class in the camp of the people and disarming the revolutionary forces ideologically?

8. NABUDERE CRITIQUE OF MAMDANI'S POLITICS AND CLASS FORMATION IN UGANDA

At the end of January 1977, when Mamdani's book came out in book form, Nabudere brought out a critical review of it as he had promised in his critique of Shivji's *Class Struggles in Tanzania.*

He began by pointing out that the terms like petty bourgeoisie, neo-Trotskyite etc. were not terms of abuse as Mamdani and others had taken them to be. Nabudere quoted Lenin in support of this view:

> Our opponents display remarkable shortsightedness in regarding the terms *reactionary and petty bourgeois* as polemical abuse, when they have perfectly *historical philosophical* meaning. (*Collected Works,* Vol. 2, p. 516).

Elsewhere, Lenin points out that the term "reactionary" for example is employed in its *historico-philosophical* sense:

> Describing only the ERROR of the theoreticians who take modes for their theories from obsolete forms of society. It does not apply at all to the personal qualities of the theoreticians or their programmes.

Citing examples, Lenin continued: "Everybody knows that neither Sismondi nor Proudhon were reactionaries in the normal sense of the term". Nabudere pointed out further that such other terms as neo-Marxist and neo-Trotskyist refer to trends within the international working class movement. Indeed Mamdani's publishers and *friends* who recommended his book for publication because they see it in very favourable light cannot be said to have been abusing him when they eulogised it thus:

> It is in my view very nearly a perfect piece of work, as a work of art as well as a work of scholarship. It is WITHOUT QUESTION an uncommonly fine specimen of the NEO-MARXIST UNDERDEVELOPMENT schools – indeed, probably its best fruit to date in African studies... (Spring, 1976, brochure issued by Monthly Review Press).

This description has been conveniently removed from the Heinemann edition, for circulation in East Africa although the Monthly Review edition for circulation in USA still retains it.

Mamdani's eclecticism and contradictions are difficult to disentangle and summarise. We refer the reader to Nabudere's and Tandon's critiques. Here we shall confine ourselves to the major weakness of Mamdani's thesis.

First Mahmood Mamdani abstracts class formation and class struggle in a neo-colony such as Uganda from imperialism. This is presumably because to him imperialism is external.

According to Mamdani, "The Uganda economy was an undeveloped economy integrated into the world capitalist market..." He does not show how this happened so concretely. Thus he sees the crisis of imperialism in Uganda as that of balance of payments crisis because of unequal exchange where instead of "an inflow" of capital each year there was an outflow of capital! If Uganda was integrated into the capitalist system, how then does the crisis become a balance of payments crisis and not that of imperialist exploitation and oppression?

According to Mamdani, a communal mode co-exists with the capitalist mode of production in Uganda (p. 140) whereby labour is drastically paid below its value. One wonders how labour-power could be paid below its value if it was not part of the capitalist mode for them the law of value would not apply.

Mamdani often finds himself caught up in contradictions. "Underdevelopment" is blamed on merchant capital, although its primacy is seen also as the "primacy" of metropolitan capital to which it is "tied in a dependent relation". Thus a dualism is created. Mamdani tells us that the Indian "commercial bourgeoisie" dominated production at the level of the "territorial economy" although the metropolitan bourgeoisie "dominated the entire colonial system" (p. 108). We are told that "Indian capital" as represented by Narandas Rajaram and Co. Limited "at one stroke" struck a blow to the domination of the (cotton) industry by British capital. Then we are told that the capital did not actually belong to Rajaram but to the National Bank of India whose capital, as Mamdani came to realise, was not Indian but British finance capital. The bank in spite of its name belonged to the British monopoly capitalists.

Lacking the understanding of imperialism Mamdani's "class struggles" turn out to be no "class struggles" but contradictions among the petty-bourgeoisie. A class struggle is created between the "African petty-bourgeoisie and the Indian commercial bourgeoisie" and their contradiction is postponed in 1969 to 1971 when it is "resolved by the *coup d'etat*. The passing of the Cooperative Societies Ordinance "to boost the organisational strength" of African kulaks and traders resulted in "class struggle" although there was a "contradiction" between the traders and kulaks. The principal contradiction is seen as that between the African petty-bourgeoisie and Asian capital. This "contradiction" surfaced with Amin's ascendency to power after "the state had consolidated its state apparatus" and was resolved eight months later when Amin called the Asians to a conference in January 1972 after which they were expelled. Thus the "principal contradiction" was resolved! In this way Mamdani reduces the scientific theories of "class struggles" and "contradiction" to an absurdity.

Imperialism and the proletariat hardly feature in Mamdani's class struggles and contradictions. Because Mamdani does not understand imperialism, he also does not understand what the national question means and consequently he does not know what the new democratic revolution is about. This is why he hold that those who say the enemy is imperialism will shelter the "ruling class" (which happens to be nascent commercial bourgeoisie) in the camp of the "people". Chairman Mao long ago advised us that:

> ... in studying any complex process in which there are two or more contradictions, we must devote every effort to finding its principal contradiction. Once this principal contradiction is grasped, all problems can readily be resolved. This is the method that Marx taught us in his study of capitalist society. Likewise Lenin and Stalin taught us this method when they studied *Imerialism* and the general crisis of capitalism and when they studied the Soviet Economy. There are thousands of scholars and men of action who do not understand it, and the result is that, lost in a fog, they are unable to get to the heart of the problem and naturally cannot find a way to resolve its contradictions (*Selected Works*, Vol. 1, p. 332. Emphasis added).

Such are our Mamdani's who, lost in a fog, create "principal" contradictions out of nowhere only to "resolve" some in eight months and to postpone others. These "contradictions" exist only in their brains. This is idealism *par excellence* and to us it is totally unacceptable. We hold that the principal contradiction is that between the people of Uganda and finance capital (imperialism) and its local comprador agents who oppress and exploit them. The contradiction within the petty-bourgeoisie and between the petty-bourgeoisie and the proletariat are secondary. Accordingly, the proletariat in the new democratic revolution rallies the petty-bourgeoisie behind it, forming a broad united front against imperialism, smashing the neo-colonial state and all supporters of imperialism who refuse to join the united front and establish the democratic dictatorship of the revolutionary classes and later of the proletariat.

Chairman Mao teaches us that the contradiction among the people as the case may be, can, if "properly handled be transformed into a non-antagonistic one" during the fight against imperialism. Such is the strategy of the proletariat and such is our stand! We leave 'pure theorising' to the scholars and men of action who are lost in a fog.

CONCLUSION

The debate has clarified many issues and contributed to our ideological development. We are convinced that the only way to advance is through struggle against incorrect and anti-Marxist views. This is why we have carried out a relentless struggle against the views of Mamdani, Shivji and others. It is a pity that these gentlemen have mistaken these criticisms for personal attack. That mistaken position of theirs is unacceptable and we shall continue to criticise them. While not replying to the criticisms so far made of them they have further made no effort to criticise themselves. This suggests to us that they still stick to their erroneous line. If that is so there is no platform for unity since we cannot compromise on major issues of Marxism-Leninism. This is because the two lines are diametrically opposed on these issues. We therefore request all comrades, and we cannot emphasize enough the necessity of all comrades to clarify themselves on these issues. We hope no more comrades will get "lost in a fog" or it they do, they should have the courage and initiative to break through it. This can only be done through study and further study. For as Lenin said, "Without revolutionary theory there is no revolutionary movement".

31

COMMENTS ON THE MANUSCRIPT*

Rohini Banaji

Dear Dan,

I'm sorry I didn't have much opportunity to talk to you while I was there, but I have been reading your manuscript and I would like to make a few comments on that as well as on your interventions at Marc's seminar.

You say on page 383 that, 'whereas the bourgeoisie became triumphant over feudalism and absolutism in Europe with mass support of the oppressed peasantry, no such conditions for creating this old bourgeois revolution existed in the colonies. Whereas the change from feudalism led rapidly to economic development and emancipation of the peasantry from feudal exploitation... such economic development and the emancipation of the peasant masses in the colonies and semi-colonies were impossible under imperialism'. Since you make no attempt to explain why this is so, the statement remains a mere assertion. I think this is because you fail to conceptualise the exact relations existing between big capital and the peasantry, and this impression is confirmed by your statement at the seminar that there are no intermediaries between finance capital and the petty producers. Empirically this is not correct; in fact very often those who are directly in contact with the petty producers are small traders or usurers, who often succeed in accumulating a considerable amount of money-wealth which is sometimes later invested in production. Clearly this process is quite distinct from the accumulation of capital which is simultaneously going on in the hands of the big bourgeoisie; you have to recognise that the relations of production are not purely capitalist ones, because otherwise you would be totally unable to explain the fact that capitalist laws of motion such as the tendency for the productivity of labour to rise do not operate in these cases. On the other hand, your argument has an element of truth, since whatever accumulation of money-wealth, and even of capital, that takes place is not completely unfettered but operates within the limits, the framework, set by big capital. It is this precise relationship which has to be investigated, and I think that if you modify your argument in this way it will be much, much stronger than the argument you have been trying to put forward, which is easy to pull apart both empirically and theoretically.

I have been referring to big capital rather than imperial or metropolitan capital. I think you very seriously underestimate the degree and the possiblity of capital accumulation taking place locally, with the curious result that although explicitly you throw out that dependency-under-development thesis, you inadvertently let it in through the backdoor. Let us take a few examples. On page 406 you say, 'In some countries where industrial capital had enabled it, there developed a national industrial bourgeoisie (e.g., India, Brazil). But with the rise of finance capital this bourgeoisie became dependent on international monopoly capital. The result was that such "national bourgeoisie" could not develop the productive forces in these

---

The Political Economy of Imperialism, Dan Wadada Nabudere.

countries on its own and consequently ended up serving monopoly interests of the financial oligarchies'. Here you could be saying one of two things. you may be saying that if the bourgeoisie of the countries were completely cut off from all other capital it would find it difficult or impossible to develop the productive forces. If so, then it is a banality, because what capital is not dependent on other capital in this sense, and also serves the interests of other capital at the same time? Commodity production, and therefore necessarily capitalist commodity production, is by its nature an interdependent system. But if you are arguing that such capital has <u>no</u> independence and has no option but to serve the interests of foreign capital, then you are wrong. Really big Indian capital (Tatas, Birlas, etc.) can bargain with European, American and Japanese capital both directly and through the state, and at times get the better of them; it can compete on equal terms internationally, get contracts in third countries at their expense, and so on.

I think your argument is the latter, because you later state that 'we have shown throughout our analysis that since the colony, semi-colony and neo-colony has no "national capital" of its own, or if it has any, it is very insignificant, if follows that a "national bourgeoisie", whether private or public, is bound to be subservient to imperialism, since their "national industry" is objectively a part of monopoly enterprise in the sense that it serves it', (p. 504). And again: 'We assert that although this "national bourgeoisie" objectively serves monopoly interests, it nevertheless has a contradiction with imperialism and finance capital, because it is precisely this domination by finance capital that makes it impossible for it to emerge fully as a national bourgeoisie. This therefore is a subjective contradiction, because, as we maintain, historically no conditions exist for its emergence as such a bourgeoisie'. What these passages betray is a failure to conceptualise relations internal to the capitalist class, i.e., relations between one capital and another. <u>All</u> capital is objectively dependent on other capital, since <u>no</u> capital could exist without other capital. At the same time <u>all</u> capital has an objective contradiction with other capital one capitalist always kills many, as Marx says. There is nothing here that is peculiar to 'national capital', in 'colonies, semi-colonies and neo-colonies'. Concepts like 'subservient', 'domination', etc., are more reminiscent of Samir Amin than Marx and do not really help us to understand the relations between different capitals.

This last passage quoted refers to 'subjective' contradictions which do not correspond to any 'objective' contradictions and therefore spring, presumably, out of the heads of the 'subservient' capitalists. The same theory of ideology (or rather lack of such a theory) lies at the back of the following passage: 'These forms of exploitation are objectively ascertainable and constitute the material reality with which we are concerned. The monopoly bourgeoisie, like their henchmen the petty bourgeoisies, are not interested in bringing out this reality to the people because this would expose them as an exploiting class', (p. 400). Ideology is seen here as a <u>conscious deception,</u> hence as something proceeding out of the evil brains of the bourgeoisie. What is lacking from this conception is a theory of fetishism, of the <u>necessary</u> transformation which takes place when the relations of capitalist production are manifested in the world of phenomena (the value-form, the wage-form, etc. See esp. Marx's *Capital*, Vol. 1, Chap. 1, section 4 and the chapter on the wage-form; also the addenda to Part 3 of the "Theory of Surplus Value"). This mystification therefore has objective causes and can be penetrated only by the use of Marx's scientific method. The monopoly bourgeoisie and their petty-bourgeois henchmen are as much victims of it as the exploited masses—unless, that is, they spend their spare time secretly studying Marx and applying his method of analysis!

One final point. Your failure to examine anywhere the role of the Russian state would seem to be pure opportunism to the Indian proletariat, for examle, since it is as much exploited by Russian 'capital' (let us call it that provisionally) as by any other – perhaps more so. But in order to understand that Russian role, you would not only have to be better equipped theoretically, but also you would have to take a slightly more careful look at Russian history. Unless you have done that, you are not really in a position to write an account of imperialism today.

To sum up, then: your book gives the impression that you have studied Lenin on imperialism with some care, but using it as a short-cut to a study of Marx's *Capital* rather than as a supplement. Thus many key concepts are either missing or misused in your analysis, and your formulations often have a non-Marxist ring. Going carefully through all three volumes of *Capital* before writing a book on imperialism may sound like a laborious way of doing things but, to quote Marx himself, "there is no royal road to science, and only those who do not dread the fatiguing climb of its steep paths have a chance of gaining its luminous summit's—(Preface to the French edition). Maybe you could discuss this with Marc, since he seems to share some of your ideas, and perhaps also with Yash, since he seems to understand the necessity for a thorough grasp and careful use of Marxist categories.

I hope you don't think I have been hypercritical. The reason I have been so critical is that I was told you might publish it as a book, and it seemed a shame to let it be published without any improvements. And now that I have taken the trouble to write you my comments on your book, perhaps you will do the same for me and let me know your comments and criticisms of my manuscript. I am sure you will find much to criticise, but I am interested to know <u>how</u> you do it, since you were absent from both the discussions. In any case, you may find some of the ideas there useful for your work, as also some of the ideas in my paper on Amin.

With fraternal greetings,
Rohini

P.S. Although I have not so far said so, I <u>do</u> think your project is a worthwhile one, and you have made a heroic attempt to tackle it! But that is all the more reason why you should make it as good as possible.

A REPLY

D.W. Nabudere

Dear Rohini,

I thank you for your letter I received a few days ago. I am sorry that during your stay I did not have the opportunity to talk to you. This was caused by circumstances beyond my control hence my inability to attend both your talks.

I am glad that you took an early opportunity to comment on my manuscript. I am also glad to hear that you did not accept my interventions with Mahmood Mamdani, author of *Politics and Class Formation in Uganda*. This debate will continue for some time and is a healthy development which will enable us to further comprehend modern imperialism, and hopefully get away from the usual scholastic sophistry of 'neo-Marxist' and Trotskyite writings.

1. Having said this, I would like to say straight away that I find some of your own comments on my manuscript scholastic, too, running away from the essence of the problem of imperialism. Firstly, I do not believe I understand what your query about my statement on p. 383 of the manuscript is all about. It seems to me self-evident that whereas the old bourgeois revolution was characterised by mass involvement in the national movement by the peasantry, this is not the case with the bourgeois-democratic movements in the neo-colony, hence the historic role of the proletariat in providing leadership to other oppressed classes. This is not only self-evident from the analysis in the manuscript, if you care to read up to page 387, wherein reference is made to Stalin and Mao Tsetung, but more importantly the statement can be explained from Lenin's analysis of the national question. It is also a historical fact.

You will therefore agree that the discussion in these pages does not amount to mere assertions!!

Secondly it seems to me that the inference you draw from my analysis on these pages has no relevance whatsoever to it. This is because you seem to infer from it (in which sense the analysis is not clear) the question of the intermediary role of other 'capitals' between the petty-producers and 'big capital'. I cannot see how your discussions of this question has any relevance to the analysis of the old and new democratic struggles, as discussed in the manuscript, and hence I am not replying to your comments on the intermediary role of other capitals in this connection. I deal with this question immediately below.

2. The assertion made by you, Mahmood and a number of 'neo-Marxists', both at this (University) Hill and elsewhere, that merchant capital plays a mediatory role in circulation of commodities in the era of imperialism under monopoly capitalism is not new. Our thesis, which is based on Lenin's definition and analysis of finance capital and the concrete manner in which finance capital operates in the colonial and neo-colonial countries, is not a matter open to mystification. I nowhere deny that petty traders, petty merchants and usurers do 'mediate' in the circulation of commodities, but what we demand is that you concretely analyse the manner in which this capital operates independently of finance capital and in which way it contradicts finance capital.

The discussion in Marc's seminar focuses finance capital on Kay's book* (which I hope you have read) in which he maintains that it is 'merchant capital' at the service of 'industrial capital' which predominates in production in the neo–colony. Kay defines finance capital as 'circulating capital'. It was this misconception that we were querying. It seems to us that when we are analysing a major movement like imperialism, it is unscientific to bring in side issues of no real significance. An analysis of a specific social formation was to investigate that extent to which 'merchant capital' and other 'small capitals' mediate, although we would add a caveat: do not create capitals and then allocate 'classes' to them. 'Class analysis' based on such mental constructs are highly pedantic and unreal.

3. You speak of the 'possibility of capital accumulation taking place locally'. This also has not been denied. What we cannot accept is that such accumulation proceeds from circulation. Any accumulation from circulation can only be a hoard. Once the hoard enters into production it is then creating real accumulation, and here it is acting as finance capital, not as merchant capital. What we have maintained is that, in the era of finance capital, in which concentration of production and capital leads to elimination of trade between monopolised industries and the present era in which the transnational monopoly is increasingly

*Development and underdevelopment: A Marxist Analysis, Geoffrey Kay.

integrated both vertically and horizontally, it is unscientific to talk of merchant capital. We hold that any capital accumulated locally which may form part of 'national capital', being in this case the total capital of the total exploiting class, is increasingly centralised and put to use by the financial oligarchy of the imperialist countries in the neo-colony. To this extent such 'national capital' becomes part of capitalist accumulation on a world scale, and 'national capital' can be analysed and understood as such. An analysis of finance capital in the neo-colony is also an analysis of 'national capital' and of the classes that engage in its production and appropriation.

Your use of the word 'big capital' instead of 'metropolitan or imperial capital' is not understood in view of Lenin's concept of finance capital, and is indeed an effort on the part of many 'neo-Marxists' and Trotskyites to underplay Lenin's analysis. Your reference to the Birlas and Tatas as being capable of competing 'on equal terms' with the monopolies is subjectivist and in fact contradicts your case of the interdependence of capital. Of course the Birlas will operate in the US and European markets and even exploit third countries, for example Tanzania. But they do so not as 'Indian capital' but as part and parcel of finance capital. This is evidenced by the fact that the most dynamic sector of Indian industry today is the one which operates on foreign monopoly licences and to which technology is 'sold'. In fact, what is happening is that, because of the extreme form of present-day monopoly concentration, these licences, patents and other technological inputs are tied to exports of finance capital to India and are processes through which 'Indian capital' is centralised and put to use by the financial oligarchies. What therefore appear as Indian production and competition in world markets is finance capital in its global aspect and its reproduction and accumulation. That is why we maintain that your 'conceptualisation' of the Birlas, Tatas and whatever other 'national bourgeoisie' as having 'independence' and having 'option' not to 'serve the interests of foreign capital' is subjectivist; it does not accord with reality.

Moreover this conceptualisation is unscientific and ahistorical because the rise of 'national bourgeoisies' in history is not distinguished, as Lenin aptly points out in his *Critical Remarks on the National Question*. The rise of the English national bourgeoisie, which erects itself on the tomb of feudalism and brings itself up on the basis of a national and international markets, whose national capital is formed on the basis of internal and external primitive accumulation, and which leads an entirely transformed society, cannot be compared to a so-called Indian 'national bourgeoisie' which only arises under the armpit of finance capital, with no developed home market of its own, heading a lopsided economy and an untransformed society and which itself survives and operates so long as finance capital exists in India. This is why we think you over-emphasize 'the objective contradictions of capitals' *inter se*. All capital has a basic unity and it is this unity which is of interest to us in analysing the principal contradiction between capital and labour on a world scale. Such analysis is only possible with Lenin's concept of finance capital.

In our view, relations internal to the bourgeoisie are important but not determinant in the struggles that we characterise as anti-imperialist. The intra-class struggles are united in their objective role of exploiting labour. These are therefore minor or secondary contradictions which, nevertheless, the proletariat ought to exploit. You are right however in pointing out that the words 'subjective contradiction' might have the implication you indicate. Our point however is a valid one; it is that the aspiration of a 'national bourgeoisie' to develop a national capital independent of finance capital is historically out of the question in the colony, semi-colony or neo-colony.

Thus words like subservient or domination must be understood in this context, and have no moral connotations that are reminiscent of Samir Amin. We do not accept the mere engagement in abstractions that are not related to reality by hiding behind the 'pure categories' with which Trotskyism and 'neo-Marxism' have recently become so fascinated since the appearance of the *Grundrisse*. We know that there is no field in which Trotskyism excels more than in 'pure abstractions' which result in sophistry and pedantic debates that have led to more hair-splitting than anything else. We can refer you to many passages in *Capital* and other writings where Marx uses words like "subjugation" or "domination"; similarly, Lenin. These are not reminiscent of Samir Amin. The context must be understood. Our attack on Amin is based on more than mere use of words; his whole analysis is eclectic and unscientific. It is petty bourgeois.

4. Finally, we do not accept your unprincipled accusation that our work is opportunistic to the working class in India because it does not deal with social-imperialism. First of all, it was never our purpose to do so, since our explicit aim was to restate Lenin's thesis. We had not the time nor the material to grapple with the issue of social-imperialism – a phenomenon which is still evolving and an area on which not enough theoretical work has been done. I understand you have written on this issue and no doubt we shall learn from it. But that should be no excuse for imputing opportunism on our part. Any careful study of the manuscript will reveal our ideological position (despite your assertion of our lacking one), and the issue of social-imperialism will be adequately handled when the time for it comes. You would seem to imply by this criticism that social-imperialism exploits India 'perhaps more so' than western imperialism. While we agree that social-imperialism is increasingly challenging western imperialism in India, we would not accept this implication. In our view, western imperialism under US-led finance capital still accounts for far more of the exploitation of the Indian working class than social-imperialism.

Finally, while appreciating your comments very much we would like to say that a little more of the substance would have been even more helpful. We also detect an element of 'aristocratic intellectualism' which is alien to us and is most unacceptable.

32

FOOTNOTE TO A CONFUSED DEBATE

Rohini Banaji

Having been consistently attacked for years by authentic Trotskyites, I was amused to see myself described as 'the Trotskyite Rohini Banaji' in D.W. Nabudere's 'The Politics and Political Economy of Imperialism: A Reply'. I presume the cause of this reference is my 'advocating the Trotskyist nonsense of 'world revolution'(see D.W. Nabudere, 'A Caricature of Marxism-Leninism'). I will take this opportunity, therefore, of putting the record straight.

To my knowledge, the first person to popularise all this 'nonsense' of 'world revolution' was a comrade by the name of Karl Marx, together with his collaborator, Frederick Engels. In Chapter I of *The German Ideology*, they explained how capitalism has created a class, the proletariat, whose interests in all countries are the same, and thus 'has put world-historical, empirically universal individuals in place of local ones'. They went on to claim that the proletariat can thus only exist world-historically, just as communism, its activity, can only have a 'world-historical' existence (p. 56).

In conformity with this conception of communism as the world-historical activity of the proletariat they later, in *The Communist Manifesto,* issued the slogan: 'Workers of all countries, unite'! They even went to the extent of organising and taking up the leadership of the International Workingmen's Association, also known as the First International. In *The Civil War in France,* Marx explained that:

> Our Association is, in fact, nothing but the international bond between the most advanced working men in the various countries of the civilized world. Wherever, in whatever shape, and under whatever conditions the class struggle obtains any consistency, it is but natural that members of our Association should stand in the foreground. The soil out of which it grows is modern society itself. It cannot be stamped out by any amount of carnage. To stamp it out, the Governments would have to stamp out the despotism of capital over labour – the condition of their own parasitical existence (p. 98-9).

The argument is quite simple. The development on a world scale of capitalist big industry, which is an inevitable result of the working of the laws of motion of capitalist production, objectively makes 'each nation dependent on the revolutions of others' (*The German Ideology,* p. 56) and thus creates an objective bond between the working people of these countries. The most advanced and class-conscious of these workers become conscious of this objective inter-independence – this too, must inevitably occur – and form an international organisation. This international organisation is thus in the forefront of the working class struggle: it is the purest embodiment of communism, the 'world-historical' activity of the proletariat.

So much for Marx and Engels. After their death there were others who continued to propagate this "rubbish" about world revolution. Among them was Comrade V.I. Lenin. In the '*Proletarian Revolution and the Renegade Kautsky*' he wrote:

The Socialist, the revolutionary proletarian, the internationalist, argues differently. He says: 'The character of the war (whether it is reactionary or revolutionary) does not depend on where the attacked was, or in whose country the "enemy" is stationed; it depends on what class is waging the war, and of what politics this war is a continuation'. If the war is a reactionary, imperialist war, that is, if it is being waged by two world groups of the imperialist, rapacious, predatory, reactionary bourgeoisie, then every bourgeoisie (even of the smallest country) becomes a participant in the plunder, and my duty as a representative of the revolutionary proletariat is to prepare for the world proletarian revolution as only escape from the horrors of a world war. I must argue, not from the point of view of 'my' country (for that is the argument of a wretched, stupid, petty-bourgeois nationalist who does not realize that he is only a play thing in the hands of the imperialist bourgeoisie), but from the point of view of my share in the preparation, in the propaganda, and in the acceleration of the world proletarian revolution (p. 800).

Lenin more than anyone else, was aware of the contradictions among different sections of the bourgeoisies, and especially those between the bourgeoisie of oppressed nations and the bourgeoisie of oppressor nations. Yet this did not obscure his consciousness of the inevitability, in the long term, of the primary contradiction in the world becoming that between the world proletariat and world bourgeoisie. It was this understanding of the long-term tendencies of capitalist development which led him to insist that 'an' internationalist must appraise the war as a whole from the point of view of the world bourgeoisie and the world proletariat'. (p. 79). It was the same understanding which showed itself in his unremitting efforts to set up a Communist International after the collapse of the Second Internatioal into social chauvinism. To Lenin, who recognized the need for a revolutionary war by the proletarians of all countries, against the bourgeoisies of all countreis, it seemed self-evident that this 'revolutionary' war needed a united revolutionary leadership which would

> utilise the organizational experience and links of the working class so as to create illegal forms of struggle for socialism, forms appropriate to a period of crisis, and to unite the workers, not with the chauvinist bourgeoisie of their respective countries, but with the workers of all countries.

Hence his firm conviction that 'the proletarian International has not gone under will not go under. Notwithstanding all obstacles, the masses of the workers will create a new International' (*Collected Works*, Vol. 21, p. 23).

It seems that, repugnant though the thought of world revolution might be to all those who retain the traces of petty bourgeois nationalist ideology, for revolutionary communists, on the contrary, it is simply taken for granted as one of the marks of distinction between scientific socialism and all forms of reactionary and utopian socialism. And in view of the extensive re-writing of history that has been undertaken precisely by such disguised nationalists, it is necessary to add here that comrades Rosa Luxemburg (one of 'the best representatives of the world proletarian International, of the unforgettable leaders of the world socialist revolution' – V.I. Lenin, *Collected Works*, Vol. 28, p. 434), and Leon Trotsky belong also to this tradition of communism revolutionaries. Whatever be their mistakes – and criticize them we must, since communists recognize no infallible popes – they lived and died in the struggle to bring about the proletarian-socialist world revolution, and no amount of vilification or distortion can prevent their memory being held in the highest honour in an authentically revolutionary working class movement.

Taking all this into account, it does not seem unreasonable to conclude that abandonment of the goal of world socialist revolution constitutes a fundamental revision of Marxism. Moreover, this abandonment of Marxist revolutionary practice is accompanied inevitably by an abandonment of the Marxist method. One striking component of the method adopted instead is its dogmatism. A proposition is made, for example a national bourgeoisie cannot develop in a former colony. All phenomena that cannot be explained by the assertion are then simply ignored or denied in an ostrich-like fashion. The existence, for example, of the bourgeoisie of India, some of whose members stand among the largest capitalists of the world, which can compete internationally in techologically sophisticated manufactured products, which boasts a highly efficient and up-to-date bourgeois state apparatus and which is able to carry out an election fought on basic political issues is simply denied, as though denial of its existence will make it disappear. To our regret, matters are not so easy. however, if we now try to identify the source of this dogmatic assertion, we discover an element of empiricist impressionism. It does not at all follow from the laws of motion of capital as Marx described them that a national bourgeoisie should not develop in former colonies. On the contrary, according to Marx in *The Communist Manifesto, The German Ideology* and elsewhere, the tendency of capitalism is to produce the same conditions, the same class relations, the same state structures in all countries of the world.

Where, then, does this 'law' come from? Its source is easily identifiable as a generalisation made on the basis of a knowledge of a limited number of ex-colonies examined over a limited period of time. Because a national bourgeoisie does not develop to any significant extent in these countries in this period of time, therefore it cannot ever develop in any such countries—that is the implicit reasoning behind this conclusion. Empirical observations of an impressionistic nature become the occasion of formulating a general law—the very opposite of what Marx described as the 'scientifically correct method', which is to ascend 'from the simple relations, such as labour, division of labour, need, exchange value, to the level of the state, exchange between nations and the world market'. (*Grundrisse*, p. 101).,

But if once we admit the possibility that new bourgeoisies can arise in the epoch of imperialism, are we not committed to arguing that it is possible to 'roll back the concentrating, centralizing and internationalizing tendency of capitalism' that Marx and Lenin talked about? ('A Caricature of Marxism-Leninism'—Nabudere) Not at all. All we need in order to resolve this artificial contradiction is the notion of uneven development. The two processes occur side by side. Existing capital becomes more concentrated and centralized; at the same time new capitals spring up where none existed before. Without such a process, it would be impossible to explain the emergence of the bourgeoisies of the US Australia and Japan, let alone those of the underdeveloped countries. This is so simple and obvious that it hardly needs to be stated. But the second point is that this capital, having emerged, becomes, at one level, part of world capital; at another, however, it competes with the other capitals which also constitute world capital. Let us see how Marx expresses it: 'Competition merely expresses as real, posits as an external necessity, that which lies within the nature of capital; competition is nothing more than the way in which the many capitals force the inherent determinants of capital upon one another and upon themselves'. (*Grundrisse*, p. 651) Marx is not playing around here. On the contrary, he is evolving the only method by which he will be able to reproduce in thought the reality of capitalist production and he is able to bypass false contradictions of the nature: either finance capital or national capital, either centralization of capital or the creation of new capitals.

Once we have resolved this false contradiction between finance capital and national capital, the false contradiction between world bourgeoisie and national bourgeoisies also disappears. As Lenin pointed out, in an imperialist war the bourgeoisies even of the smallest nations participate in the plunder; likewise in times of peace, even the weakest and most embryonic bourgeoisie, inasmuch as it constitutes part of the world bourgeoisie, participates in the exploitation of the proletariat and semi-proletariat. This is not to deny the importance of contradictions between emergent national bourgeoisies and powerful metropolitan bourgeoisies, nor the role they may play in furthering the working class struggle. In situations where the working class can gain from the struggle of national bourgeoisie against other bourgeoisies, it may adopt a dual tactic, on the one hand participating in the immediate struggle alongside the bourgeoisie, on the other hand simultaneously organizing itself separately in order to struggle against this same bourgeoisie. The guiding thread of its activity must always be, however, what is the best strategy from the point of view of the world proletariat? What strategy will contribute most to the progress of the world revolution? One point should be made clear here. To struggle alongside the bourgeoisie is not the same as having an alliance with it. To have an anti-imperialist alliance with the 'national' bourgeoisie means necessarily having a programme which excludes the expropriation of its capital—since no bourgeoisie will participate in a struggle to expropriate itself. Such a programme is, thus formulated on the basis of class-collaboration with the national bourgeoisie. The classic example of this is the anti-imperialist programme of the revisionist, class-collaborationist, opportunist, 'Communist' Party of India, which despite its revolutionary rhetoric is forced, by the logic of its position, to trail behind the bourgeoisie. It is one indication of the more advanced character of the class struggle in India that this old revisionist strategy has there already been decisively rejected by the working masses, while in East Africa it is still being served up as something original and revolutionary.

Let us take one more example. To the proposition that: 'Peasants are not transformed into proletarians. The peasant doesn't sell his labour-power, he sells his product', is counterposed by the proposition that: 'his so-called under-valued price of the product is no more than a wage paid for his labour... This is how a capital-labour relation exists at this level of articulation of the labour process'. Since an absolute contradiction is seen between these two, it must be because the peasant is regarded in the first proposition as a petty-bourgeois producer, in the second as a wage-labour—either wage labour or no wage labour. Yet, as we all know, the process of primitive accumulation consists precisely in the separation of the petty producers from their means of production. This is a protracted process by which a gradual quantitative separation from the means of production becomes at a certain point a qualitative transformation from petty bourgeois to proletariat. What is the situation in the process of transition? Obviously, so long as we stick to the rigid categories of wage labour or not wage labour, being or not being, we cannot grasp the process of becoming, the coming into being of wage labour. The point about the poor peasant in this situation is that he is neither a petty bourgeois nor a proletarian, or, to put it another way, is both a petty-bourgeois and a proletarian; in other words, a semi-proletarian. The process of proletarianization, of transition, is impossible to grasp so long as we think in terms of rigid oppositions; problems appear which simply cannot be resolved. The inevitable result his an utterly confused and confusing debate. Because the conditions for its own resolution do not lie within it, the debate inevitably degenerates into bitterness and sectarianism. Instead of leading to greater clarity, it leads to greater confusion; instead of leading to unity on a higher plane, it leads to fragmentation and disintegration; instead of laying the basis for a revolutionary strategy, it gives

310

impression that no strategy is possible where the concrete situation itself is so unclear.

In another paper ('The Historical Necessity of the Platform') we have tried to explain why this situation of sterile debate, sectarianism and fragmentation prevails in the left today on an international scale. That situation is explained, like the widespread prevalence on the left of disguised firms of nationalist ideology, by the objective conditions of capitalist expansion on a world scale, which is not beginning to come up against its own barriers. However, we argue there that the situation does not by any means call for gloom and despair. For the very condition which lead to the disintegration and disarray of the traditional leftist currents are the conditions for the rebirth of an authentic Marxist revolutionary tradition. And in order to become part of this historic process of regeneration, comrades must make the effort to reappropriate Marx's dialectical method. This is not an intellectual luxury which they can afford to bypass. It is the crucial weapon which alone enables the elaboration of a critique both of all forms of bourgeois theory and of bourgeois society itself. And this critique, let us remember, is not merely theoretical.

> The question whether objective truth can be attributed to human thinking is not a question of theory but is a practical question. Man must prove the truth, i.e. the reality and power, the thissidedness of his thinking, in practice. The dispute over the reality or non-reality of thinking that is isolated from practice is a purely scholastic question. (Marx, *Theses on Ferbach*, II).

By this criterion, the 'dispute' which has been going on in the University (of Dar es Salaam) left is surely scholastic through and through, and will remain so until the ideas expressed are concretized into strategy and attempts are made to prove their truth, their reality and power, their this-sidedness, in practice. Apart from practice, it is possible to set up and knock down theories by the dozen, but with no possibility of making judgements as to their objective truth. Hence the significance of 'revolutionary', of 'practical-critical' activity. (Marx, *Thesis on Ferbach*, I). 'Marxist' intellectuals have spent too long contemplating the world. Let them try, now, to change it.